Jump comics usually come out on the fourth of each month, but it looks like this volume is coming out a little early, at the end of the previous month and in time for the end of the year. So I'd like to take this opportunity to look back at the year. Hmm...I feel like I spent every day watching *Onegai! Ranking*.

—HIROSHI SHIIBASHI,
2010

HIROSHI SHIIBASHI debuted in BUSINESS JUMP magazine with *Aratama*. NURA: RISE OF THE YOKAI CLAN is his breakout hit. He was an assistant to manga artist Hirohiko Araki, the creator of *Jojo's Bizarre Adventure*. *Steel Ball Run* by Araki is one of his favorite manga.

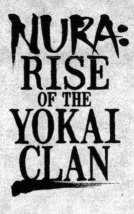

NURA: RISE OF THE YOKAI CLAN
VOLUME 14
SHONEN JUMP Manga Edition

Story and Art by HIROSHI SHIIBASHI

Translation – John Werry
Touch-up Art and Lettering – Gia Cam Luc
Graphics and Cover Design – Fawn Lau
Editor – Joel Enos

NURARIHYON NO MAGO © 2008 by Hiroshi
Shiibashi. All rights reserved. First published in
Japan in 2008 by SHUEISHA Inc., Tokyo. English
translation rights arranged by SHUEISHA Inc.

The rights of the author(s) of the work(s) in this
publication to be so identified have been asserted
in accordance with the Copyright, Designs and
Patents Act 1988. A CIP catalogue record for this
book is available from the British Library.

Printed in the U.S.A.

Published by VIZ Media, LLC
P.O. Box 77010
San Francisco, CA 94107

10 9 8 7 6 5 4 3 2 1
First printing, April 2013

www.viz.com   www.shonenjump.com

NURA: RISE OF THE YOKAI CLAN

14

TO NIJO CASTLE

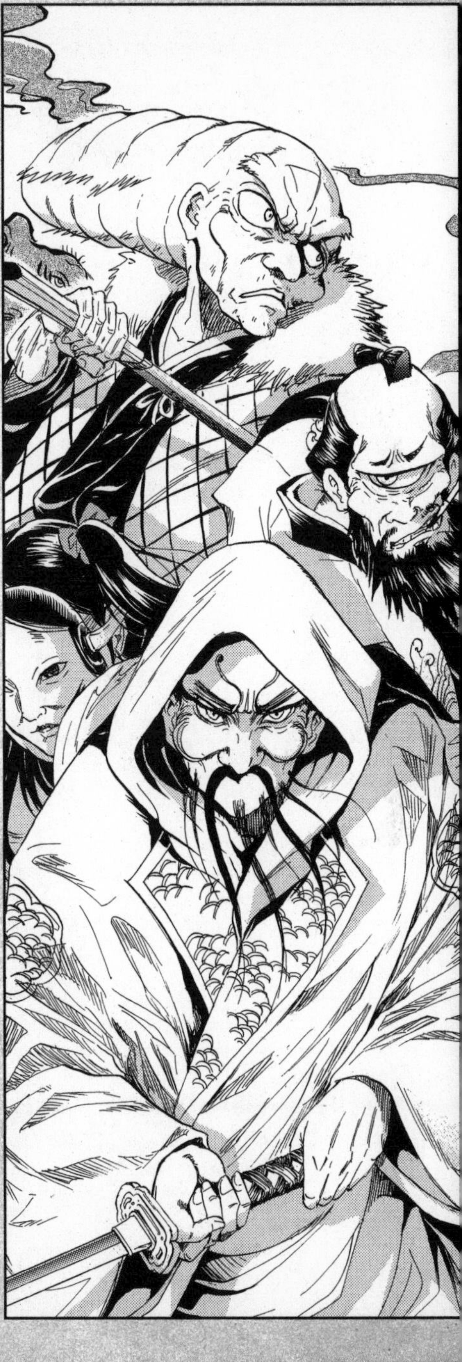

STORY AND ART BY
HIROSHI SHIIBASHI

CHARACTERS

NURARIHYON

Rikuo's grandfather and the Lord of Pandemonium. He intends to pass leadership of the Nura clan—leaders of the yokai world—to Rikuo. He's mischievous and likes to dine and ditch.

RIKUO NURA

Though he appears to be a human boy, he's actually the grandson of Nurarihyon, a yokai. His grandfather's blood makes him one-quarter yokai, and he transforms into a yokai at times.

KIYOTSUGU

Rikuo's classmate. He has adored yokai ever since Rikuo saved him in his yokai form, leading him to form the Kiyojuji Paranormal Patrol.

KANA IENAGA

Rikuo's classmate and a childhood friend. Even though she hates scary things, she's a member of the Kiyojuji Paranormal Patrol for some reason.

YUKI-ONNA

A yokai of the Nura clan who is in charge of looking after Rikuo. She disguises herself as a human and attends the same school as Rikuo to protect him from danger. When in human form, she goes by the name Tsurara Oikawa.

YURA KEIKAIN

Rikuo's classmate and a descendant of the Keikain family of onmyoji. She transferred into Ukiyoe Middle School to do field training in yokai exorcism. She has the power to control her shikigami and uses them to destroy yokai.

AWASHIMA

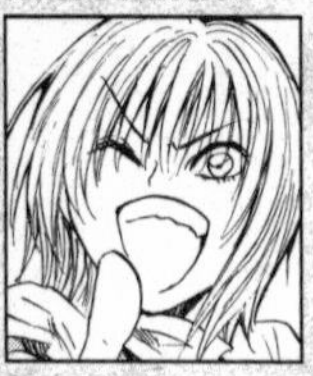

A yokai from Tono. He's a boy by day and a girl at night. As an amanojaku born of an angel and demon, he can use Possess moves with different characteristics from each side.

ITAKU

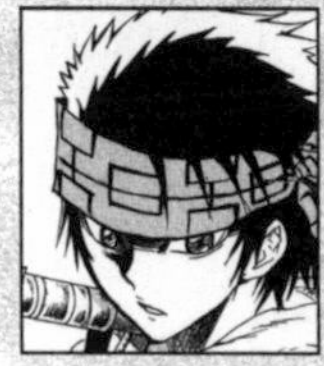

A yokai from Tohoku yokai village, Tono. When he was in charge of Rikuo's training there, he taught Rikuo the move Possess. His weapons are scythes.

TSUCHIGUMO

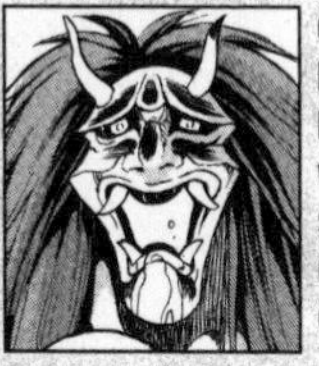

One of the Kyoto yokai, but instead of obeying Hagoromo-Gitsune, he does what he wants. He is so strong that people say he is an ayakashi you definitely don't want to meet!

HAGOROMO-GITSUNE

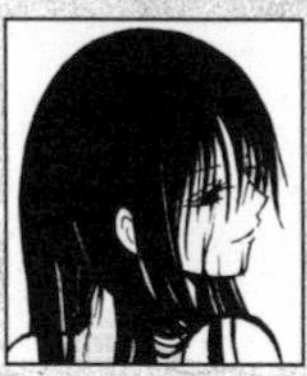

A great yokai in Kyoto who has a connection to Nurarihyon and the Keikain clan. She possesses humans and then commits foul deeds. She has returned to life after a 400-year absence.

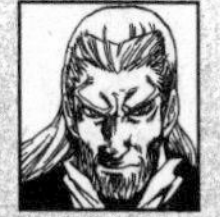

KIDOMARU

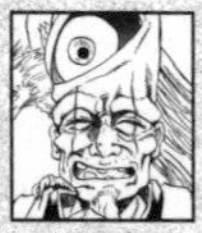

MINAGOROSHI-JIZO

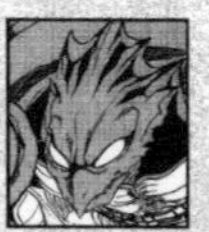

AMEZO

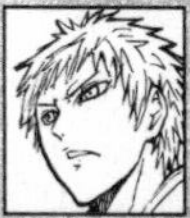

ZEN

STORY SO FAR

Rikuo Nura is a seventh-grader at Ukiyoe Middle School. At a glance, he appears to be just another average, normal boy. But he's actually the grandson of the yokai Overlord Nurarihyon. He's also the Underboss of the powerful Nura clan. He spends his days as a human, despite the clan's hopes that he will someday become a great Overlord like his grandfather.

The heretical Kyoto yokai named Shokera attacks the Keikain clan main family! When Aotabo fights back, Shokera reveals his grotesque true form. Overcome with a desire to protect the children, Aotabo makes a stand.

Meanwhile, Rikuo is learning a new technique on Mt. Kurama when the tengu suddenly attack. He tries to handle them on his own, but Zen convinces him of the importance of relying on comrades. Rikuo finally manages to pull off Hidden Technique of the Lord of the Hundred Demons: Equip, allowing him to overcome the challenge.

Now that training is over, Rikuo confronts the yokai Tsuchigumo again at Sokokuji Temple in an effort to rescue his friend Tsurara. He does Equip with Tsurara and it appears they have dealt Tsuchigumo a decisive blow, but then Tsuchigumo gets serious for the first time in one thousand years and overwhelms them. Then backup in the form of Itaku and the other yokai from Tono rush in!!

TABLE OF CONTENTS

NURA: RISE OF THE YOKAI CLAN

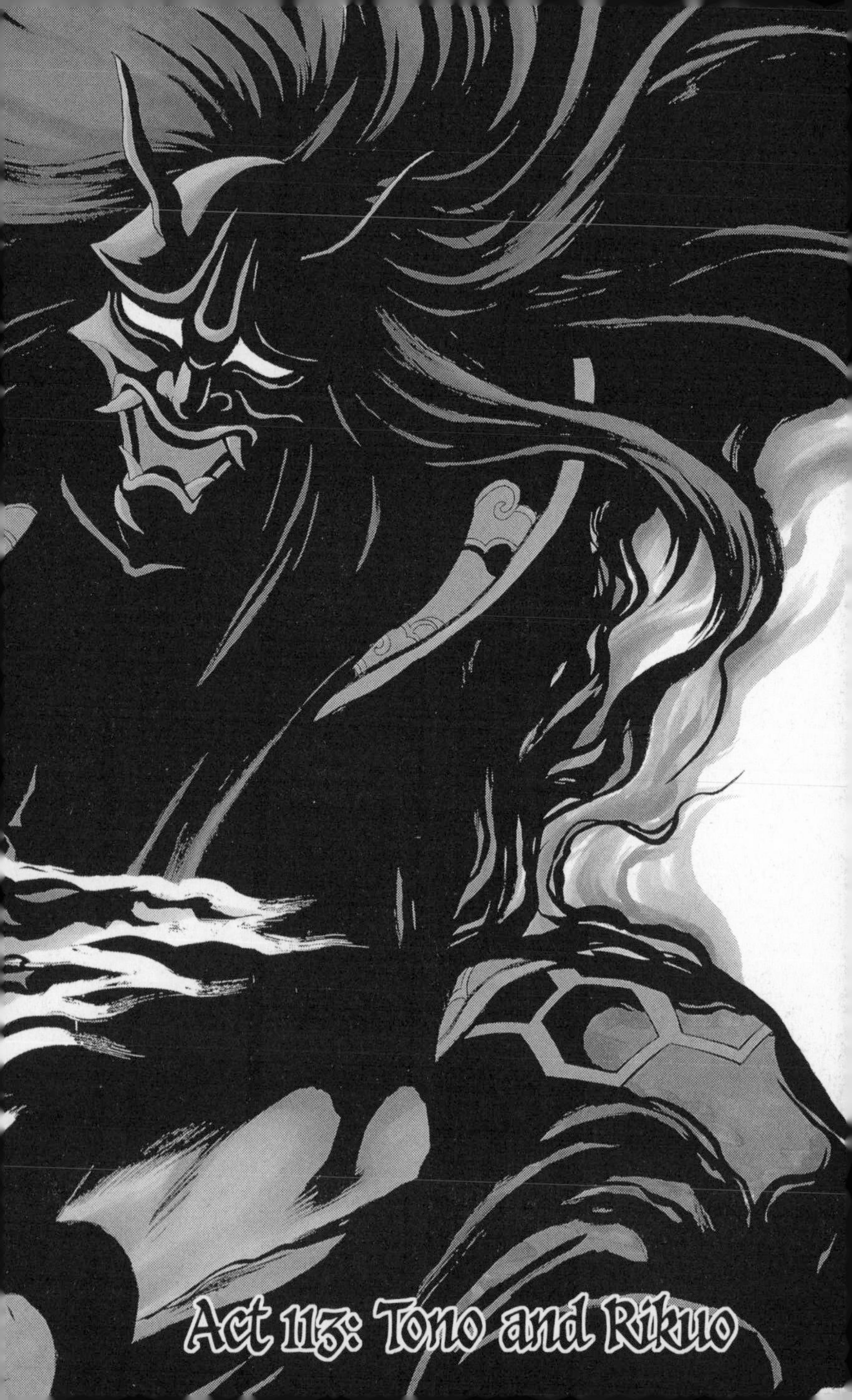

Act 113: Tono and Rikuo

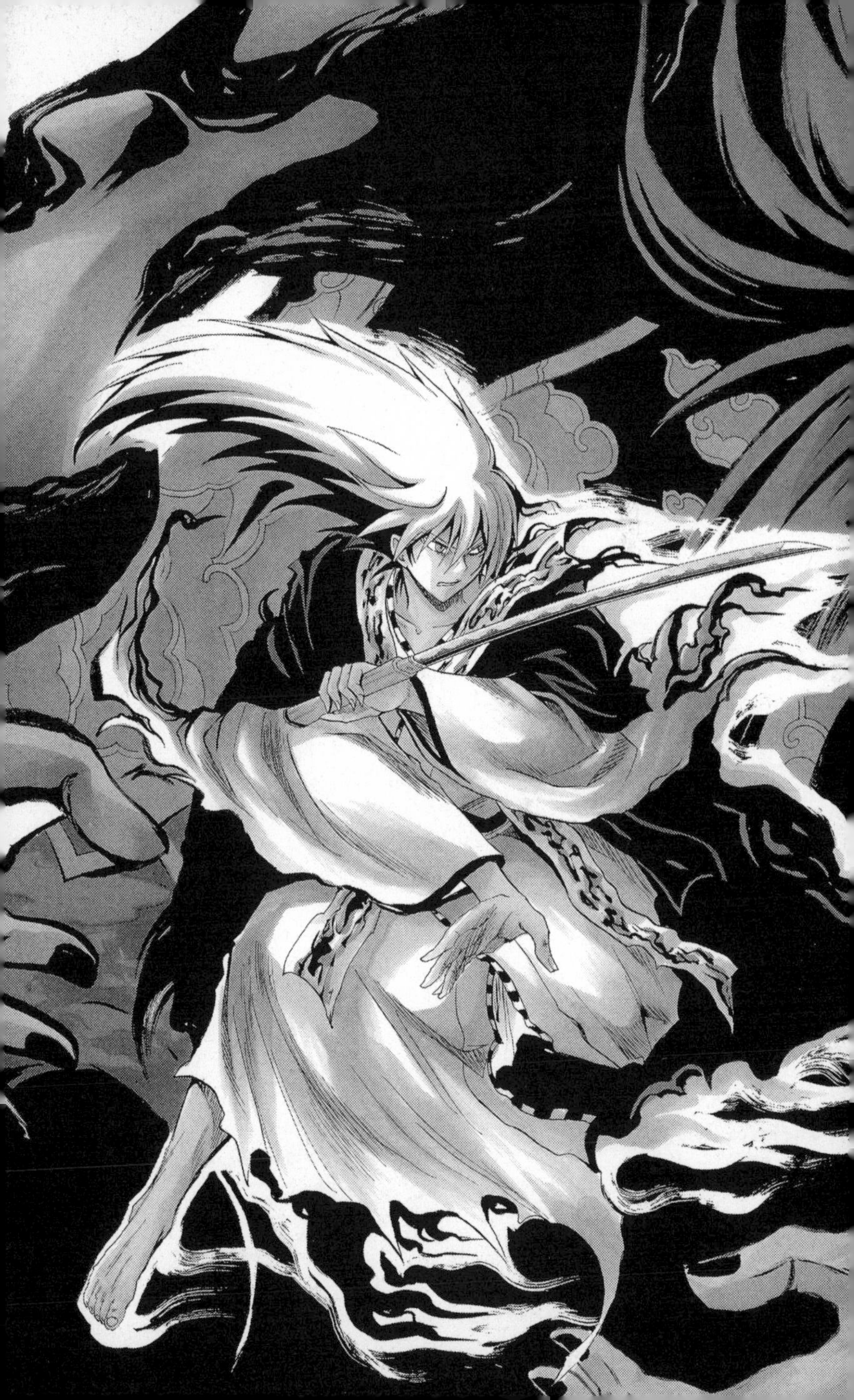

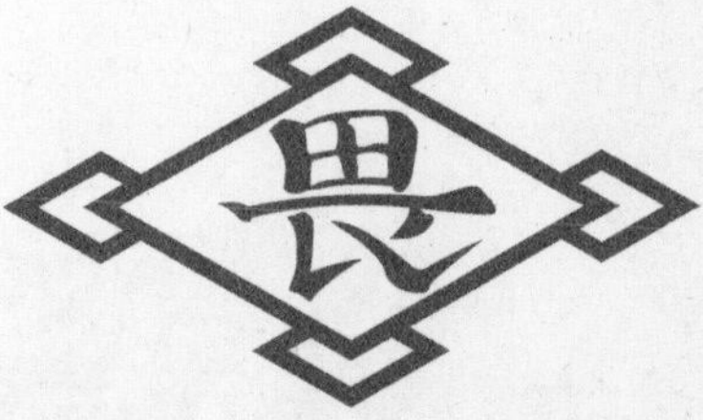
畏

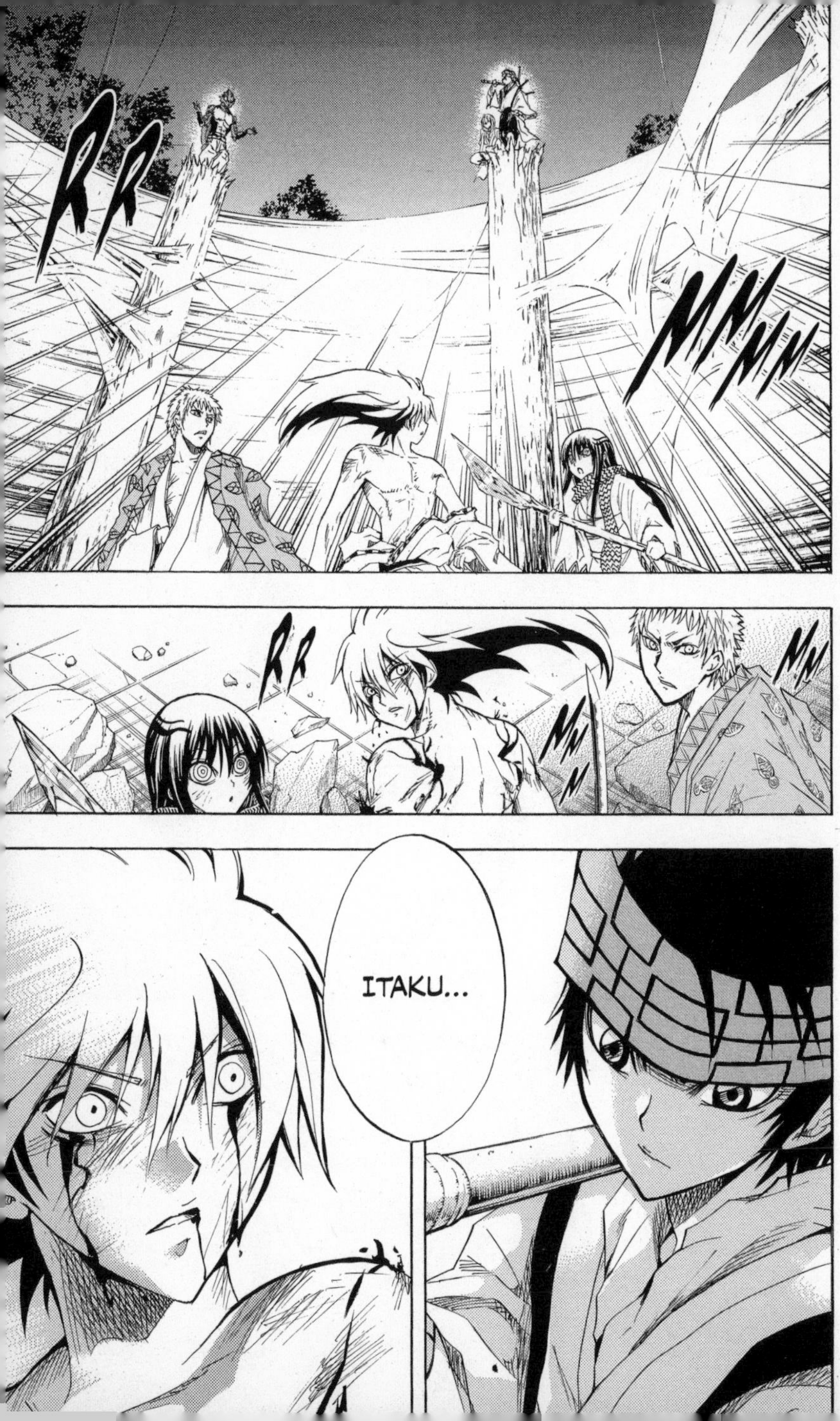
MMMMM
RR
MM
MM
RR
ITAKU...

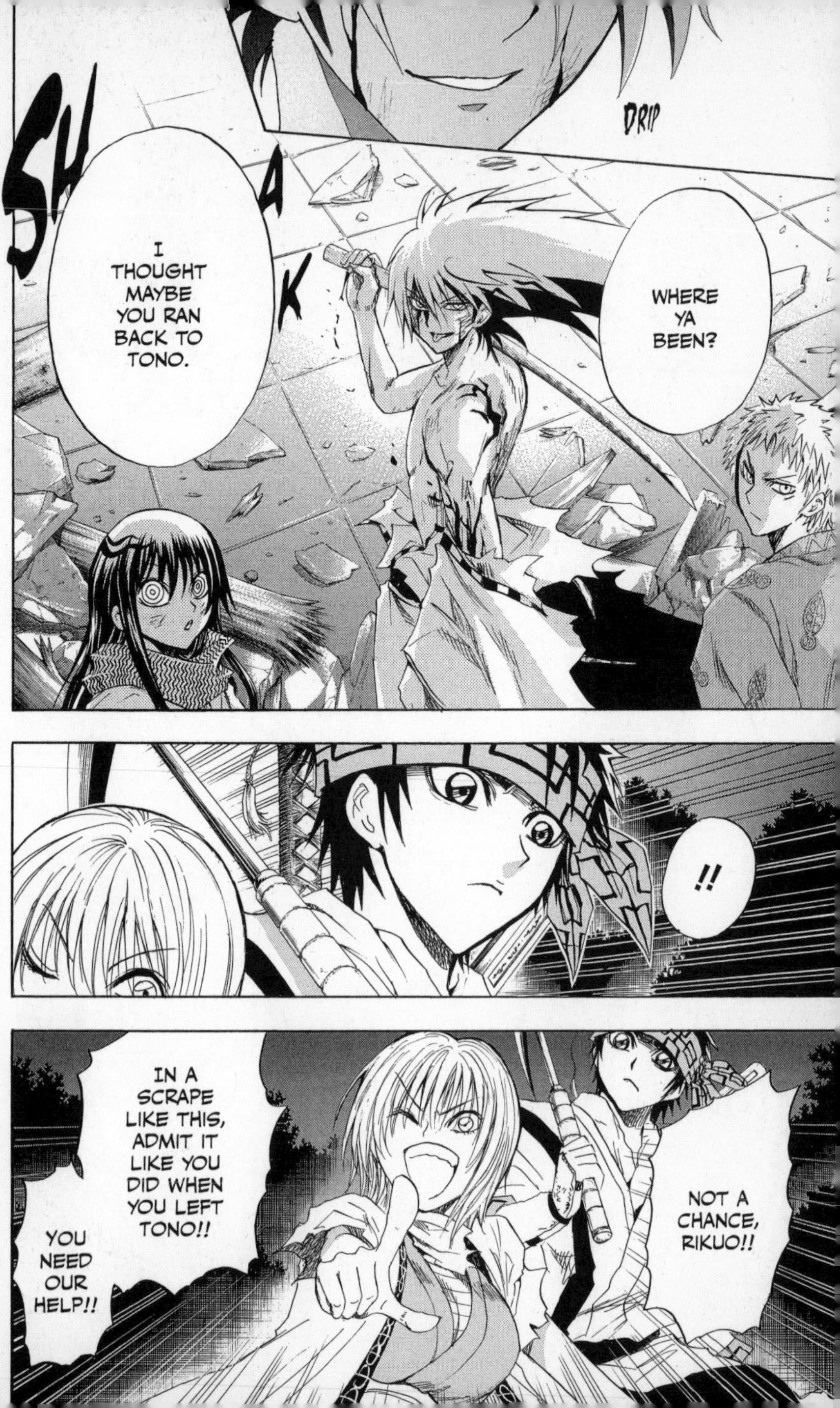
DRIP
WHERE YA BEEN?
SHAK
I THOUGHT MAYBE YOU RAN BACK TO TONO.
!!
NOT A CHANCE, RIKUO!!
IN A SCRAPE LIKE THIS, ADMIT IT LIKE YOU DID WHEN YOU LEFT TONO!!
YOU NEED OUR HELP!!

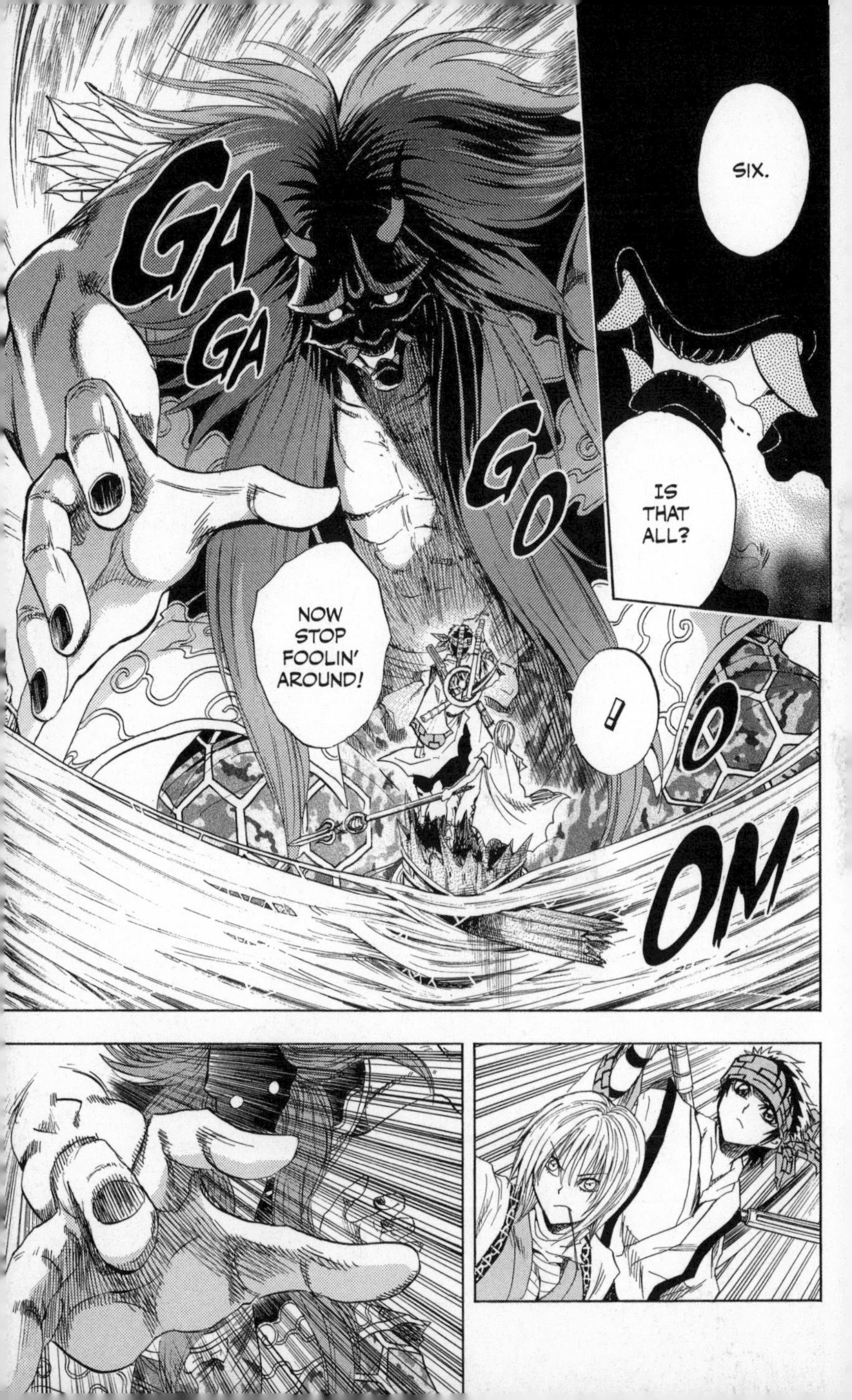
SIX.
IS THAT ALL?
!
NOW STOP FOOLIN' AROUND!
GAGA
GO
O
OM

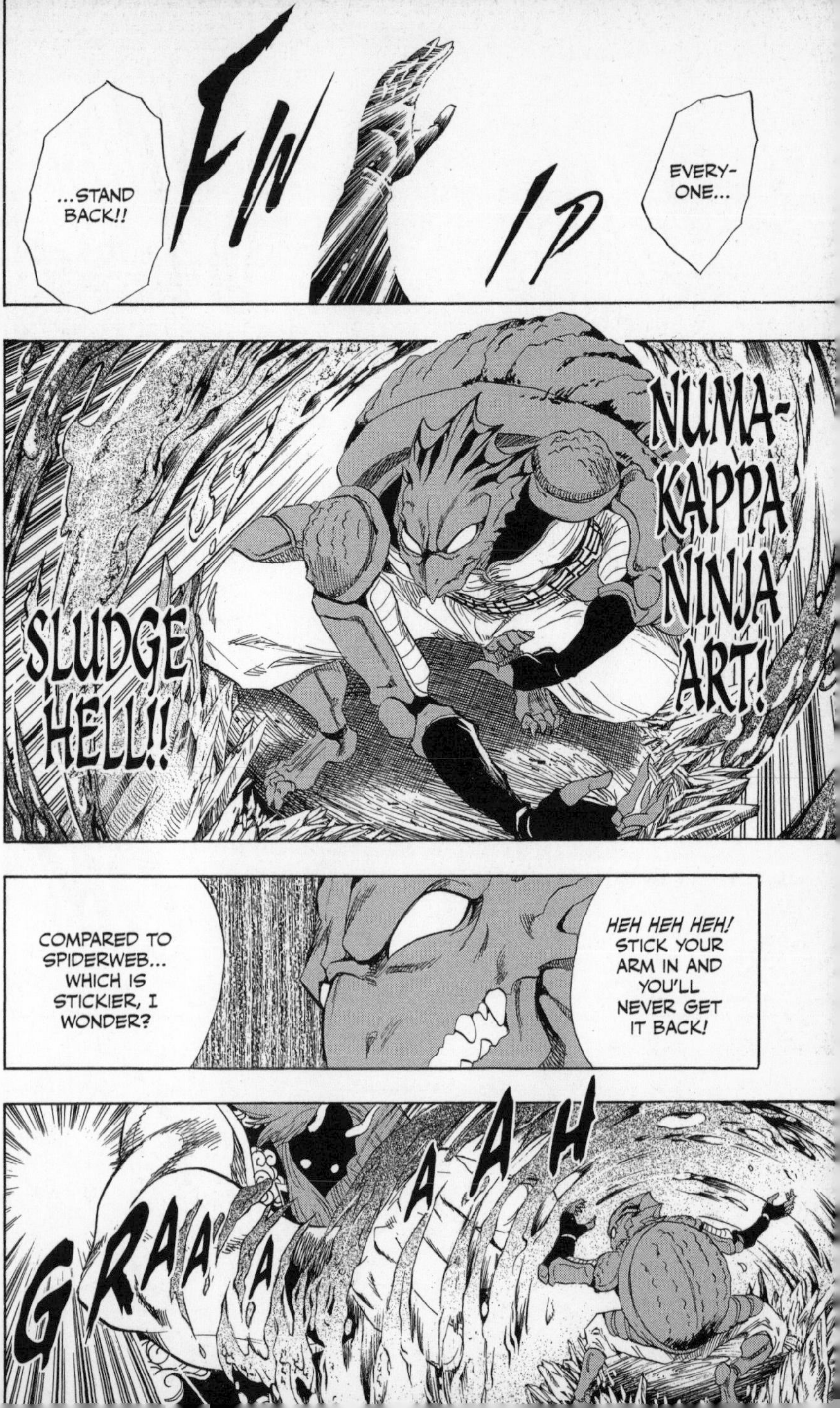
EVERY-ONE...
FWIP
...STAND BACK!!
NUMA-KAPPA NINJA ART!
SLUDGE HELL!!
HEH HEH HEH! STICK YOUR ARM IN AND YOU'LL NEVER GET IT BACK!
COMPARED TO SPIDERWEB... WHICH IS STICKIER, I WONDER?
GRAAAAAAH

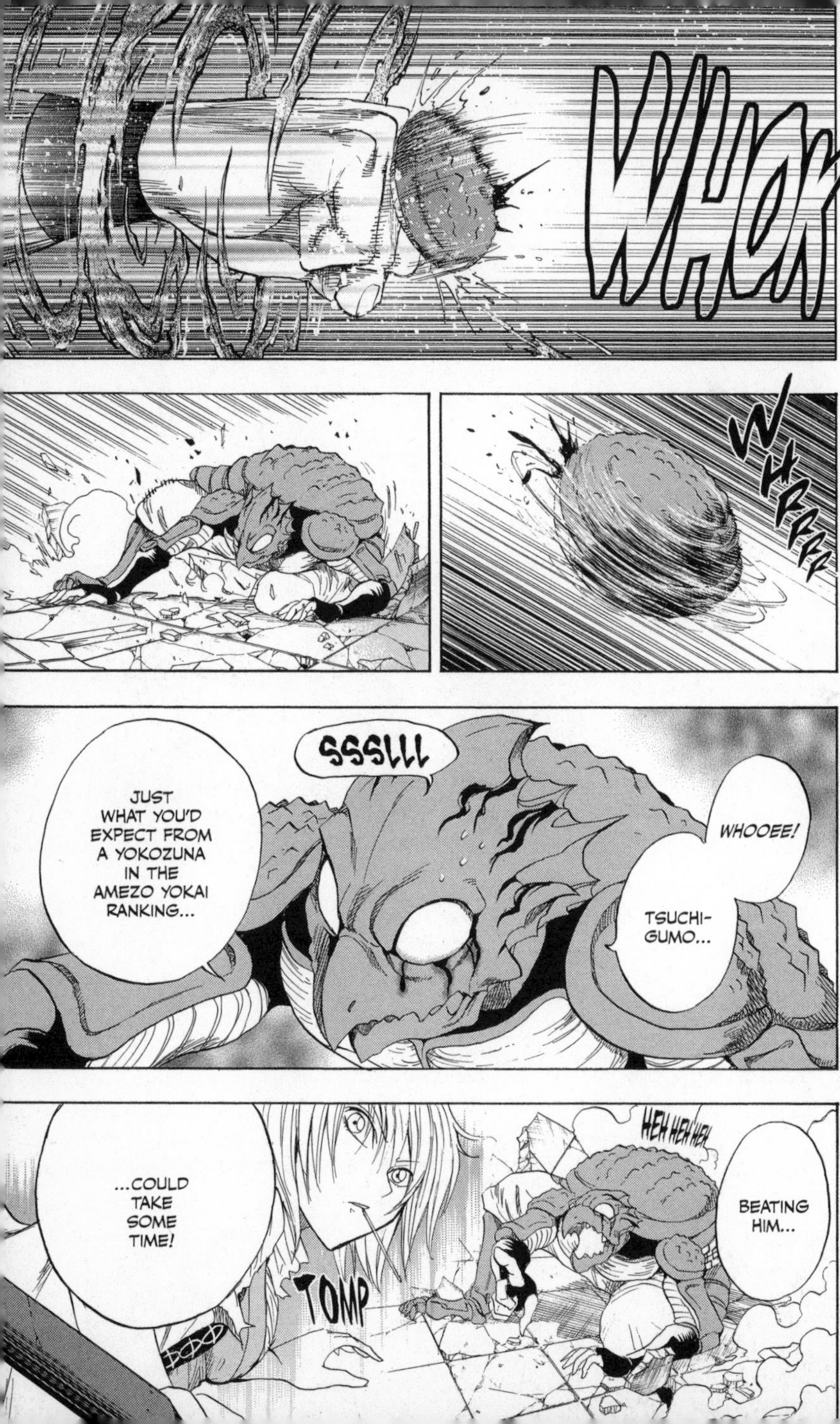
WHOCK
WHRRRR
WHOOEE!
TSUCHI-GUMO...
SSSLLL
JUST WHAT YOU'D EXPECT FROM A YOKOZUNA IN THE AMEZO YOKAI RANKING...
HEH HEH HEH
BEATING HIM...
...COULD TAKE SOME TIME!
TOMP

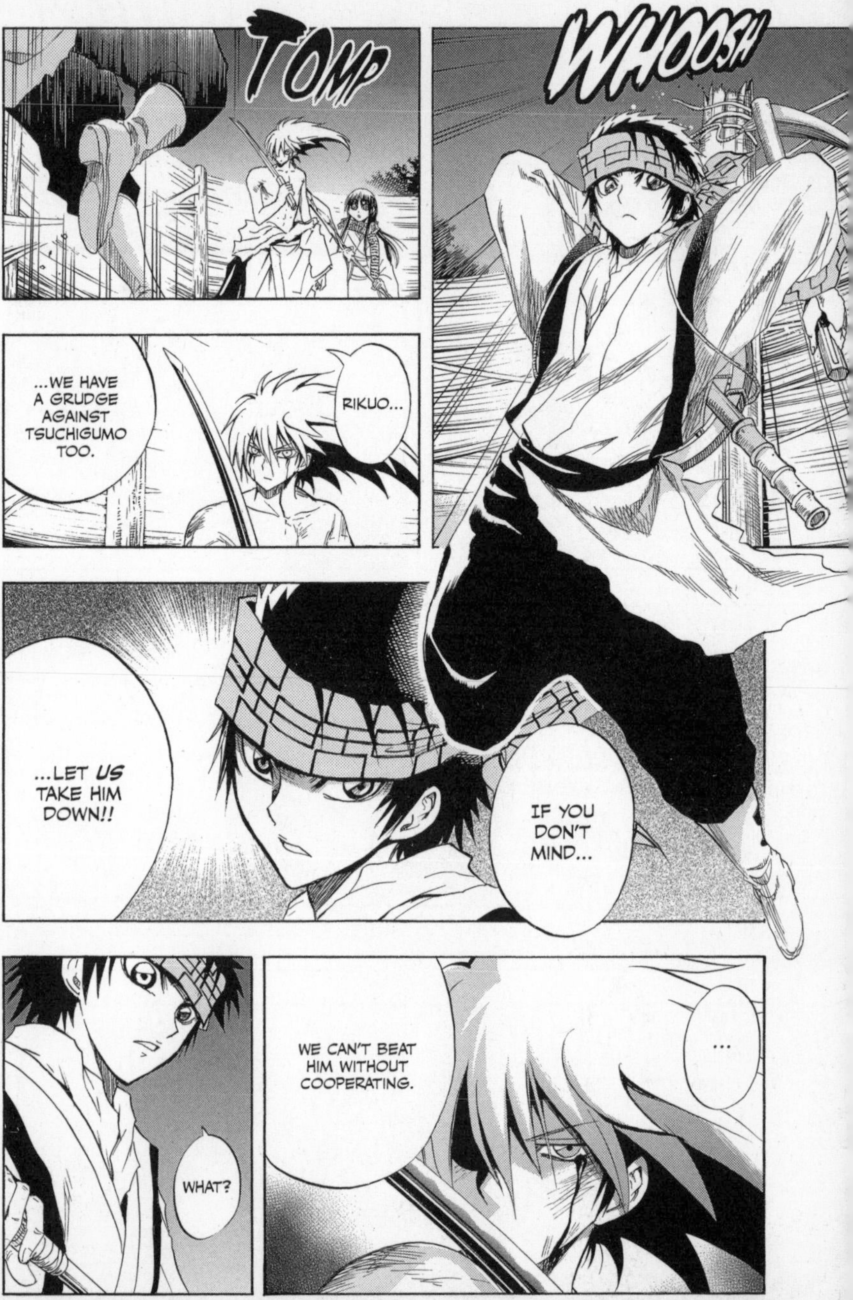

WHOOSH
TOMP
RIKUO...
...WE HAVE A GRUDGE AGAINST TSUCHIGUMO TOO.
IF YOU DON'T MIND...
...LET *US* TAKE HIM DOWN!!
...
WE CAN'T BEAT HIM WITHOUT COOPERATING.
WHAT?

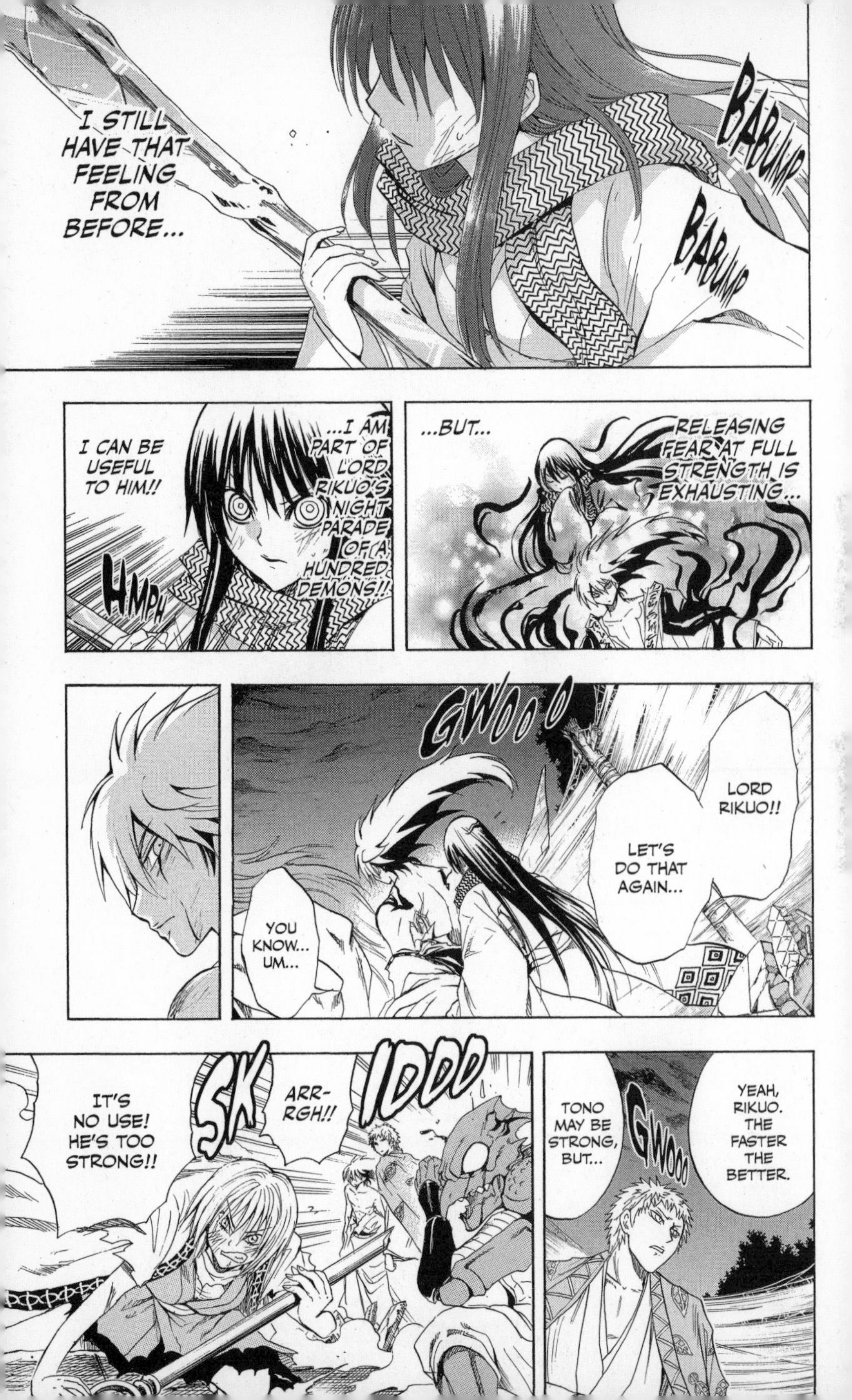
BABUMP
BABUMP
I STILL HAVE THAT FEELING FROM BEFORE...
...BUT...
RELEASING FEAR AT FULL STRENGTH IS EXHAUSTING...
...I AM PART OF LORD RIKUO'S NIGHT PARADE OF A HUNDRED DEMONS!!
I CAN BE USEFUL TO HIM!!
HMPH
GWOOO
LORD RIKUO!!
LET'S DO THAT AGAIN...
YOU KNOW... UM...
YEAH, RIKUO. THE FASTER THE BETTER.
GWOOO
TONO MAY BE STRONG, BUT...
SKIDDD
ARR-RGH!!
IT'S NO USE! HE'S TOO STRONG!!

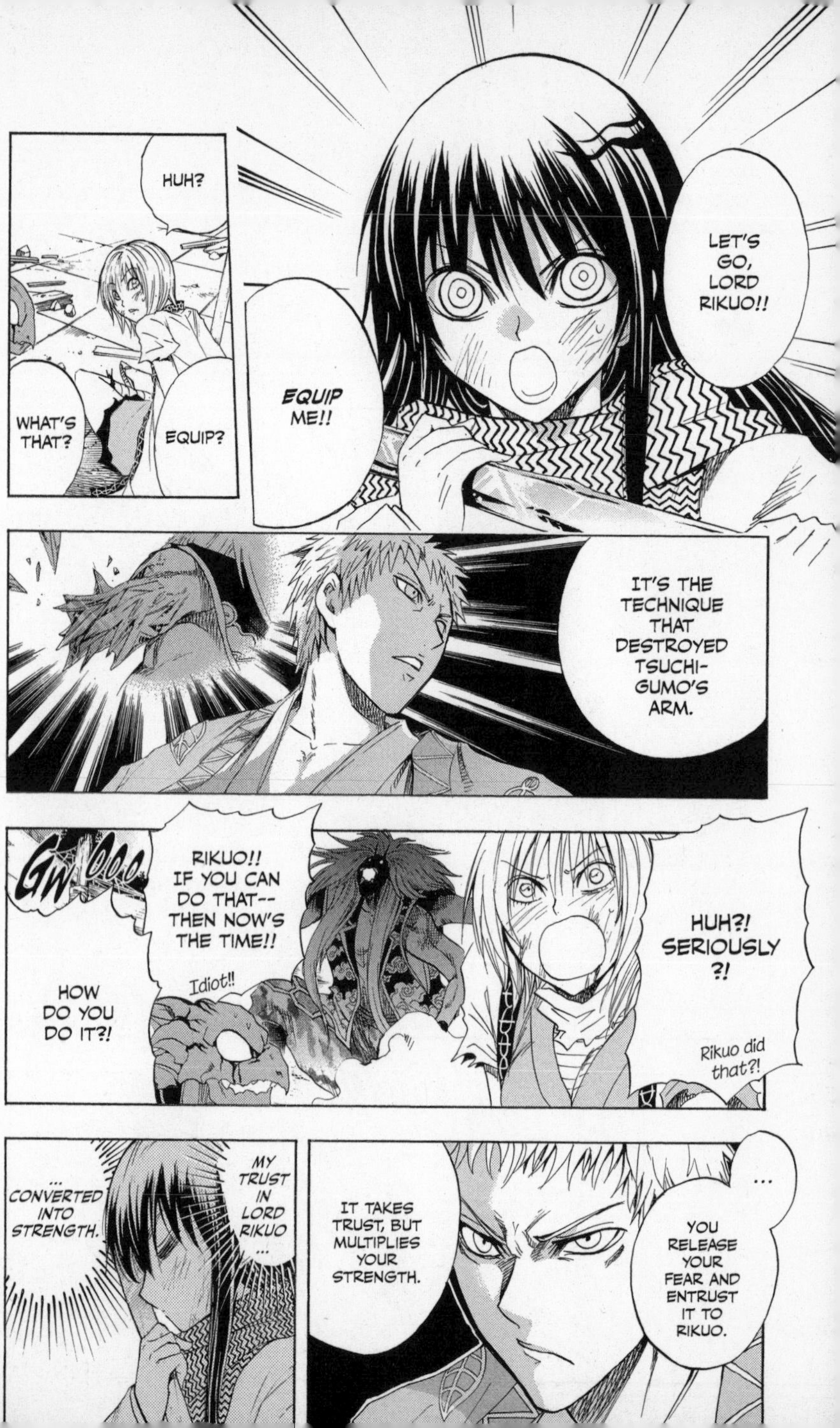
LET'S GO, LORD RIKUO!!
EQUIP ME!!
HUH?
EQUIP?
WHAT'S THAT?
IT'S THE TECHNIQUE THAT DESTROYED TSUCHI-GUMO'S ARM.
HUH?! SERIOUSLY?!
Rikuo did that?!
RIKUO!! IF YOU CAN DO THAT-- THEN NOW'S THE TIME!!
Idiot!!
GWOOO
HOW DO YOU DO IT?!
...
YOU RELEASE YOUR FEAR AND ENTRUST IT TO RIKUO.
IT TAKES TRUST, BUT MULTIPLIES YOUR STRENGTH.
MY TRUST IN LORD RIKUO...
...CONVERTED INTO STRENGTH.

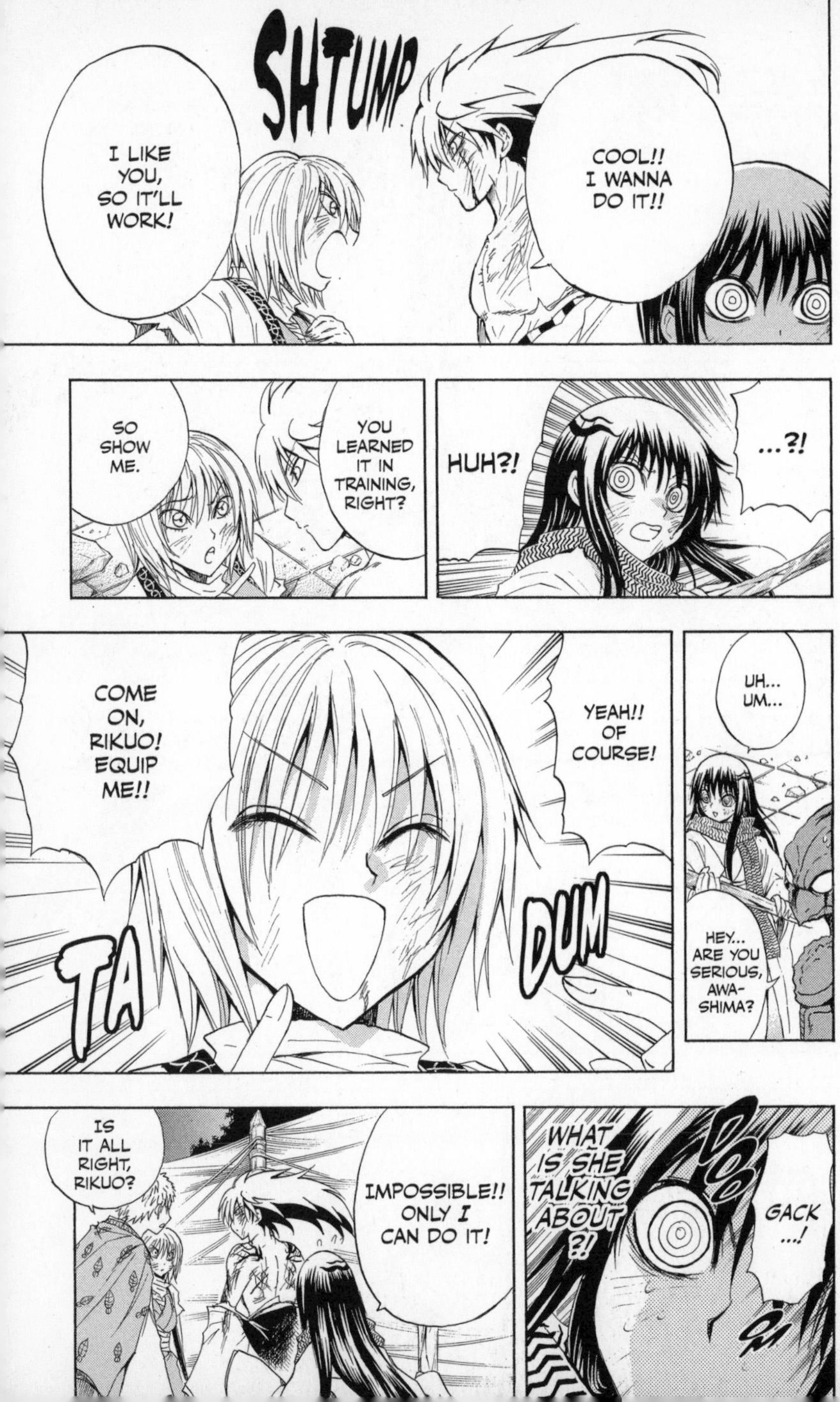
COOL!! I WANNA DO IT!!
SHTUMP
I LIKE YOU, SO IT'LL WORK!
...?!
HUH?!
YOU LEARNED IT IN TRAINING, RIGHT?
SO SHOW ME.
UH... UM...
HEY... ARE YOU SERIOUS, AWA-SHIMA?
YEAH!! OF COURSE!
COME ON, RIKUO! EQUIP ME!!
TA DUM
GACK ...!
WHAT IS SHE TALKING ABOUT?!
IMPOSSIBLE!! ONLY *I* CAN DO IT!
IS IT ALL RIGHT, RIKUO?

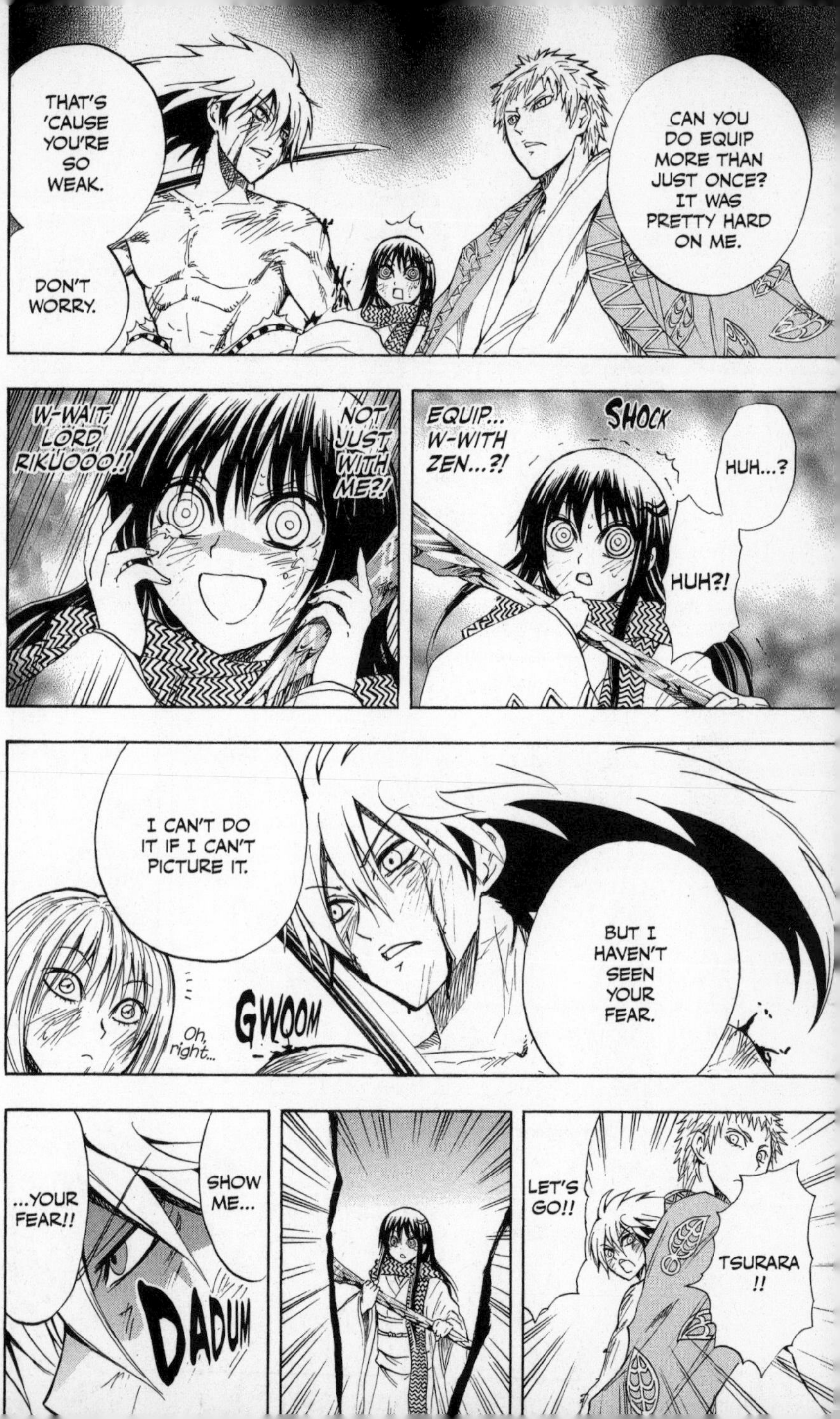
CAN YOU DO EQUIP MORE THAN JUST ONCE? IT WAS PRETTY HARD ON ME.
THAT'S 'CAUSE YOU'RE SO WEAK.
DON'T WORRY.
SHOCK
HUH...?
EQUIP... W-WITH ZEN...?!
HUH?!
NOT JUST WITH ME?!
W-WAIT, LORD RIKUOOO!!
I CAN'T DO IT IF I CAN'T PICTURE IT.
BUT I HAVEN'T SEEN YOUR FEAR.
GWOOM
Oh, right...
TSURARA!!
LET'S GO!!
SHOW ME...
...YOUR FEAR!!
DADUM

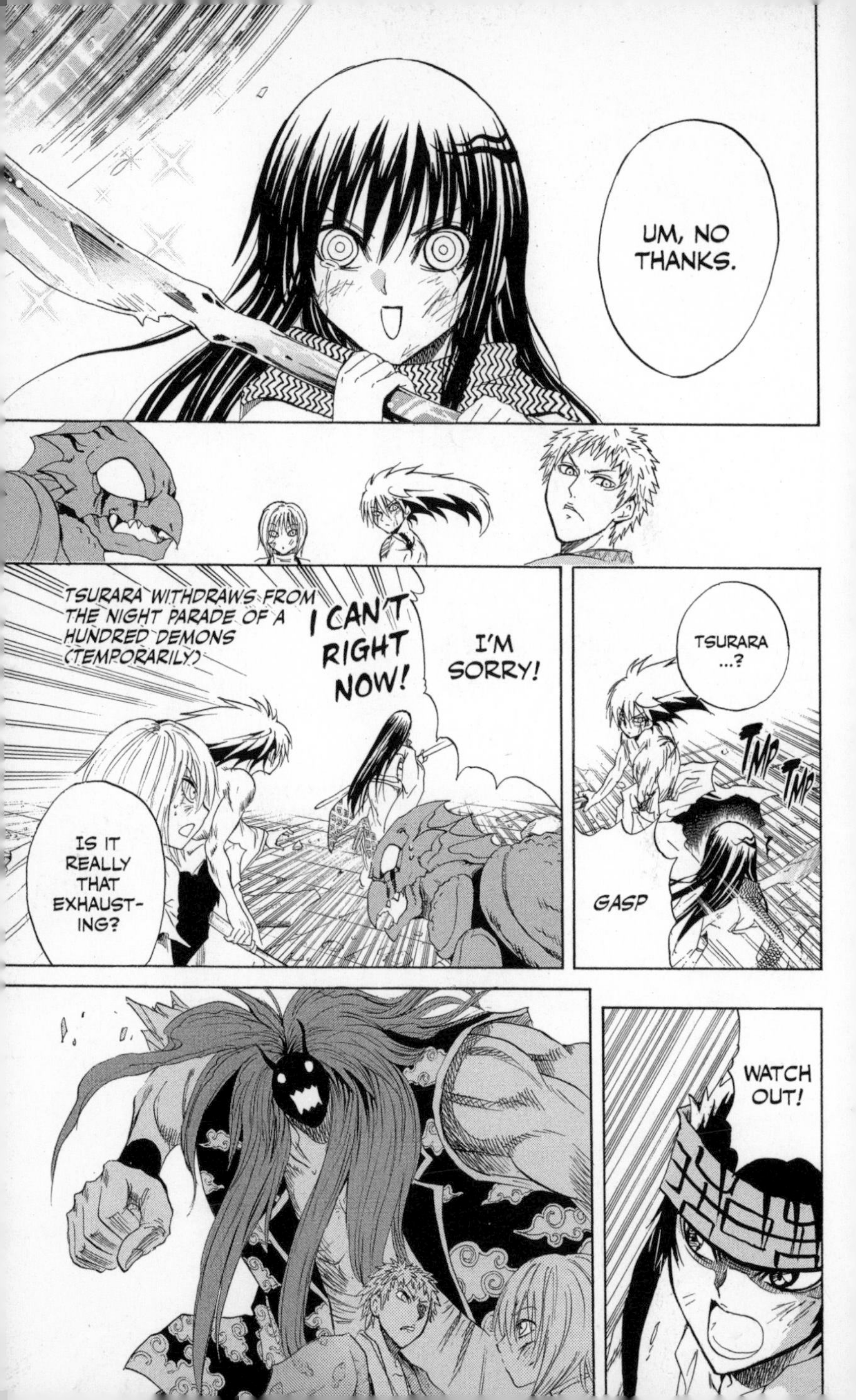
UM, NO THANKS.
TSURARA ...?
TMP TMP
GASP
I'M SORRY!
I CAN'T RIGHT NOW!
TSURARA WITHDRAWS FROM THE NIGHT PARADE OF A HUNDRED DEMONS (TEMPORARILY)
IS IT REALLY THAT EXHAUSTING?
WATCH OUT!

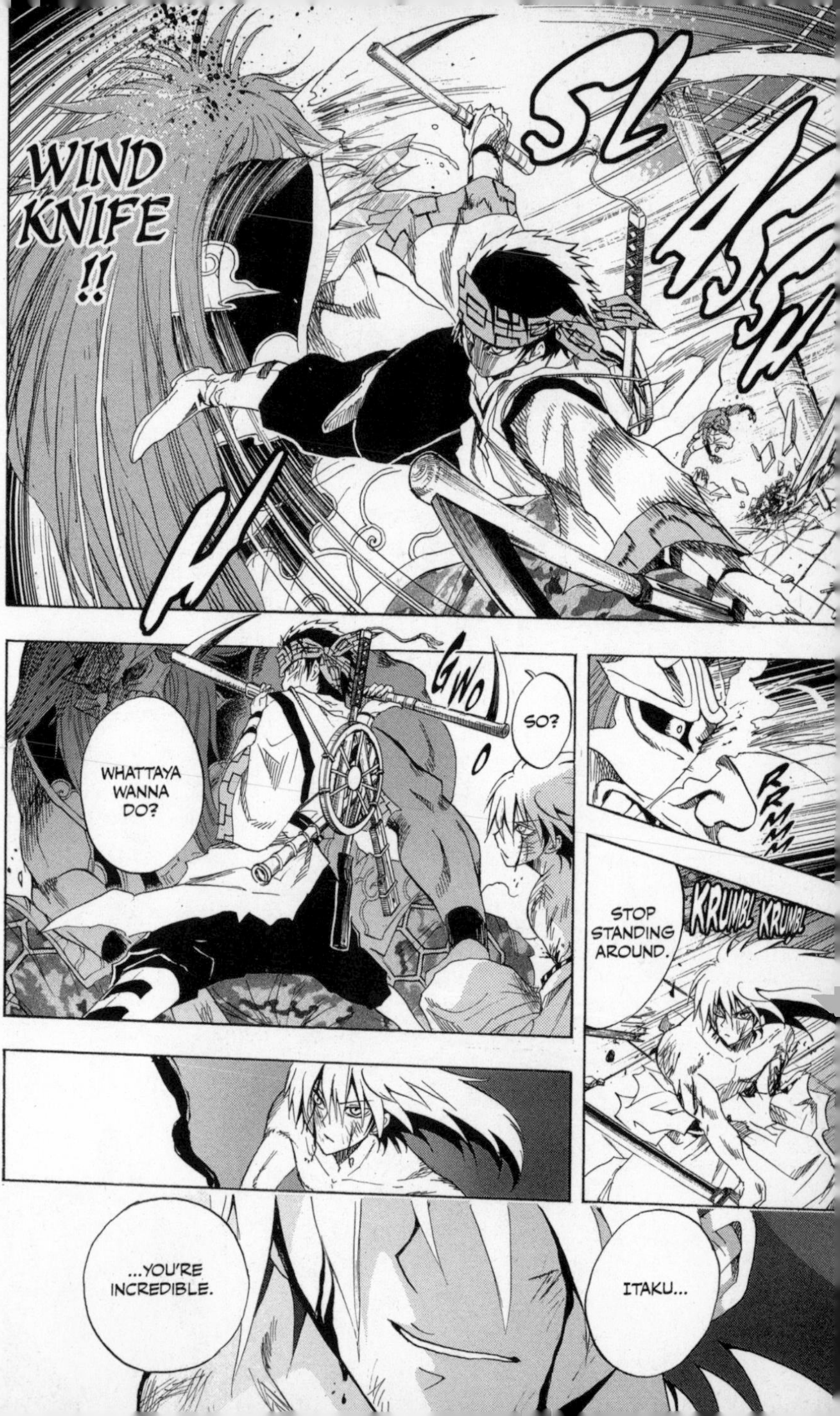
SLASH
WIND KNIFE!!
ARMMM
GWO
SO?
WHATTAYA WANNA DO?
STOP STANDING AROUND.
KRUMBL KRUMBL
ITAKU...
...YOU'RE INCREDIBLE.

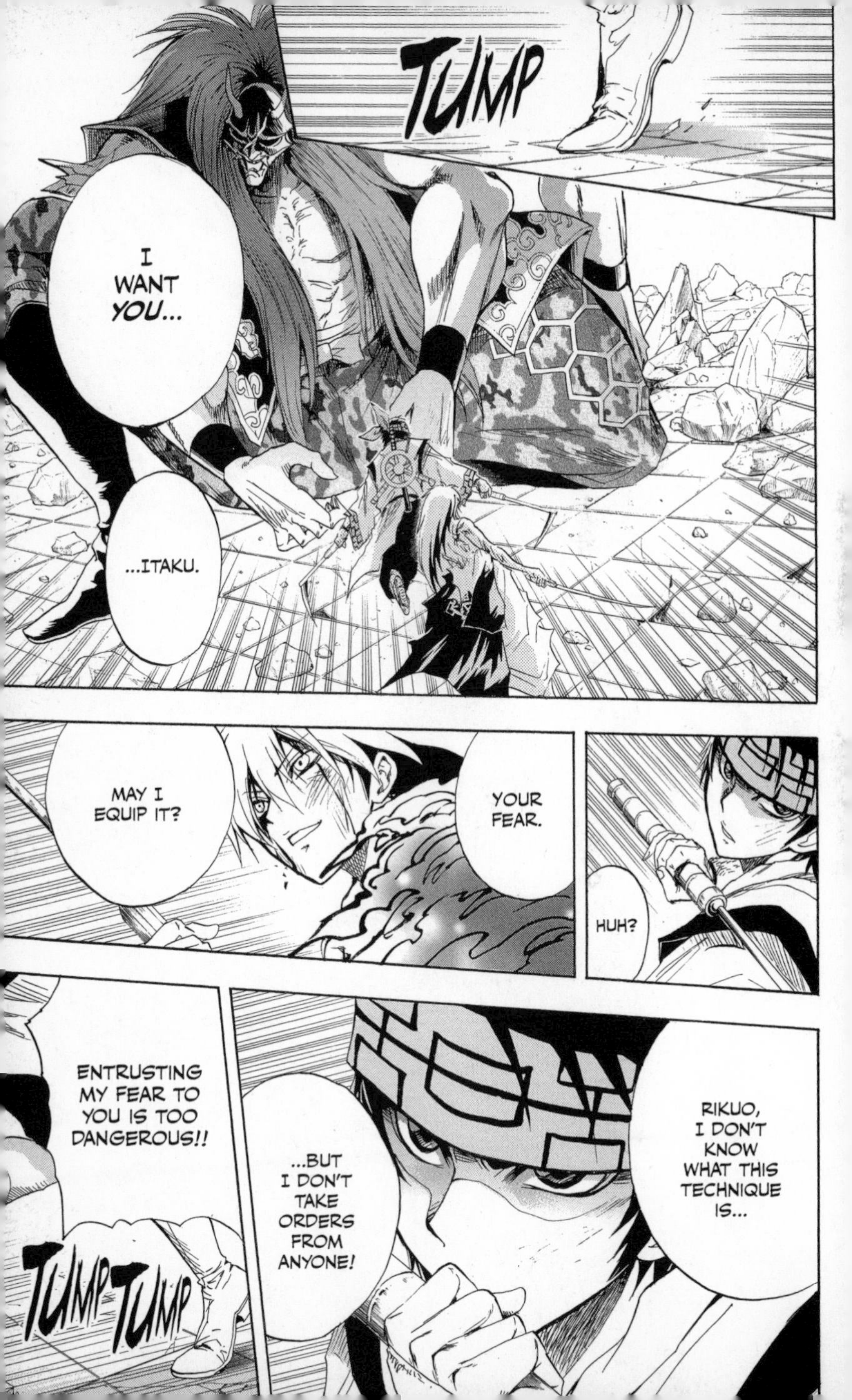
TUMP
I WANT YOU...
...ITAKU.
HUH?
YOUR FEAR.
MAY I EQUIP IT?
RIKUO, I DON'T KNOW WHAT THIS TECHNIQUE IS...
...BUT I DON'T TAKE ORDERS FROM ANYONE!
ENTRUSTING MY FEAR TO YOU IS TOO DANGEROUS!!
TUMP TUMP

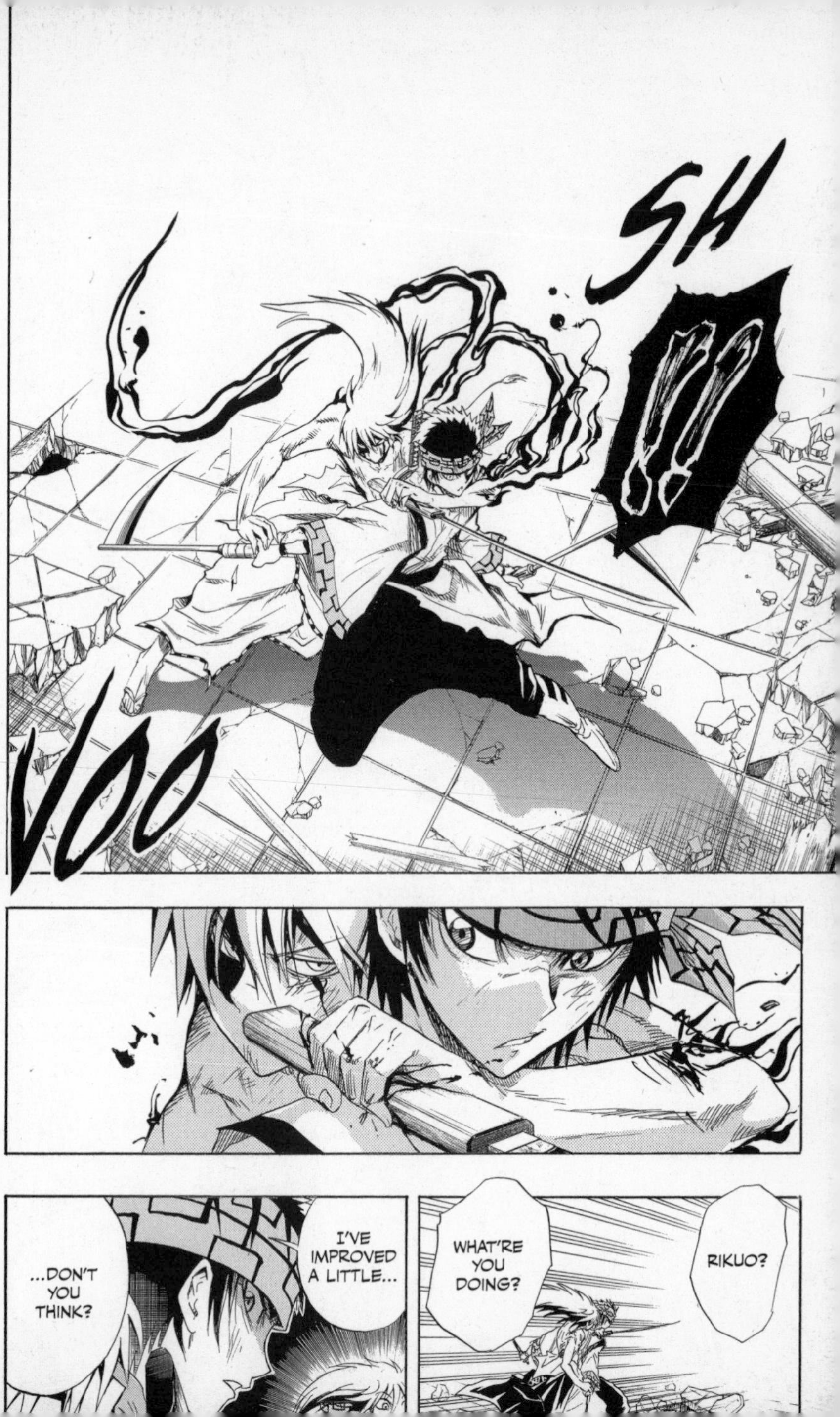
SH
!!
VOO
RIKUO?
WHAT'RE YOU DOING?
I'VE IMPROVED A LITTLE...
...DON'T YOU THINK?

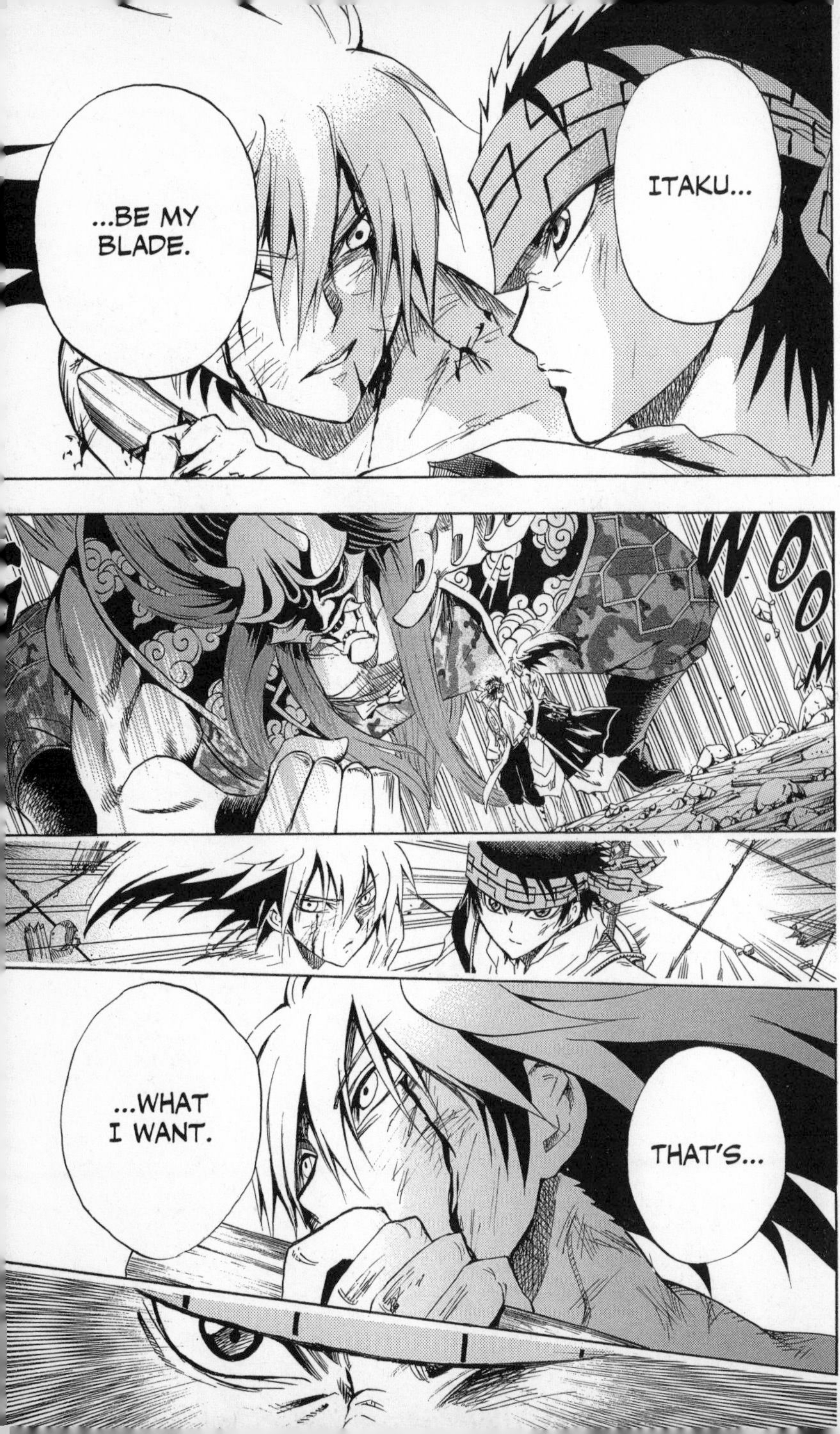
ITAKU...
...BE MY BLADE.
WOOOM
THAT'S...
...WHAT I WANT.

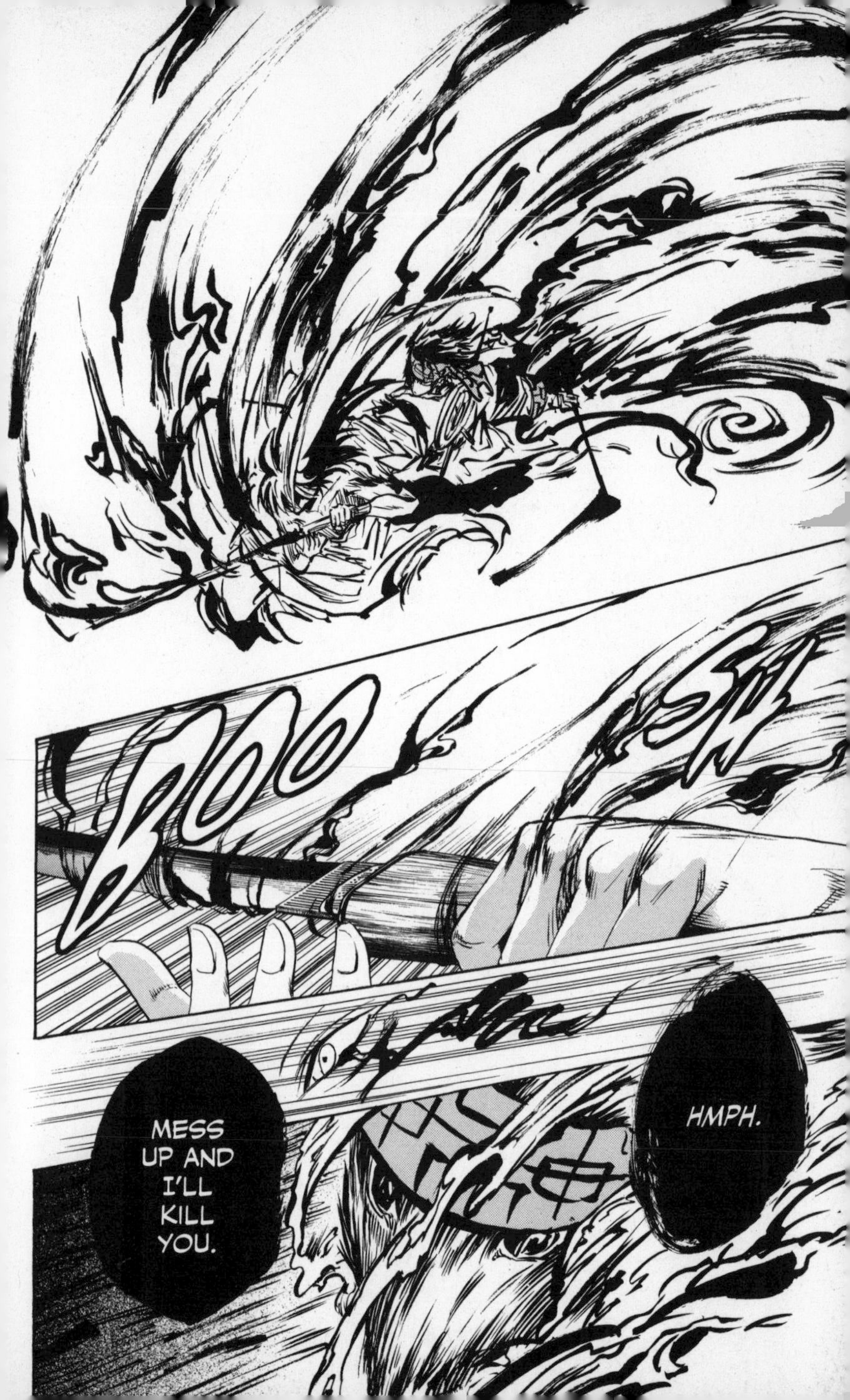
HMPH.
MESS UP AND I'LL KILL YOU.

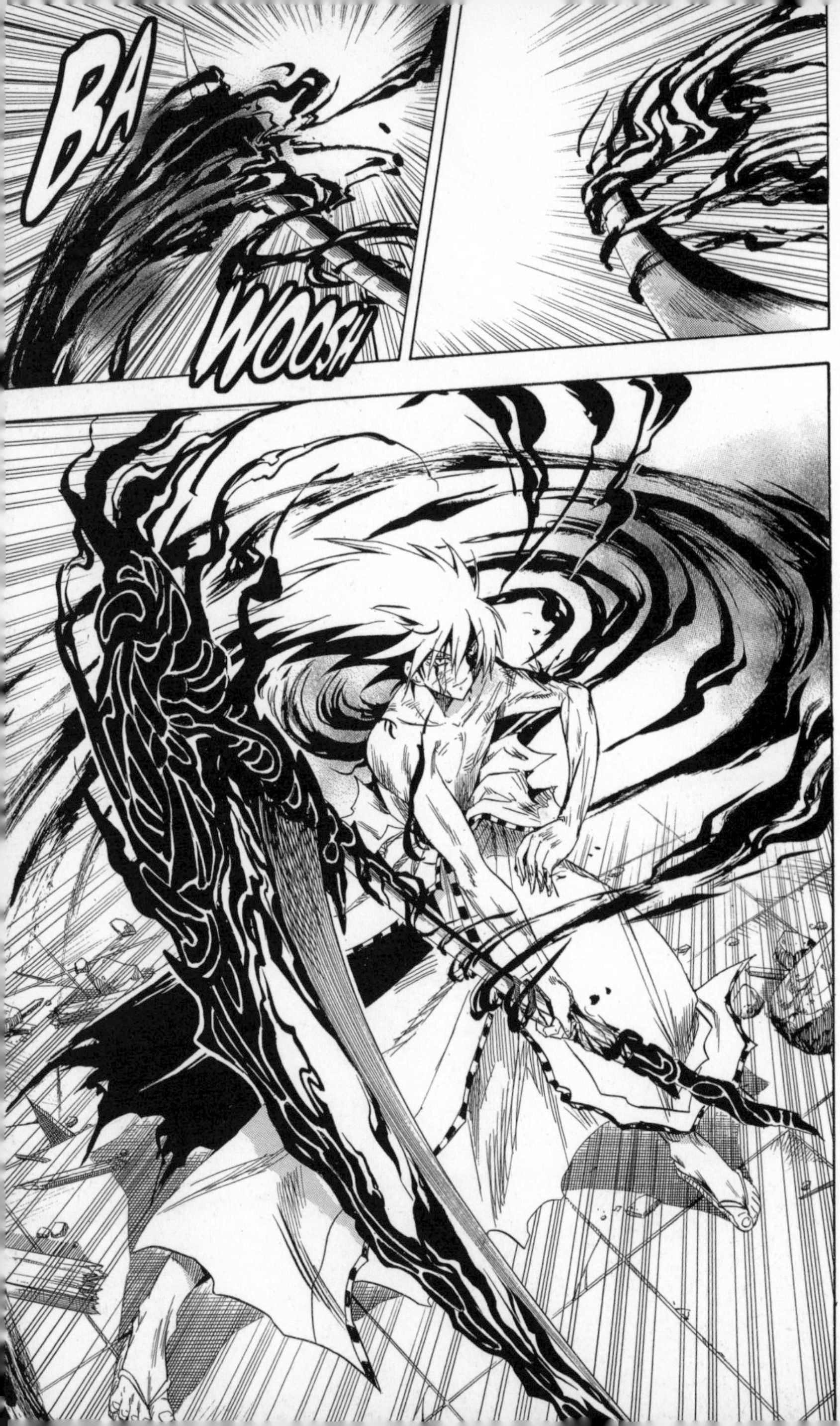
BA
WOOSH

I didn't
mean
to say
that.

The
words
just
slipped
out.

Waah...
I don't
under-
stand it.

Sorry,
Lord
Rikuo...

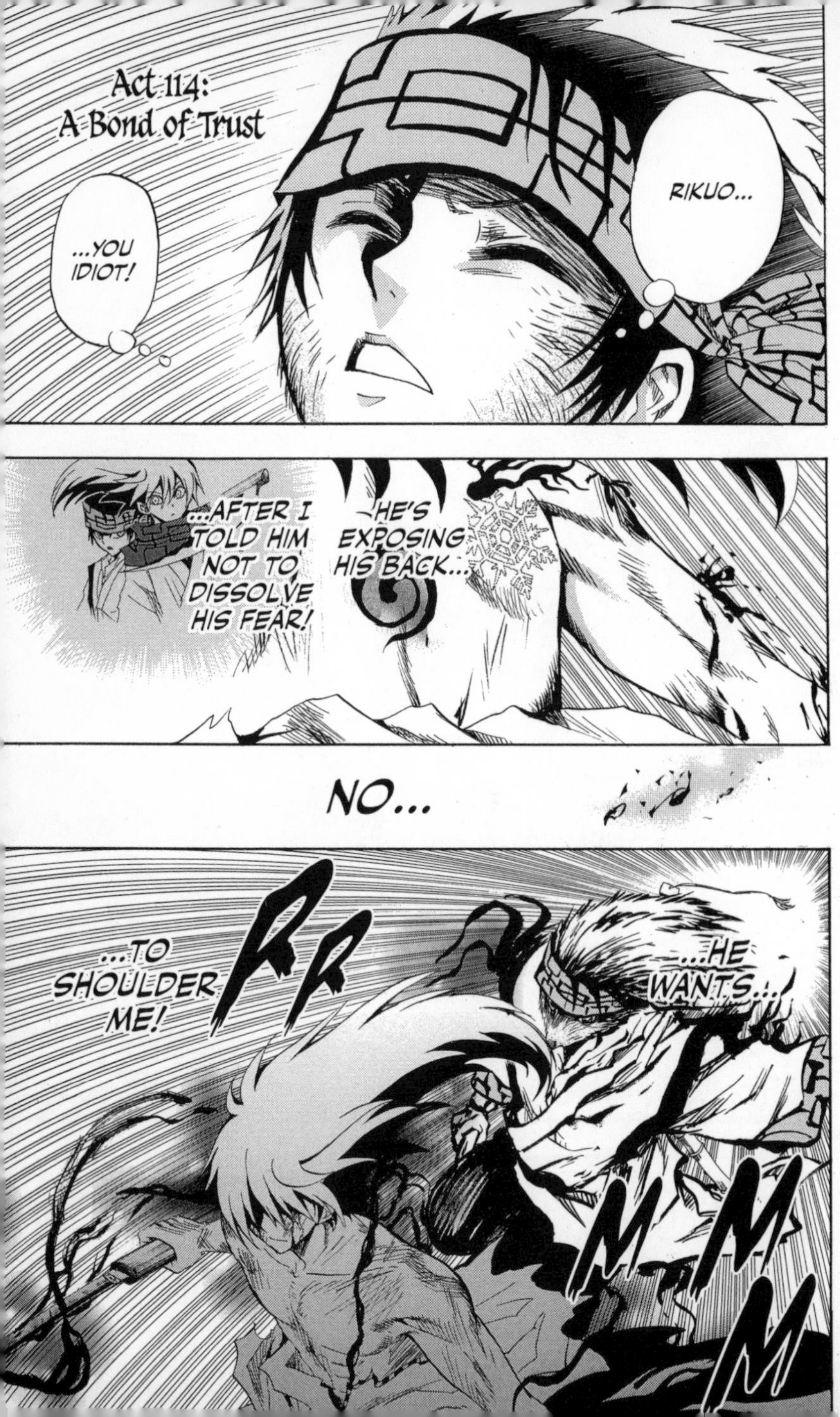
Act 114: A Bond of Trust
RIKUO...
...YOU IDIOT!
HE'S EXPOSING HIS BACK...
...AFTER I TOLD HIM NOT TO DISSOLVE HIS FEAR!
NO...
...HE WANTS...
RR
...TO SHOULDER ME!
MMMM

Act 114: A Bond of Trust

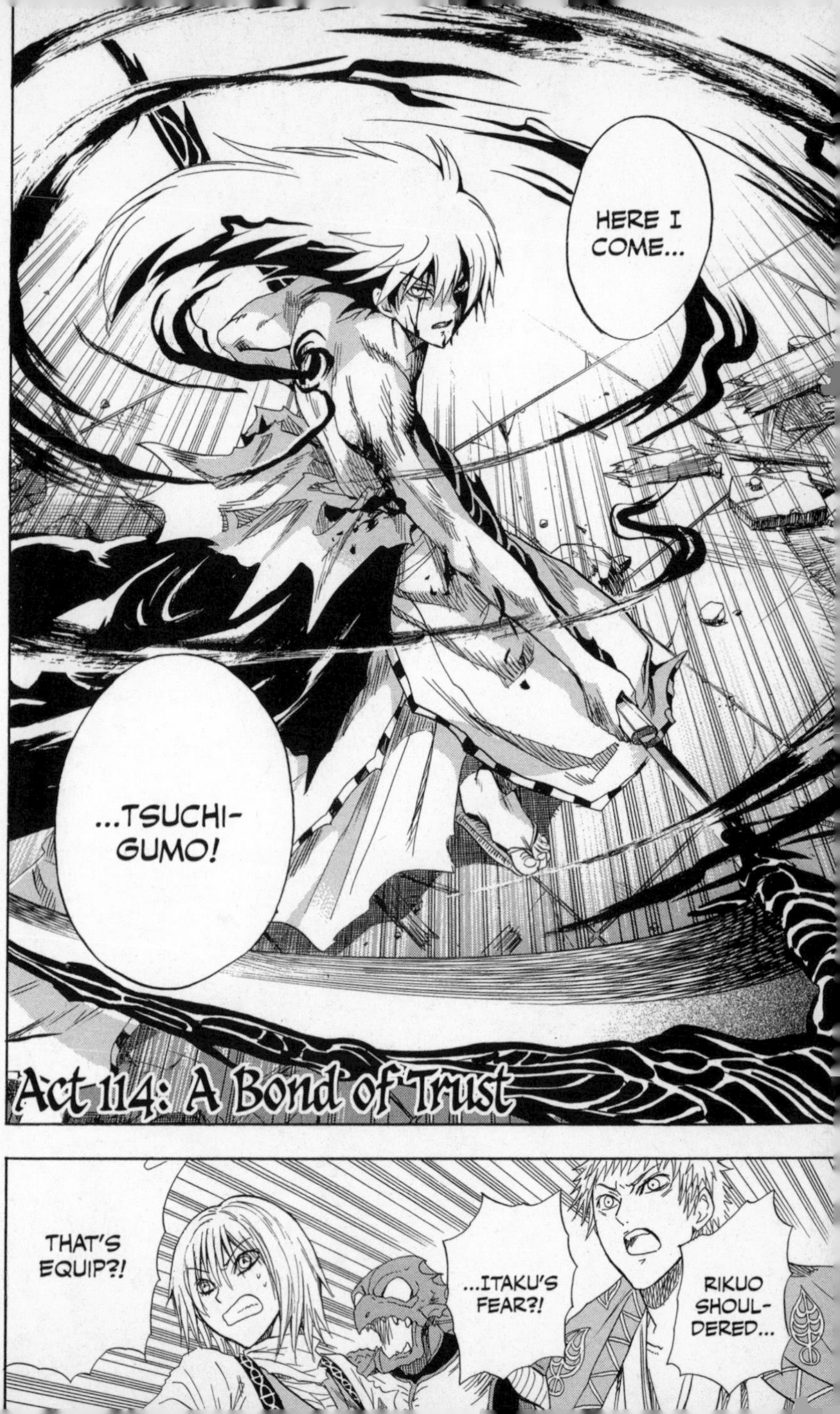
HERE I COME...
...TSUCHI-GUMO!
RIKUO SHOULDERED...
...ITAKU'S FEAR?!
THAT'S EQUIP?!

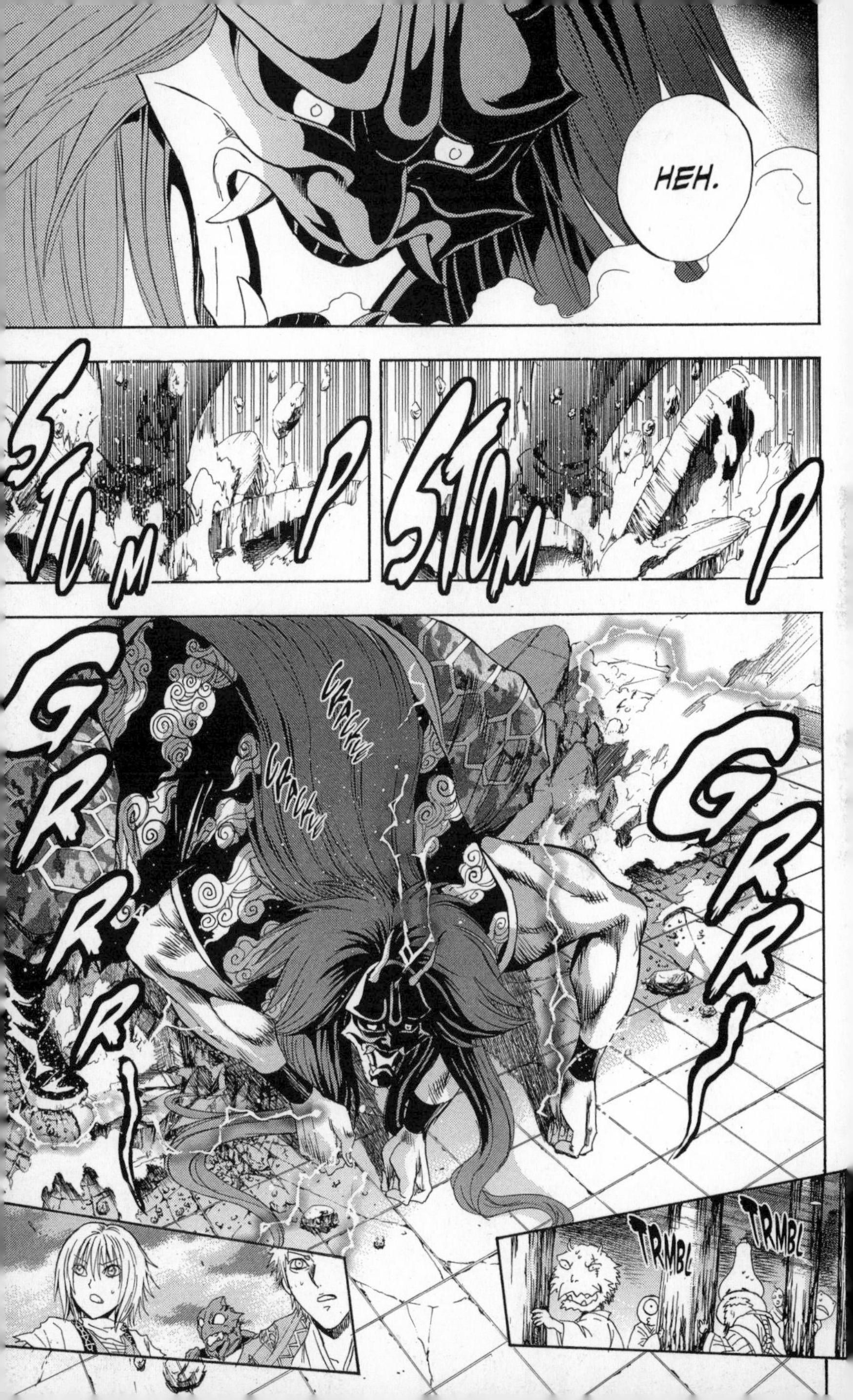
HEH.
STOMP
STOMP
GRRR
GRRRR
TRMBL
TRMBL

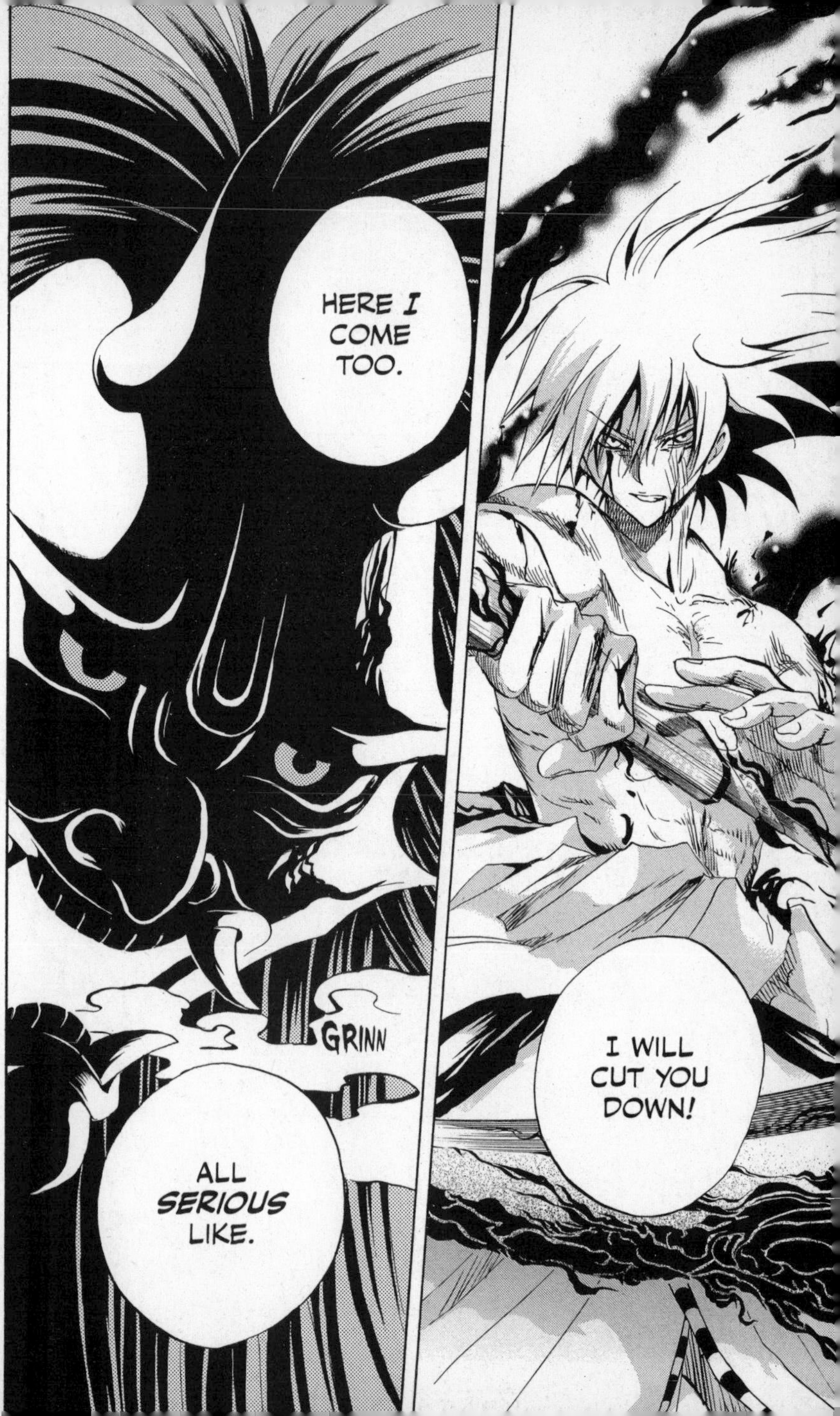
I WILL CUT YOU DOWN!
HERE I COME TOO.
GRINN
ALL SERIOUS LIKE.

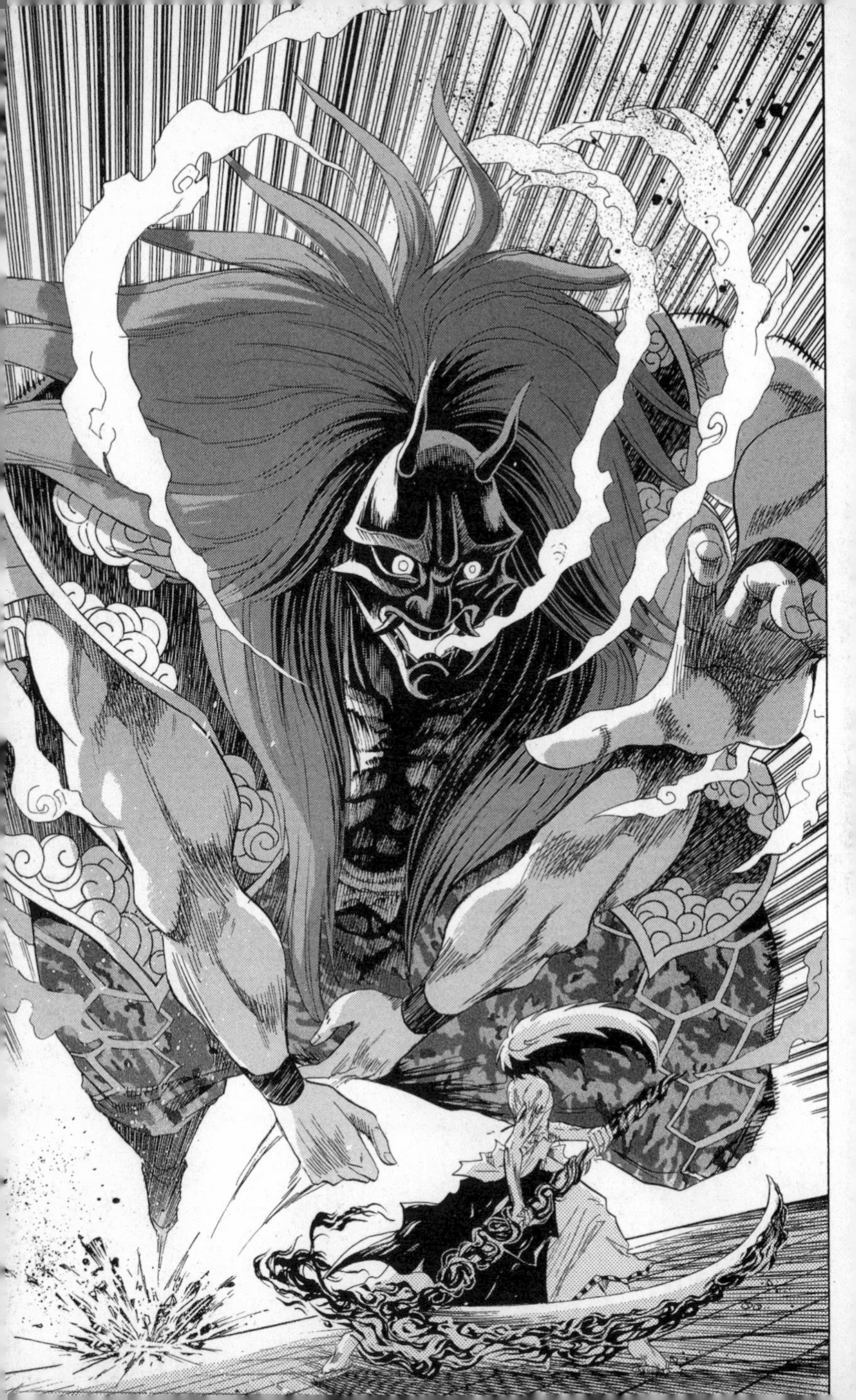

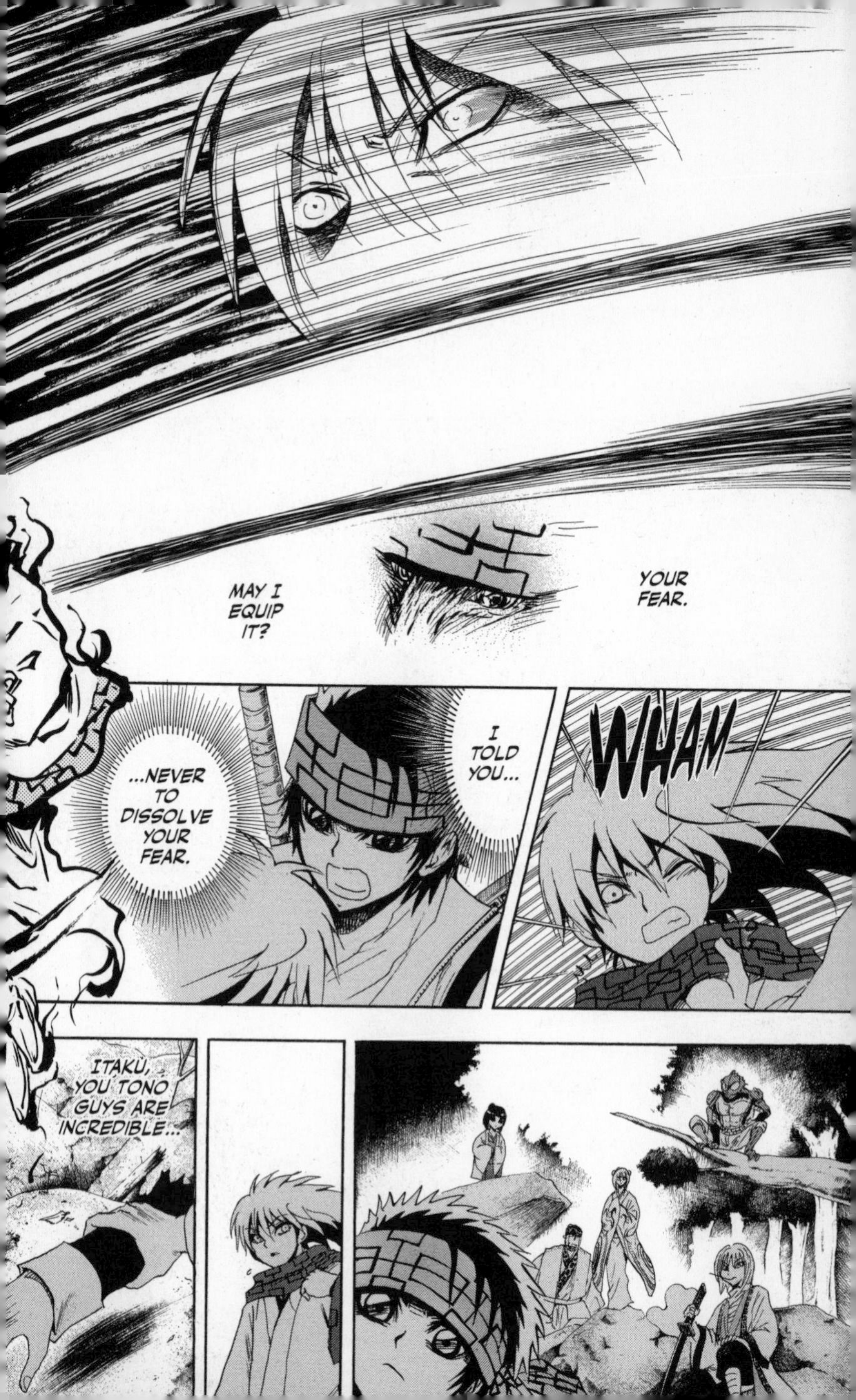
YOUR FEAR.
MAY I EQUIP IT?
WHAM
I TOLD YOU...
...NEVER TO DISSOLVE YOUR FEAR.
ITAKU, YOU TONO GUYS ARE INCREDIBLE...

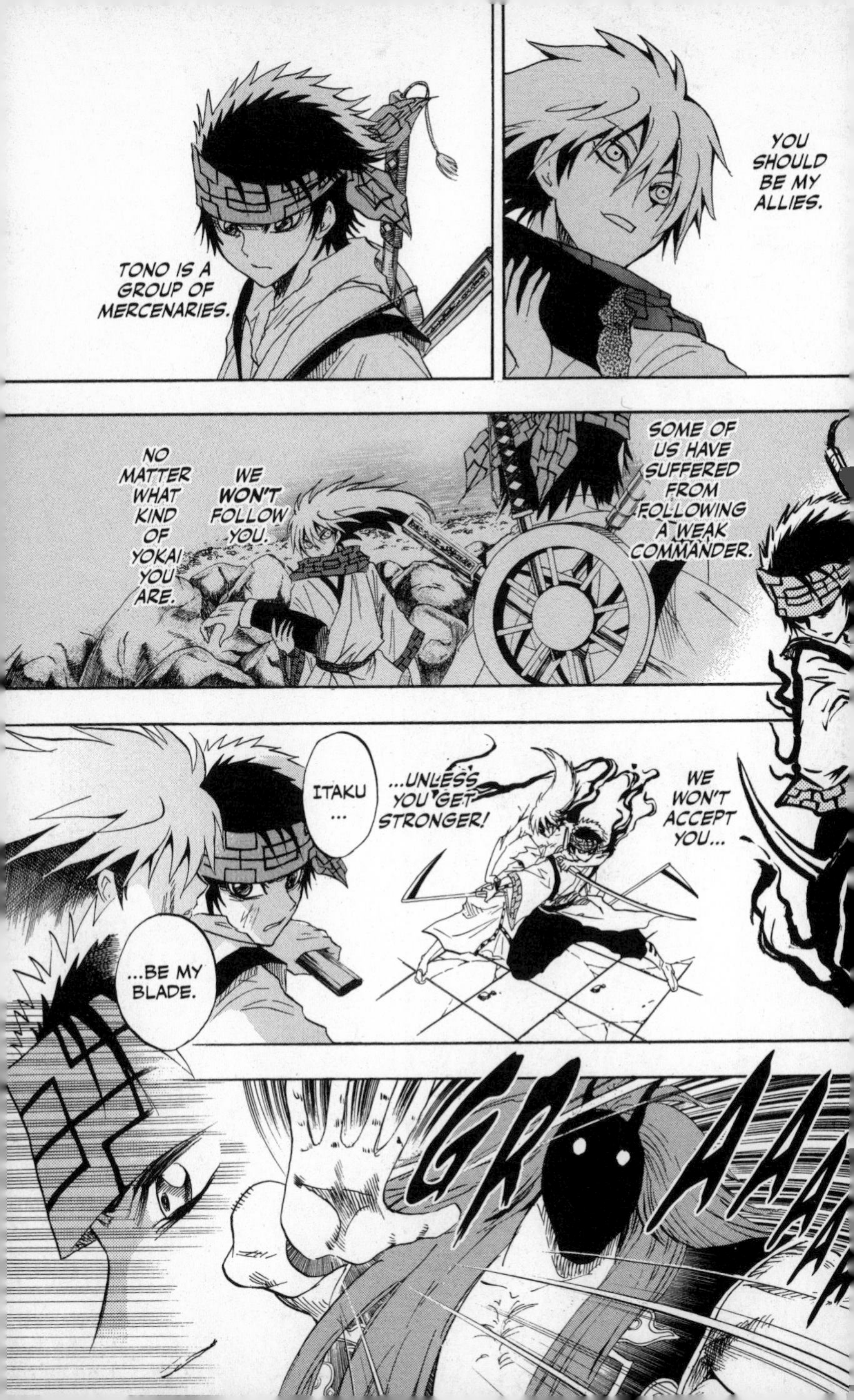
YOU SHOULD BE MY ALLIES.
TONO IS A GROUP OF MERCENARIES.
SOME OF US HAVE SUFFERED FROM FOLLOWING A WEAK COMMANDER.
WE WON'T FOLLOW YOU.
NO MATTER WHAT KIND OF YOKAI YOU ARE.
WE WON'T ACCEPT YOU...
...UNLESS YOU GET STRONGER!
ITAKU...
...BE MY BLADE.

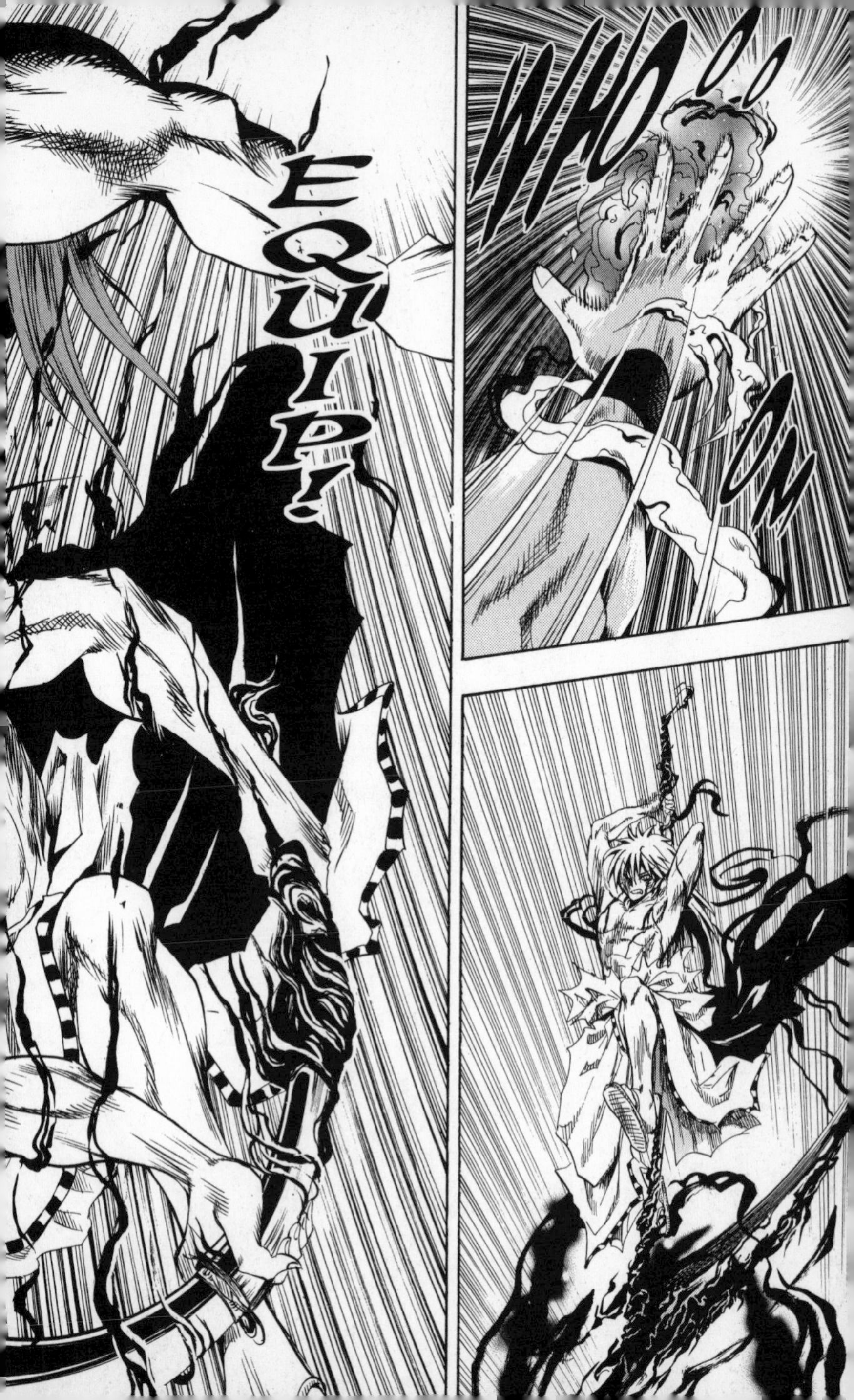
WHOOoo
OOM
EQUIP!

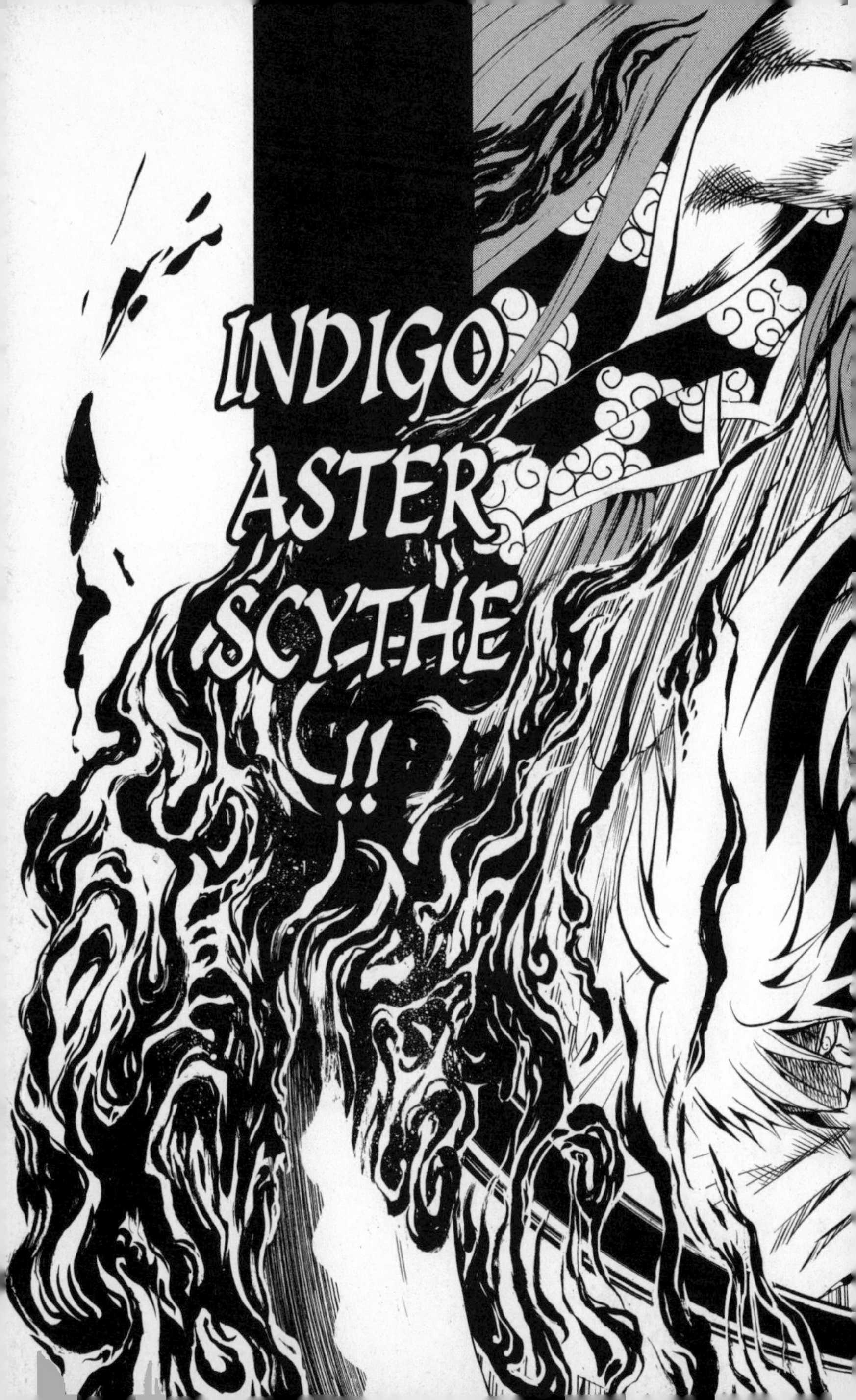
INDIGO ASTER SCYTHE!!

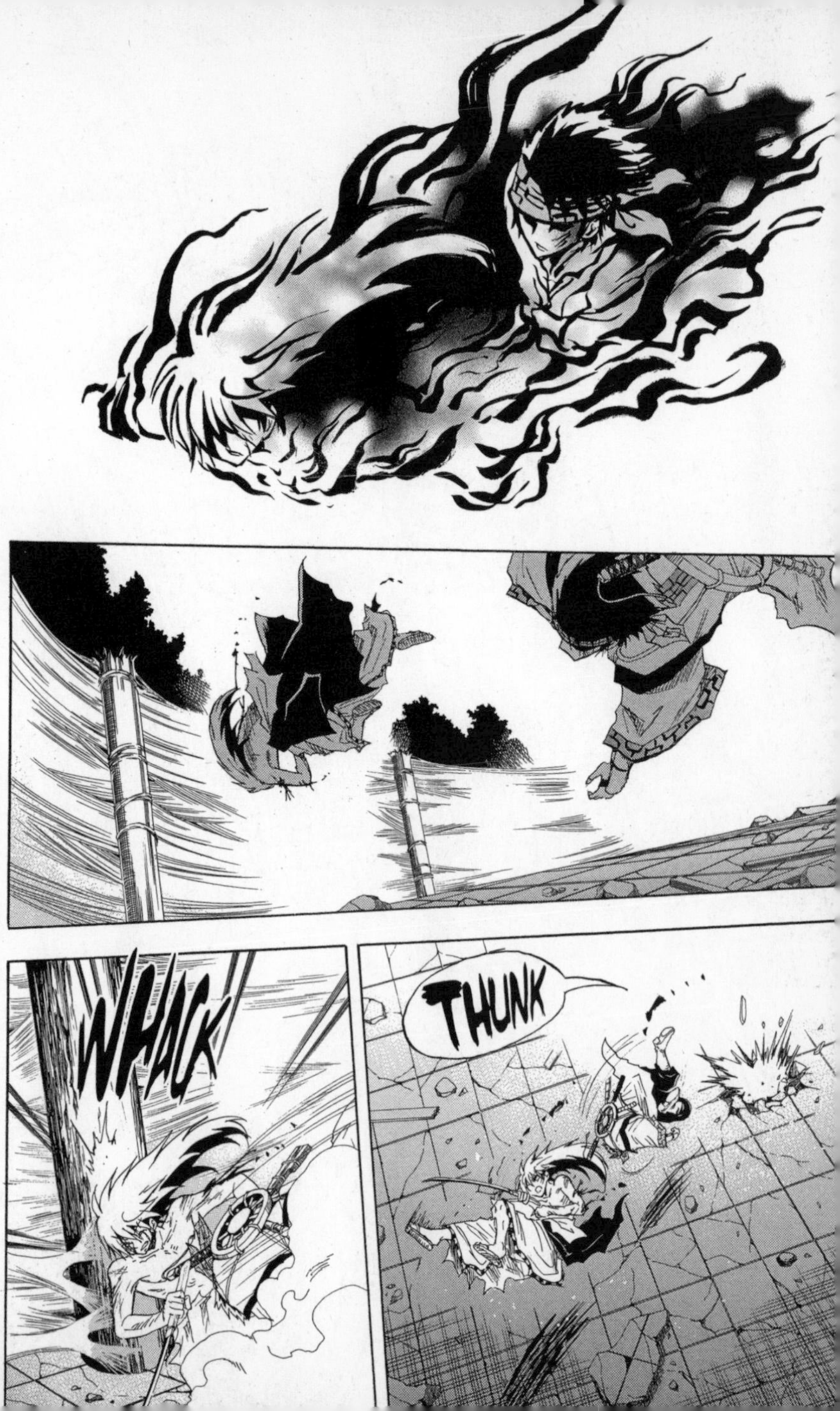
THUNK
WHACK

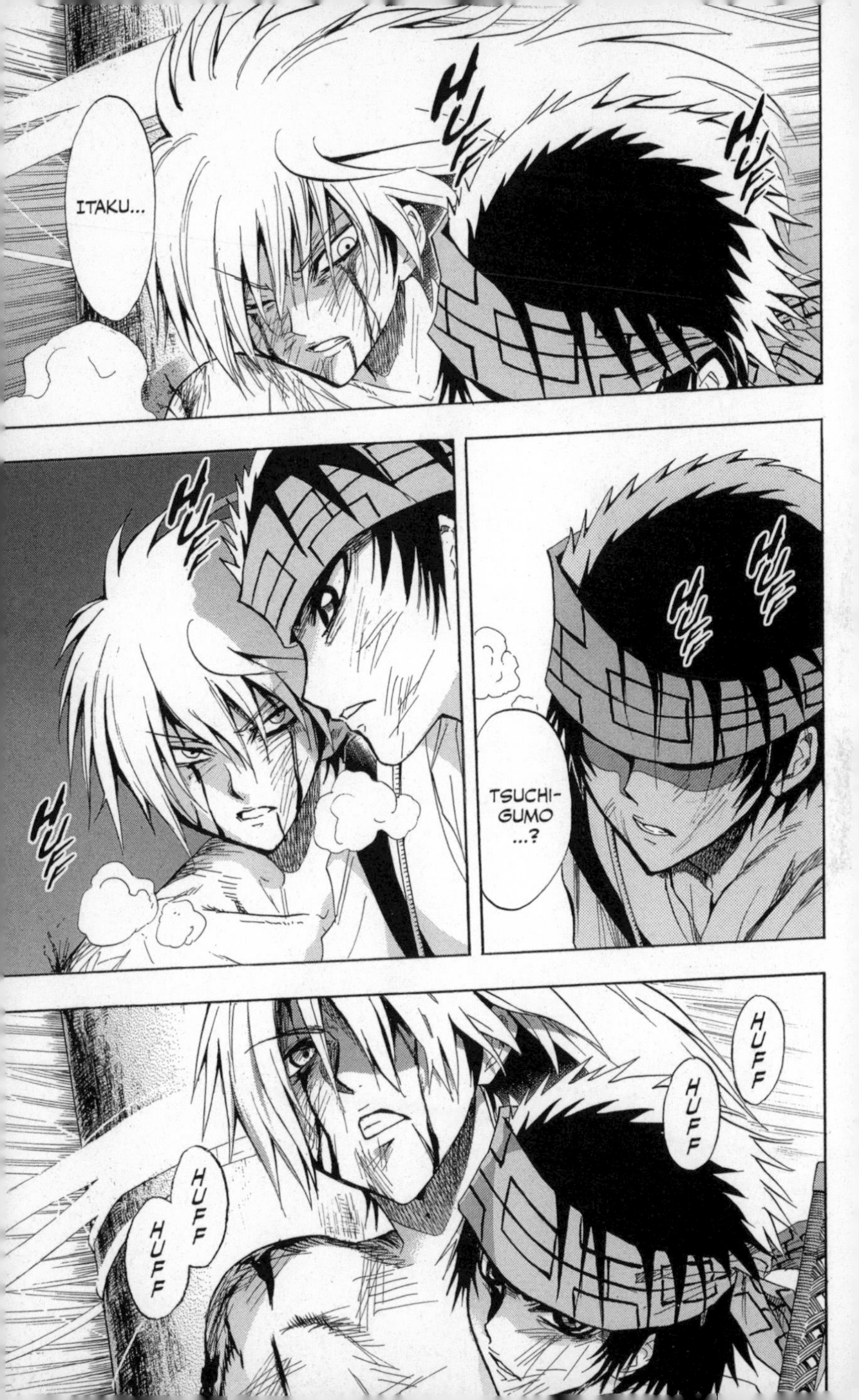
HUFF
HUFF
ITAKU...
TSUCHI-
GUMO
...?
HUFF
HUFF
HUFF
HUFF
HUFF
HUFF

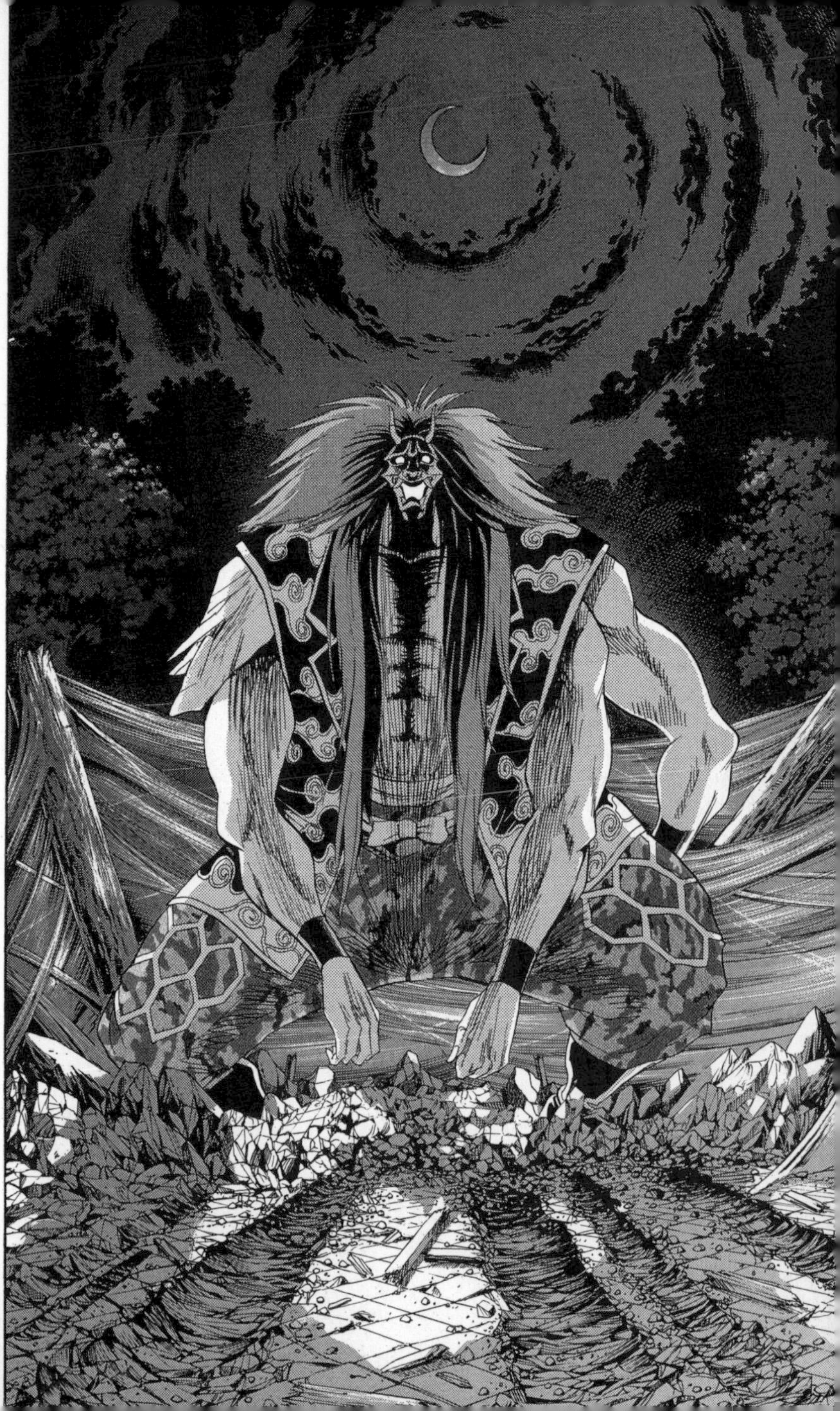

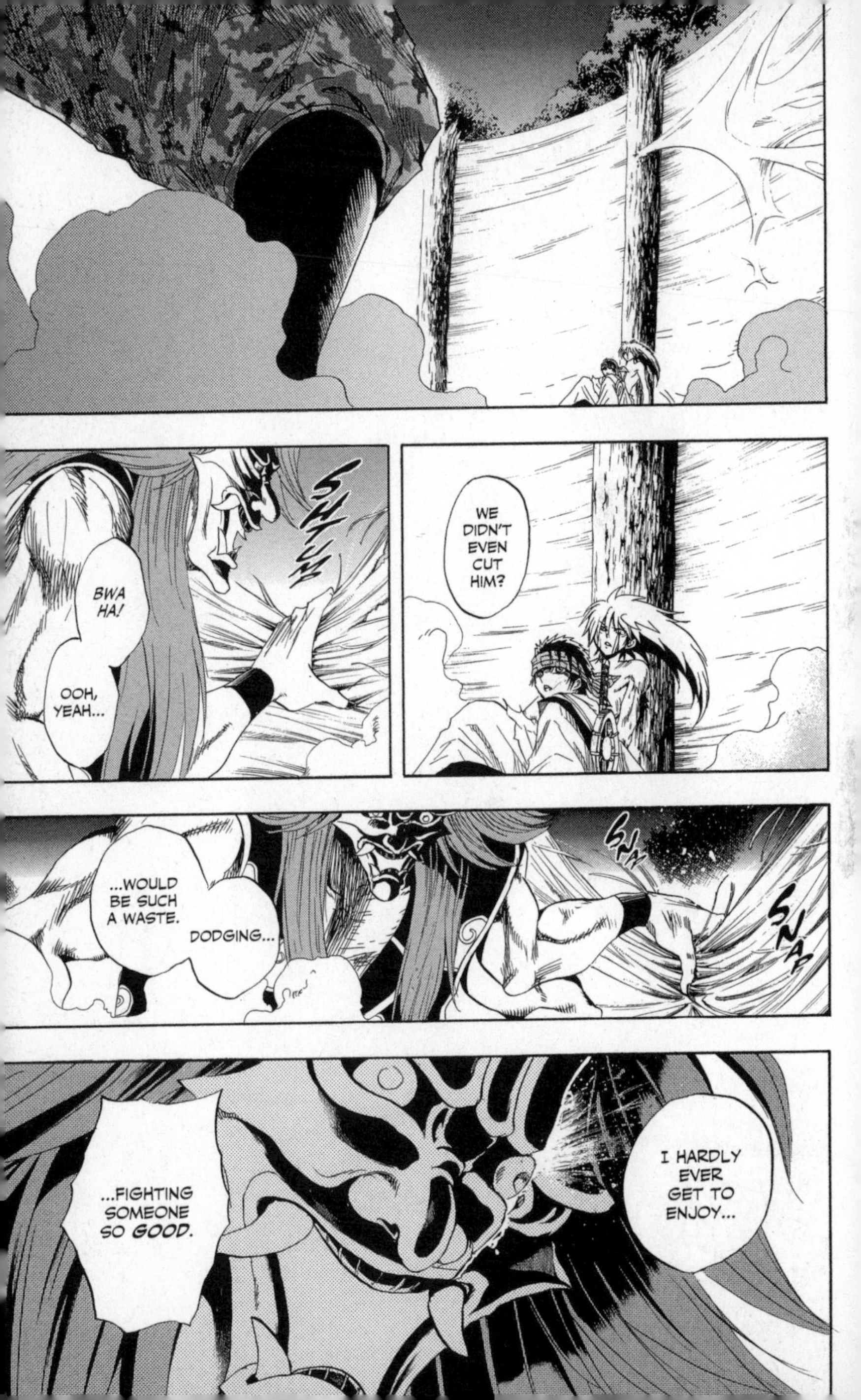
WE DIDN'T EVEN CUT HIM?
SHFUM
BWA HA!
OOH, YEAH...
SNAP
SNA
DODGING...
...WOULD BE SUCH A WASTE.
I HARDLY EVER GET TO ENJOY...
...FIGHTING SOMEONE SO *GOOD*.

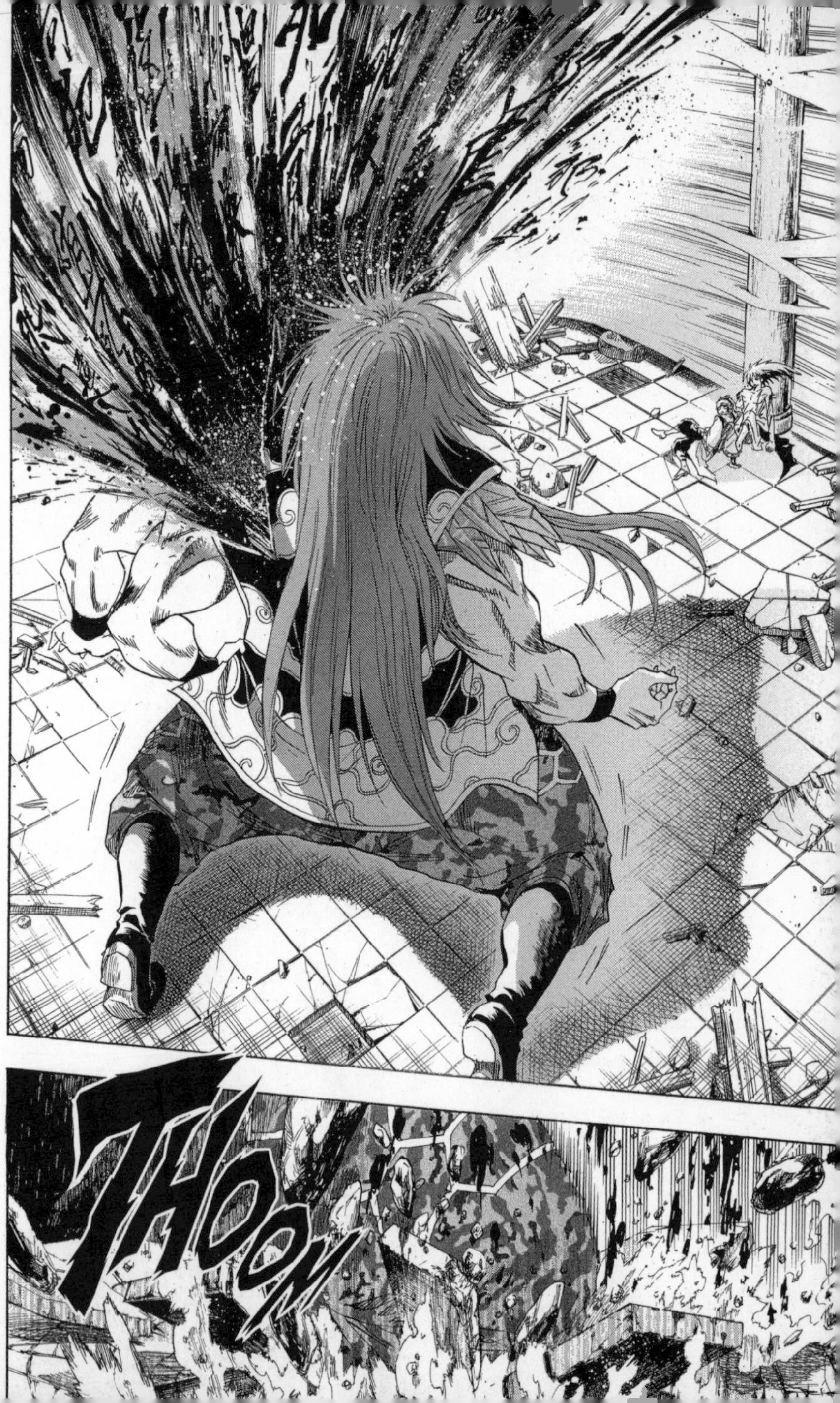
THOOM

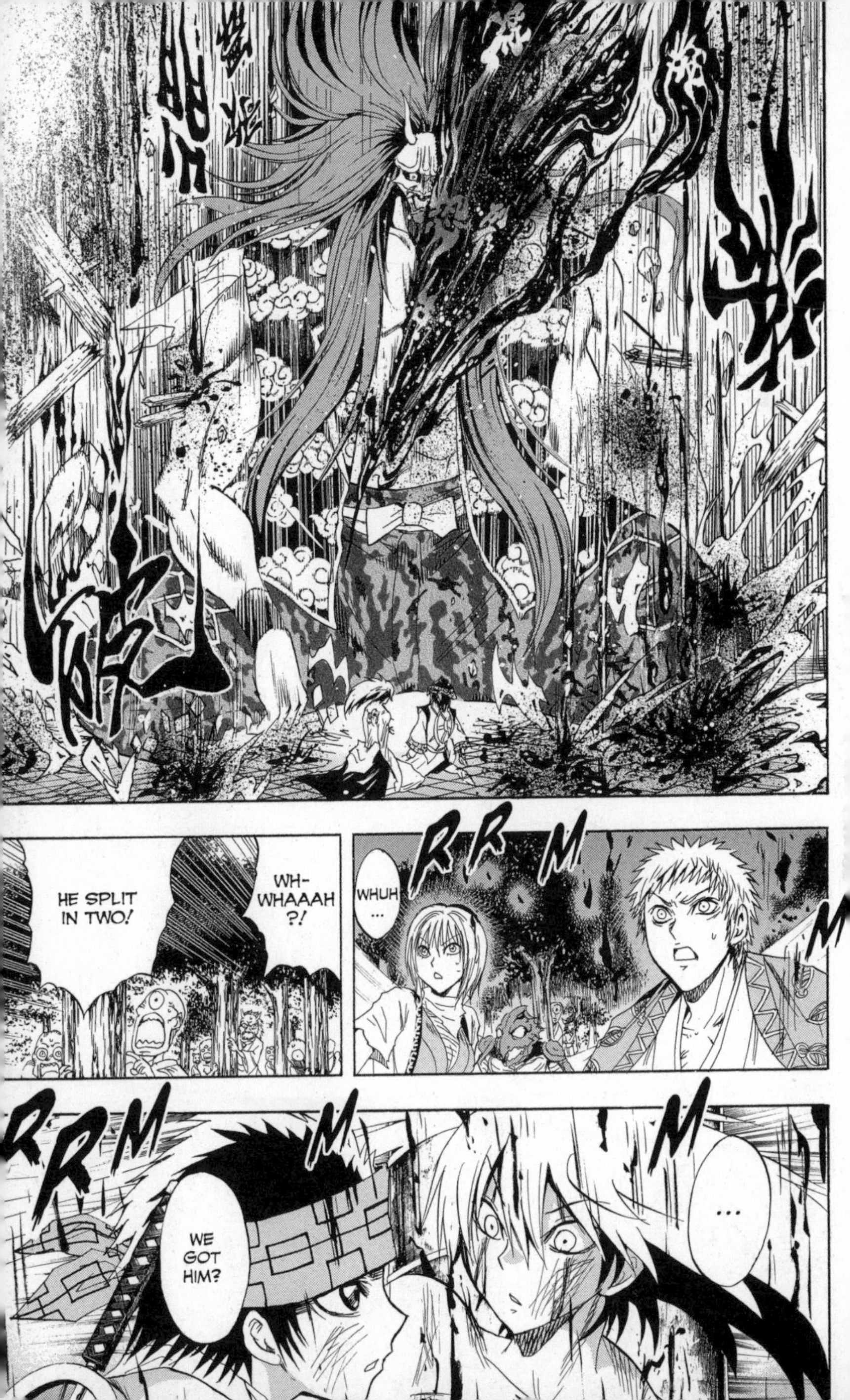

RRM
M
WHUH ...
WH- WHAAAH?!
HE SPLIT IN TWO!
RRM
M
M
M
...
WE GOT HIM?

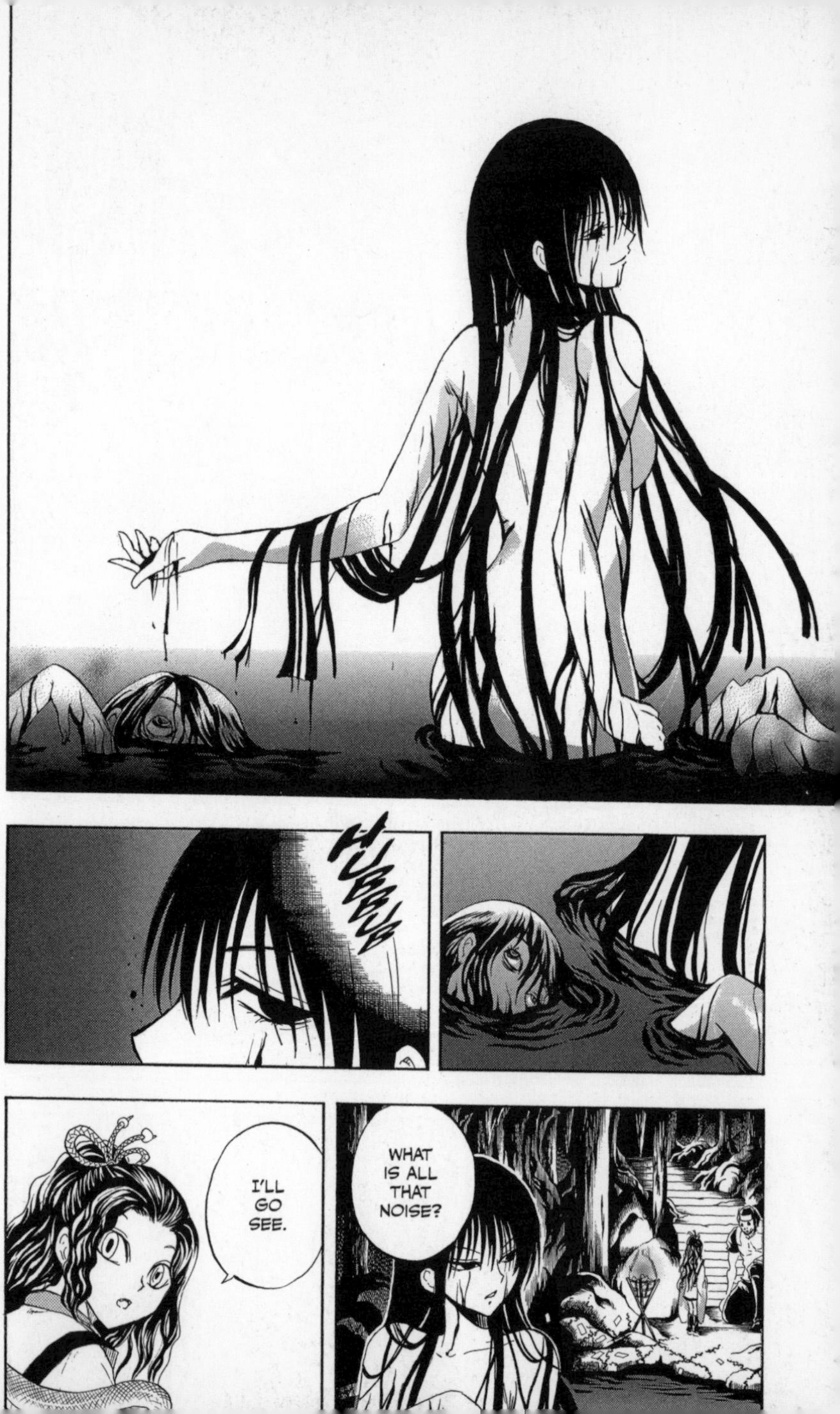
HUBBUB
WHAT IS ALL THAT NOISE?
I'LL GO SEE.

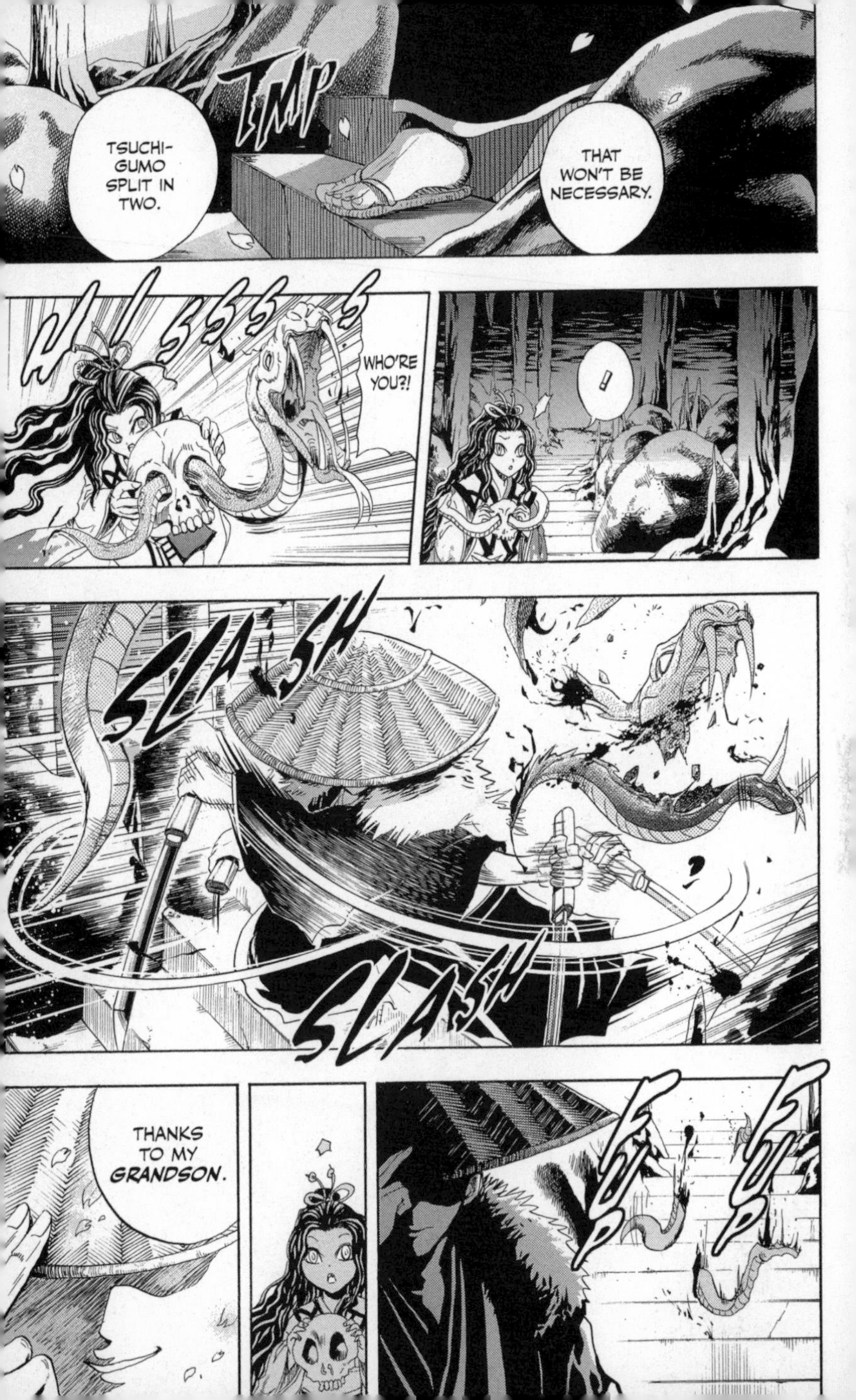
THAT WON'T BE NECESSARY.
TMP
TSUCHIGUMO SPLIT IN TWO.
!
WHO'RE YOU?!
HISSSSS
SLASH
SLASH
FWUP
FWUP
THANKS TO MY GRANDSON.

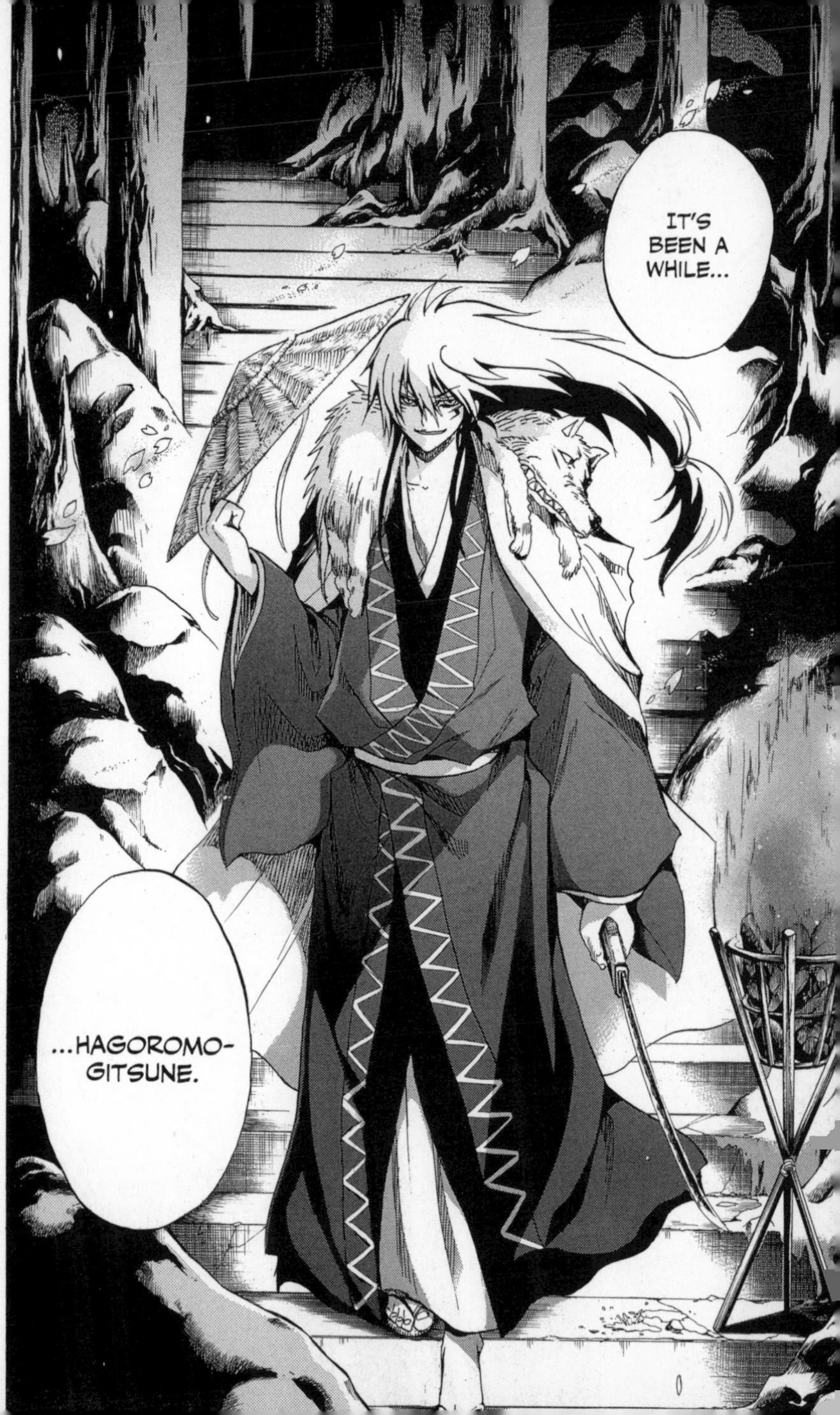
IT'S BEEN A WHILE...
...HAGOROMO-GITSUNE.

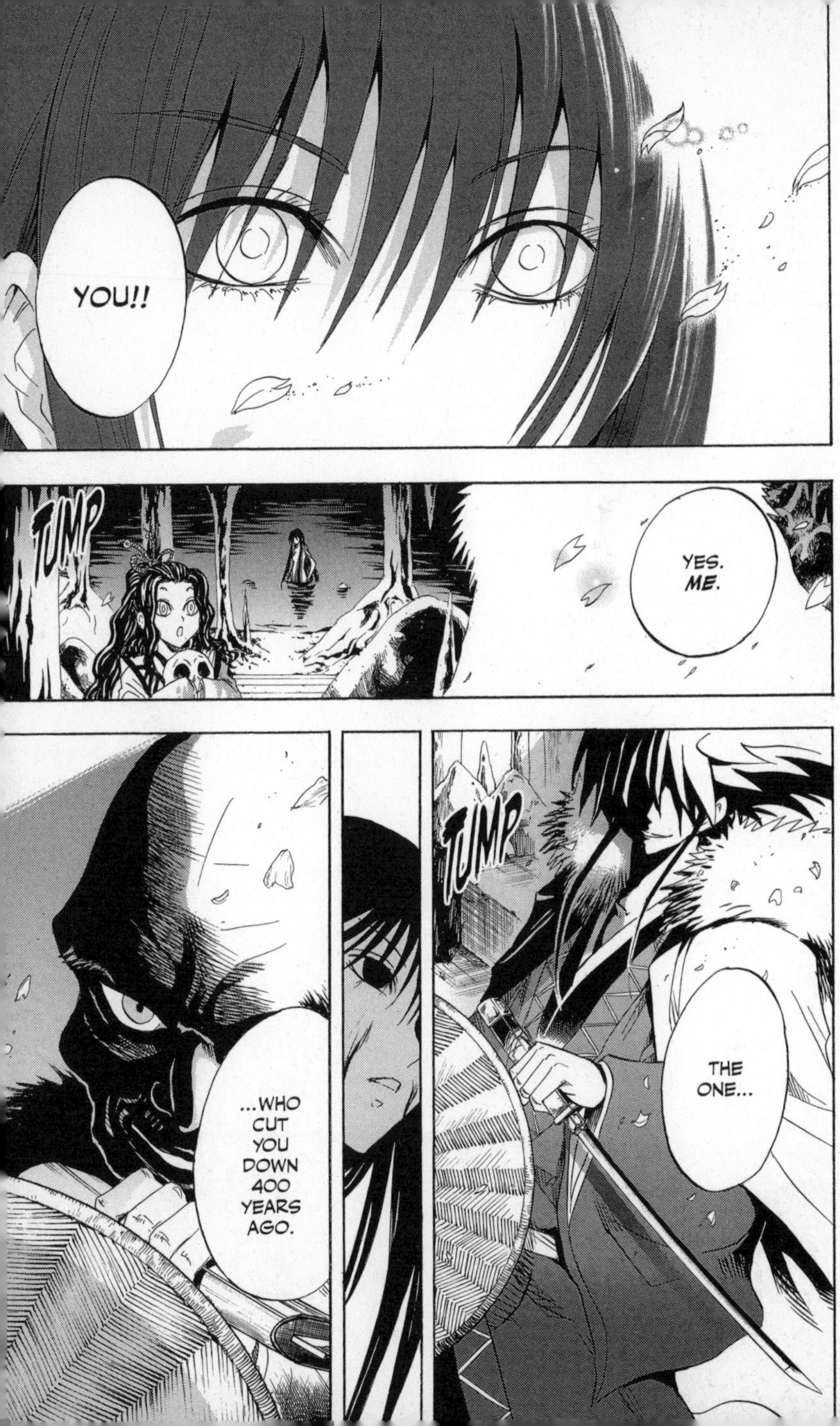
YOU!!
YES. ME.
TUMP
TUMP
THE ONE...
...WHO CUT YOU DOWN 400 YEARS AGO.

NURA: RISE OF THE YOKAI CLAN

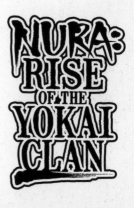

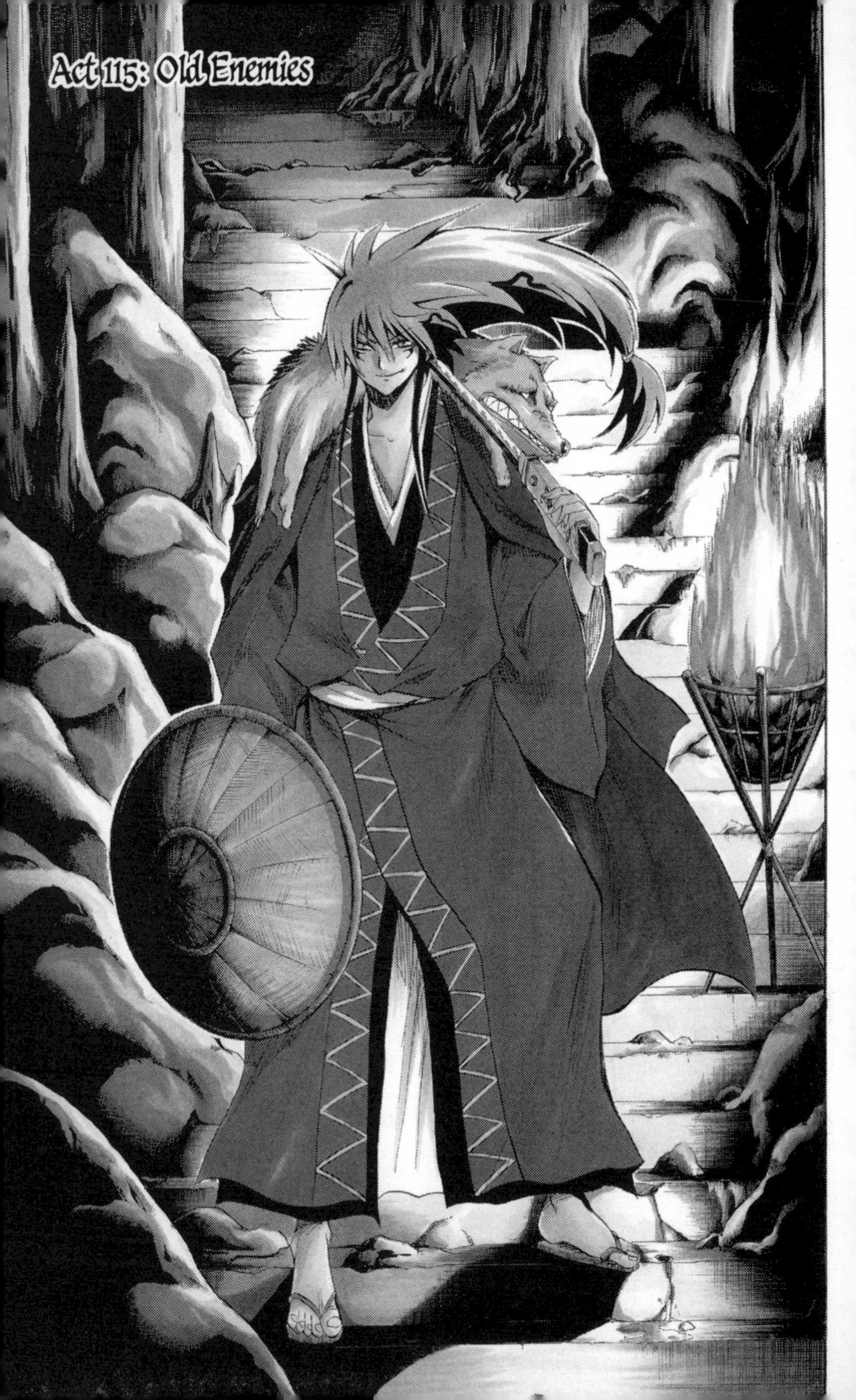
Act 115: Old Enemies

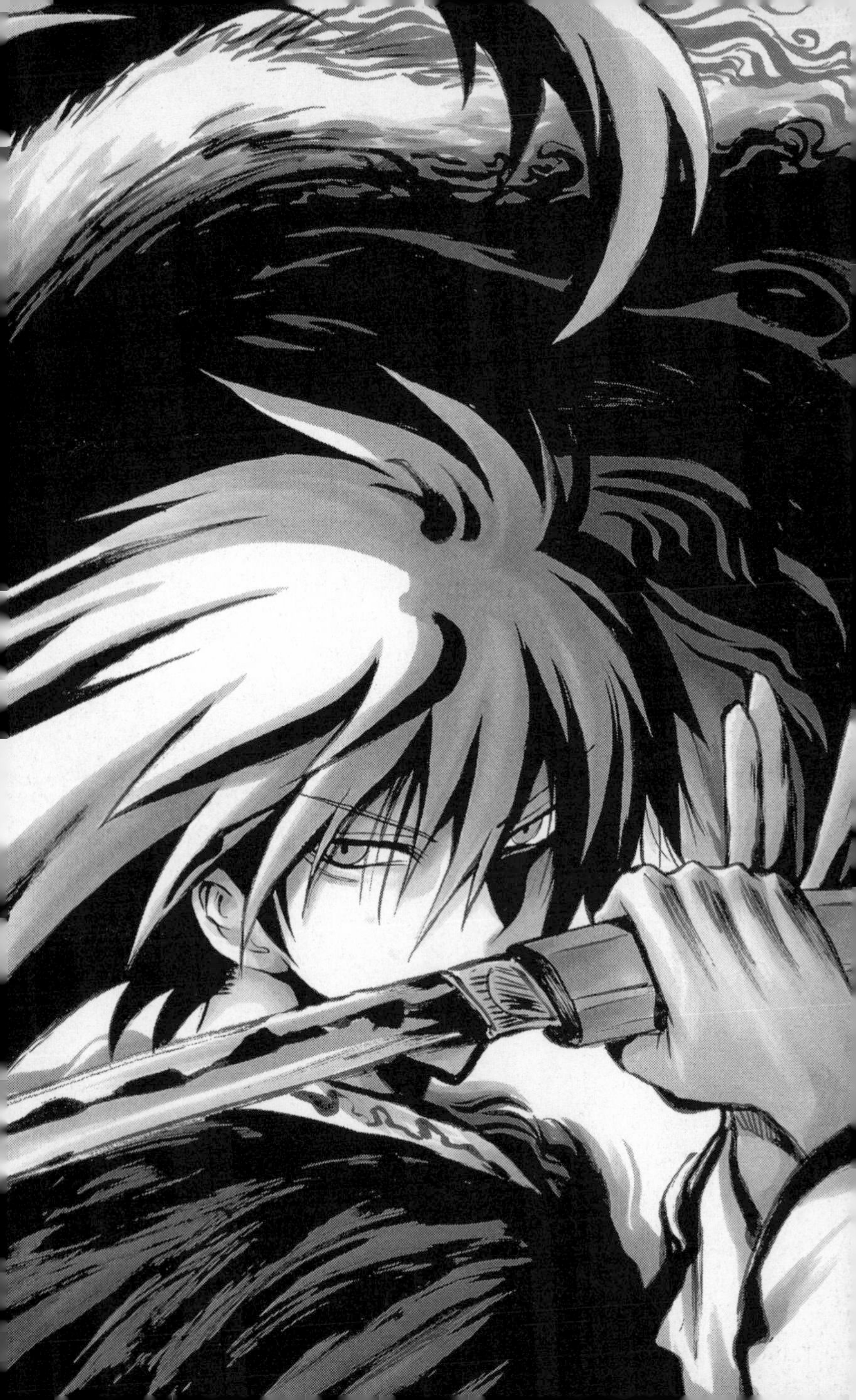

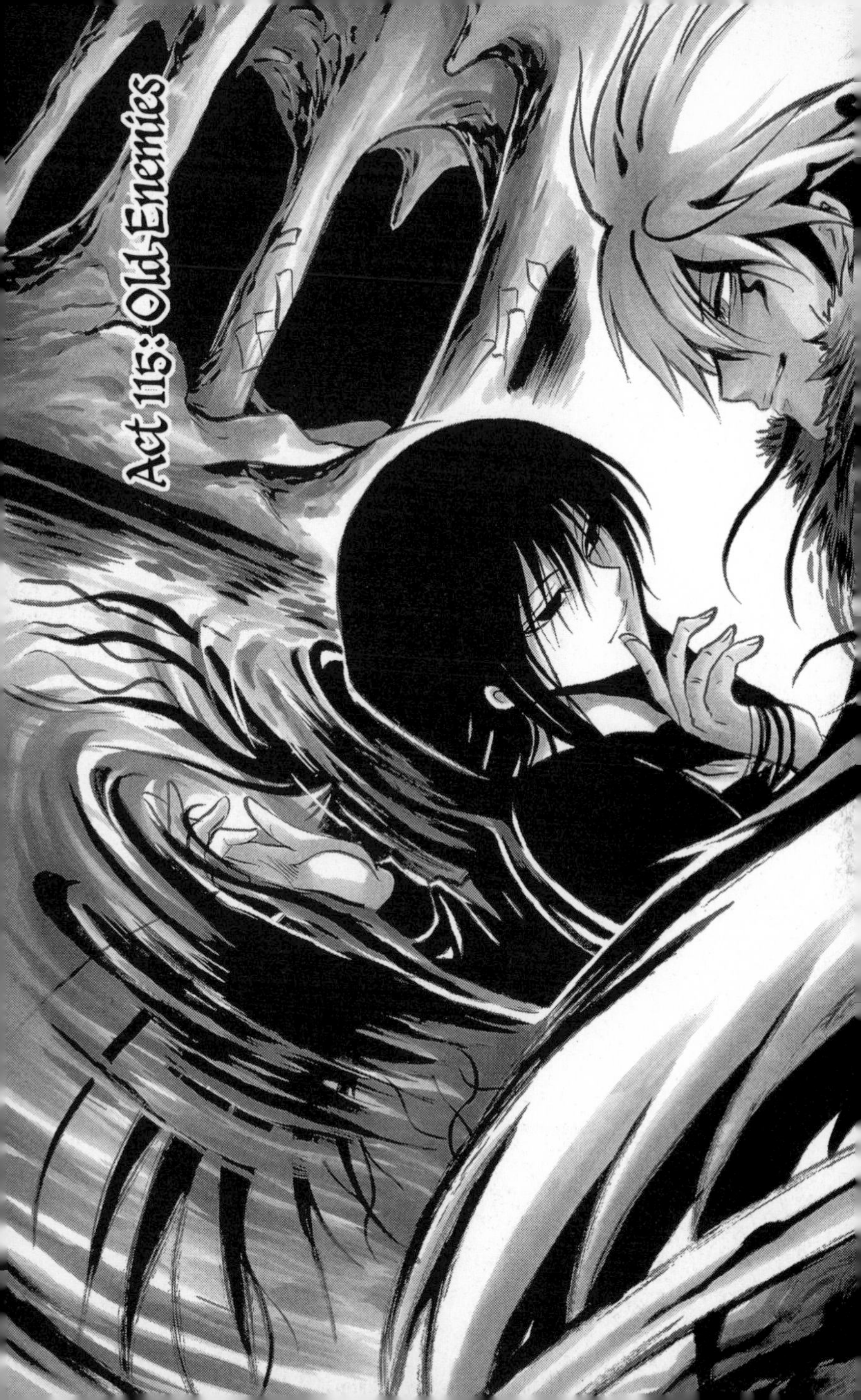
Act 115: Old Enemies

NURA: RISE OF THE YOKAI CLAN

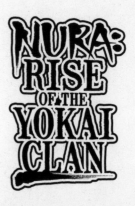

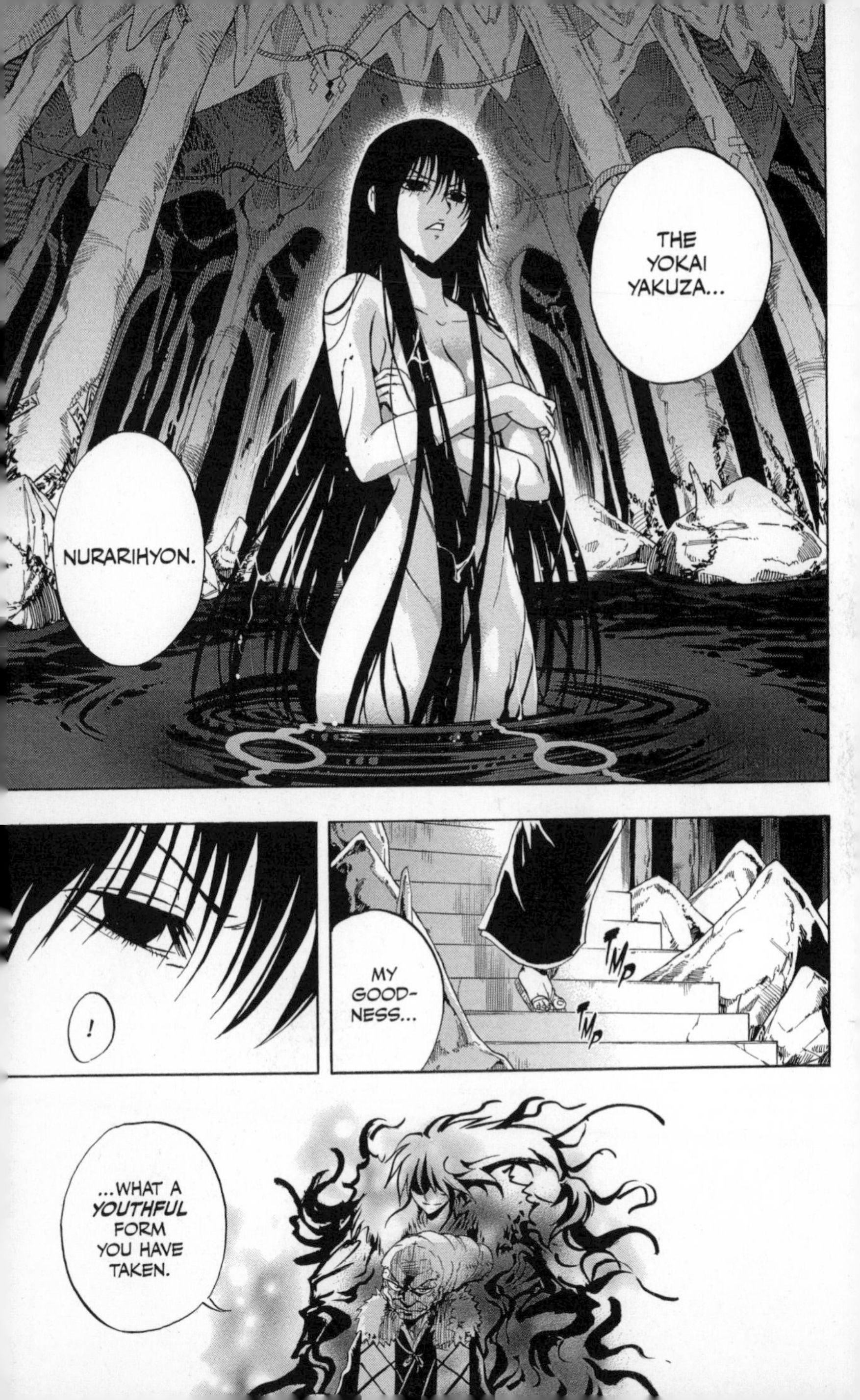
THE YOKAI YAKUZA...
NURARIHYON.
MY GOOD-NESS...
TMP
TMP
!
...WHAT A *YOUTHFUL* FORM YOU HAVE TAKEN.

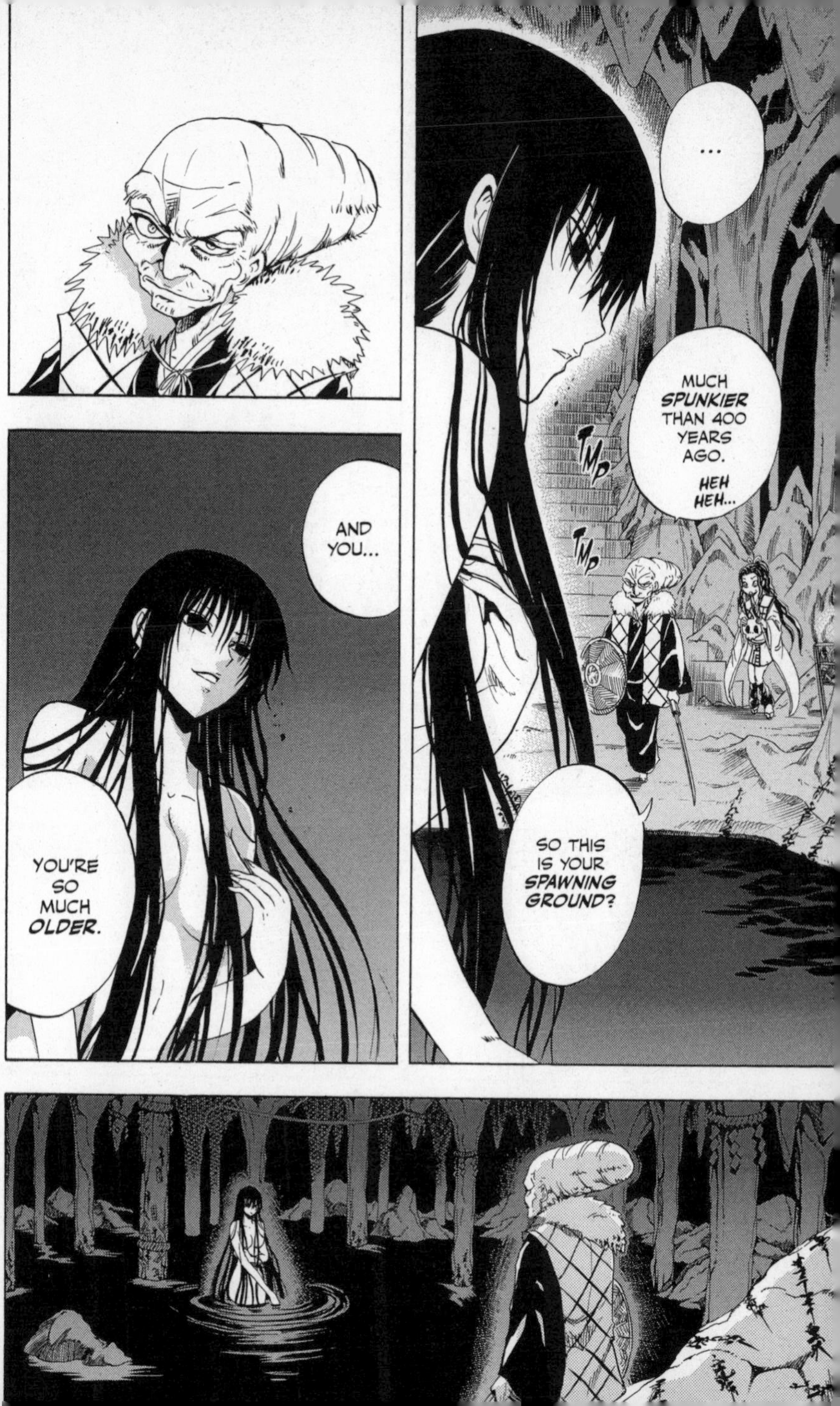
...
MUCH SPUNKIER THAN 400 YEARS AGO.
HEH HEH...
TMP
TMP
SO THIS IS YOUR SPAWNING GROUND?
AND YOU...
YOU'RE SO MUCH OLDER.

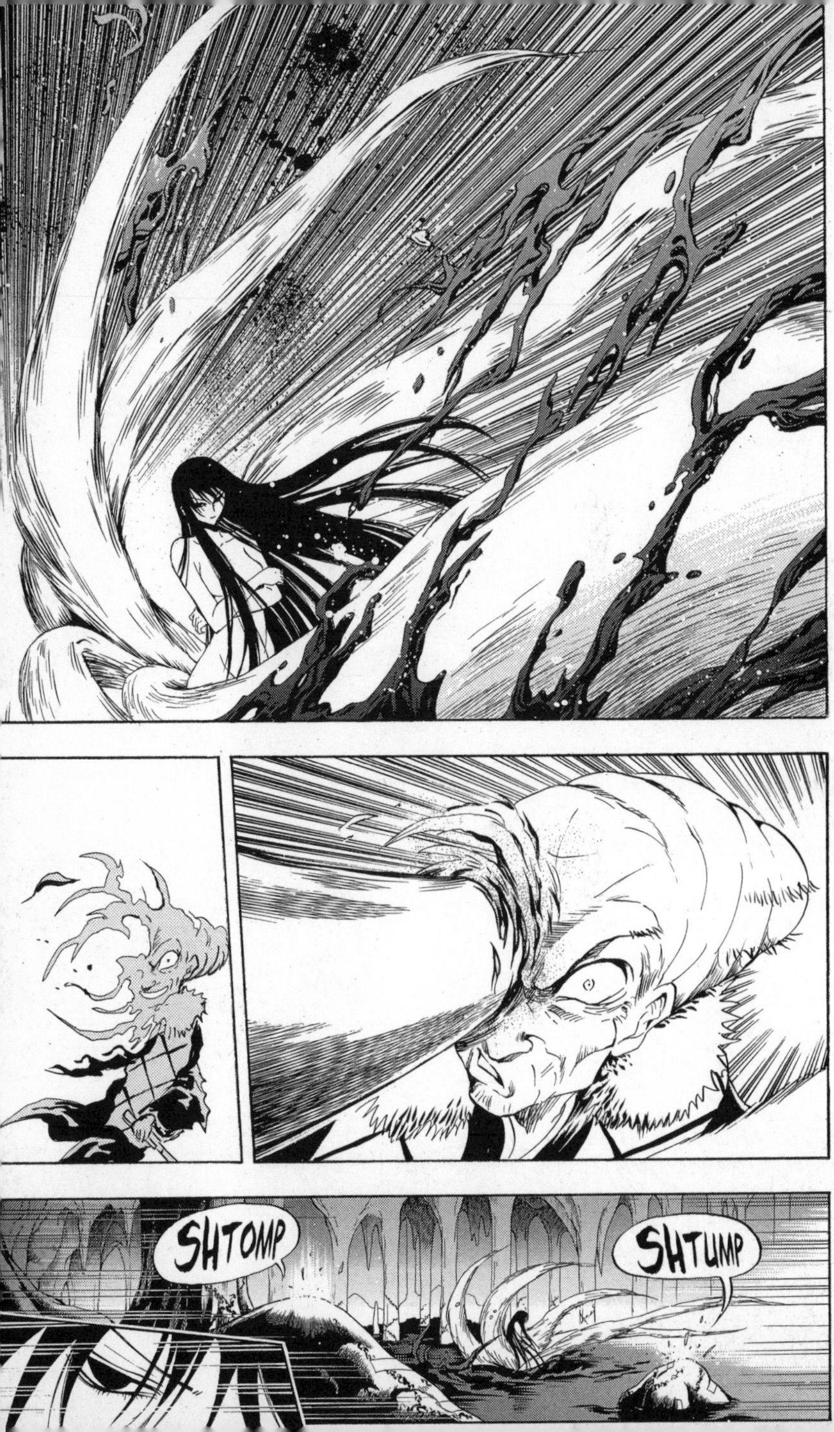
SHTUMP
SHTOMP

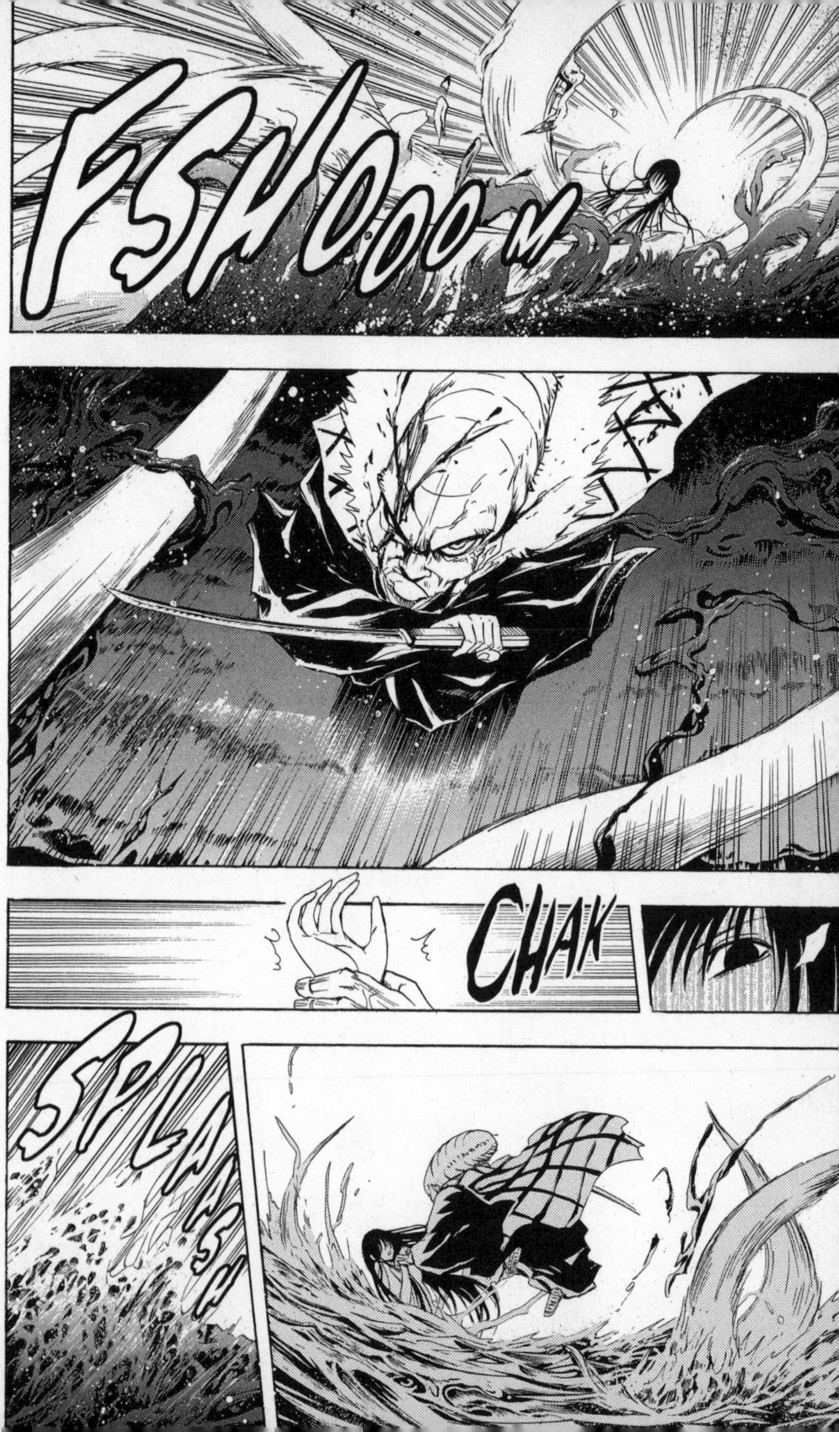
FSHOOOOM
CHAK
SPLAASH

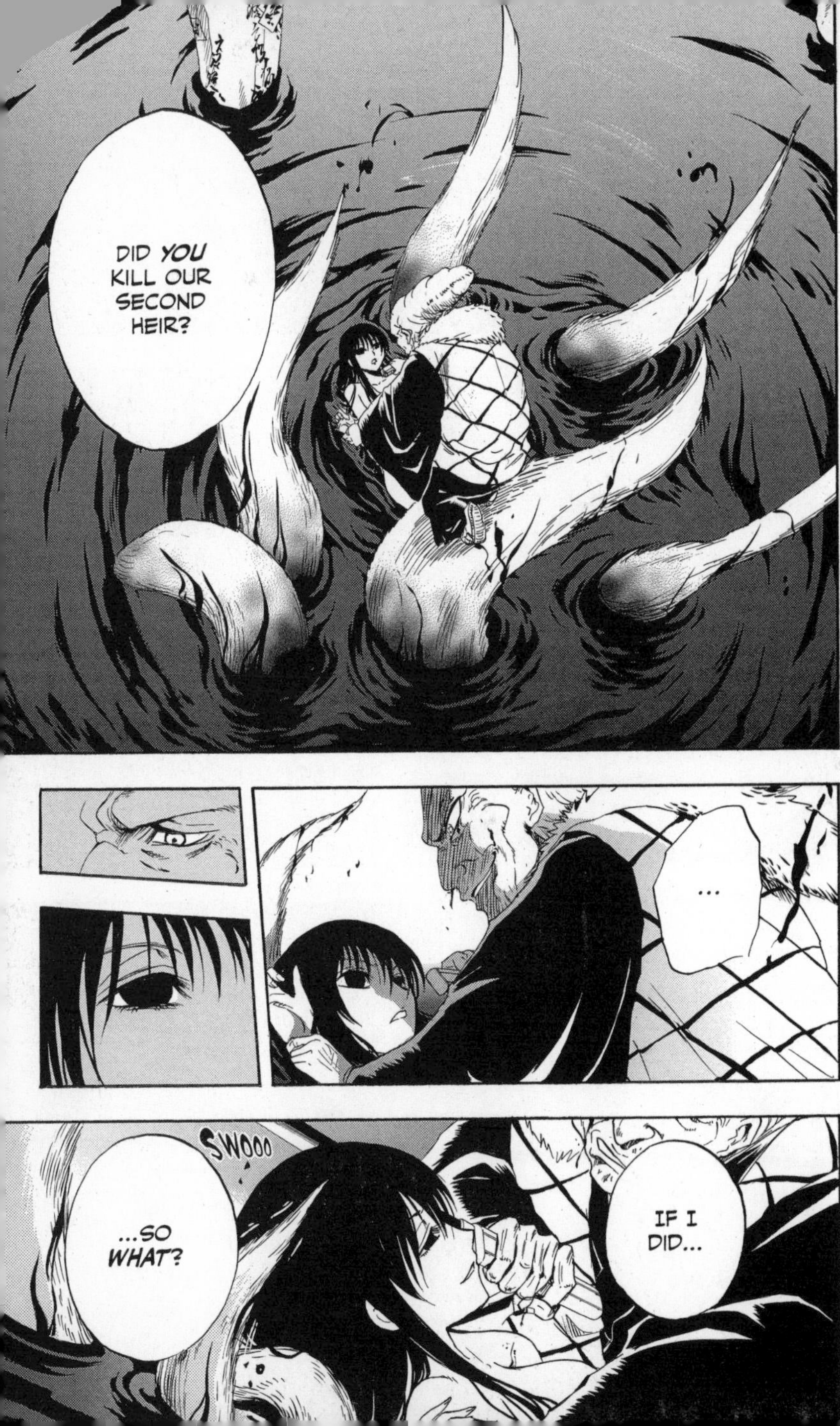
DID *YOU* KILL OUR SECOND HEIR?
...
IF I DID...
SWOOO
...SO *WHAT?*

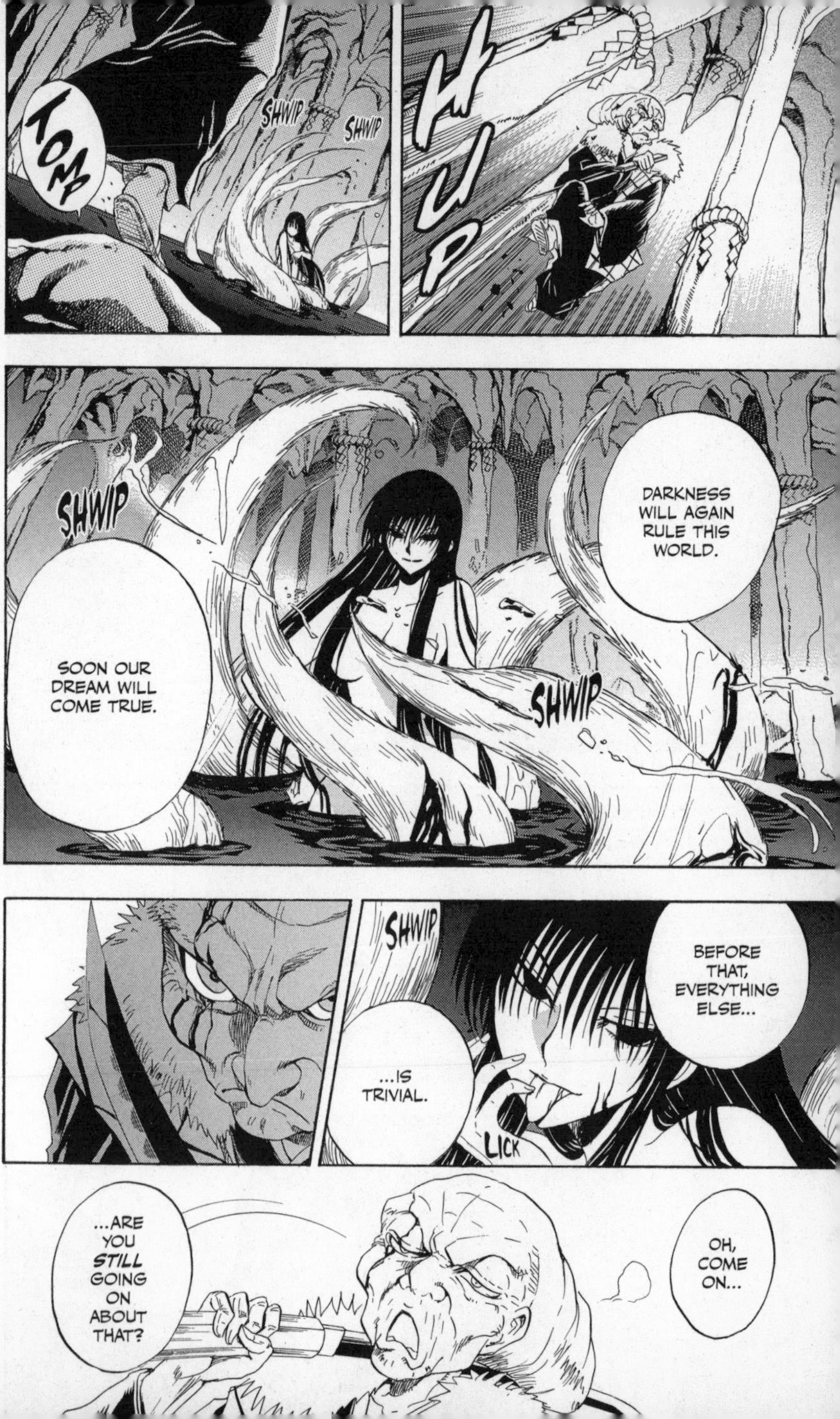

HUP
SHWIP
SHWIP
TOMP
DARKNESS WILL AGAIN RULE THIS WORLD.
SHWIP
SOON OUR DREAM WILL COME TRUE.
SHWIP
BEFORE THAT, EVERYTHING ELSE...
SHWIP
...IS TRIVIAL.
LICK
OH, COME ON...
...ARE YOU *STILL* GOING ON ABOUT THAT?

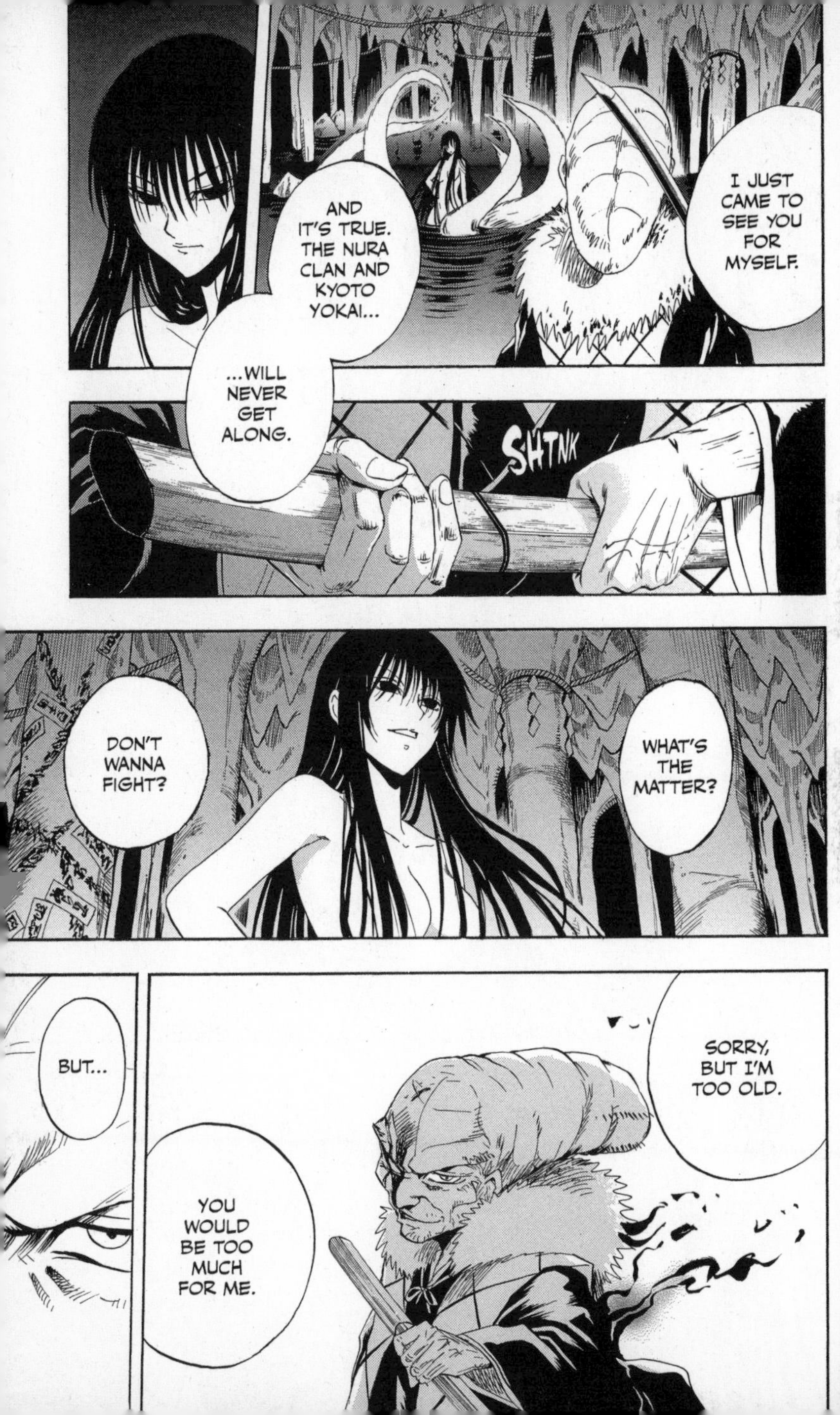
I JUST CAME TO SEE YOU FOR MYSELF.
AND IT'S TRUE. THE NURA CLAN AND KYOTO YOKAI...
...WILL NEVER GET ALONG.
SHTNK
WHAT'S THE MATTER?
DON'T WANNA FIGHT?
SORRY, BUT I'M TOO OLD.
YOU WOULD BE TOO MUCH FOR ME.
BUT...

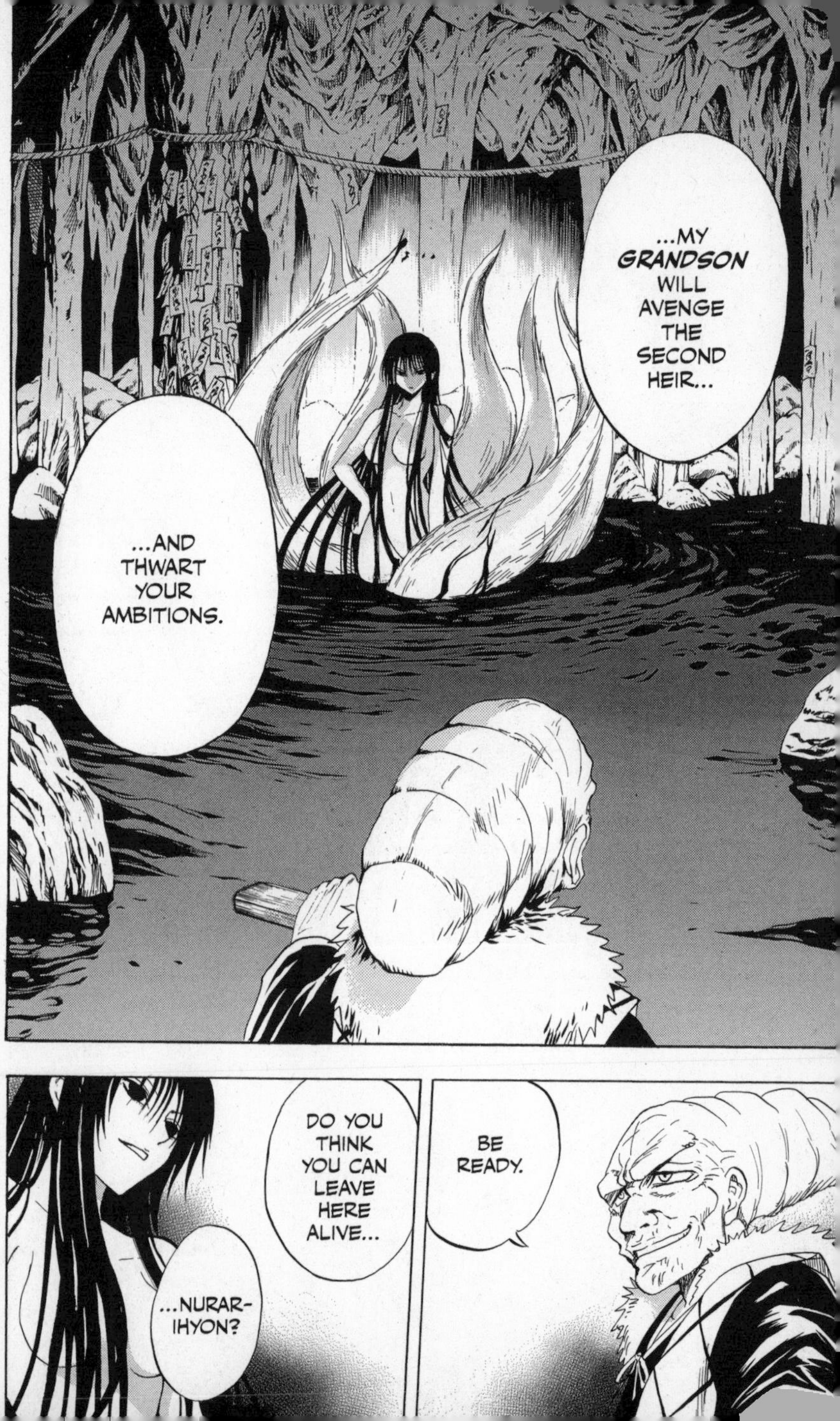
...MY GRANDSON WILL AVENGE THE SECOND HEIR...
...AND THWART YOUR AMBITIONS.
BE READY.
DO YOU THINK YOU CAN LEAVE HERE ALIVE...
...NURAR-IHYON?

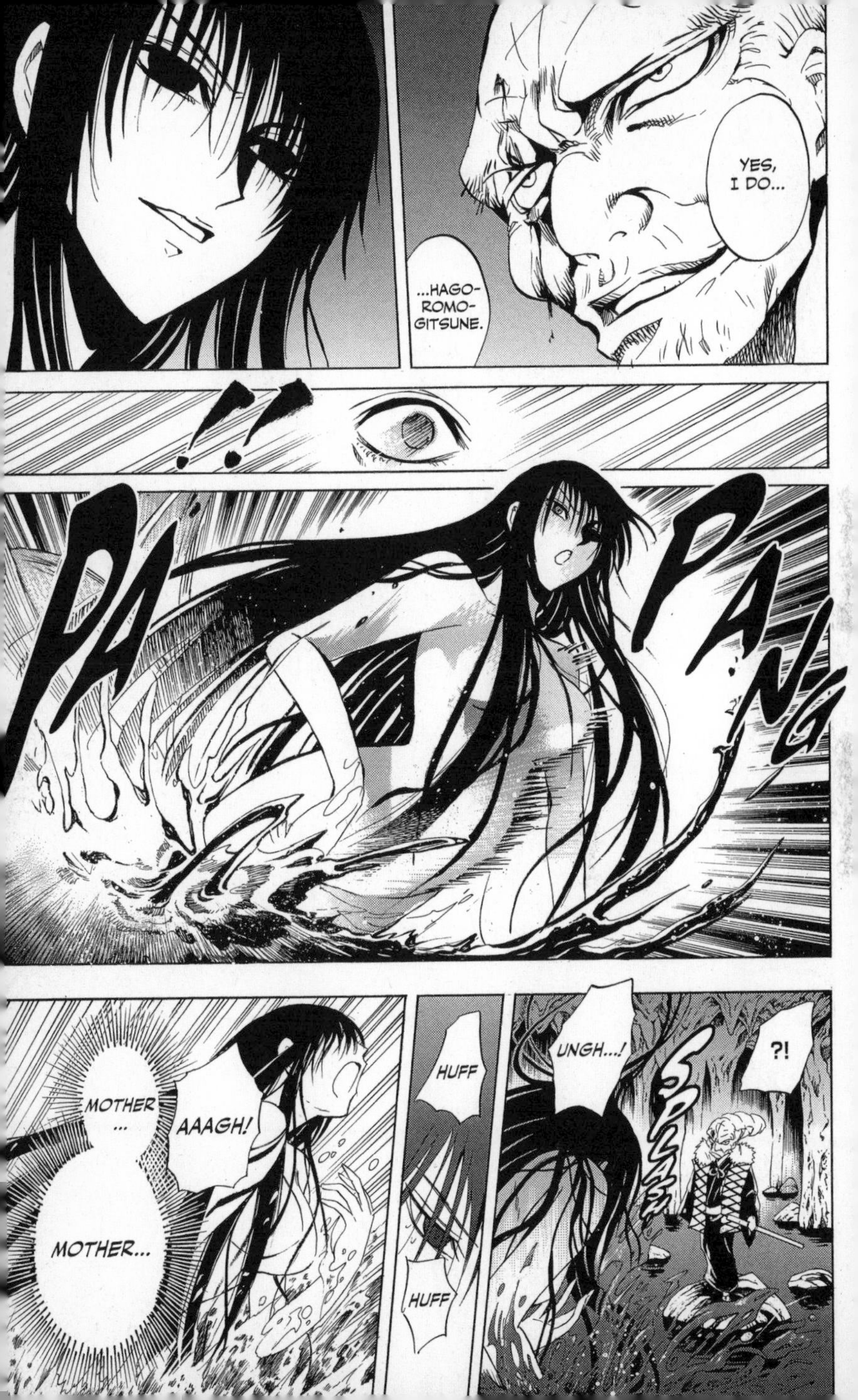
YES, I DO...
...HAGO-ROMO-GITSUNE.
!!
PANG
PA
?!
UNGH...!
HUFF
HUFF
AAAGH!
MOTHER...
MOTHER...

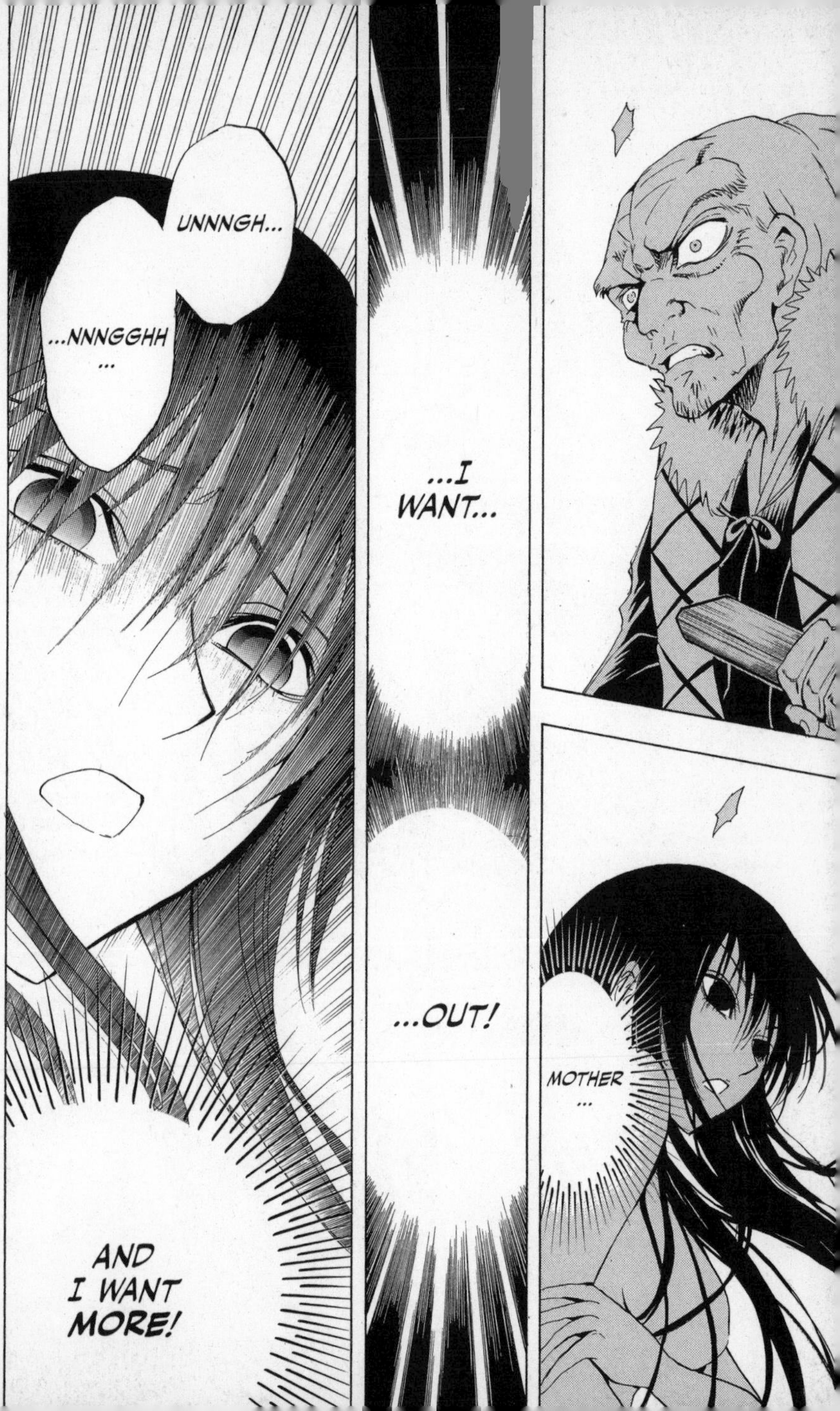
MOTHER ...
...I WANT...
...OUT!
UNNNGH...
...NNNGGHH ...
AND I WANT MORE!

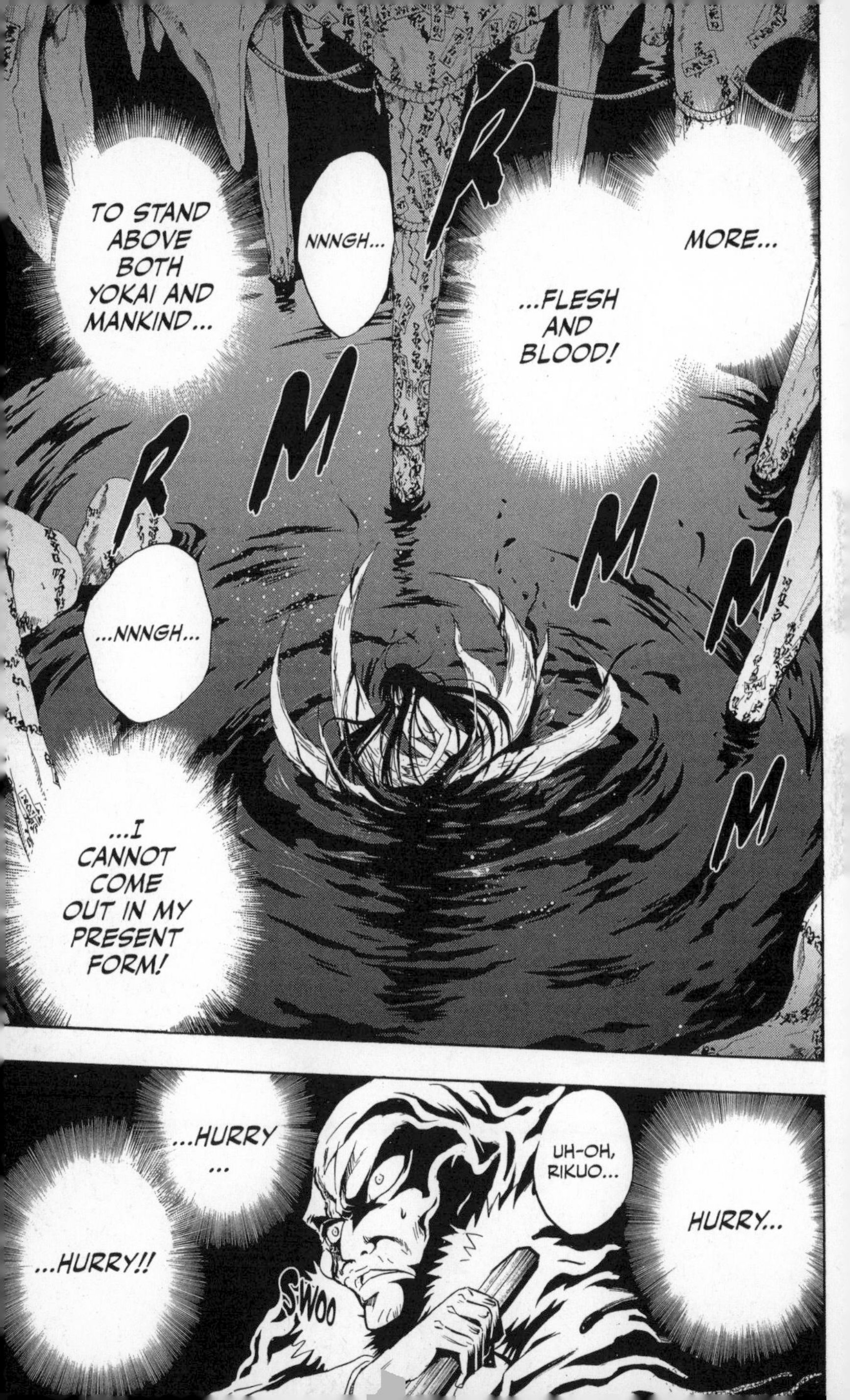
MORE...
...FLESH AND BLOOD!
NNNGH...
TO STAND ABOVE BOTH YOKAI AND MANKIND...
RRMMMMM
...NNNGH...
...I CANNOT COME OUT IN MY PRESENT FORM!
HURRY...
UH-OH, RIKUO...
...HURRY ...
...HURRY!!
SWOO

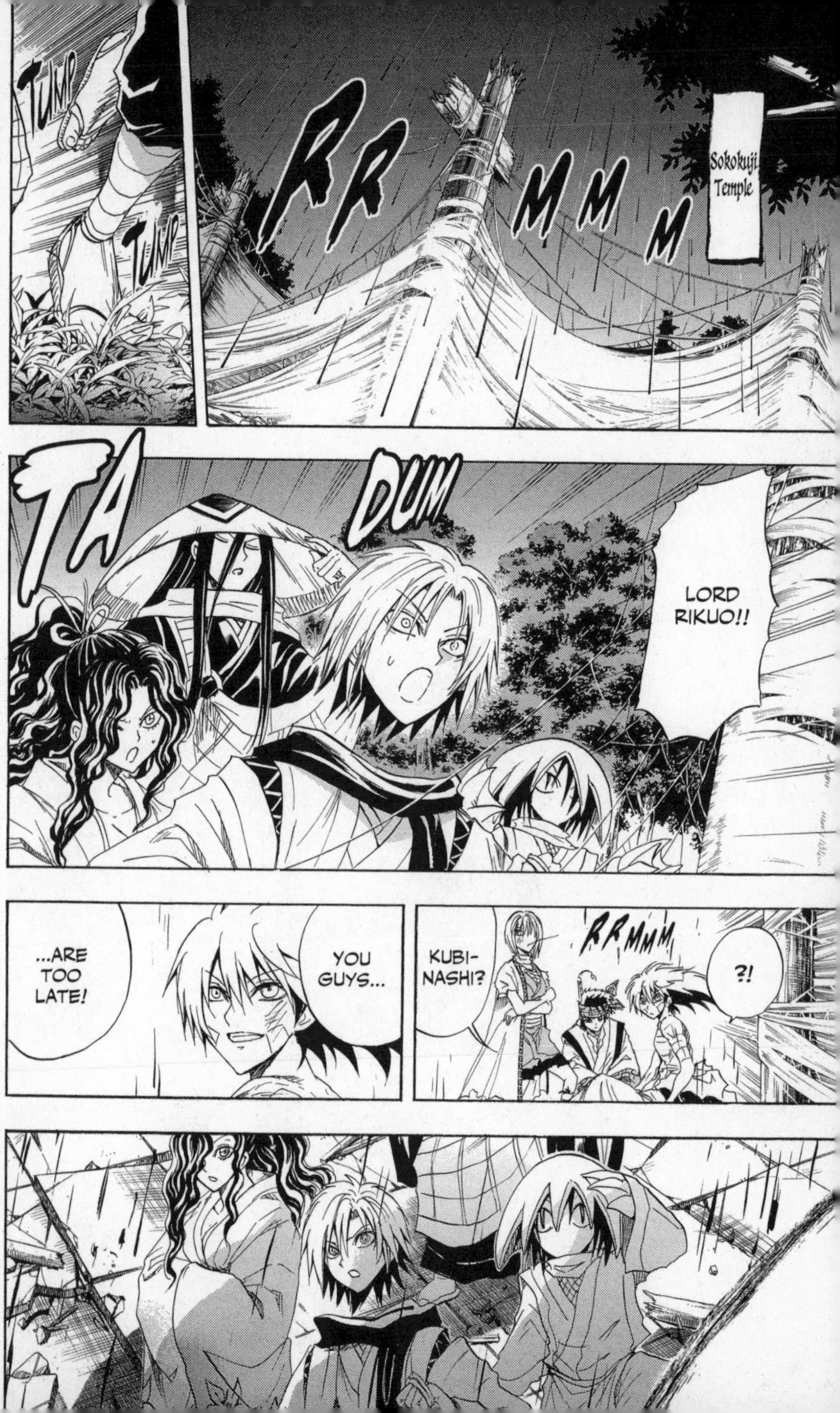
Sokokuji Temple
RRMMMM
TUMP
TUMP
TA DUM
LORD RIKUO!!
?!
RRMMM
KUBI-NASHI?
YOU GUYS...
...ARE TOO LATE!

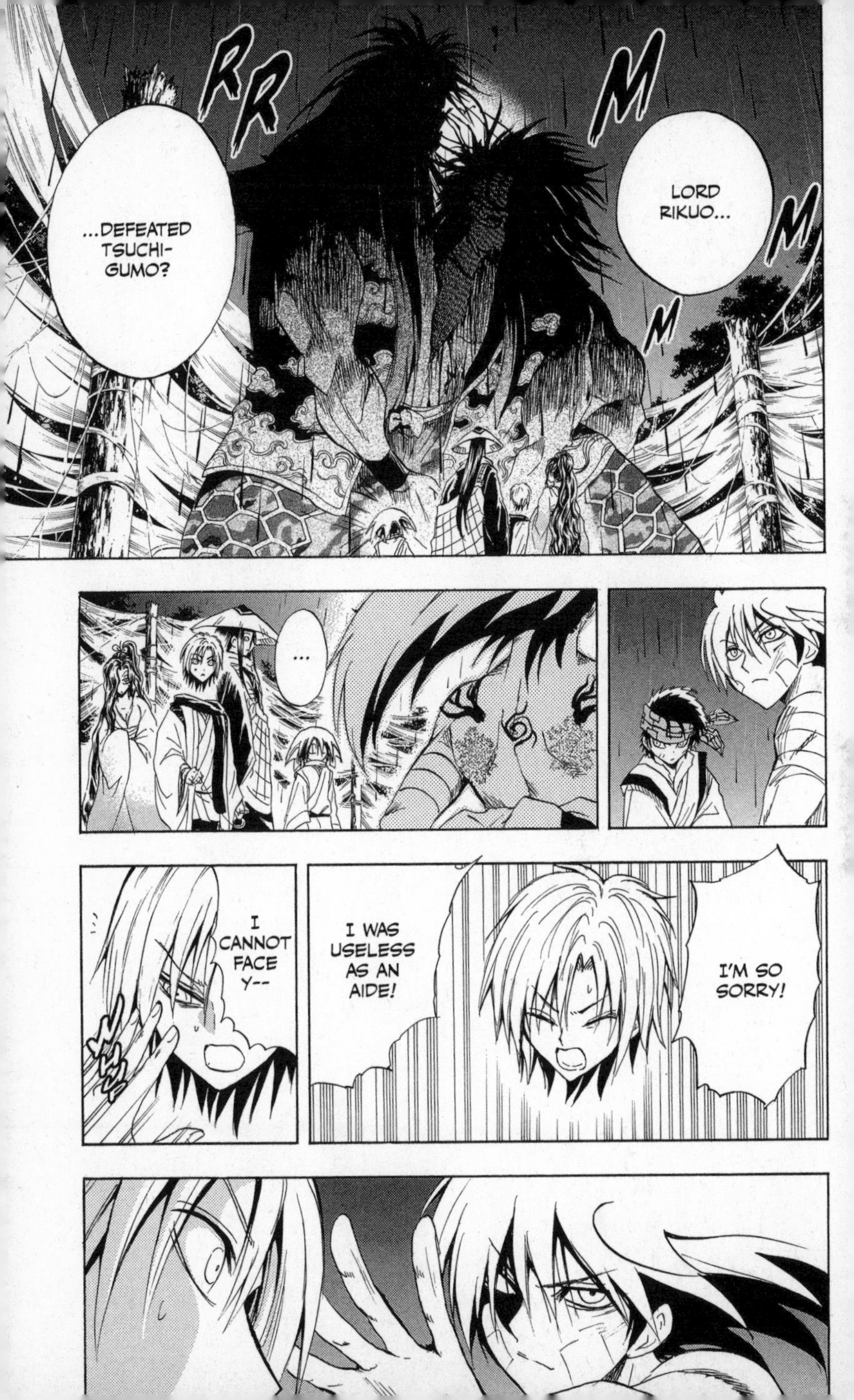
RRMMMM
LORD RIKUO...
...DEFEATED TSUCHI-GUMO?
...
I'M SO SORRY!
I WAS USELESS AS AN AIDE!
I CANNOT FACE Y--

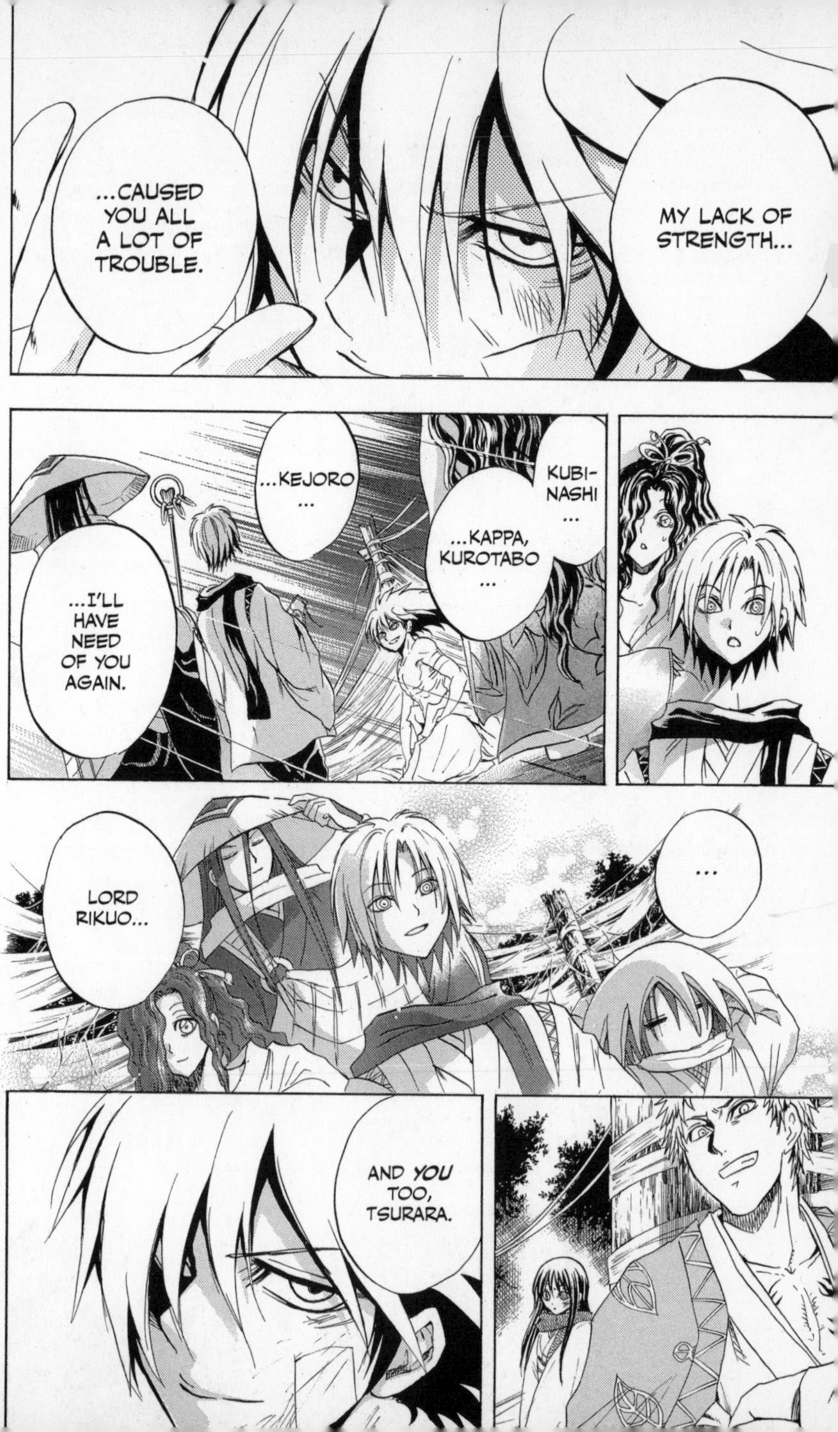
MY LACK OF STRENGTH...
...CAUSED YOU ALL A LOT OF TROUBLE.
KUBI-NASHI ...
...KEJORO ...
...KAPPA, KUROTABO ...
...I'LL HAVE NEED OF YOU AGAIN.
...
LORD RIKUO...
AND *YOU* TOO, TSURARA.

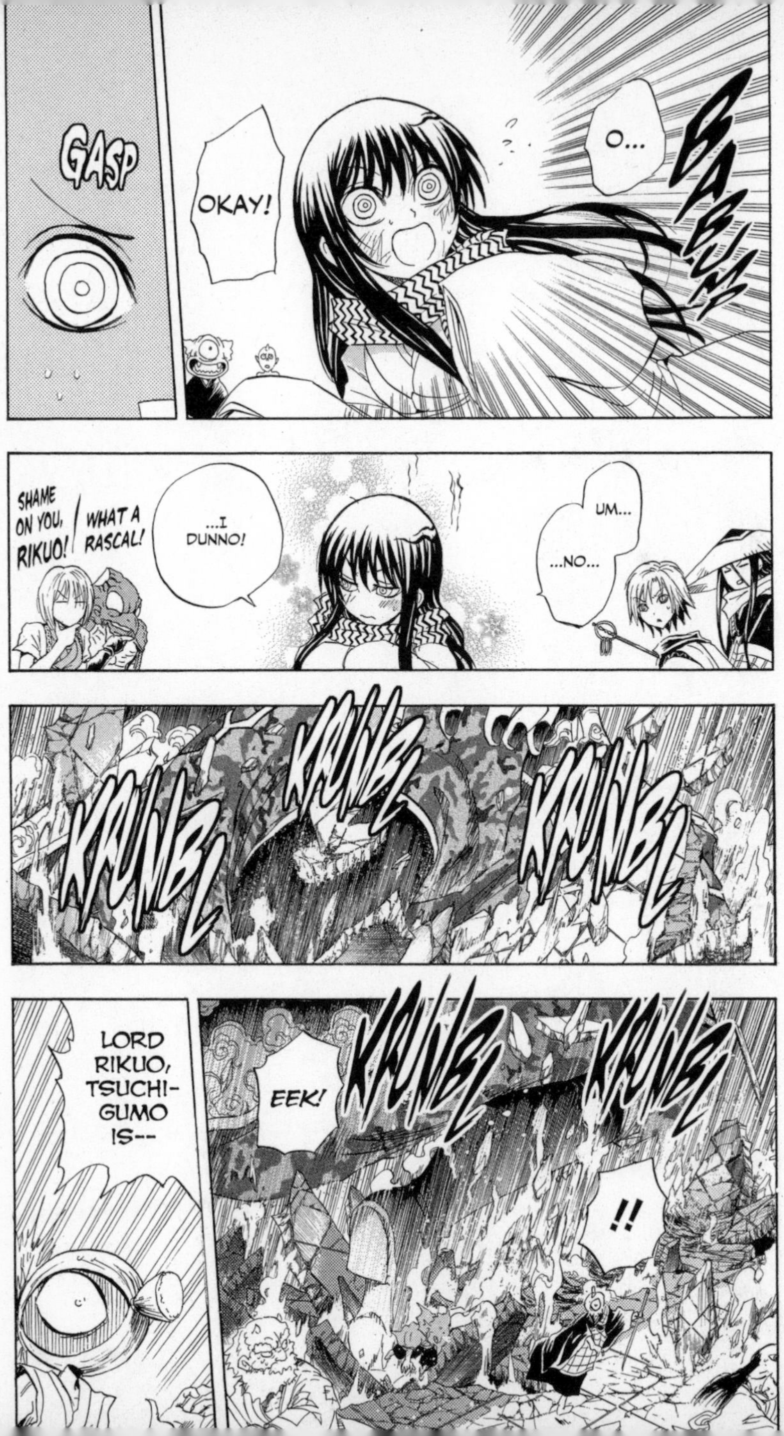
O...
OKAY!
GASP
UM...
...NO...
...I DUNNO!
WHAT A RASCAL!
SHAME ON YOU, RIKUO!
EEK!
!!
LORD RIKUO, TSUCHI-GUMO IS--

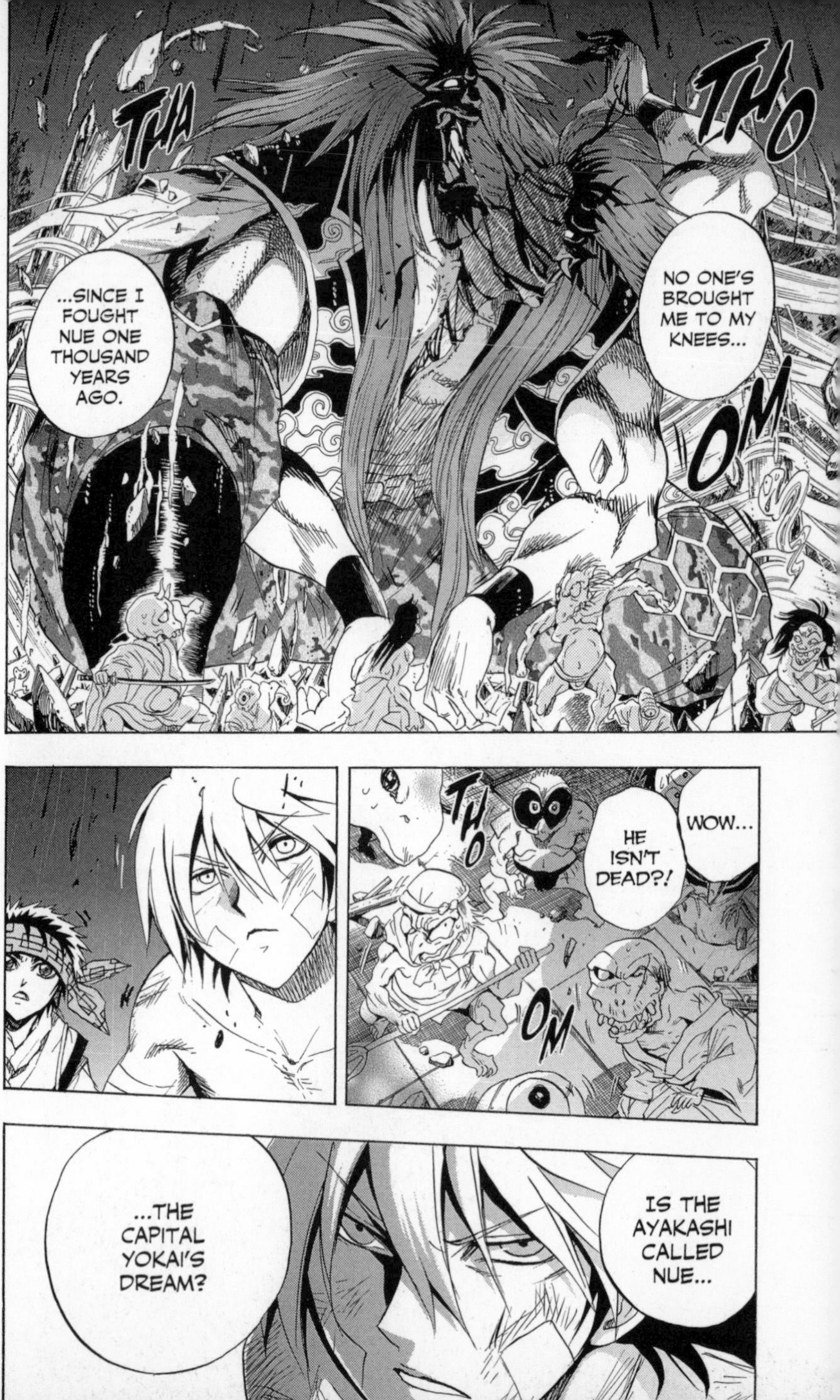
THO
NO ONE'S BROUGHT ME TO MY KNEES...
OM
...SINCE I FOUGHT NUE ONE THOUSAND YEARS AGO.
THA
WOW...
HE ISN'T DEAD?!
THO
OM
IS THE AYAKASHI CALLED NUE...
...THE CAPITAL YOKAI'S DREAM?

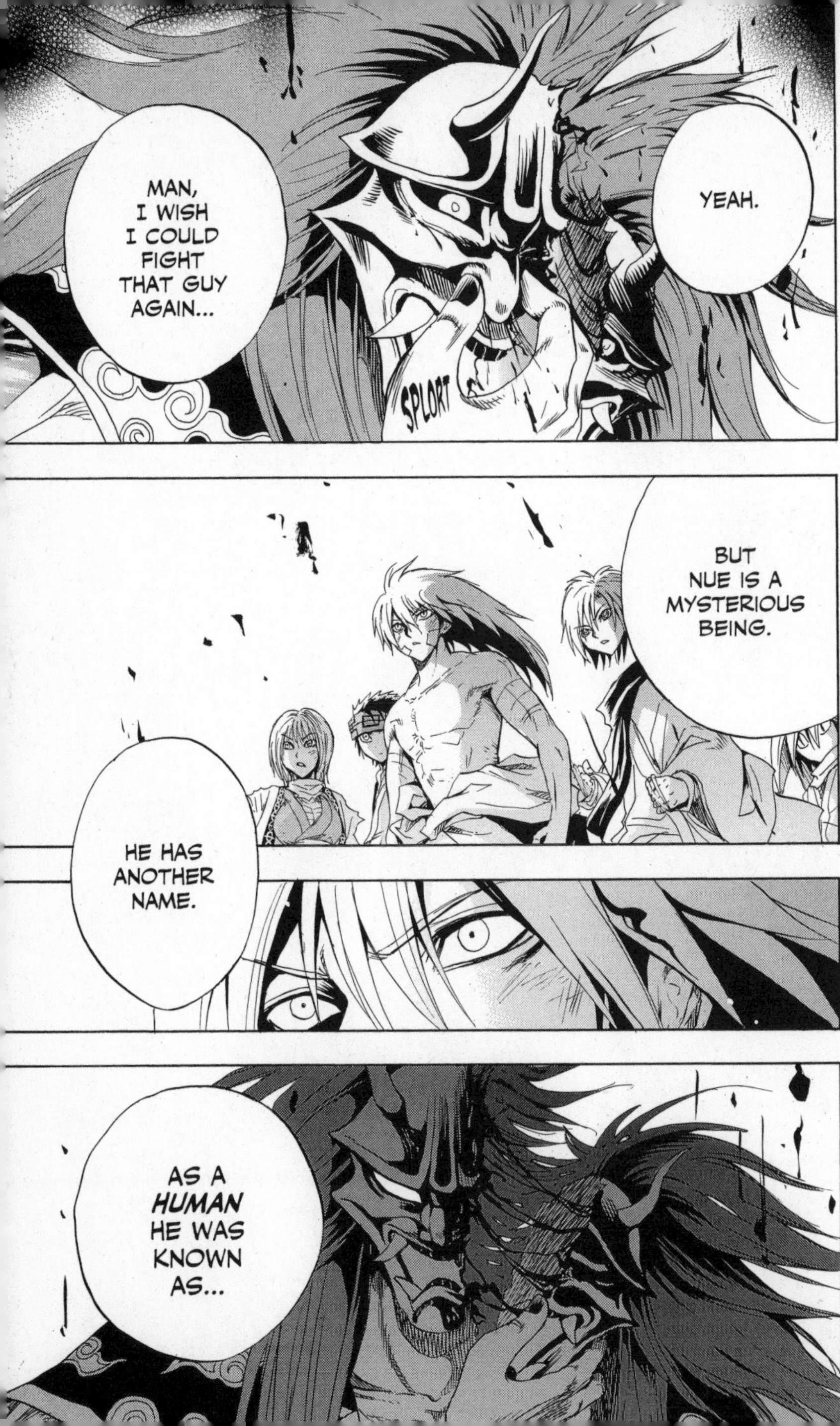
YEAH.
MAN, I WISH I COULD FIGHT THAT GUY AGAIN...
SPLORT
BUT NUE IS A MYSTERIOUS BEING.
HE HAS ANOTHER NAME.
AS A *HUMAN* HE WAS KNOWN AS...

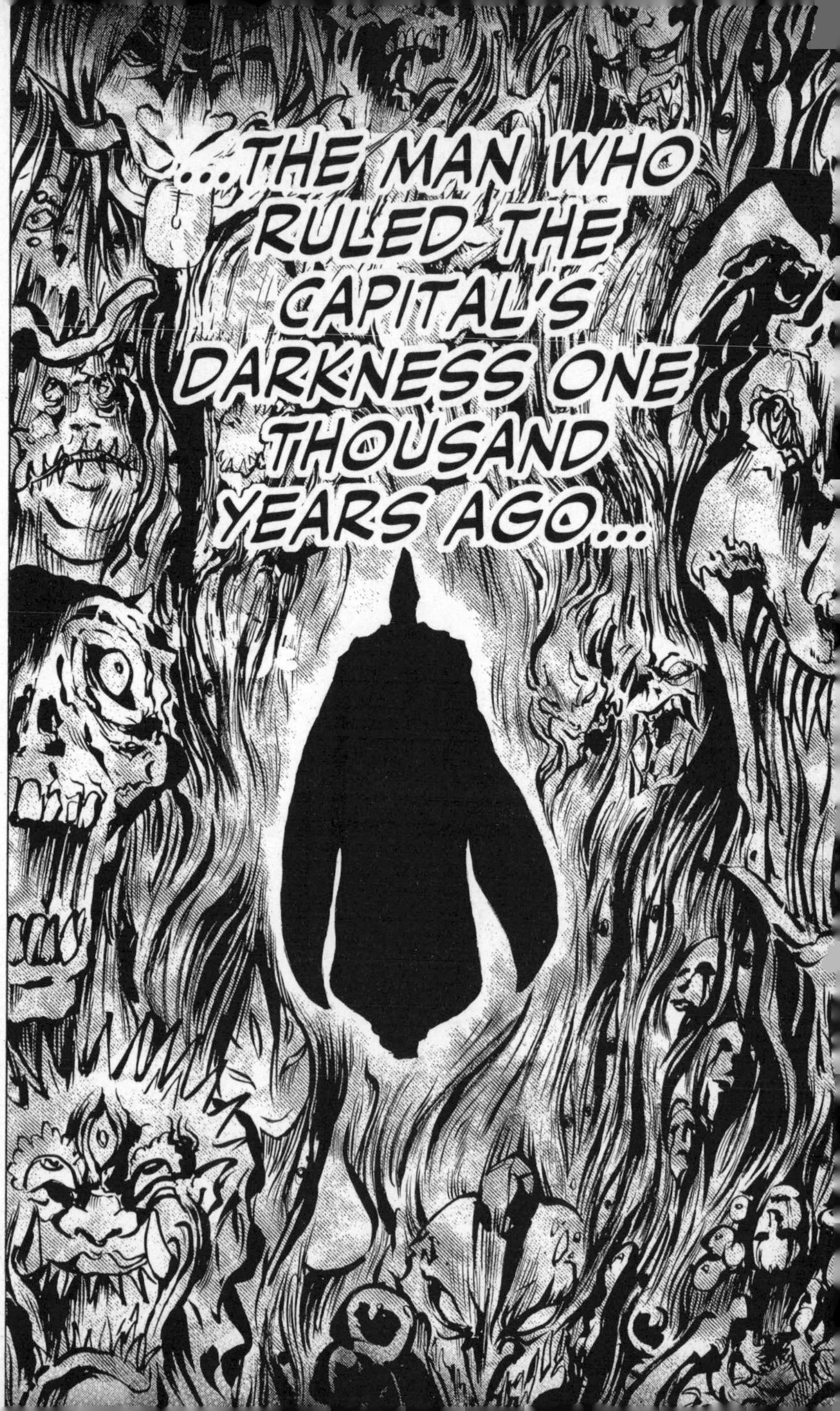
...THE MAN WHO RULED THE CAPITAL'S DARKNESS ONE THOUSAND YEARS AGO...

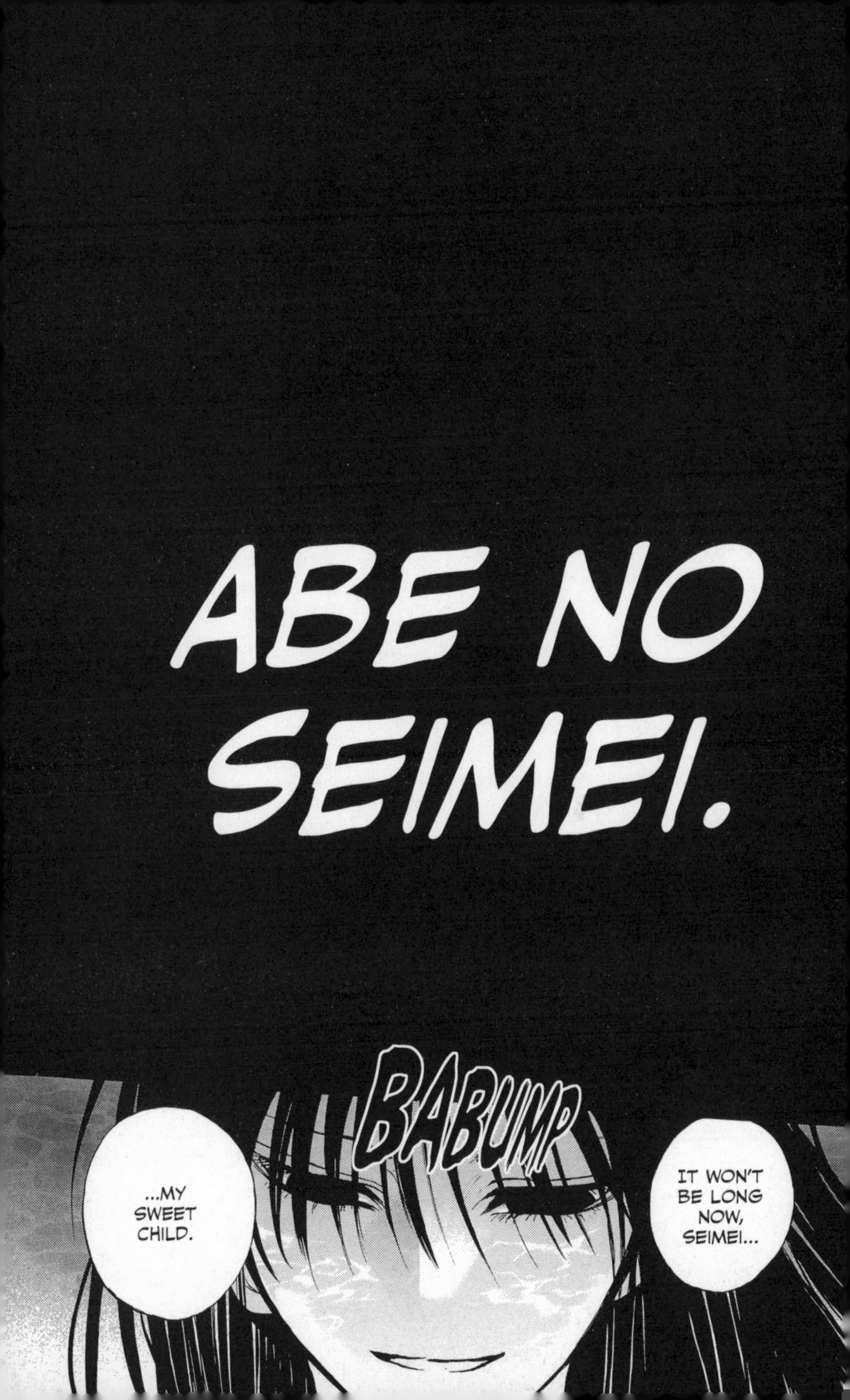
ABE NO SEIMEI.
BABUMP
IT WON'T BE LONG NOW, SEIMEI...
...MY SWEET CHILD.

KIYOTSUGU'S
YOKAI BRAIN
#13 BY KIYO

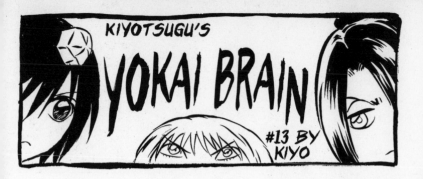

Question: Awashima has his own sword, so how long is he going to carry around Kurotabo's spear?
—*Ruu, Kanagawa Prefecture*

Awashima: Huh? Me? My sword disappeared somewhere along the way. And besides, I like this spear! Erotabo has lots of weapons, so I doubt he'll notice that I took it!

Question: How did Hagoromo-Gitsune get such beautifully smooth skin and silky hair?
—*Arisu, Fukui Prefecture*

Hagoromo-Gitsune: Is my hair beautiful? *Tee hee.* That's because I take good care of it every day. I have to use a ton of shampoo!

Question: Here's a question for Ibaraki-Doji. Do you wear that stupa all the time--even when you eat or take a bath? Can you even take it off?

Ibaraki-Doji: Lombrosooo! It's for my deceased father's grave, so I never take it off. Not even when I eat.

Question: I want to pass entrance exams with Maiden's Dance, so please come!
—*Kyokotsu's Older Sister, Miyagi Prefecture*

Awashima: Sure thing!! I'll be there!! Miyagi isn't far!

Question: Does Kuromaru have a girlfriend? If not, start by being friends with me!
(attached tanka poem:
I suddenly fell
In love with a yokai man
Oh what shall I do
With these romantic feelings
That I can barely contain?)
—*Yukina Imafuku, Kanagawa Prefecture*

Gozumaru: *Gah ha ha!* That crow sure is popular with the chicks! What a loser!

Mezumaru: He's a serious guy. Whenever I climb a tree, he makes me get down. Maybe that's what's good about him.

Kuromaru: Th-thanks. Let's be friends. But don't be surprised if I suddenly turn into a crow.

Question: This is a question for Gozumaru!♡ I love Gozumaru! Marry me!♡♡
—*Renkyun♡, Aichi Prefecture*

Gozumaru: Hunh?!

Mezumaru: *Ha ha ha ha ha!!* **You're** popular with the chicks, too!!

Gozumaru: Shut up!! What is this?! Some kind of bulletin board for finding love?!

Kuromaru: Answer the question, Gozumaru.

Gozumaru: Gimme a break!! I won't marry you!! We'll be friends!!

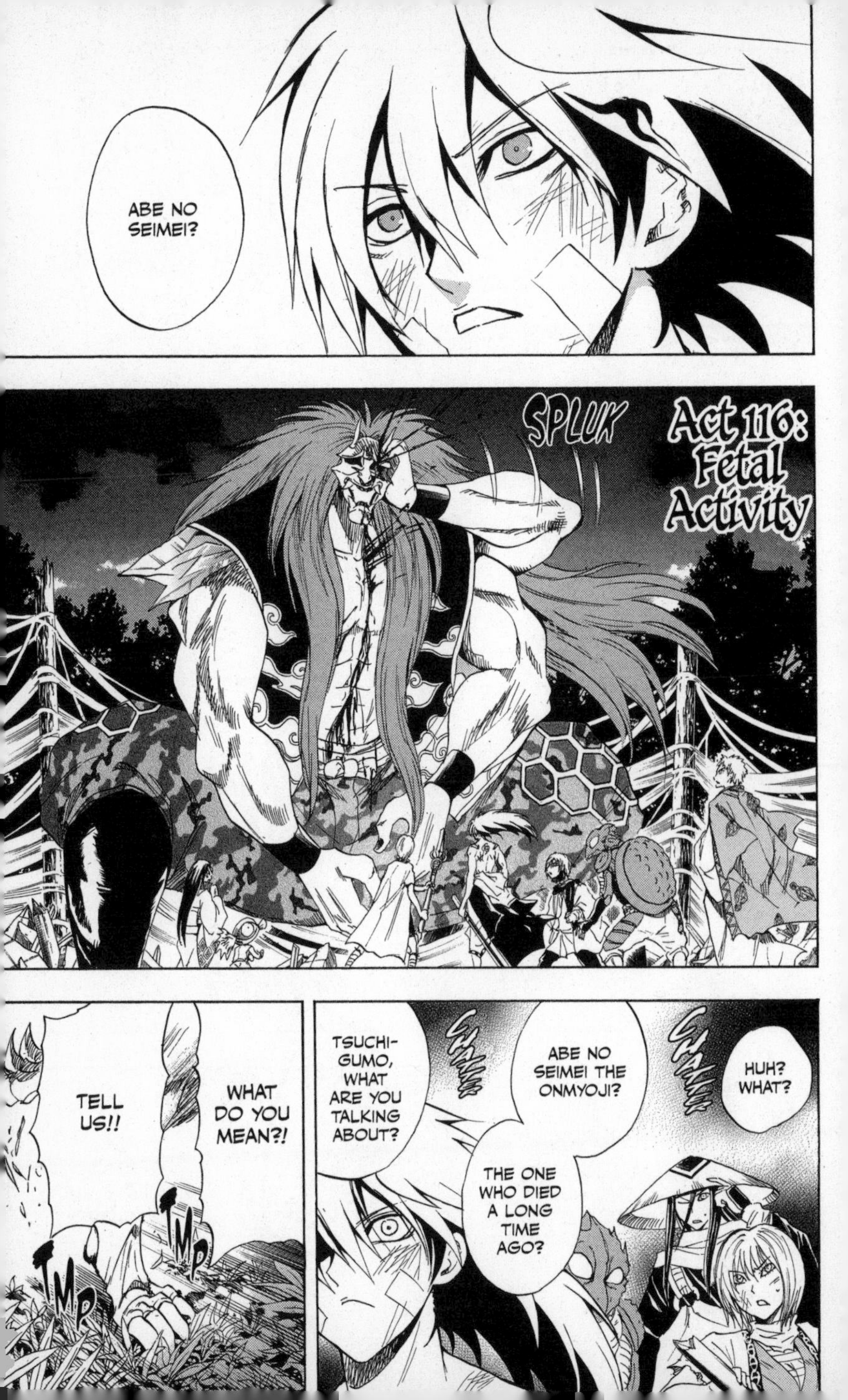
ABE NO SEIMEI?
Act 116: Fetal Activity
SPLUK
HUH? WHAT?
ABE NO SEIMEI THE ONMYOJI?
TSUCHI-GUMO, WHAT ARE YOU TALKING ABOUT?
THE ONE WHO DIED A LONG TIME AGO?
WHAT DO YOU MEAN?!
TELL US!!
TMP
TMP

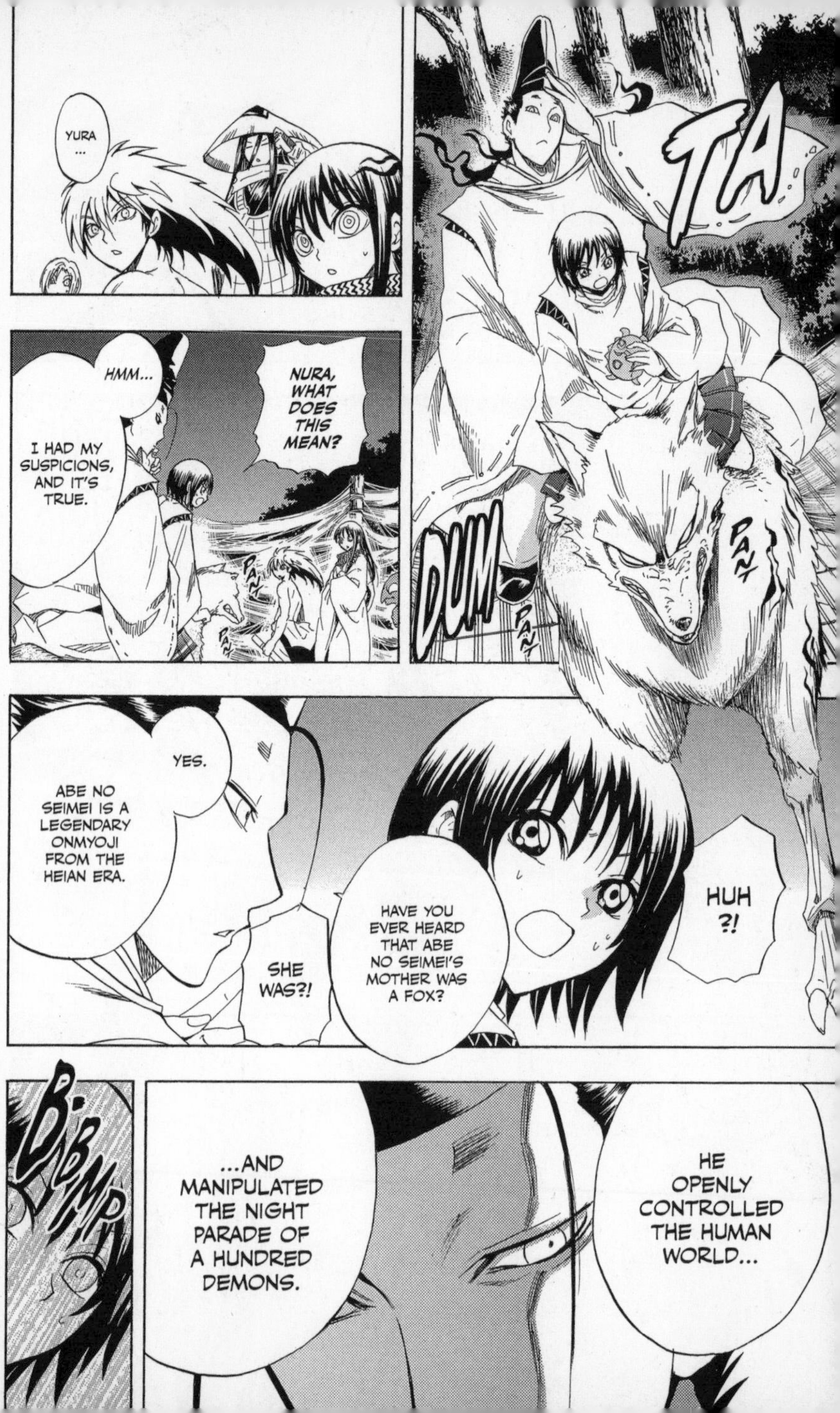
TA
DUM
PANT
PANT
YURA ...
NURA, WHAT DOES THIS MEAN?
HMM...
I HAD MY SUSPICIONS, AND IT'S TRUE.
PANT
PANT
HUH ?!
HAVE YOU EVER HEARD THAT ABE NO SEIMEI'S MOTHER WAS A FOX?
SHE WAS?!
YES.
ABE NO SEIMEI IS A LEGENDARY ONMYOJI FROM THE HEIAN ERA.
HE OPENLY CONTROLLED THE HUMAN WORLD...
...AND MANIPULATED THE NIGHT PARADE OF A HUNDRED DEMONS.

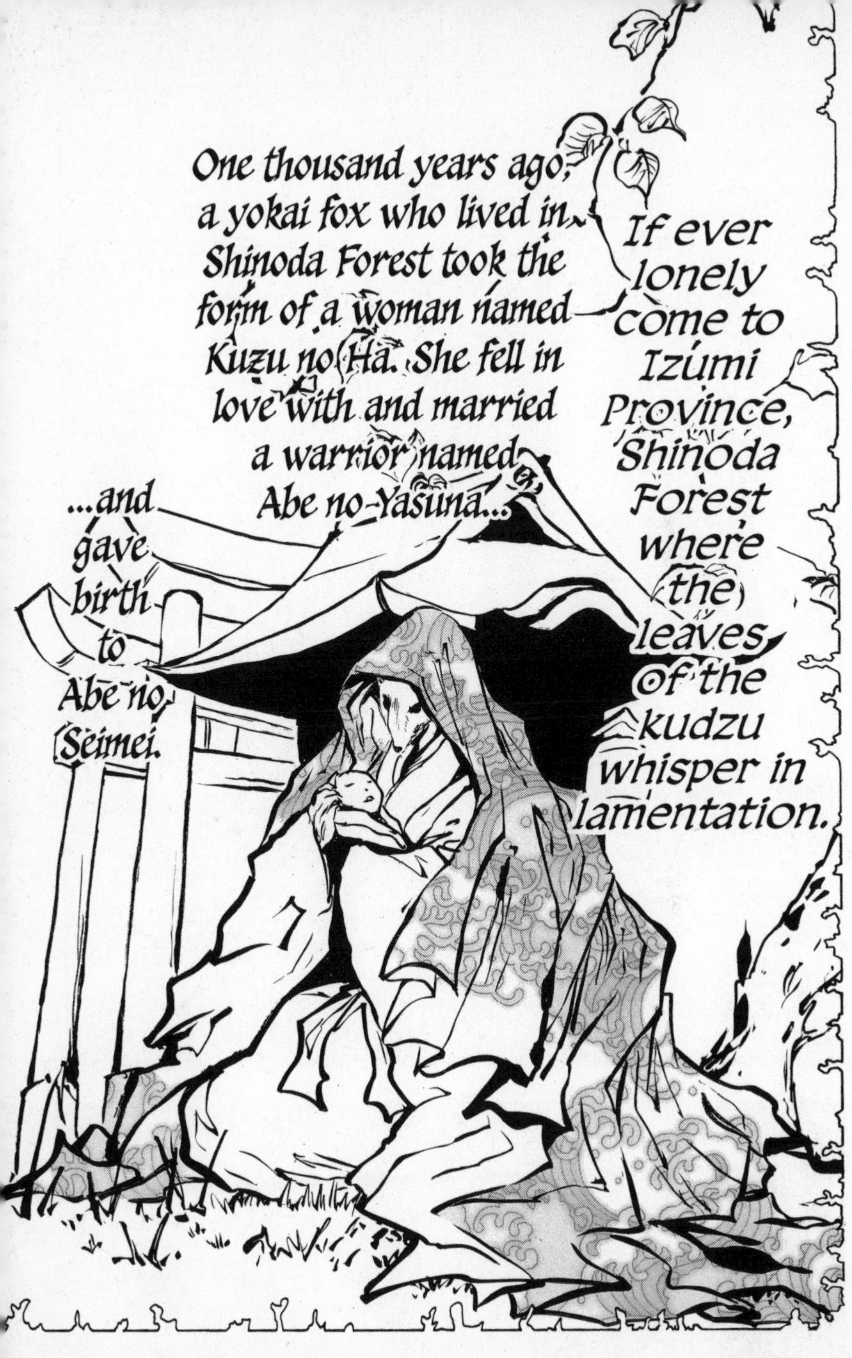
If ever lonely come to Izumi Province, Shinoda Forest where the leaves of the kudzu whisper in lamentation.
One thousand years ago, a yokai fox who lived in Shinoda Forest took the form of a woman named Kuzu no Ha. She fell in love with and married a warrior named Abe no-Yasuna...
...and gave birth to Abe no Seimei.

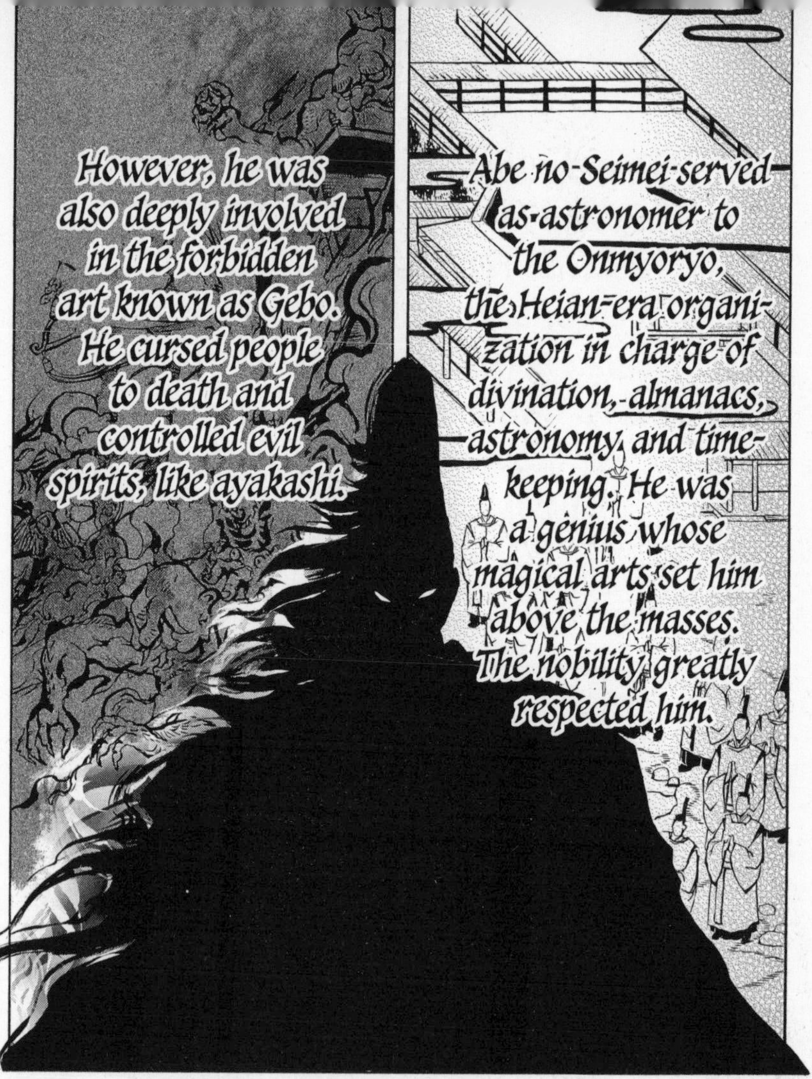
Abe no Seimei served as astronomer to the Onmyoryo, the Heian-era organization in charge of divination, almanacs, astronomy and timekeeping. He was a genius whose magical arts set him above the masses. The nobility greatly respected him.
However, he was also deeply involved in the forbidden art known as Gebo. He cursed people to death and controlled evil spirits, like ayakashi.
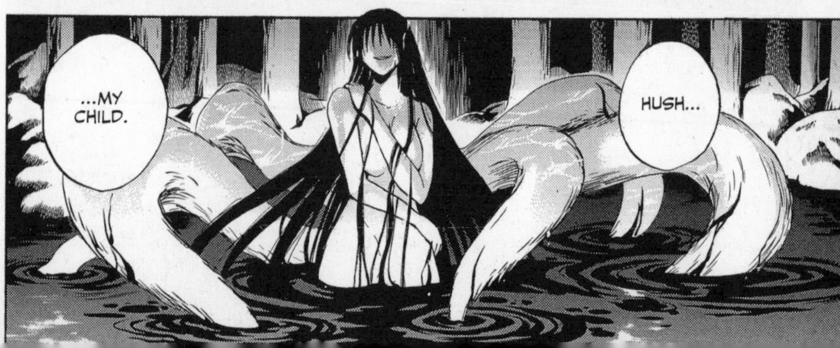
HUSH...
...MY CHILD.

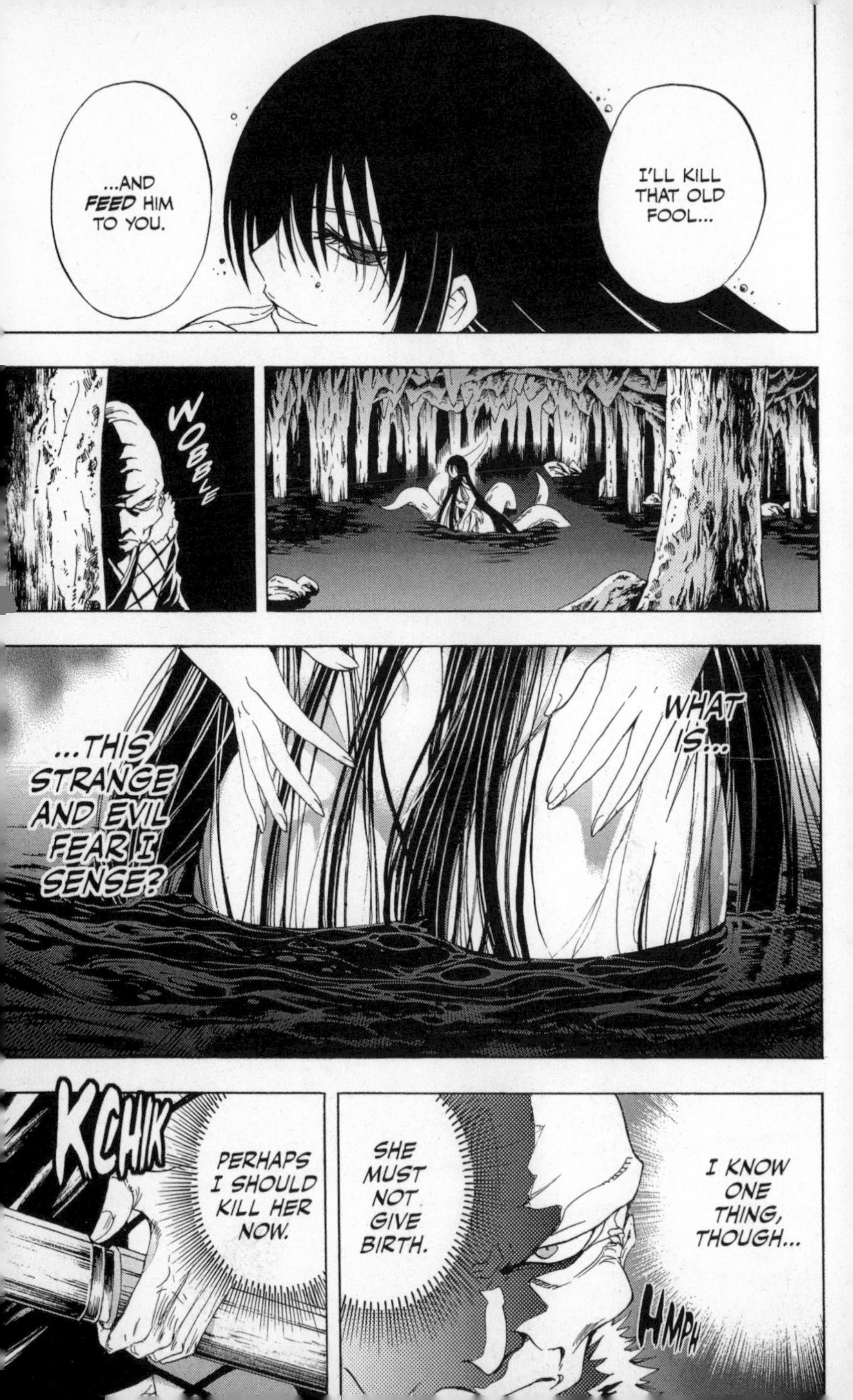
I'LL KILL THAT OLD FOOL...
...AND FEED HIM TO YOU.
WOBBLE
WHAT IS...
...THIS STRANGE AND EVIL FEAR I SENSE?
I KNOW ONE THING, THOUGH...
SHE MUST NOT GIVE BIRTH.
HMPH
PERHAPS I SHOULD KILL HER NOW.
KCHIK

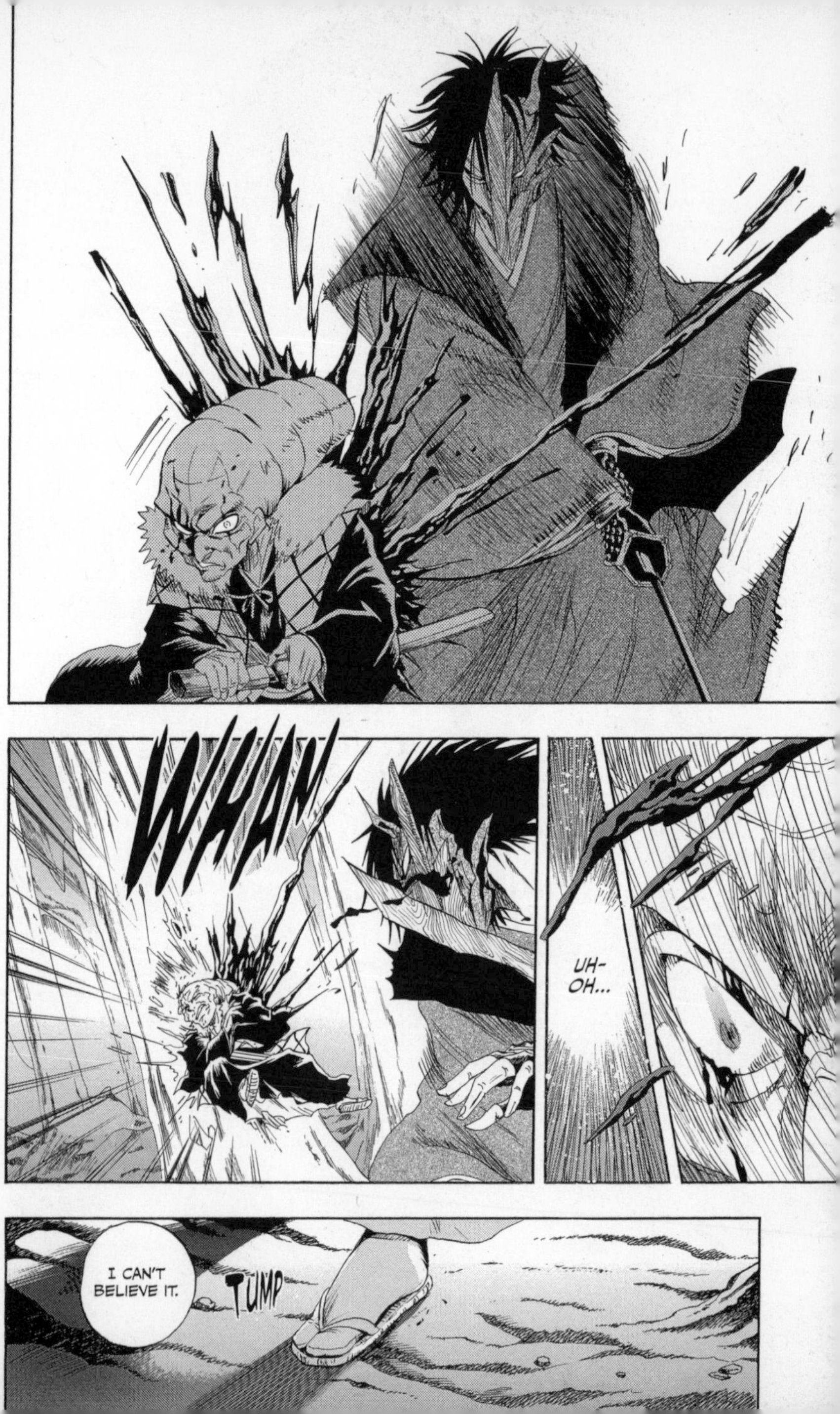
UH-OH...
WHAM
I CAN'T BELIEVE IT.
TUMP

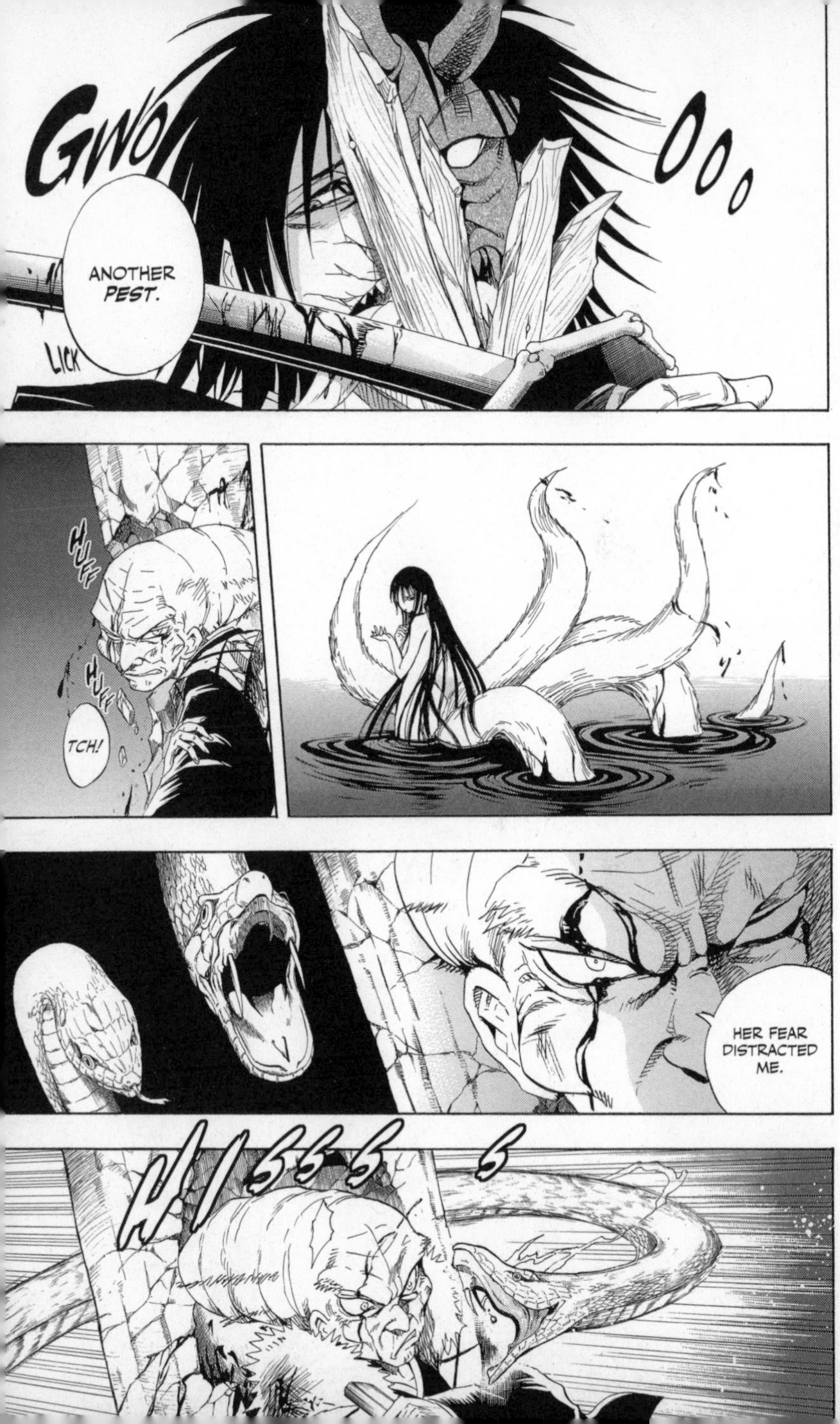
GWOOOO
ANOTHER PEST.
LICK
HUFF
HUFF
TCH!
HER FEAR DISTRACTED ME.
HISSSS

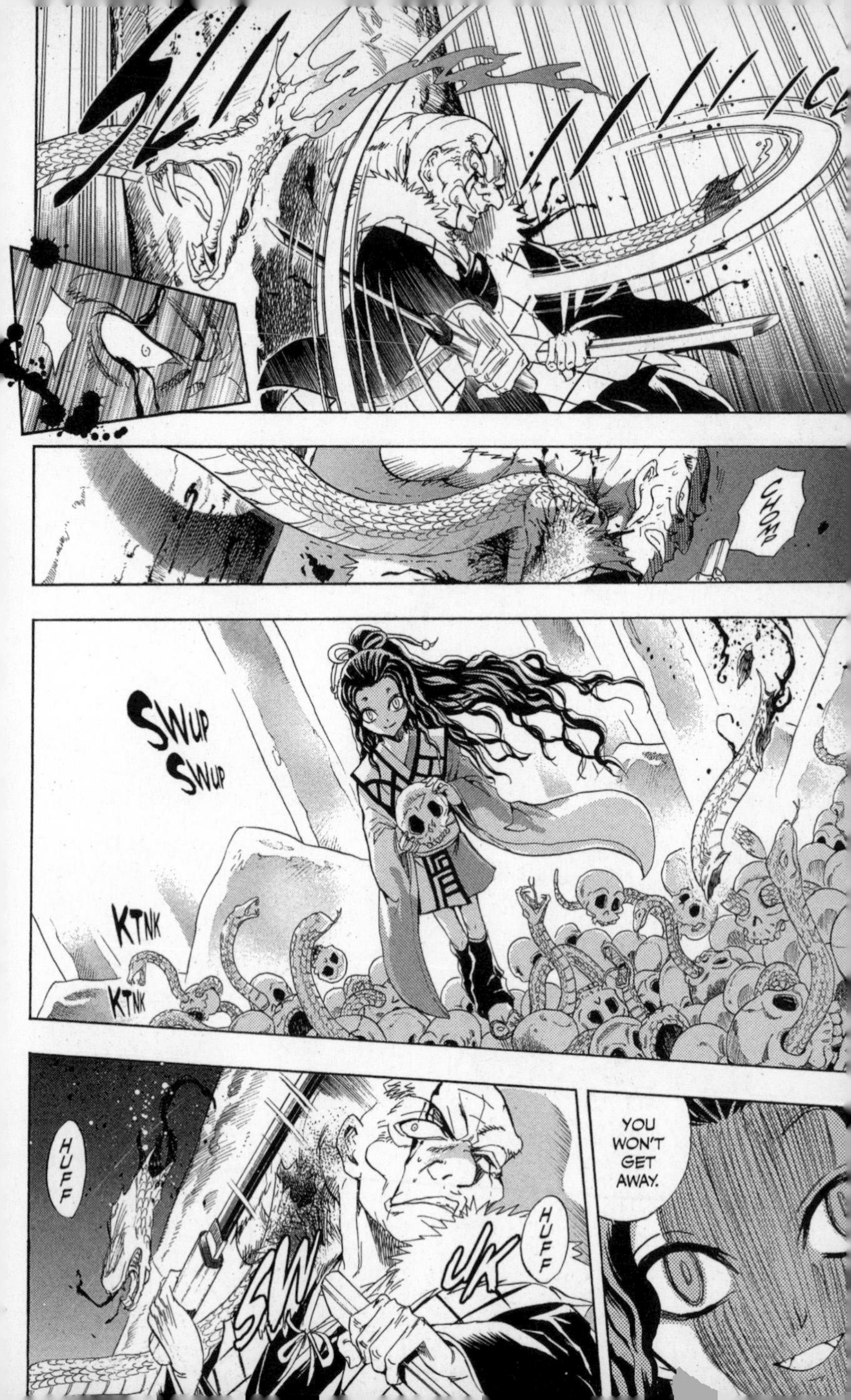
SHUNK
CHOMP
SWUP
SWUP
KTNK
KTNK
YOU WON'T GET AWAY.
HUFF
UK
SHN
HUFF

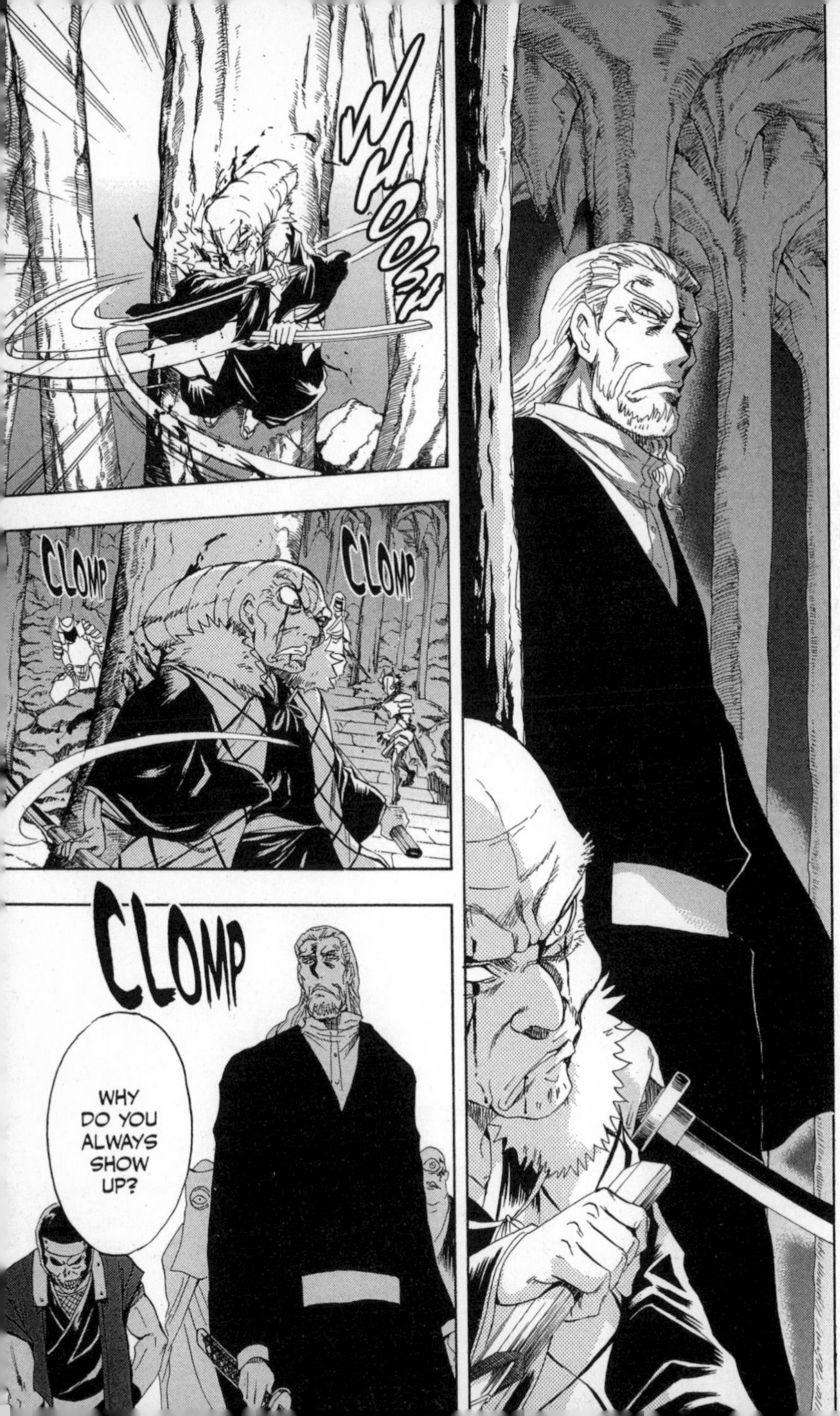
WHOOOSH!
CLOMP
CLOMP
CLOMP
WHY DO YOU ALWAYS SHOW UP?

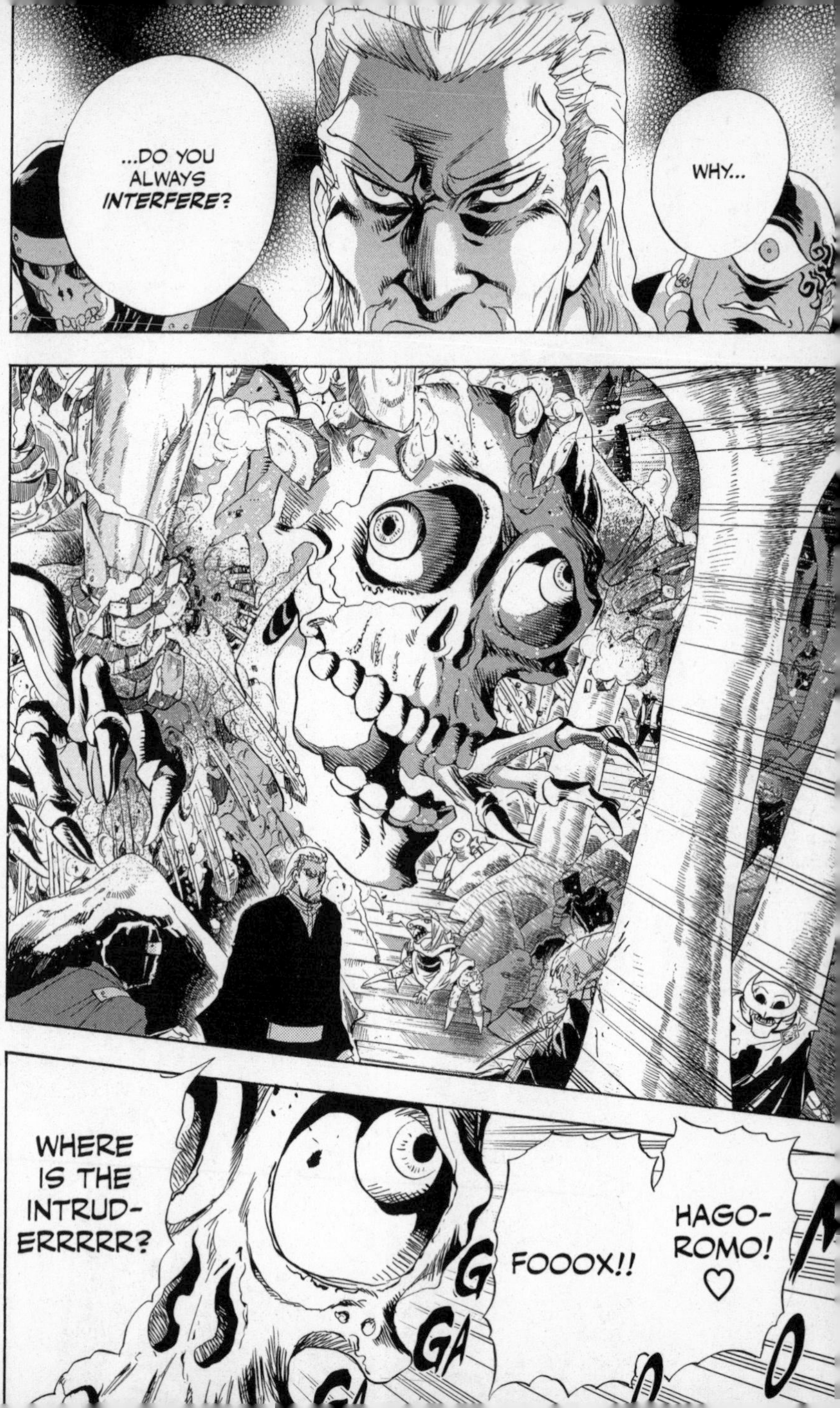
WHY...
...DO YOU ALWAYS INTERFERE?
HAGO-ROMO! ♡
FOOOX!!
G GA GA
WHERE IS THE INTRUD-ERRRRR?

URGH
...

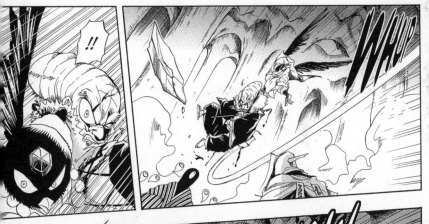

!!

WHUP

I'M
GONNA
EAT
YOUUU!
♡

WHOOOM

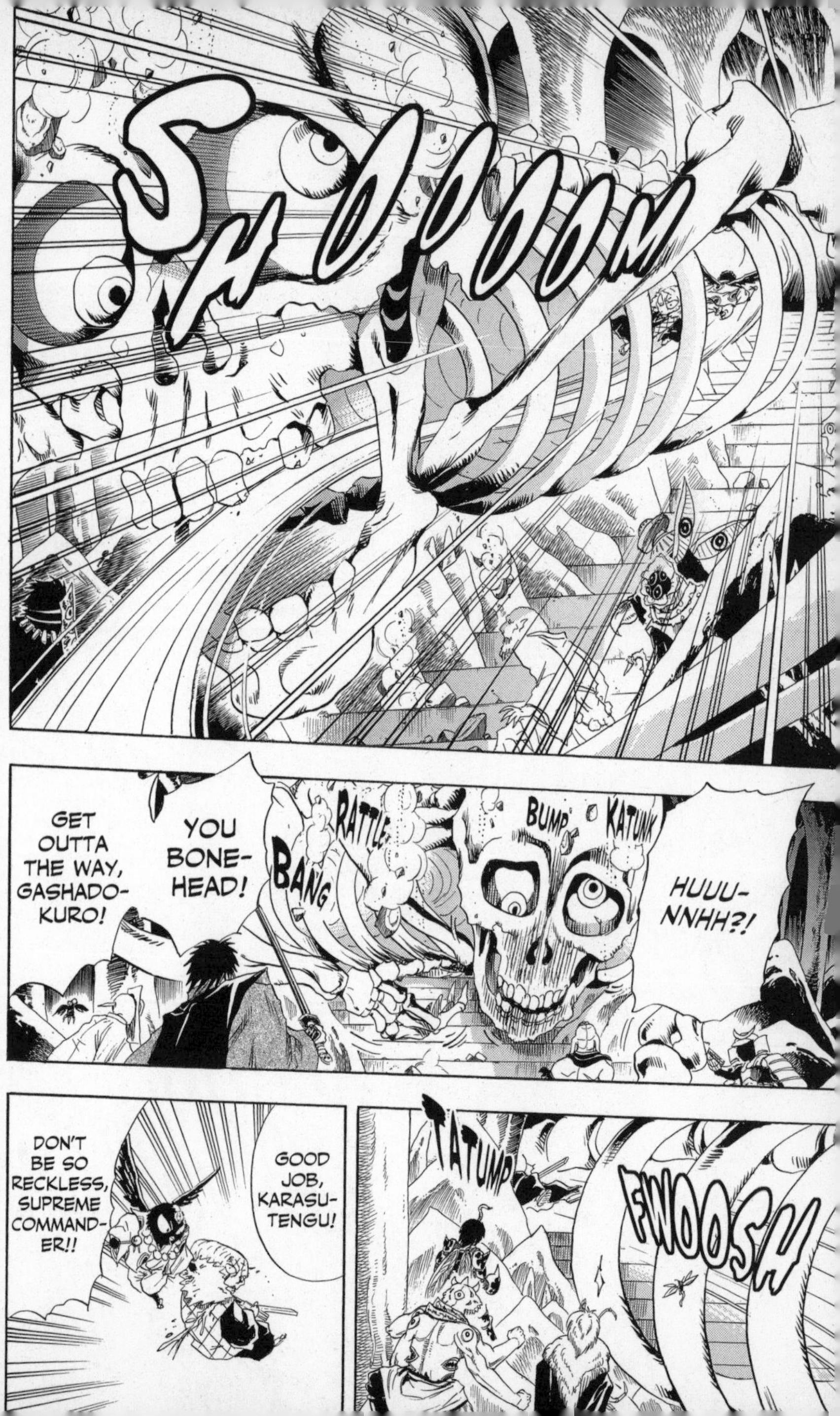
SHOOOOM
HUUU-NNHH?!
KATUNK
BUMP
RATTLE
BANG
YOU BONE-HEAD!
GET OUTTA THE WAY, GASHADO-KURO!
FWOOSH
TATUMP
GOOD JOB, KARASU-TENGU!
DON'T BE SO RECKLESS, SUPREME COMMAND-ER!!

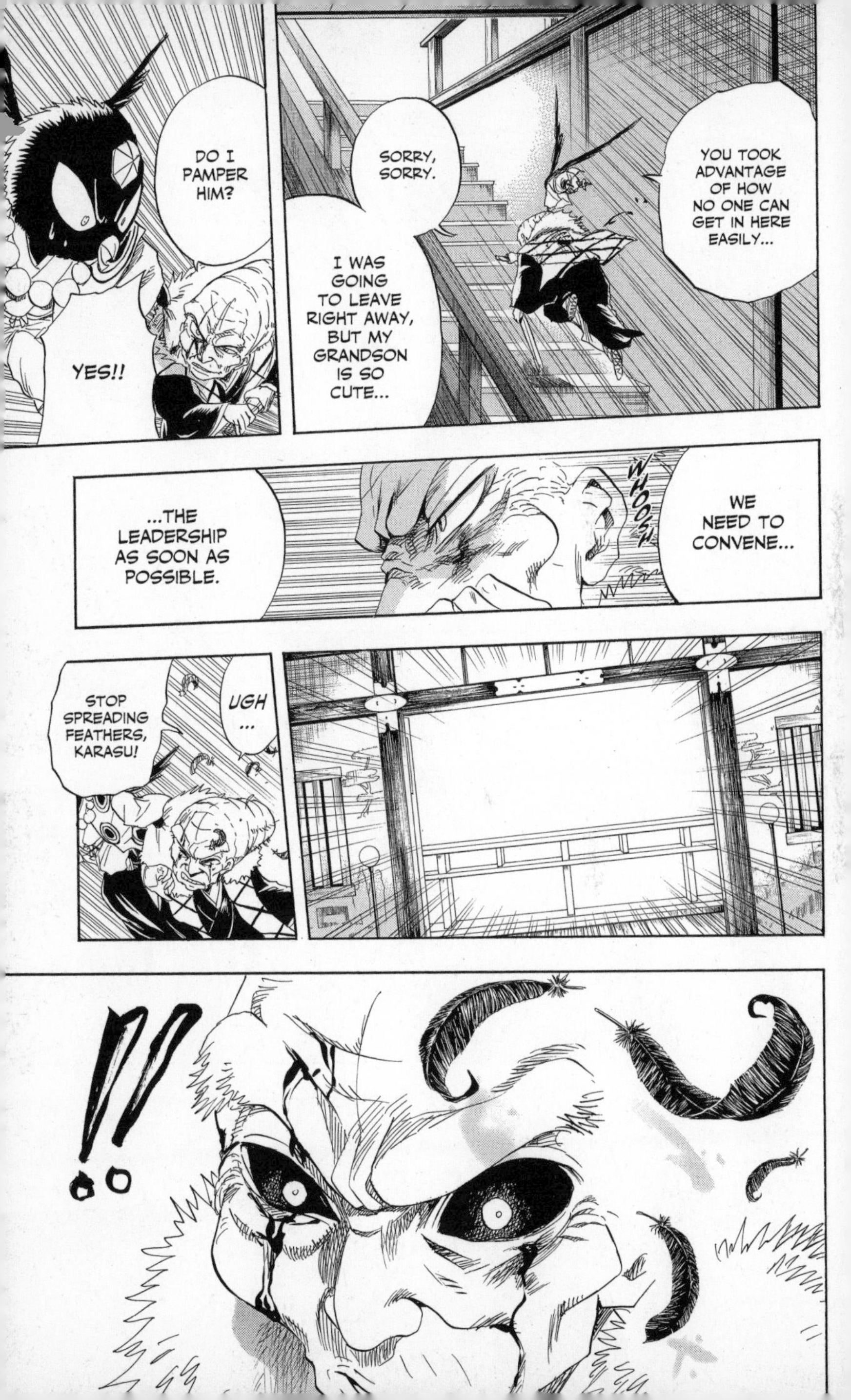
YOU TOOK ADVANTAGE OF HOW NO ONE CAN GET IN HERE EASILY...
SORRY, SORRY.
I WAS GOING TO LEAVE RIGHT AWAY, BUT MY GRANDSON IS SO CUTE...
DO I PAMPER HIM?
YES!!
WE NEED TO CONVENE...
WHOOSH
...THE LEADERSHIP AS SOON AS POSSIBLE.
UGH...
STOP SPREADING FEATHERS, KARASU!
!!

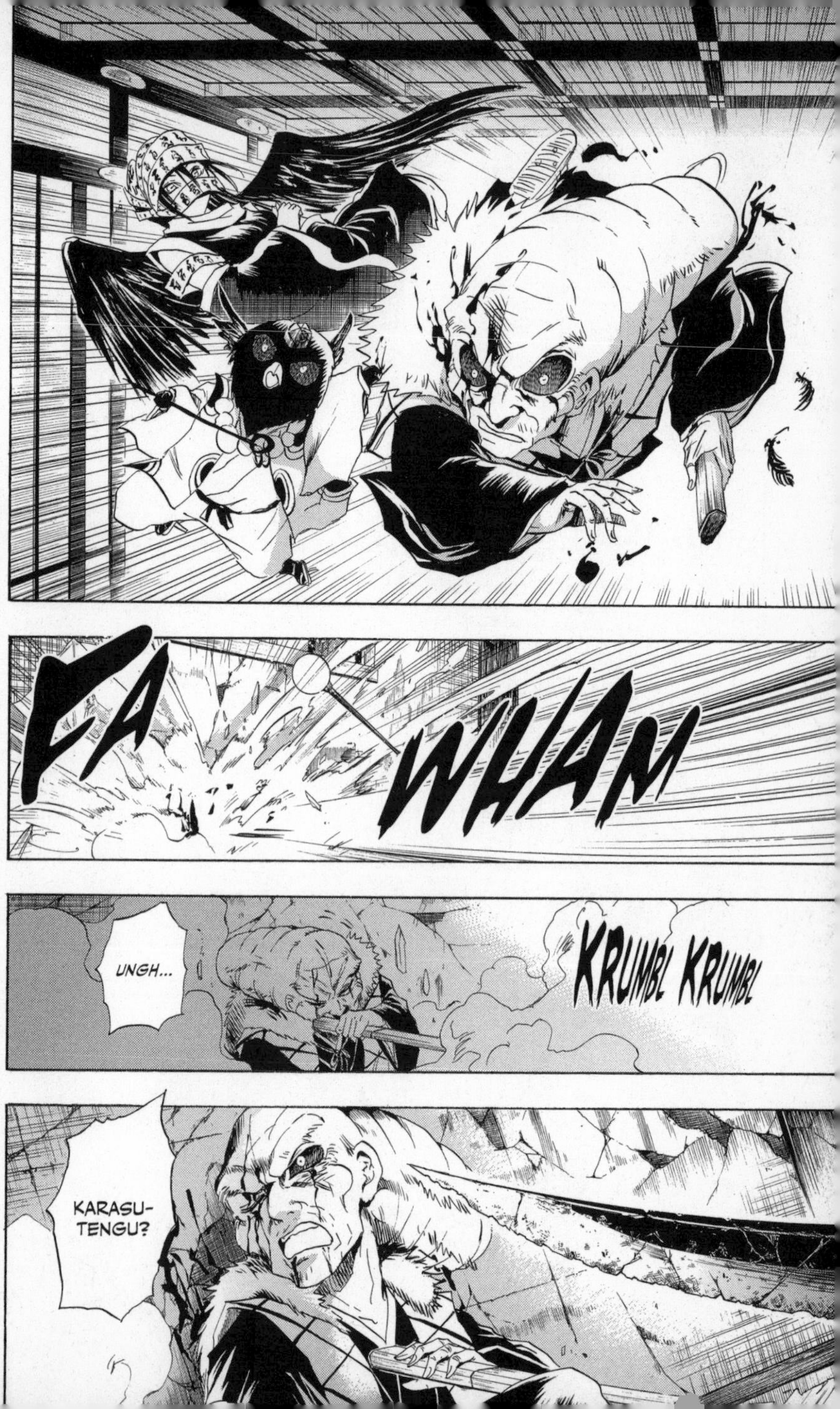
KA
WHAM
KRUMBL KRUMBL
UNGH...
KARASU-TENGU?

AGH ...!

S...

SUPREME COMMANDER ?!

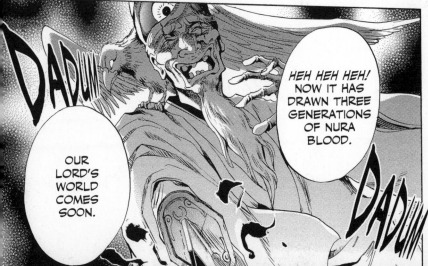

HEH HEH HEH! NOW IT HAS DRAWN THREE GENERATIONS OF NURA BLOOD.

OUR LORD'S WORLD COMES SOON.

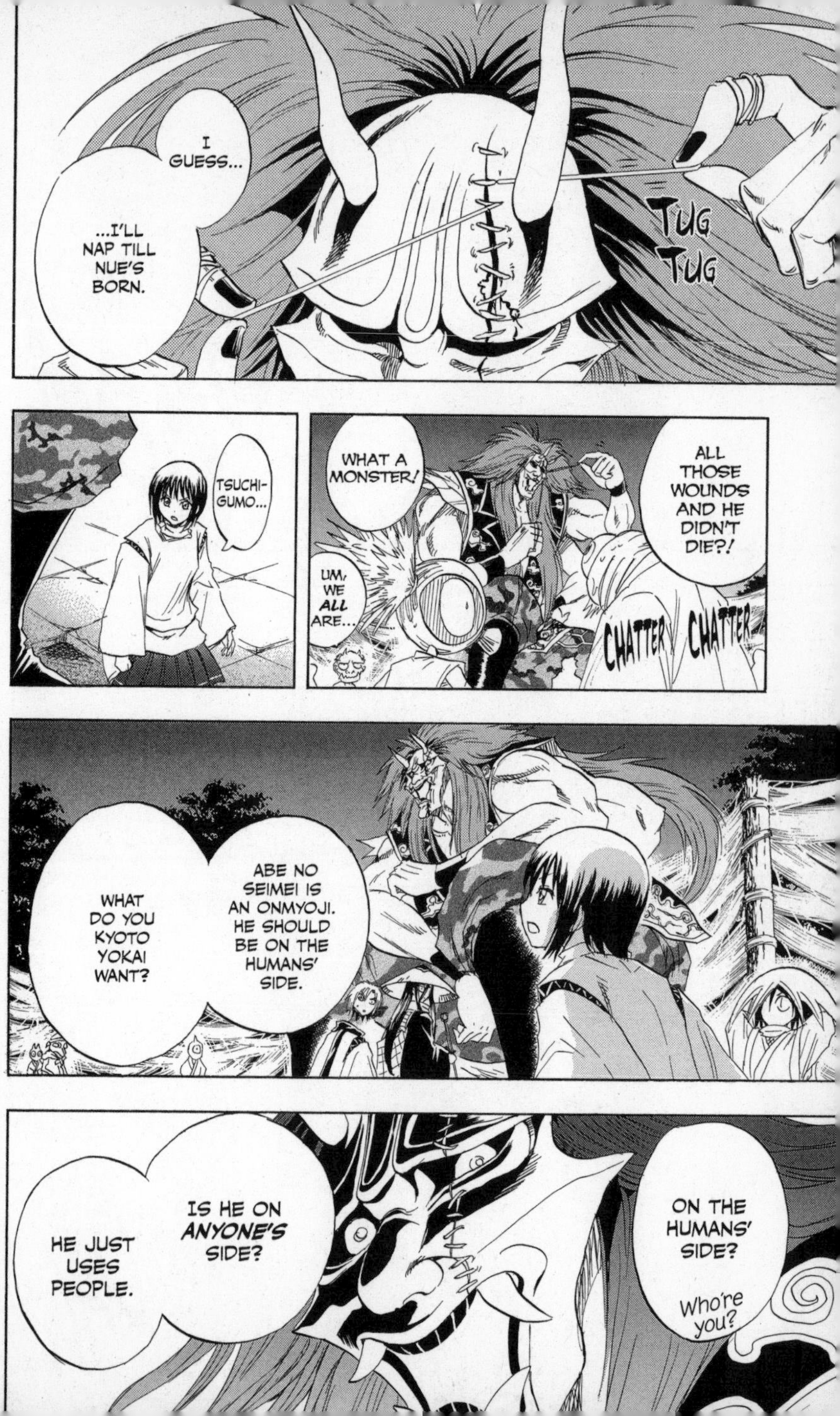
TUG TUG
I GUESS...
...I'LL NAP TILL NUE'S BORN.
ALL THOSE WOUNDS AND HE DIDN'T DIE?!
CHATTER CHATTER
WHAT A MONSTER!
UM, WE ALL ARE...
TSUCHI-GUMO...
ABE NO SEIMEI IS AN ONMYOJI. HE SHOULD BE ON THE HUMANS' SIDE.
WHAT DO YOU KYOTO YOKAI WANT?
ON THE HUMANS' SIDE?
Who're you?
IS HE ON ANYONE'S SIDE?
HE JUST USES PEOPLE.

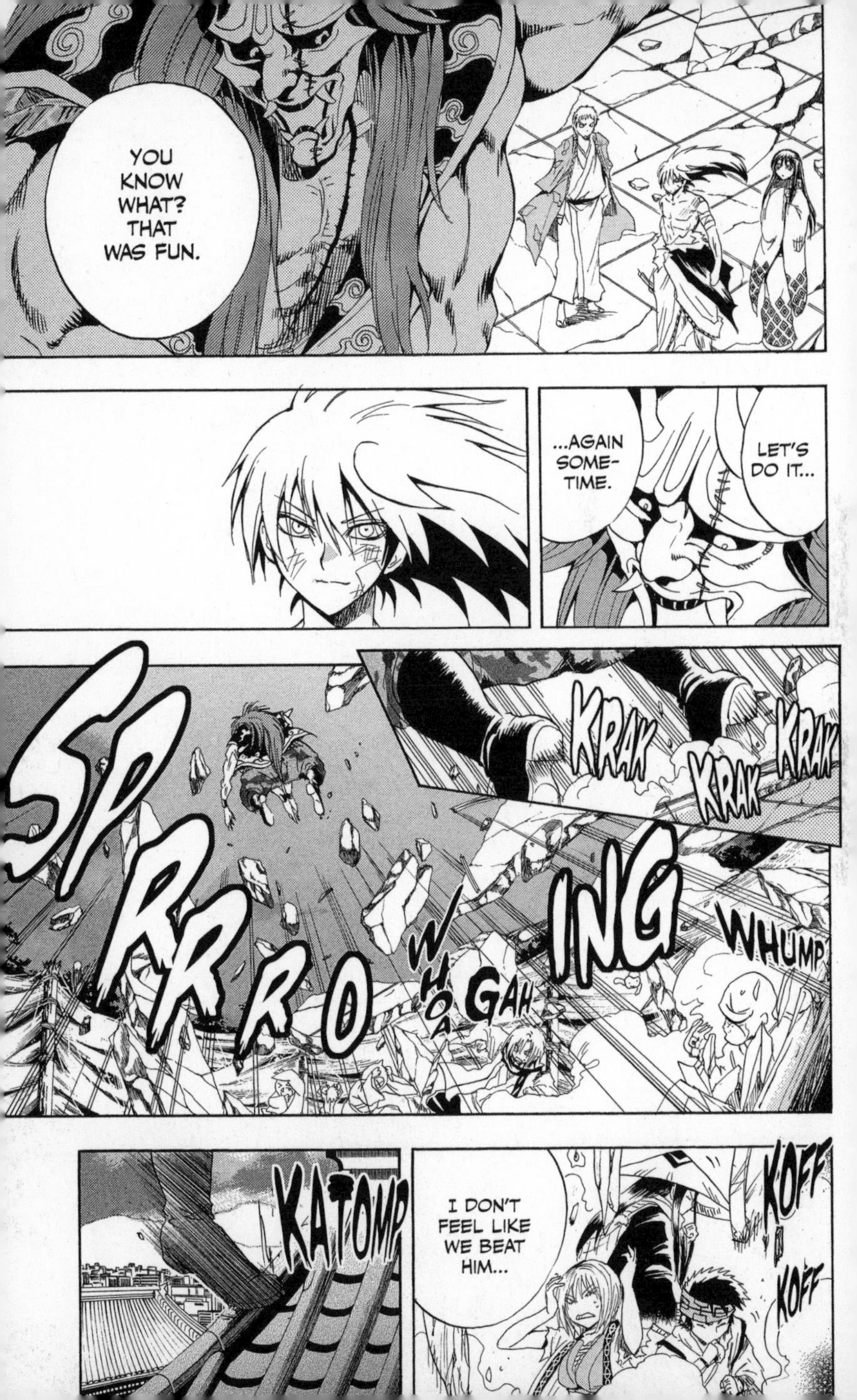
YOU KNOW WHAT? THAT WAS FUN.
LET'S DO IT...
...AGAIN SOME-TIME.
KRAK KRAK KRAK
SPRRRO ING
WHUMP
GAH
WHOA
I DON'T FEEL LIKE WE BEAT HIM...
KOFF KOFF
KATOMP

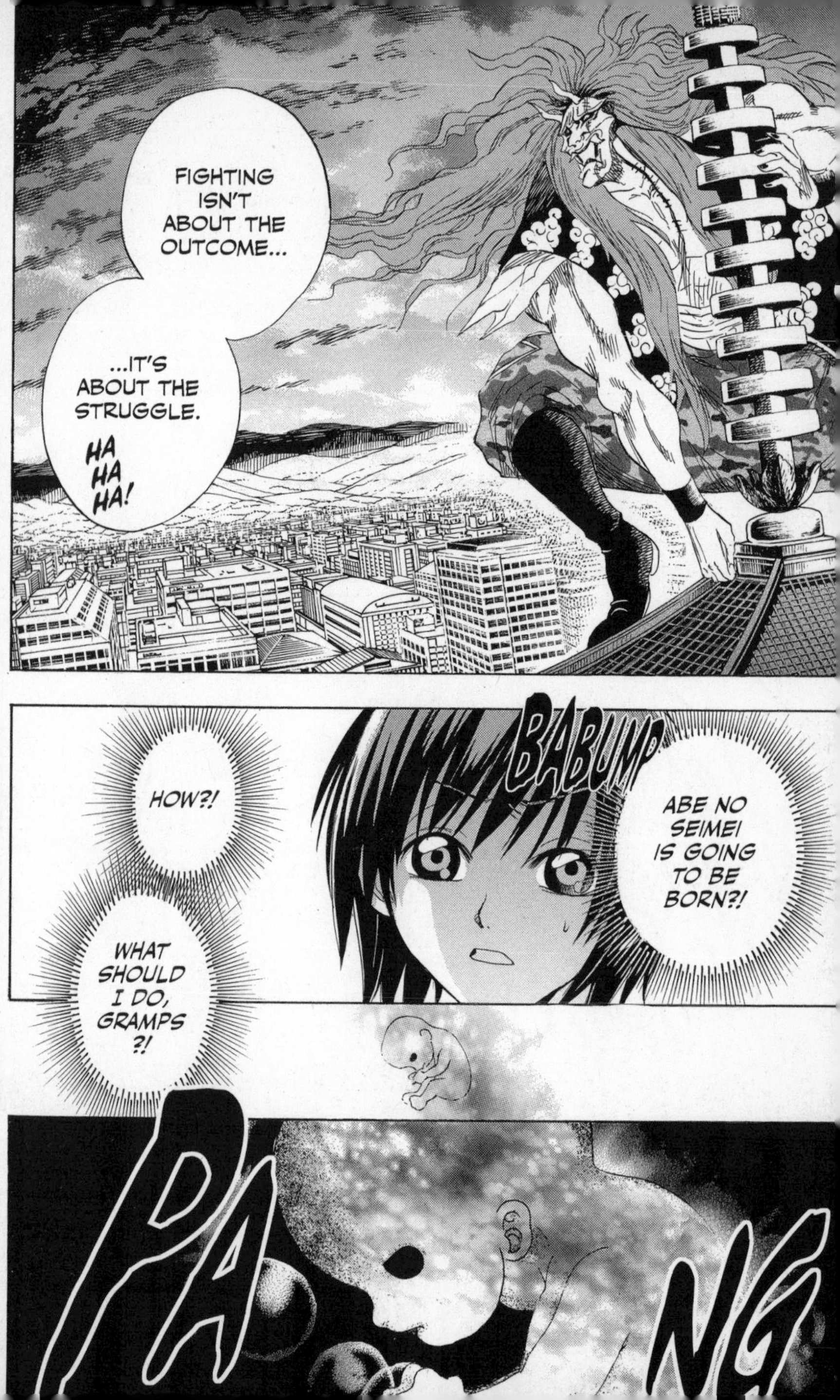
FIGHTING ISN'T ABOUT THE OUTCOME...
...IT'S ABOUT THE STRUGGLE.
HA HA HA!
BABUMP
ABE NO SEIMEI IS GOING TO BE BORN?!
HOW?!
WHAT SHOULD I DO, GRAMPS?!
PANG

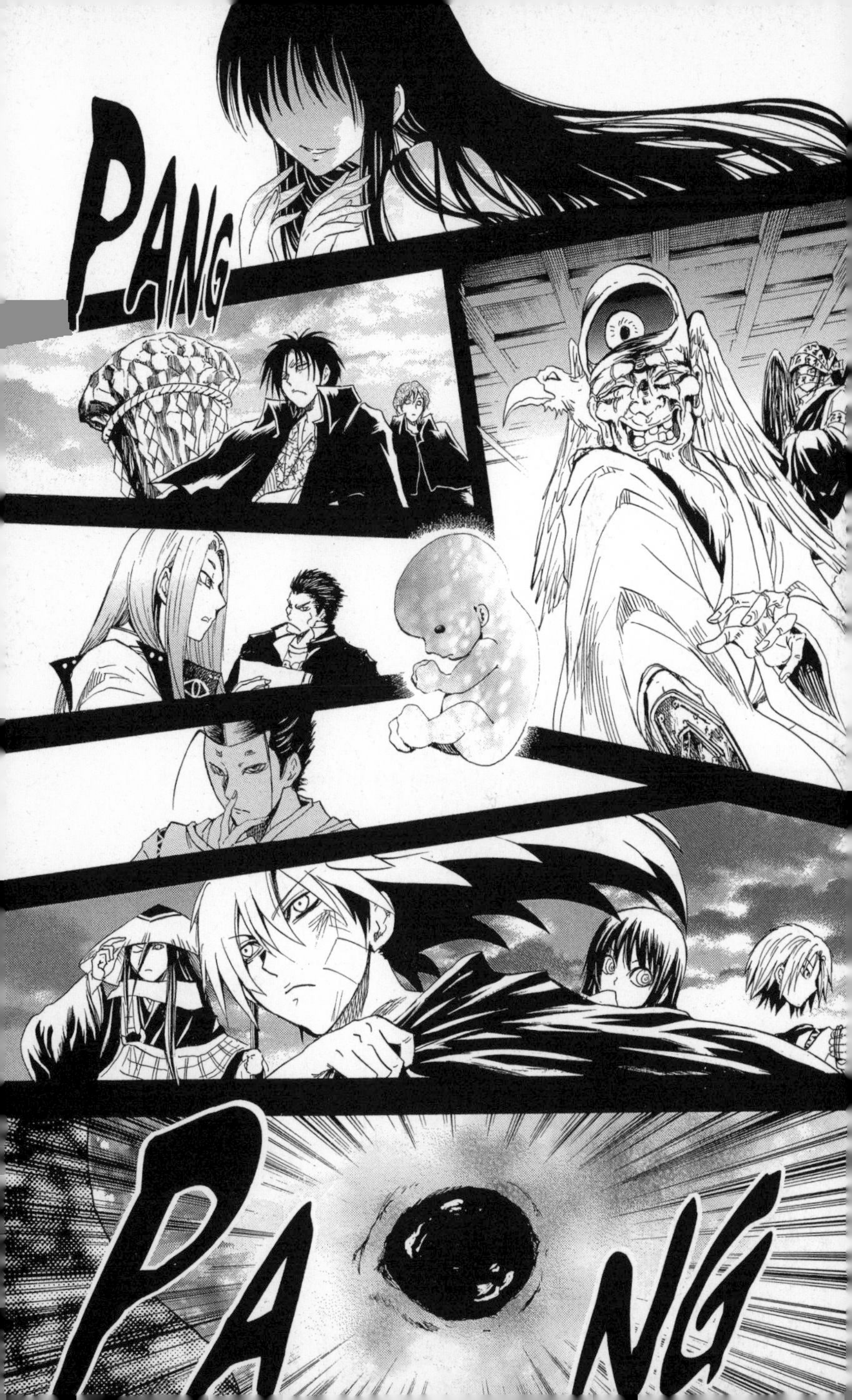
PANG
PA NG

NURA: RISE OF THE YOKAI CLAN

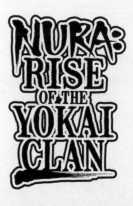

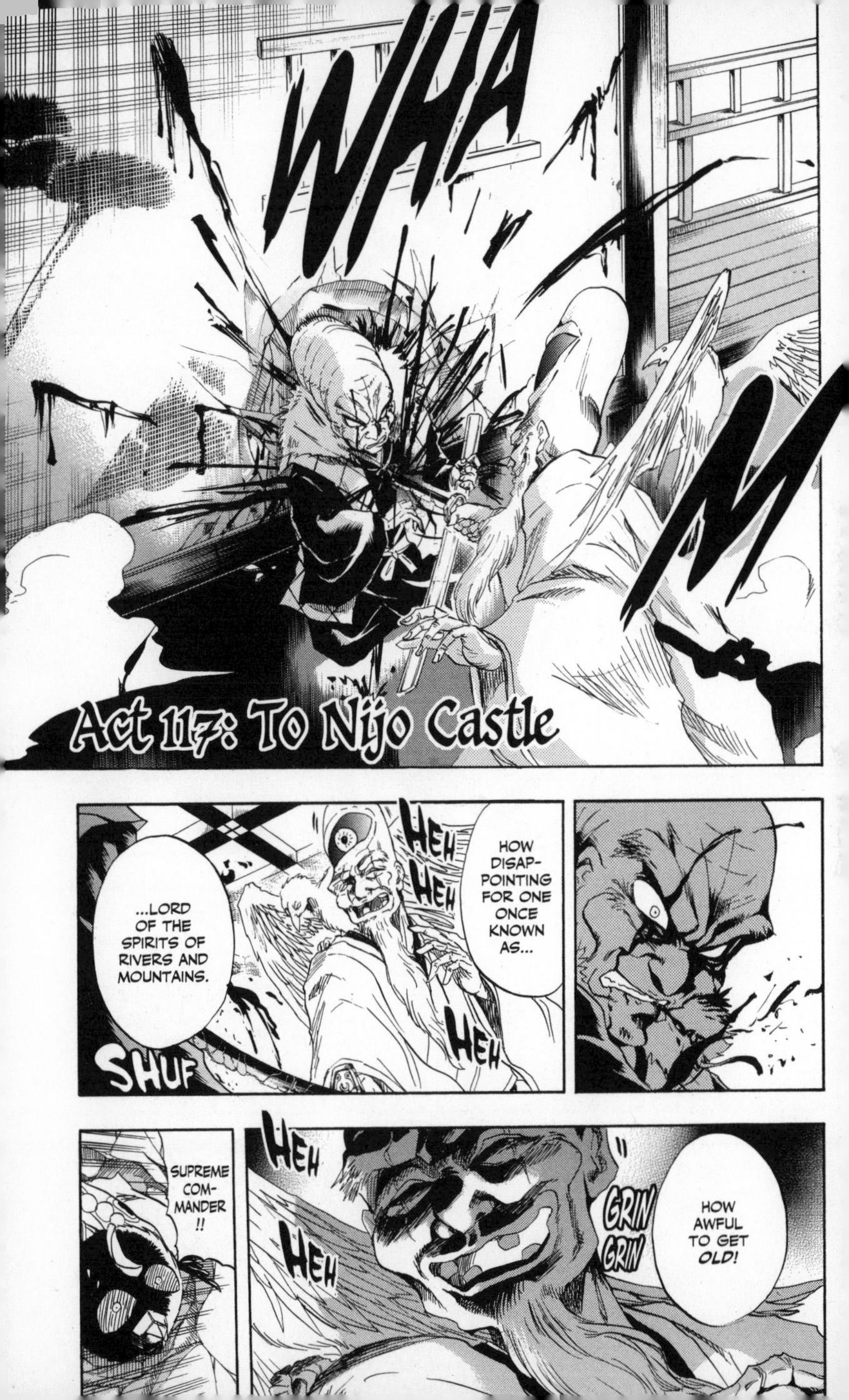
WHAM
Act 117: To Nijo Castle
HOW DISAP-POINTING FOR ONE ONCE KNOWN AS...
HEH HEH
...LORD OF THE SPIRITS OF RIVERS AND MOUNTAINS.
HEH
SHUF
GRIN GRIN
HOW AWFUL TO GET OLD!
HEH HEH
SUPREME COM-MANDER !!

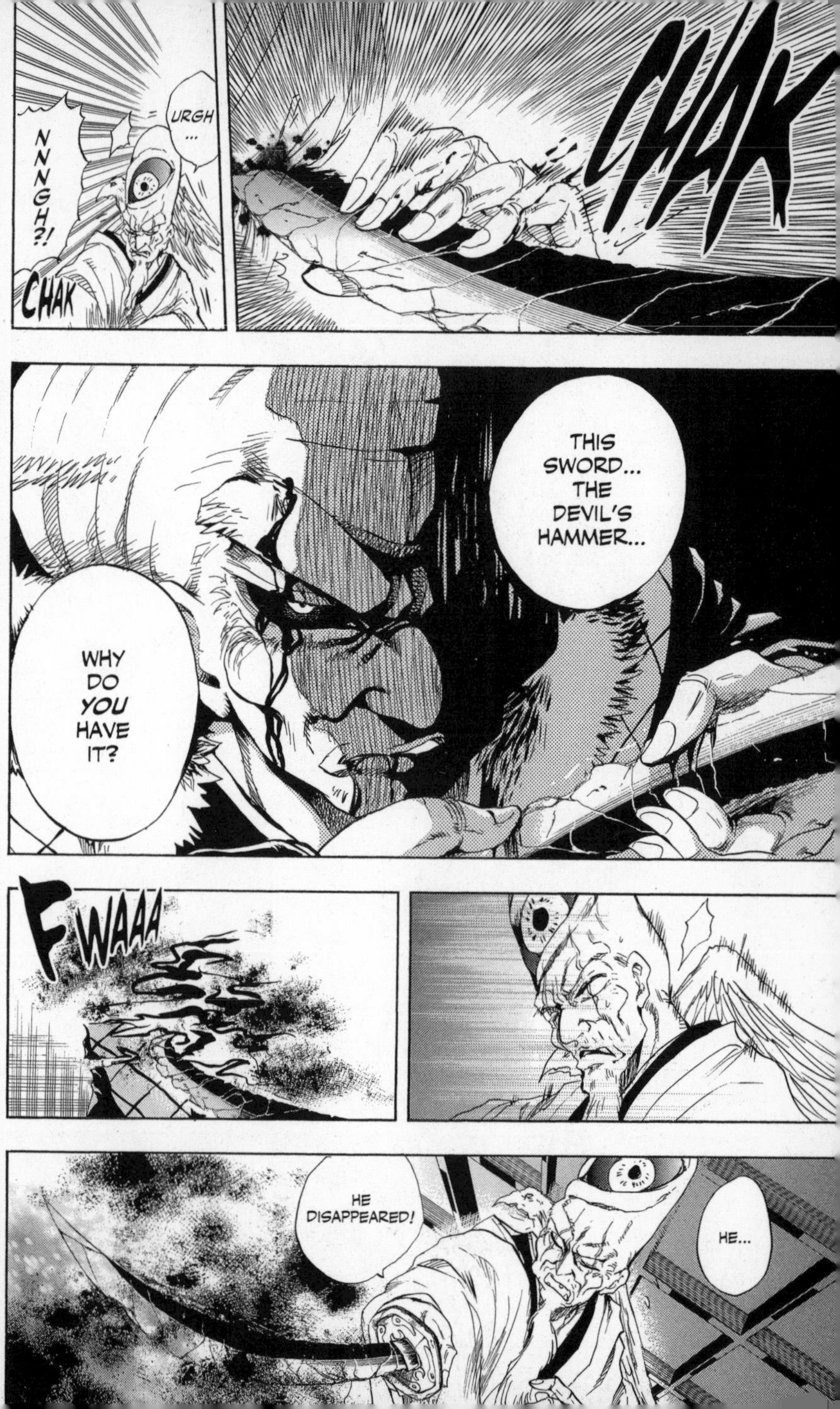
CHAK
URGH...
NNNGH?!
CHAK
THIS SWORD... THE DEVIL'S HAMMER...
WHY DO *YOU* HAVE IT?
FWAAA
HE...
HE DISAPPEARED!

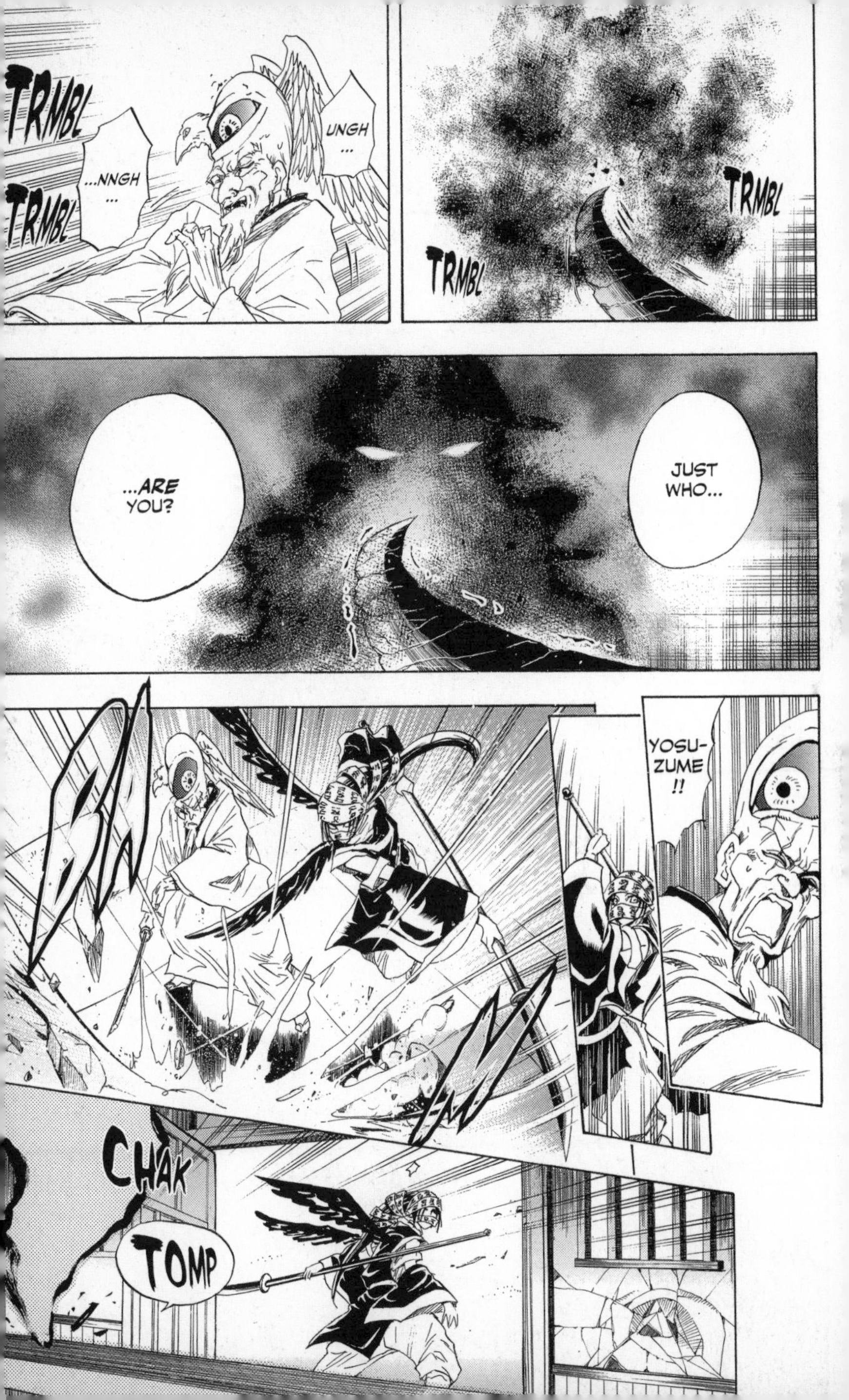
TRMBL
TRMBL
UNGH ...
...NNGH ...
TRMBL
TRMBL
JUST WHO...
...ARE YOU?
YOSU-ZUME!!
CHAK
TOMP

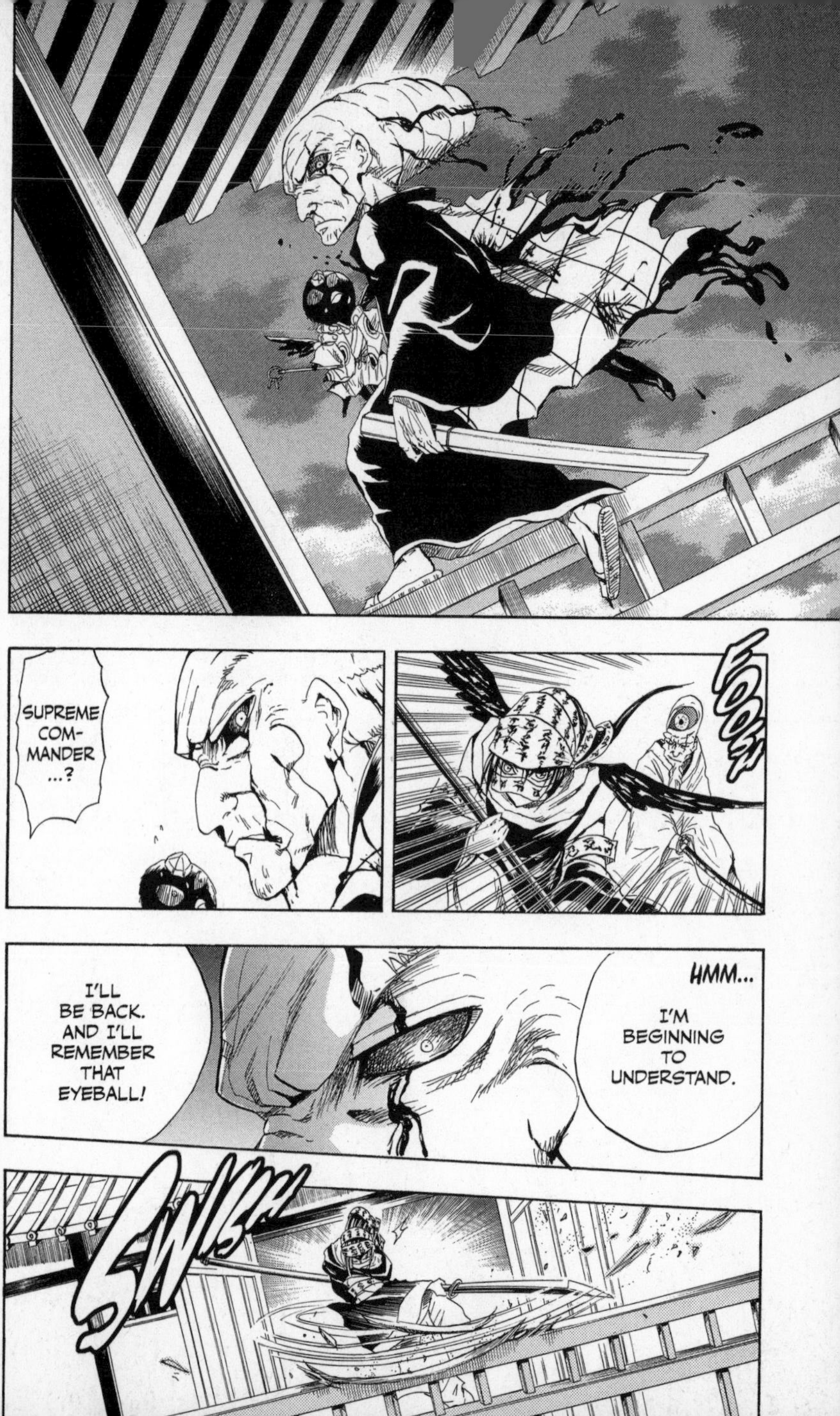
FOOM
SUPREME COM-MANDER ...?
HMM...
I'M BEGINNING TO UNDERSTAND.
I'LL BE BACK. AND I'LL REMEMBER THAT EYEBALL!
SWISH

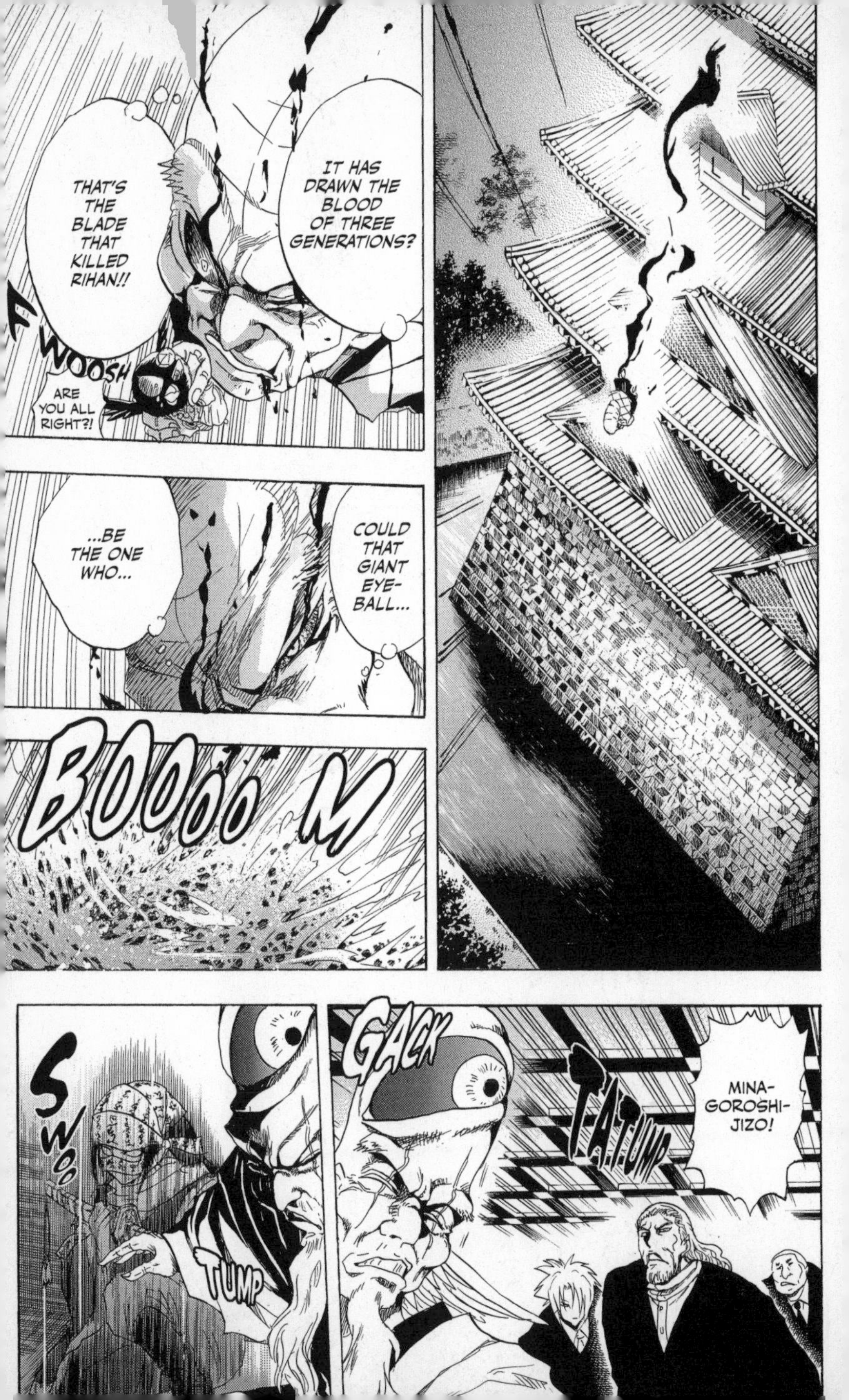
IT HAS DRAWN THE BLOOD OF THREE GENERATIONS?
THAT'S THE BLADE THAT KILLED RIHAN!!
FWOOSH
ARE YOU ALL RIGHT?!
COULD THAT GIANT EYE-BALL...
...BE THE ONE WHO...
BOOOOM
MINA-GOROSHI-JIZO!
TATUMP
GACK
SWOO
TUMP

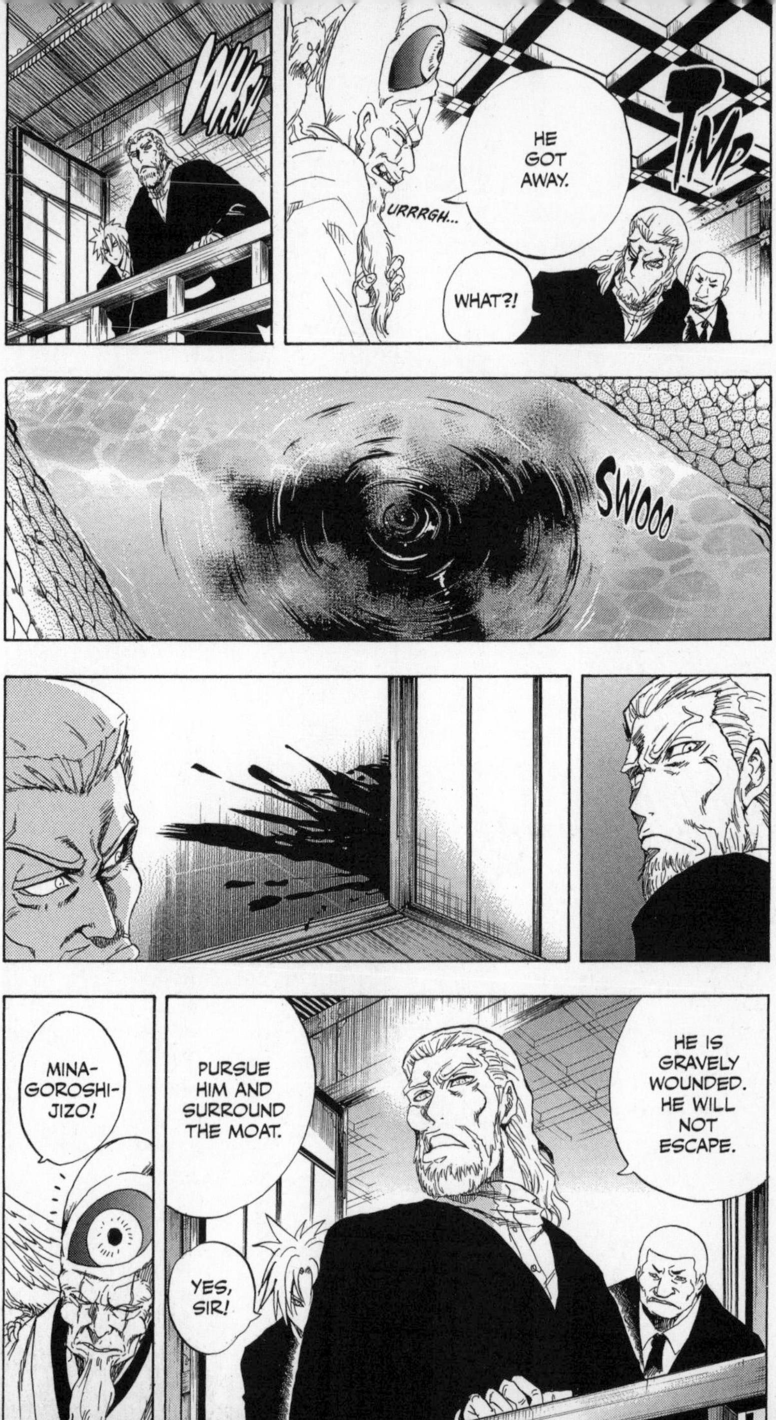
TMP
HE GOT AWAY.
URRRGH...
WHAT?!
WHSH
SWOOO
HE IS GRAVELY WOUNDED. HE WILL NOT ESCAPE.
PURSUE HIM AND SURROUND THE MOAT.
YES, SIR!
MINA-GOROSHI-JIZO!

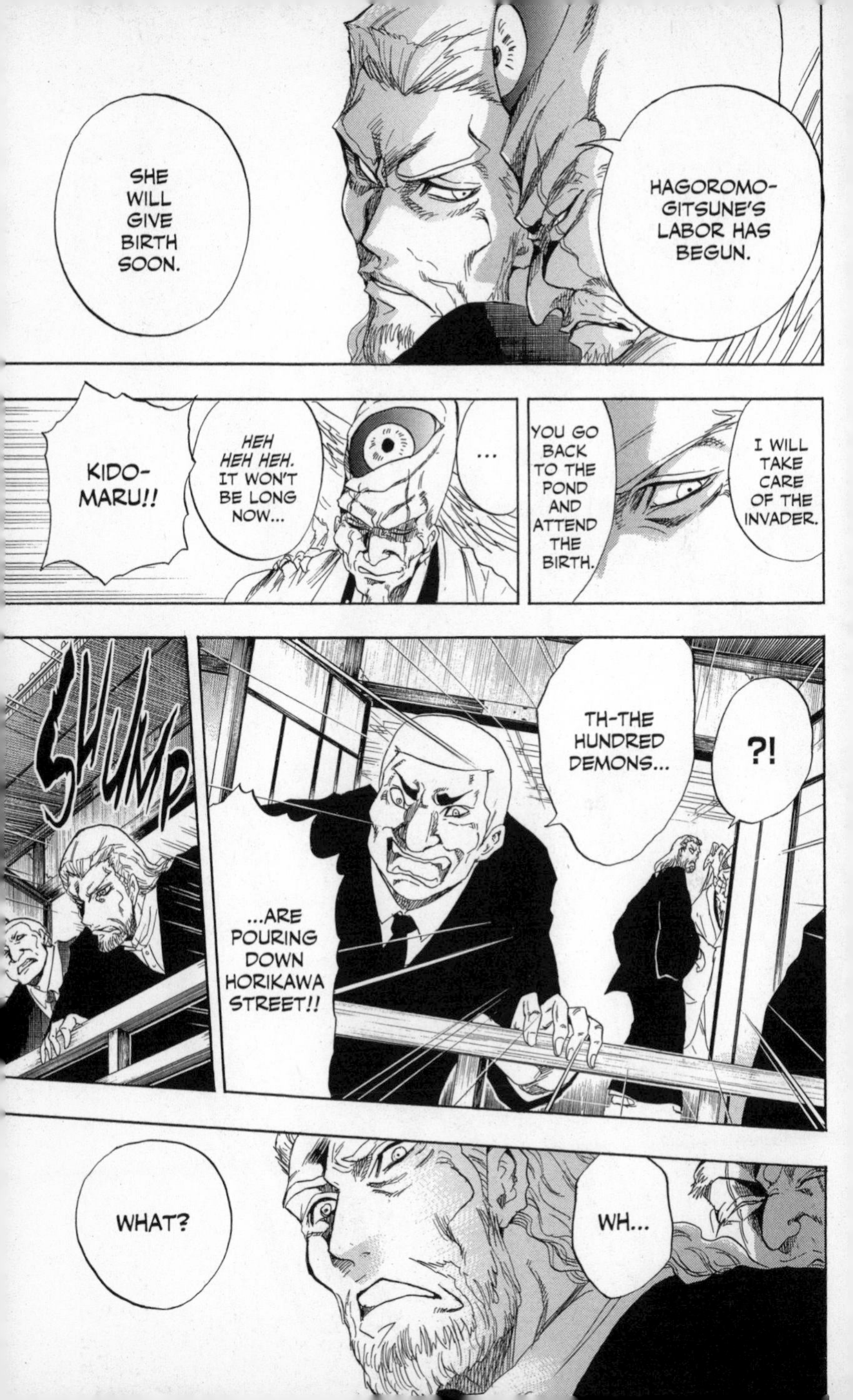
HAGOROMO-GITSUNE'S LABOR HAS BEGUN.
SHE WILL GIVE BIRTH SOON.
I WILL TAKE CARE OF THE INVADER.
YOU GO BACK TO THE POND AND ATTEND THE BIRTH.
...
HEH HEH HEH. IT WON'T BE LONG NOW...
KIDO-MARU!!
?!
TH-THE HUNDRED DEMONS...
...ARE POURING DOWN HORIKAWA STREET!!
SHUMP
WH...
WHAT?

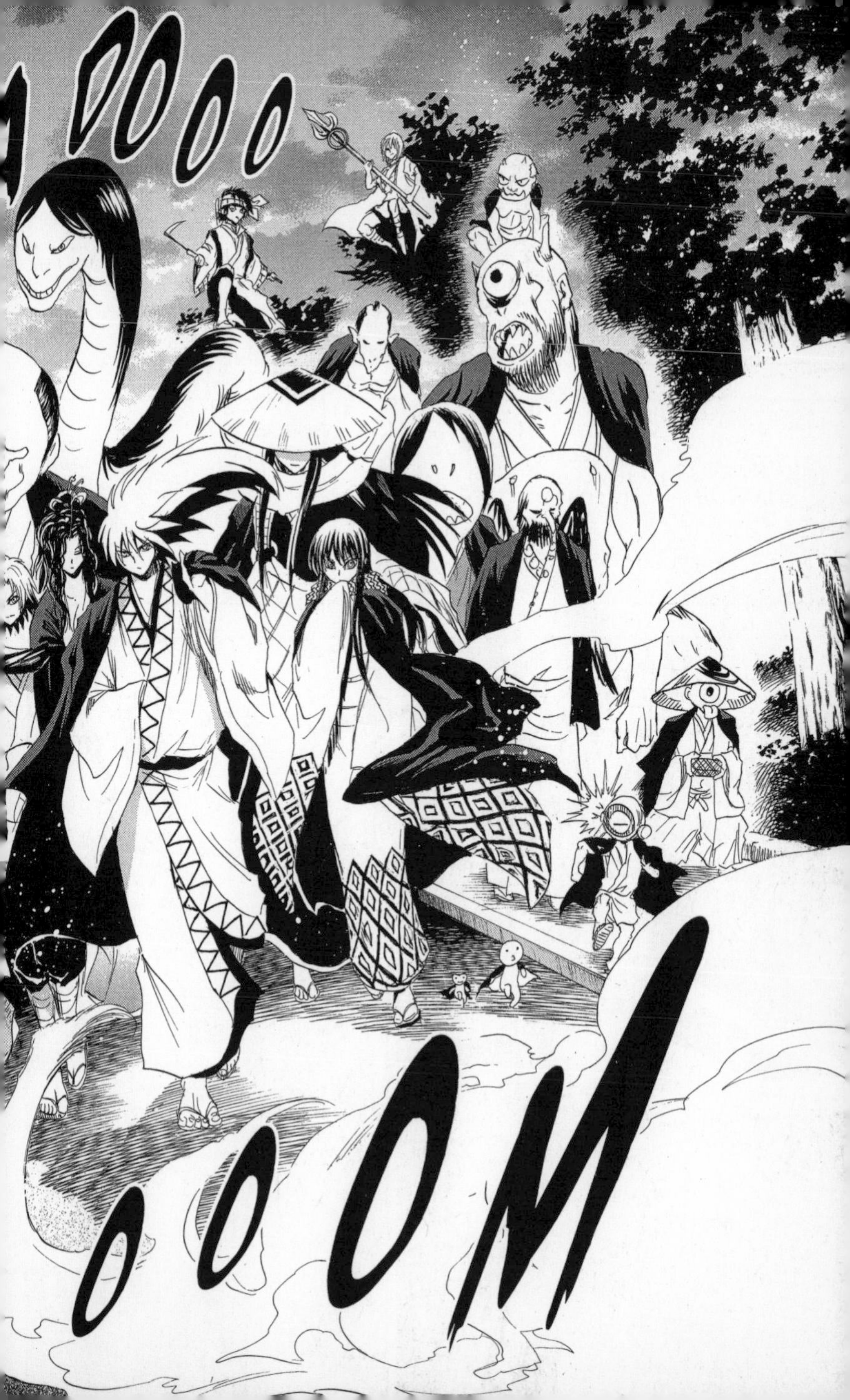
VOOOO
OOOM

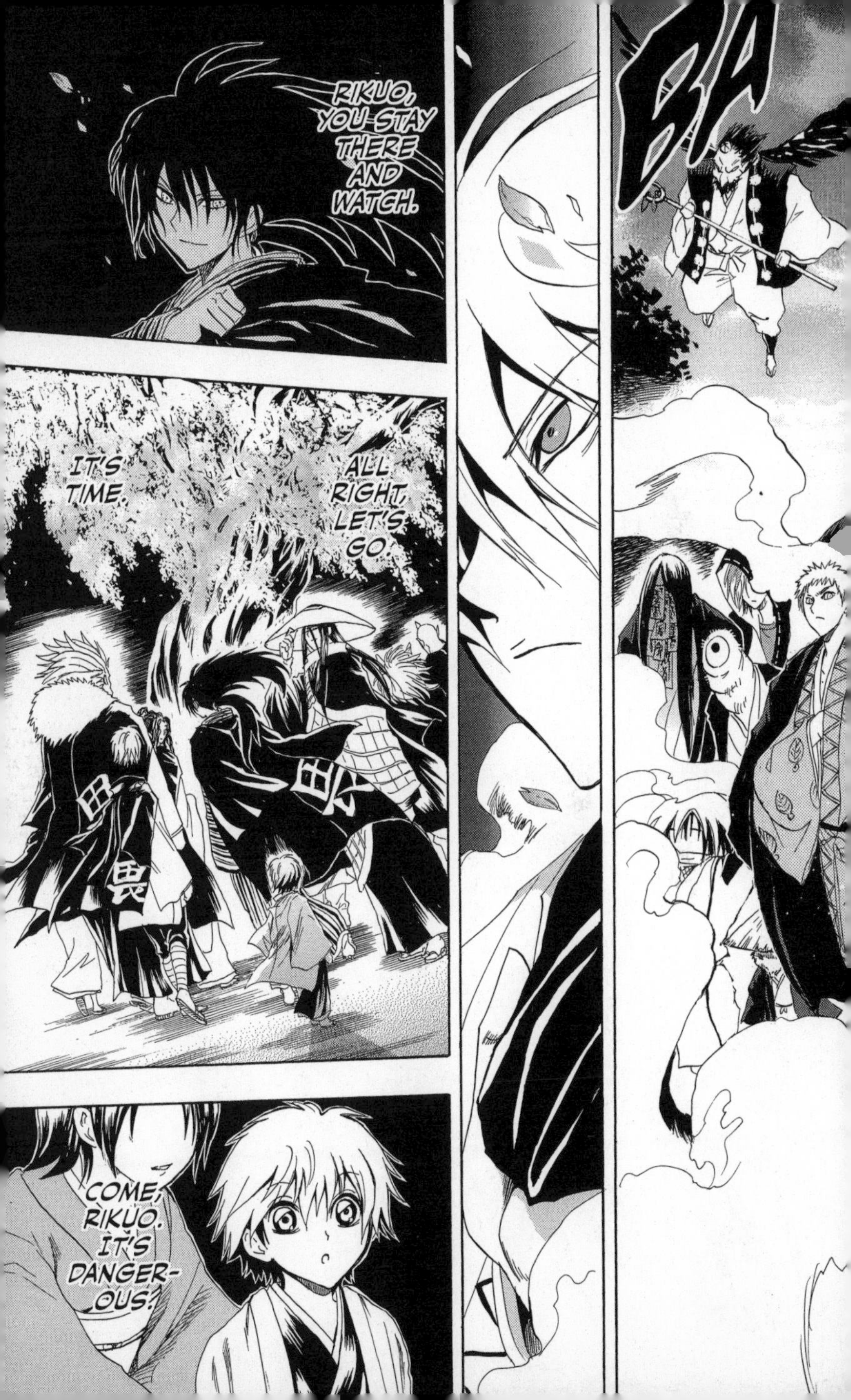
BA
RIKUO, YOU STAY THERE AND WATCH.
ALL RIGHT, LET'S GO.
IT'S TIME.
COME, RIKUO. IT'S DANGER-OUS!

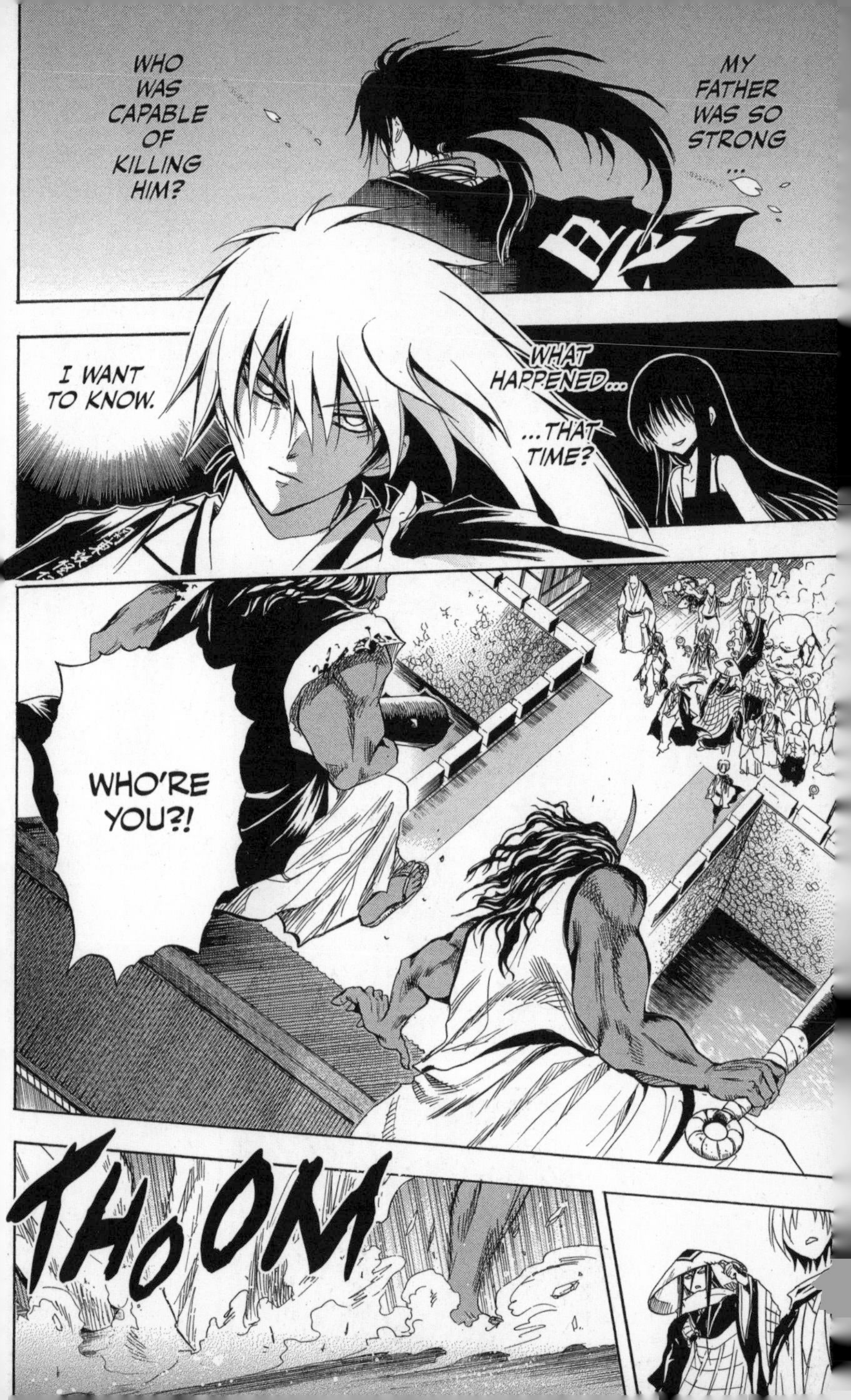
MY FATHER WAS SO STRONG ...
WHO WAS CAPABLE OF KILLING HIM?
WHAT HAPPENED...
...THAT TIME?
I WANT TO KNOW.
WHO'RE YOU?!
THOOM

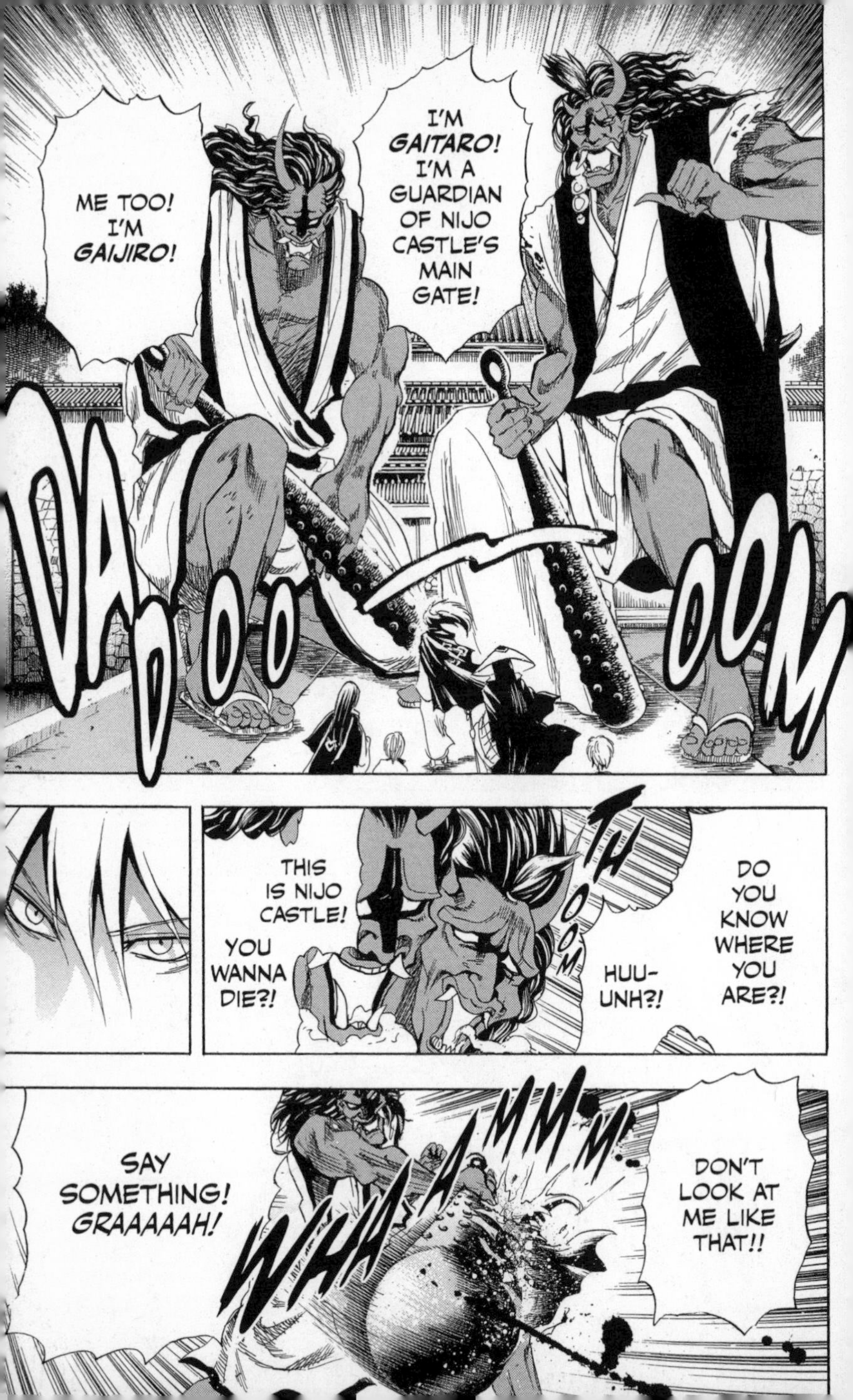
I'M GAITARO! I'M A GUARDIAN OF NIJO CASTLE'S MAIN GATE!
ME TOO! I'M GAIJIRO!
DADOOOOOM
DO YOU KNOW WHERE YOU ARE?!
HUU-UNH?!
THOOOM
THIS IS NIJO CASTLE!
YOU WANNA DIE?!
DON'T LOOK AT ME LIKE THAT!!
WHAAAMMM
SAY SOMETHING! GRAAAAAH!

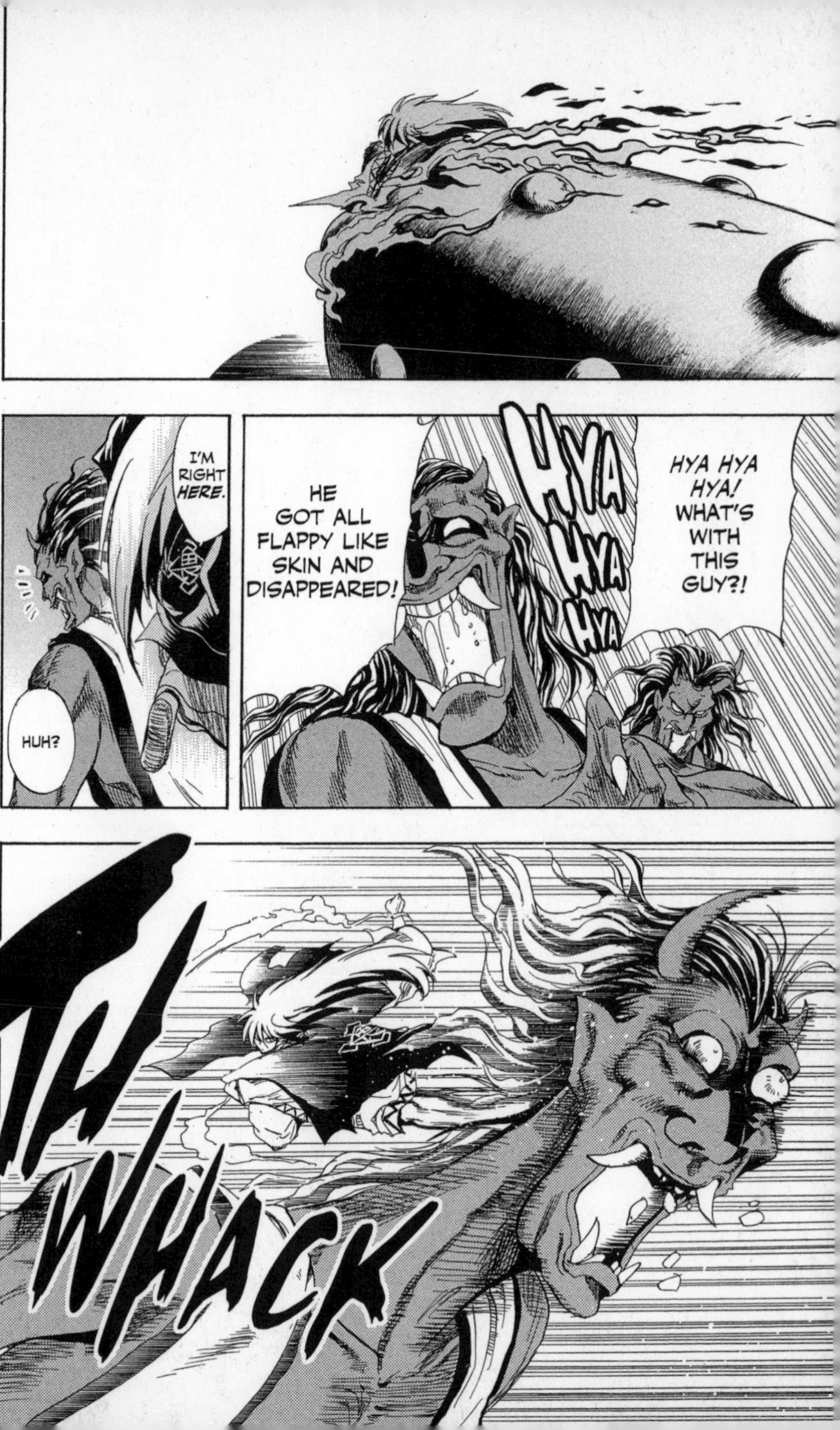
HYA HYA HYA! WHAT'S WITH THIS GUY?!
HYA HYA HYA HYA
HE GOT ALL FLAPPY LIKE SKIN AND DISAPPEARED!
I'M RIGHT HERE.
HUH?
THWACK

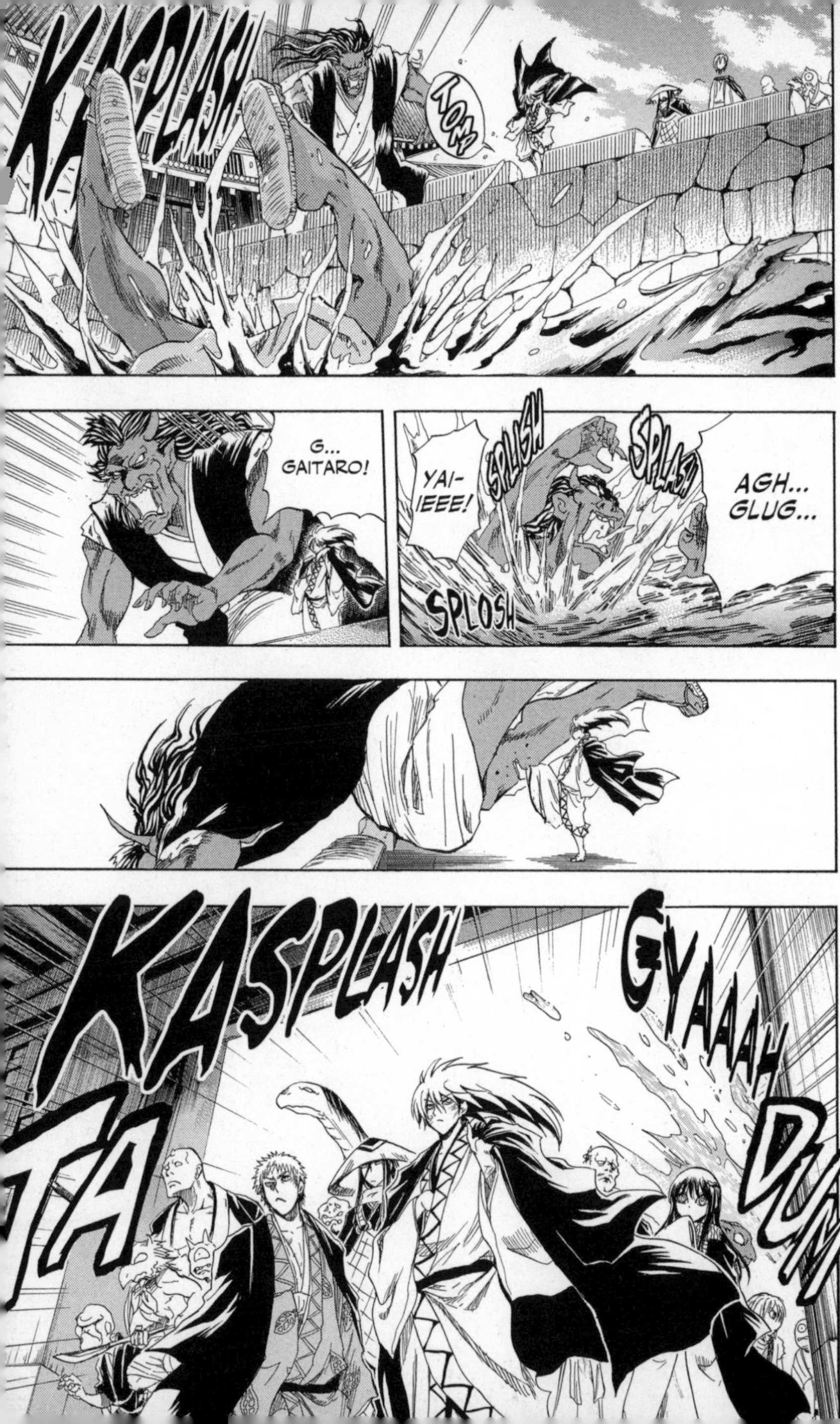
TOMP
KASPLASH
AGH... GLUG...
SPLASH
SPLASH
YAI-IEEE!
SPLOSH
G... GAITARO!
GYAAAH
DUN
KASPLASH
TA

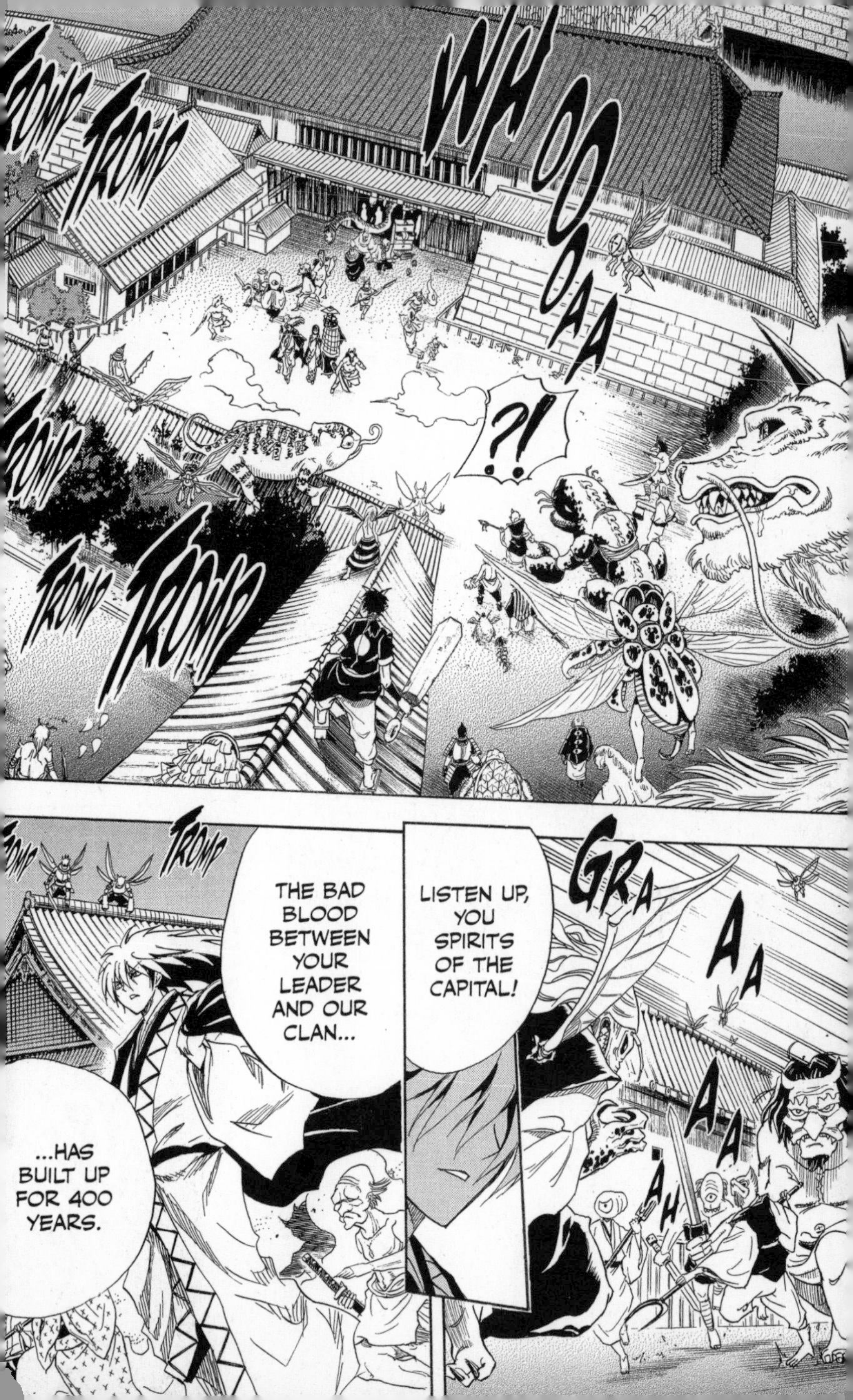
WHOOOOAAA
TROMP TROMP
TROMP
TROMP TROMP
?!
GRAAAAAAH
LISTEN UP, YOU SPIRITS OF THE CAPITAL!
THE BAD BLOOD BETWEEN YOUR LEADER AND OUR CLAN...
...HAS BUILT UP FOR 400 YEARS.
TROMP TROMP

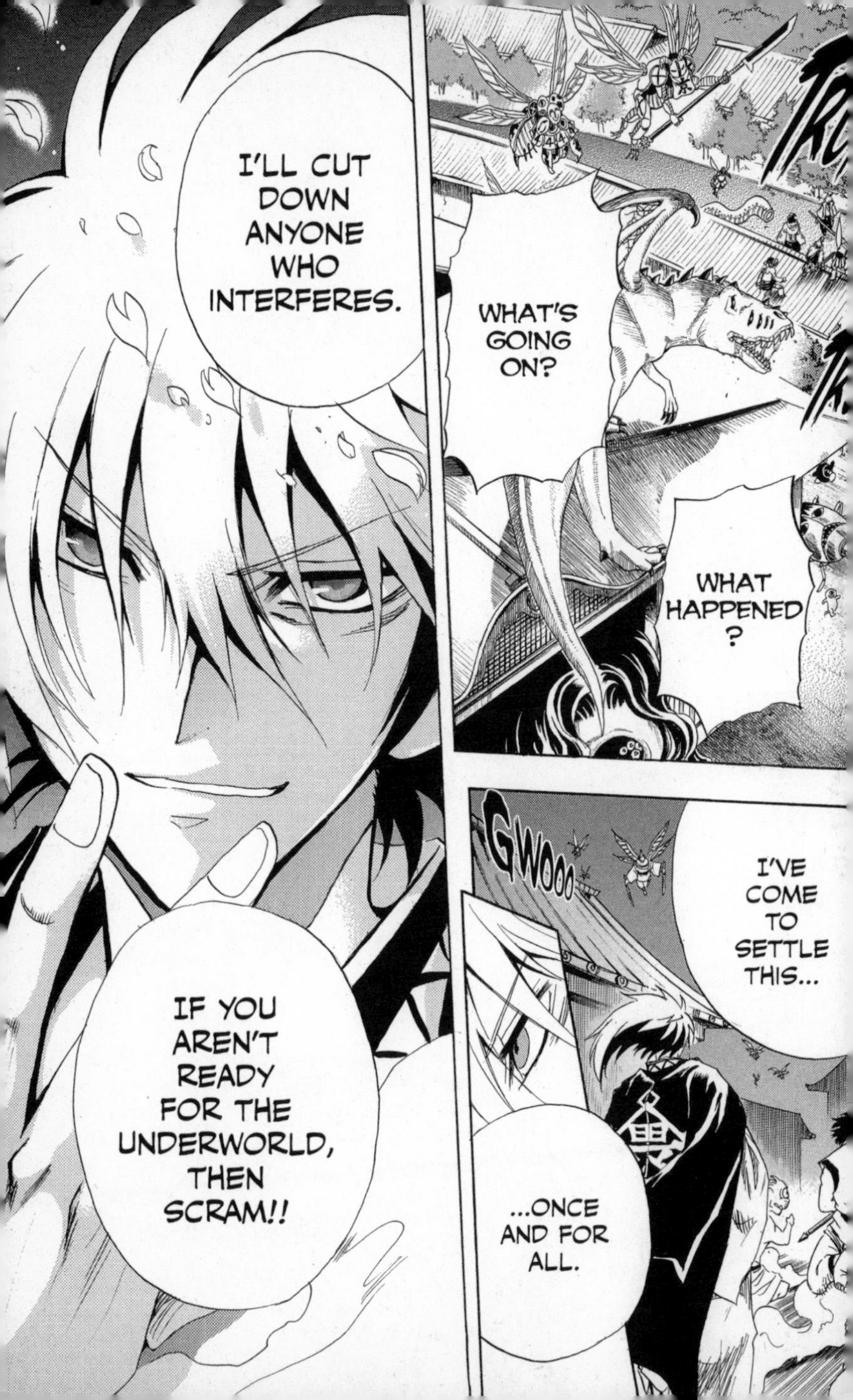
WHAT'S GOING ON?
WHAT HAPPENED?
GWOOO
I'VE COME TO SETTLE THIS...
...ONCE AND FOR ALL.
I'LL CUT DOWN ANYONE WHO INTERFERES.
IF YOU AREN'T READY FOR THE UNDERWORLD, THEN SCRAM!!

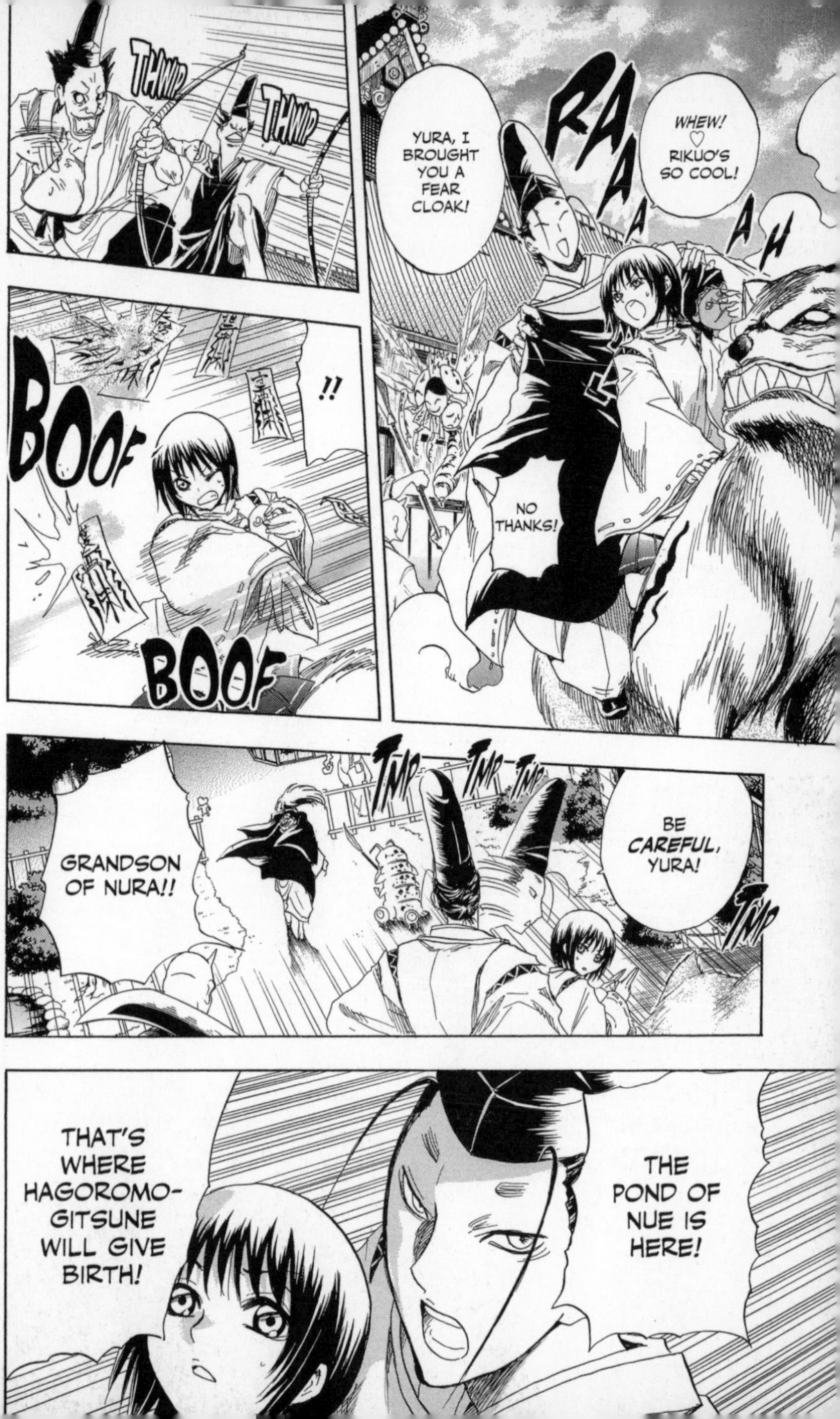
WHEW! ♡ RIKUO'S SO COOL!
RAAAAH
YURA, I BROUGHT YOU A FEAR CLOAK!
NO THANKS!
THWIP
THWIP
BOOF
!!
BOOF
BE CAREFUL, YURA!
TMP TMP TMP
TMP
GRANDSON OF NURA!!
THE POND OF NUE IS HERE!
THAT'S WHERE HAGOROMO-GITSUNE WILL GIVE BIRTH!

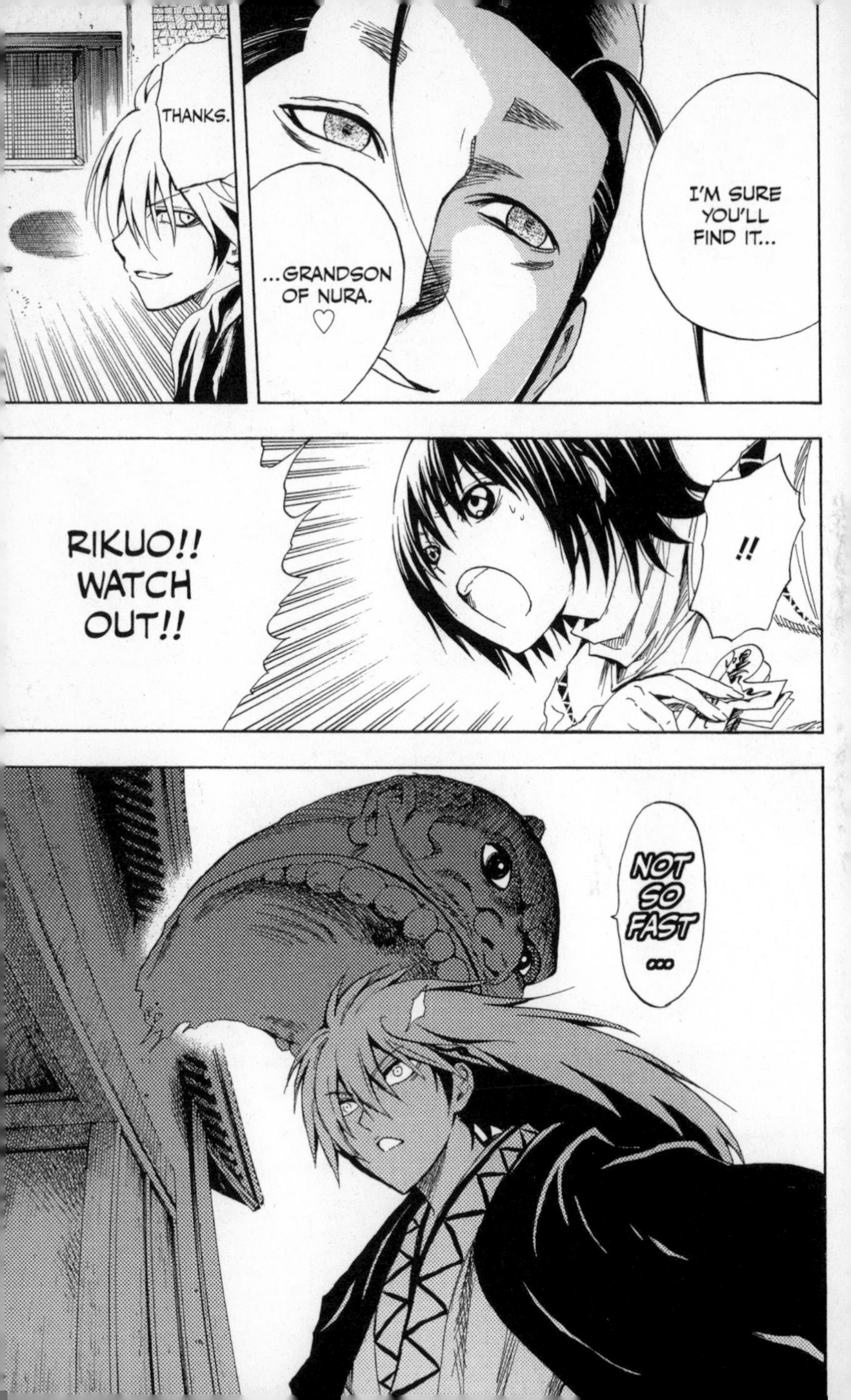
I'M SURE YOU'LL FIND IT...
...GRANDSON OF NURA. ♡
THANKS.
!!
RIKUO!! WATCH OUT!!
NOT SO FAST...

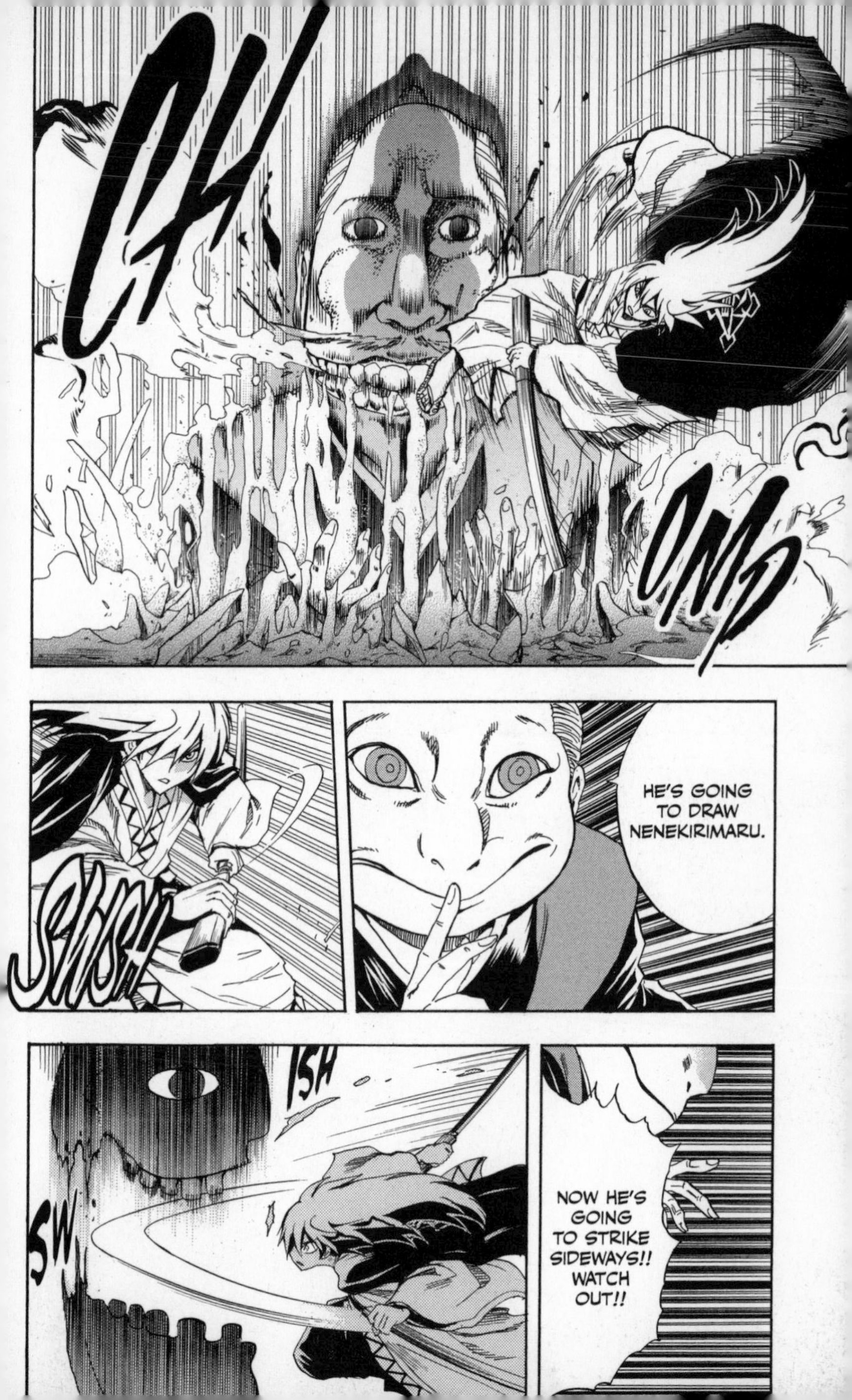
CH
OMP
HE'S GOING TO DRAW NENEKIRIMARU.
SHISH
NOW HE'S GOING TO STRIKE SIDEWAYS!! WATCH OUT!!
SW
ISH

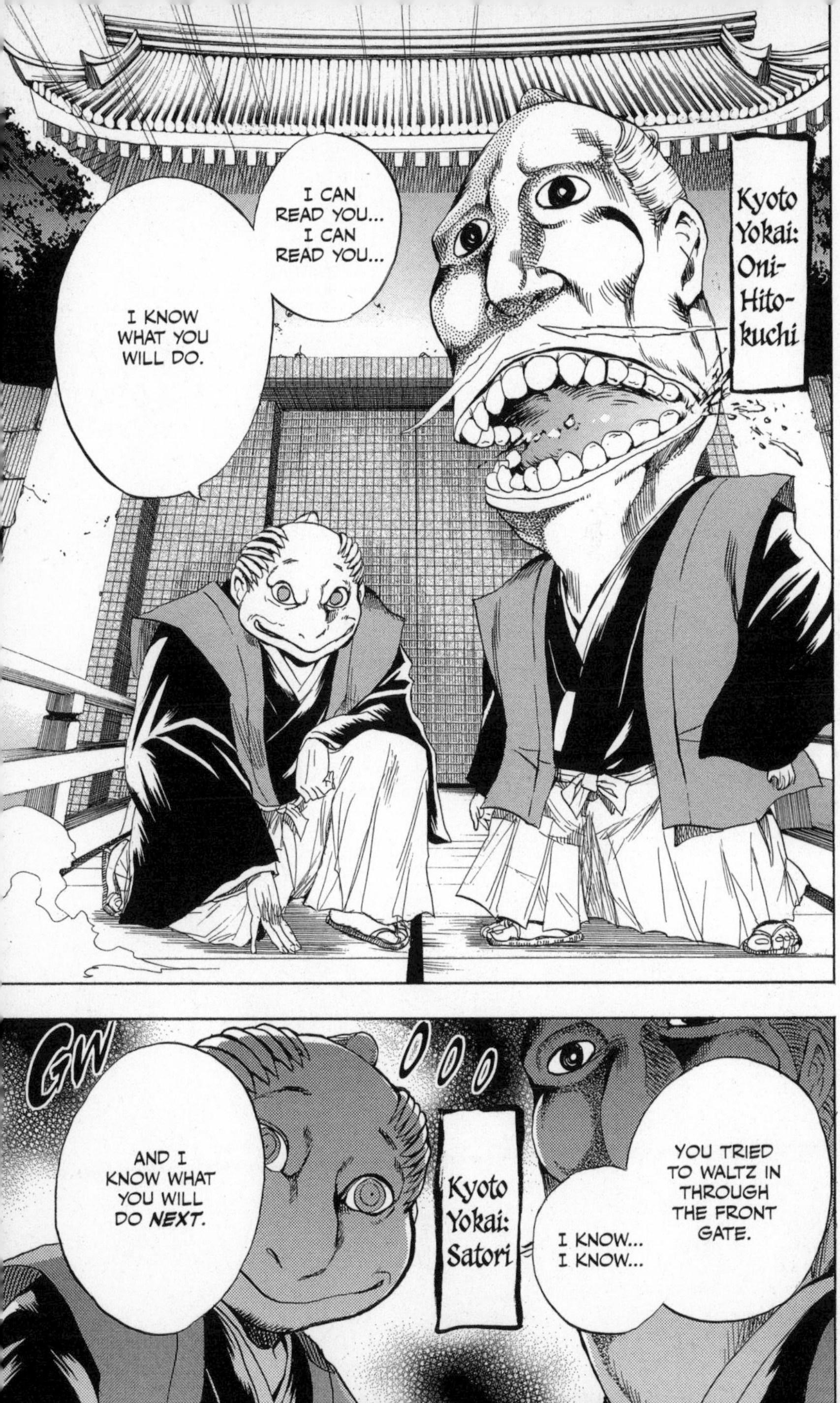
Kyoto Yokai: Oni-Hitokuchi
I CAN READ YOU... I CAN READ YOU...
I KNOW WHAT YOU WILL DO.
YOU TRIED TO WALTZ IN THROUGH THE FRONT GATE.
I KNOW... I KNOW...
Kyoto Yokai: Satori
AND I KNOW WHAT YOU WILL DO *NEXT*.
GW

Forgot these guys?
Read vol. 8!

Working hard
for 400 years.

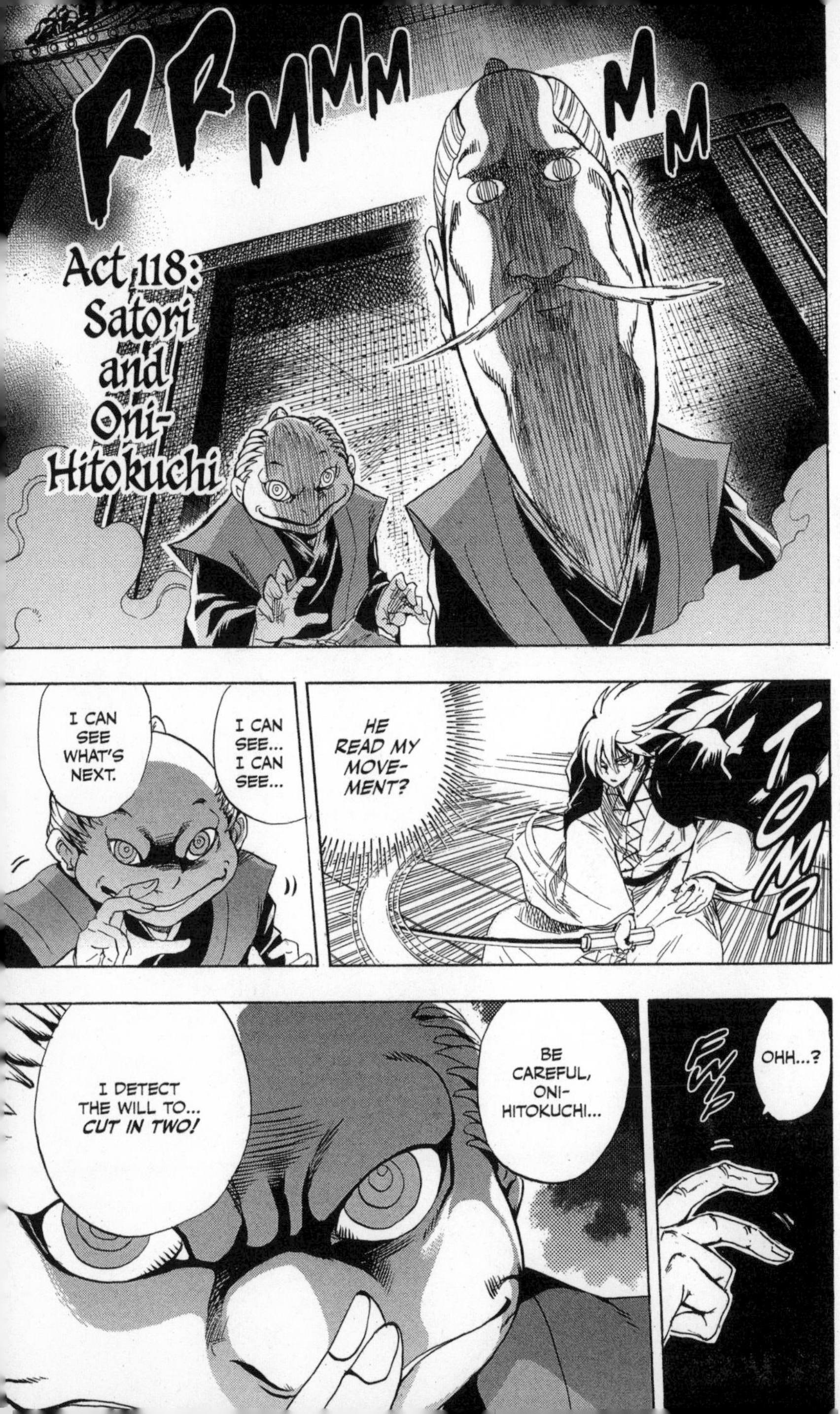
RRMMMM MM
Act 118: Satori and Oni-Hitokuchi
TOMP
HE READ MY MOVEMENT?
I CAN SEE... I CAN SEE...
I CAN SEE WHAT'S NEXT.
OHH...?
BE CAREFUL, ONI-HITOKUCHI...
I DETECT THE WILL TO... *CUT IN TWO!*

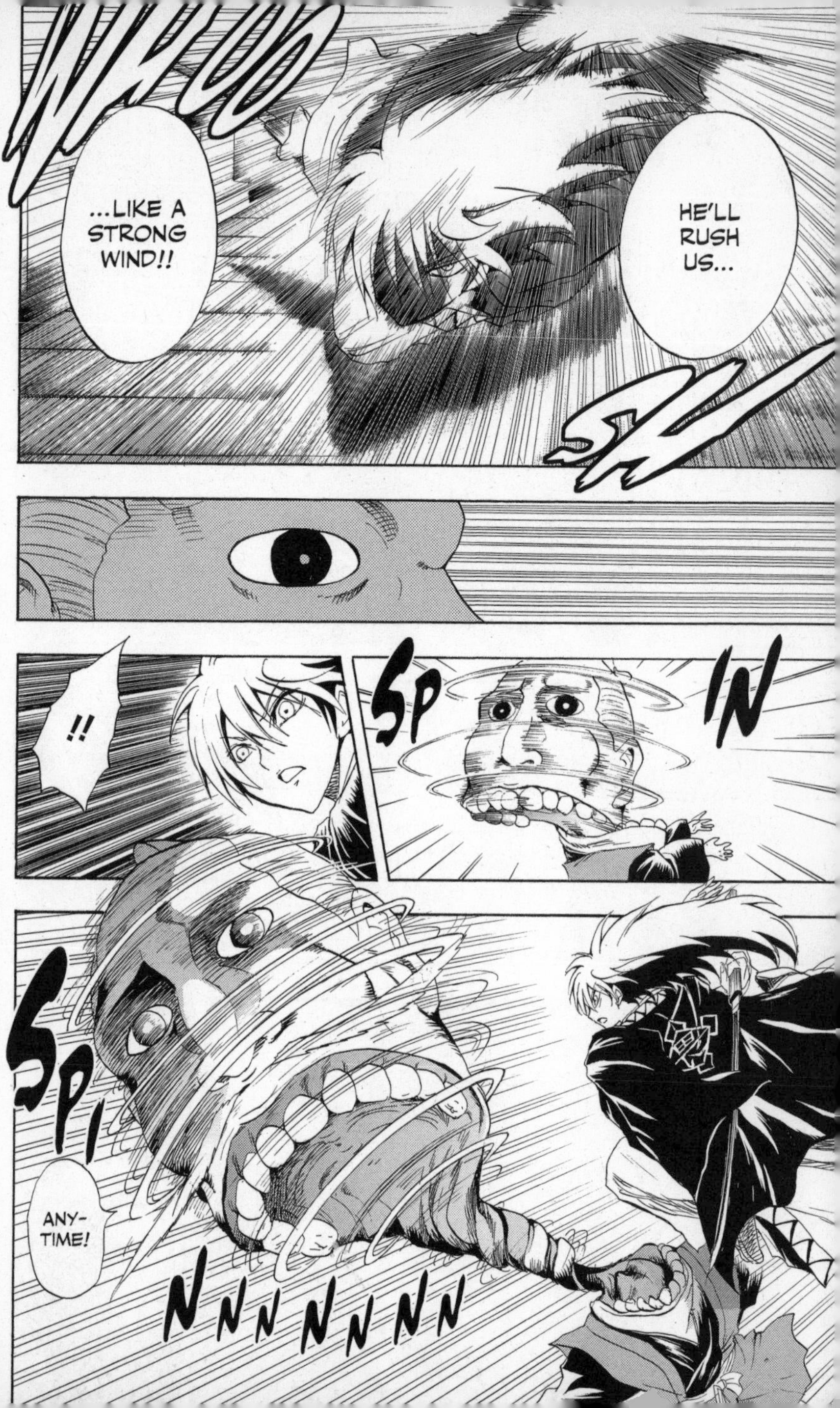
HE'LL RUSH US...
...LIKE A STRONG WIND!!
WHOO
SH
SP IN
!!
SPI NNNNNNNN
ANY-TIME!

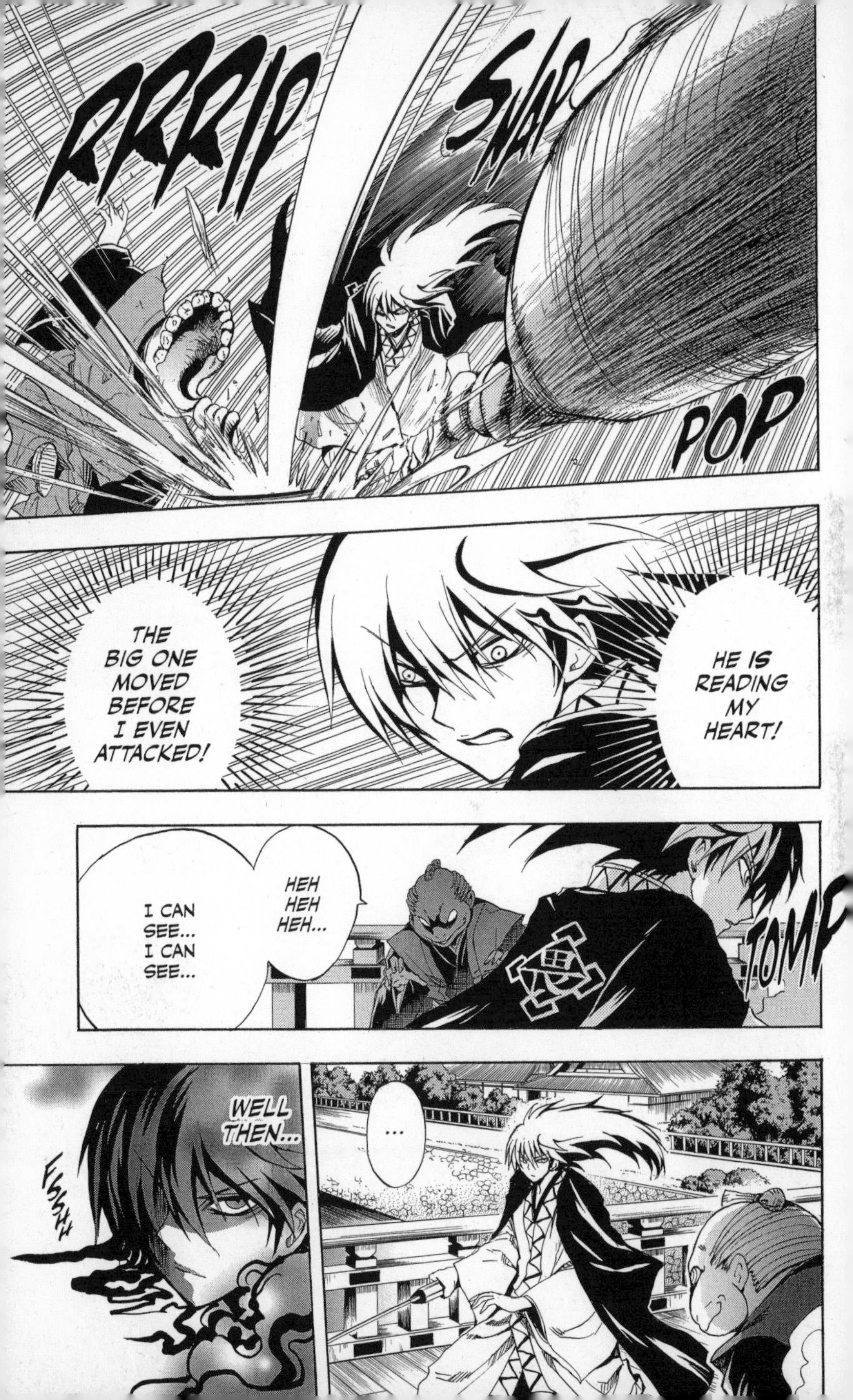
POP
SNAP
RRRIP
HE IS READING MY HEART!
THE BIG ONE MOVED BEFORE I EVEN ATTACKED!
TOMP
HEH HEH HEH...
I CAN SEE... I CAN SEE...
...
WELL THEN...
FSSHH

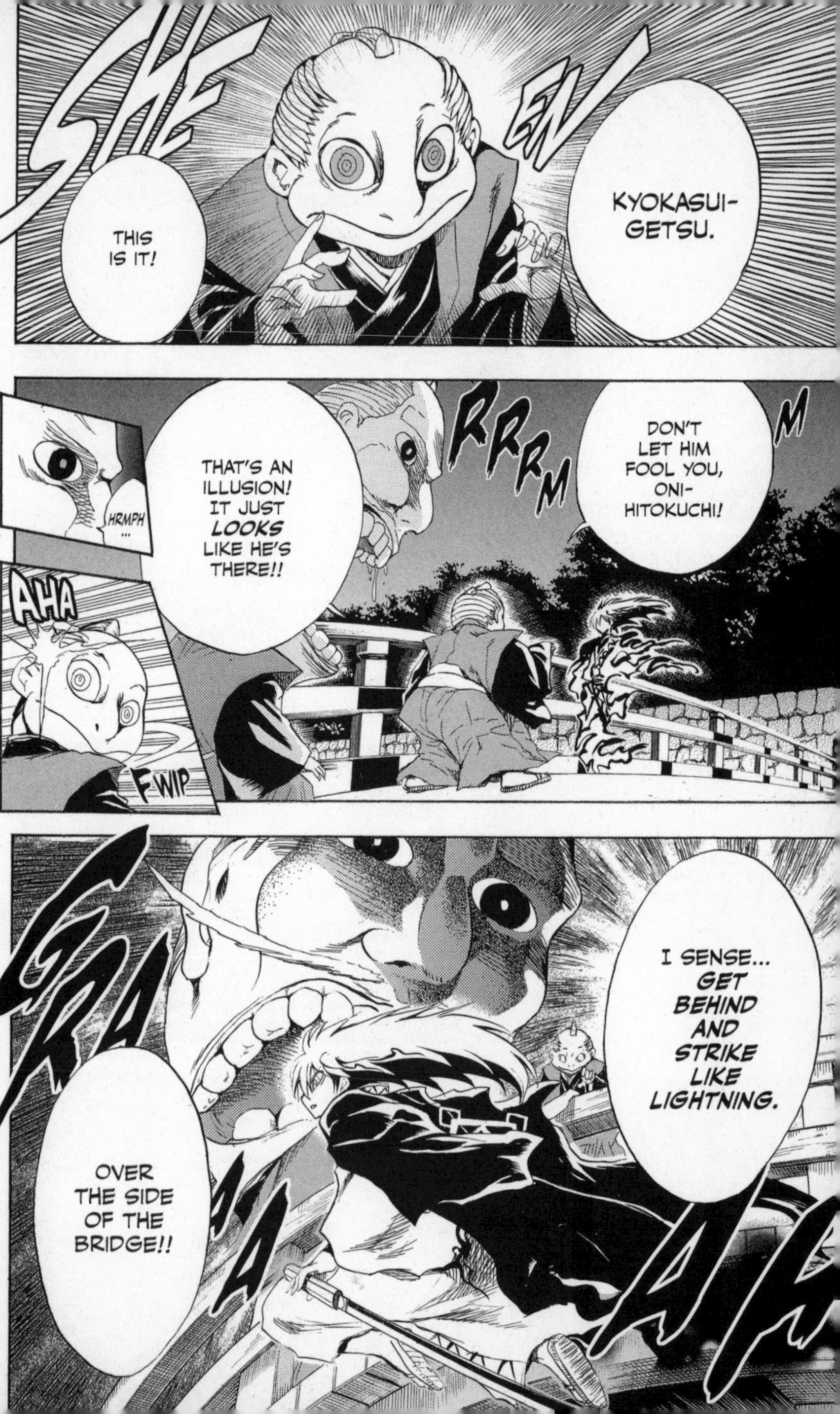
KYOKASUI-GETSU.
SHEEN
THIS IS IT!
DON'T LET HIM FOOL YOU, ONI-HITOKUCHI!
RRRM M
THAT'S AN ILLUSION! IT JUST *LOOKS* LIKE HE'S THERE!!
HRMPH ...
AHA
FWIP
I SENSE... *GET BEHIND AND STRIKE LIKE LIGHTNING.*
OVER THE SIDE OF THE BRIDGE!!

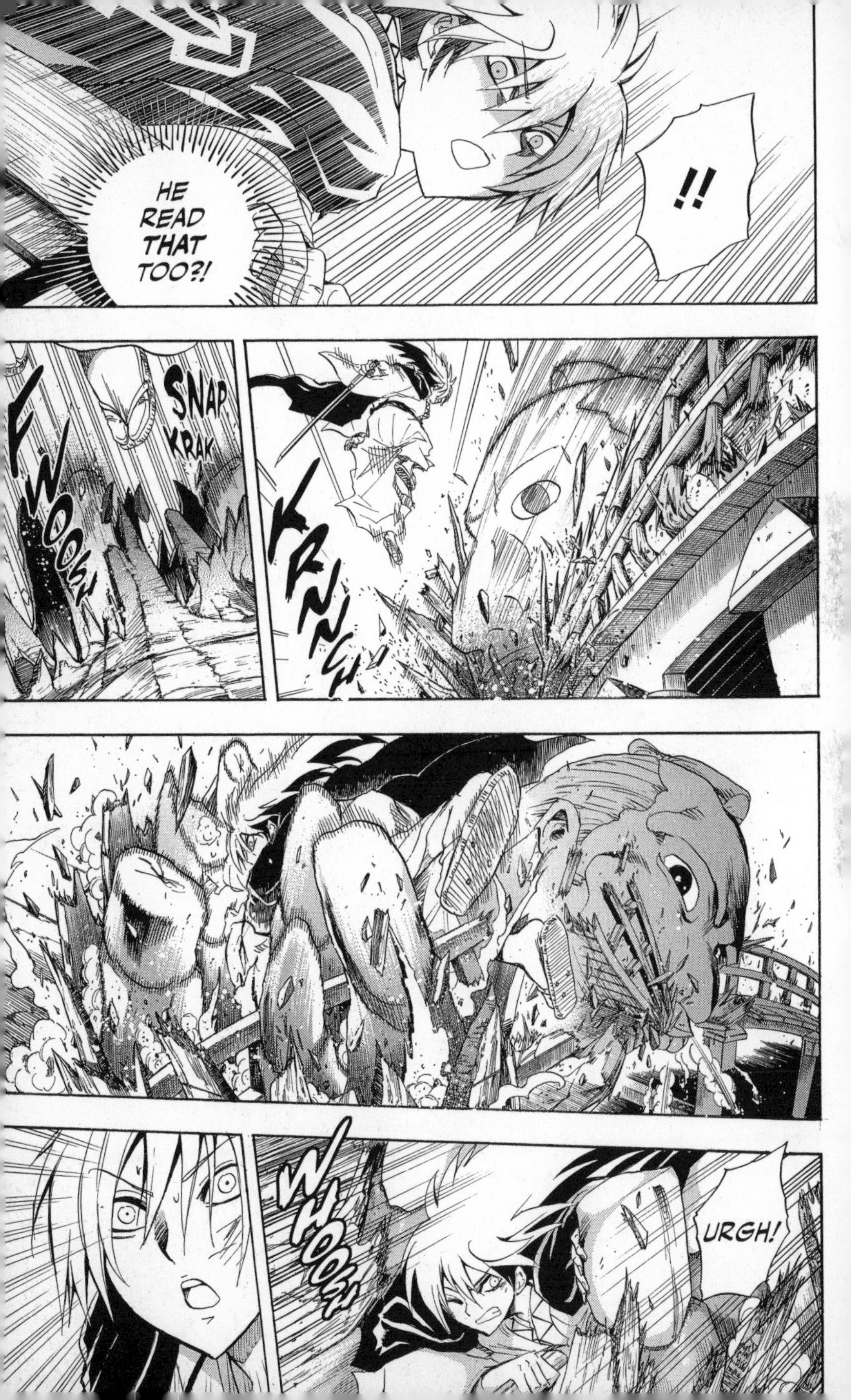
!!
HE READ THAT TOO?!
KRNNCH
SNAP
KRAK
FWOOM
URGH!
WHOOM

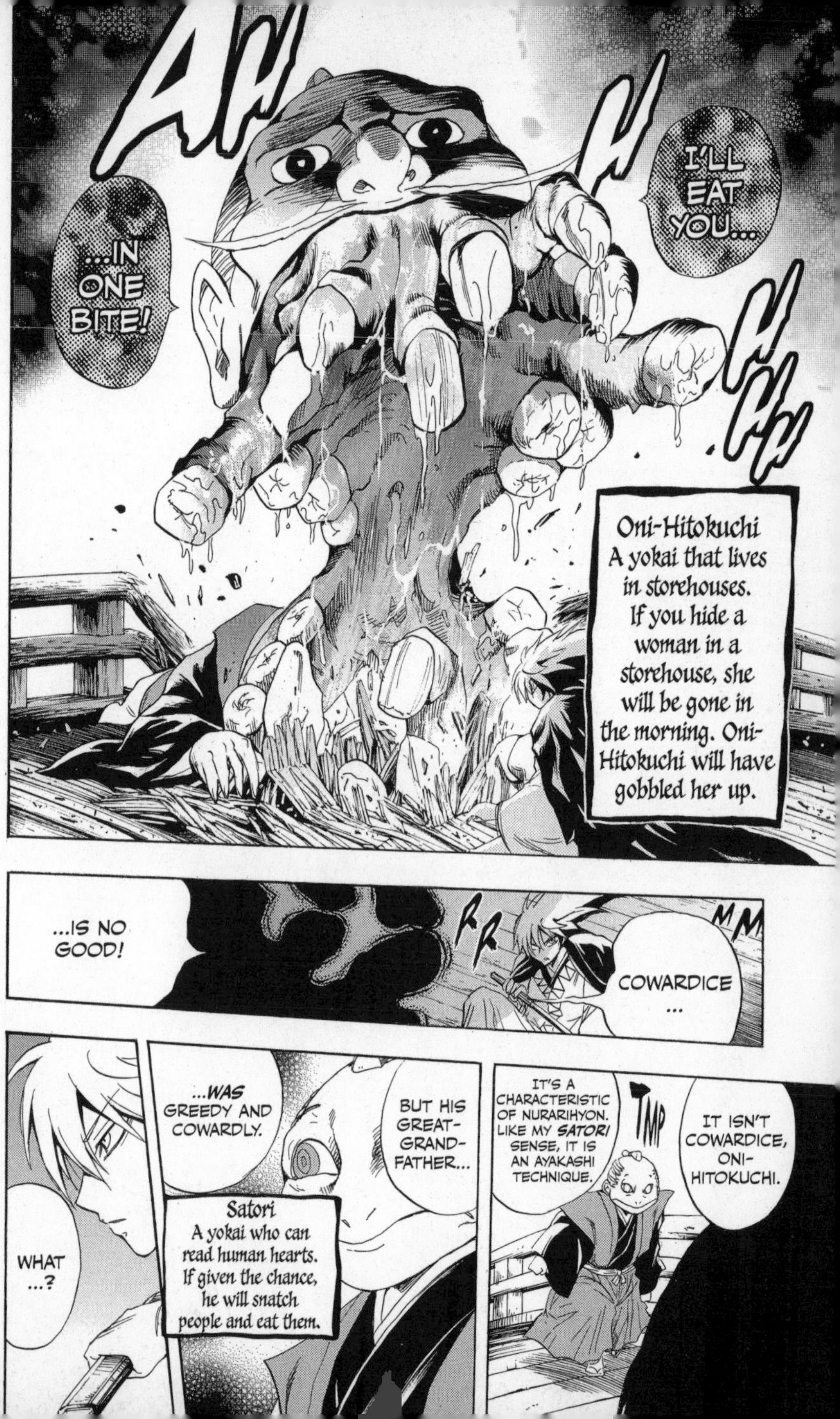
I'LL EAT YOU...
...IN ONE BITE!
Oni-Hitokuchi
A yokai that lives in storehouses. If you hide a woman in a storehouse, she will be gone in the morning. Oni-Hitokuchi will have gobbled her up.
COWARDICE ...
...IS NO GOOD!
IT ISN'T COWARDICE, ONI-HITOKUCHI.
TMP
IT'S A CHARACTERISTIC OF NURARIHYON. LIKE MY SATORI SENSE, IT IS AN AYAKASHI TECHNIQUE.
BUT HIS GREAT-GRANDFATHER...
...WAS GREEDY AND COWARDLY.
Satori
A yokai who can read human hearts. If given the chance, he will snatch people and eat them.
WHAT ...?

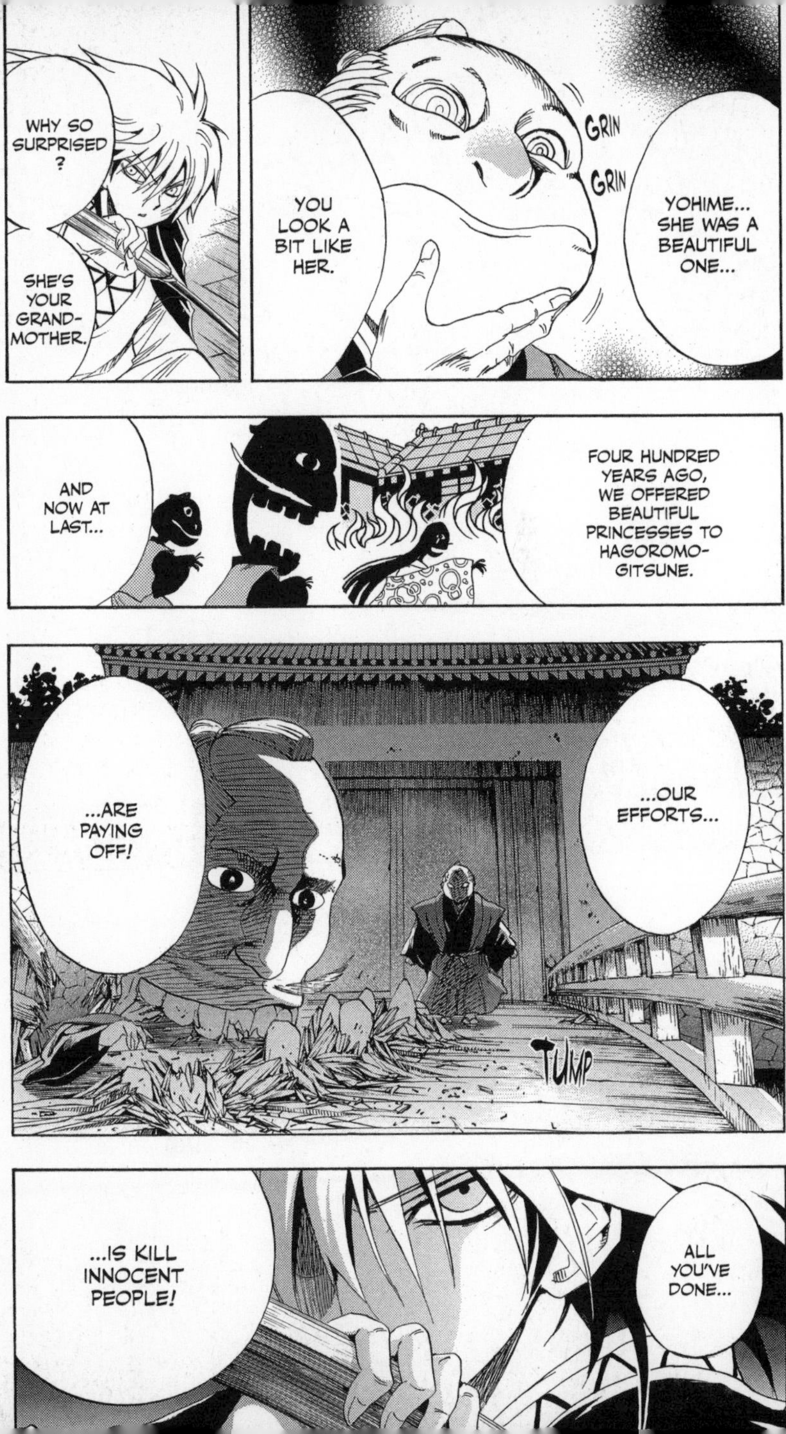
YOHIME... SHE WAS A BEAUTIFUL ONE...
GRIN
GRIN
YOU LOOK A BIT LIKE HER.
WHY SO SURPRISED ?
SHE'S YOUR GRAND-MOTHER.
FOUR HUNDRED YEARS AGO, WE OFFERED BEAUTIFUL PRINCESSES TO HAGOROMO-GITSUNE.
AND NOW AT LAST...
...OUR EFFORTS...
...ARE PAYING OFF!
TUMP
ALL YOU'VE DONE...
...IS KILL INNOCENT PEOPLE!

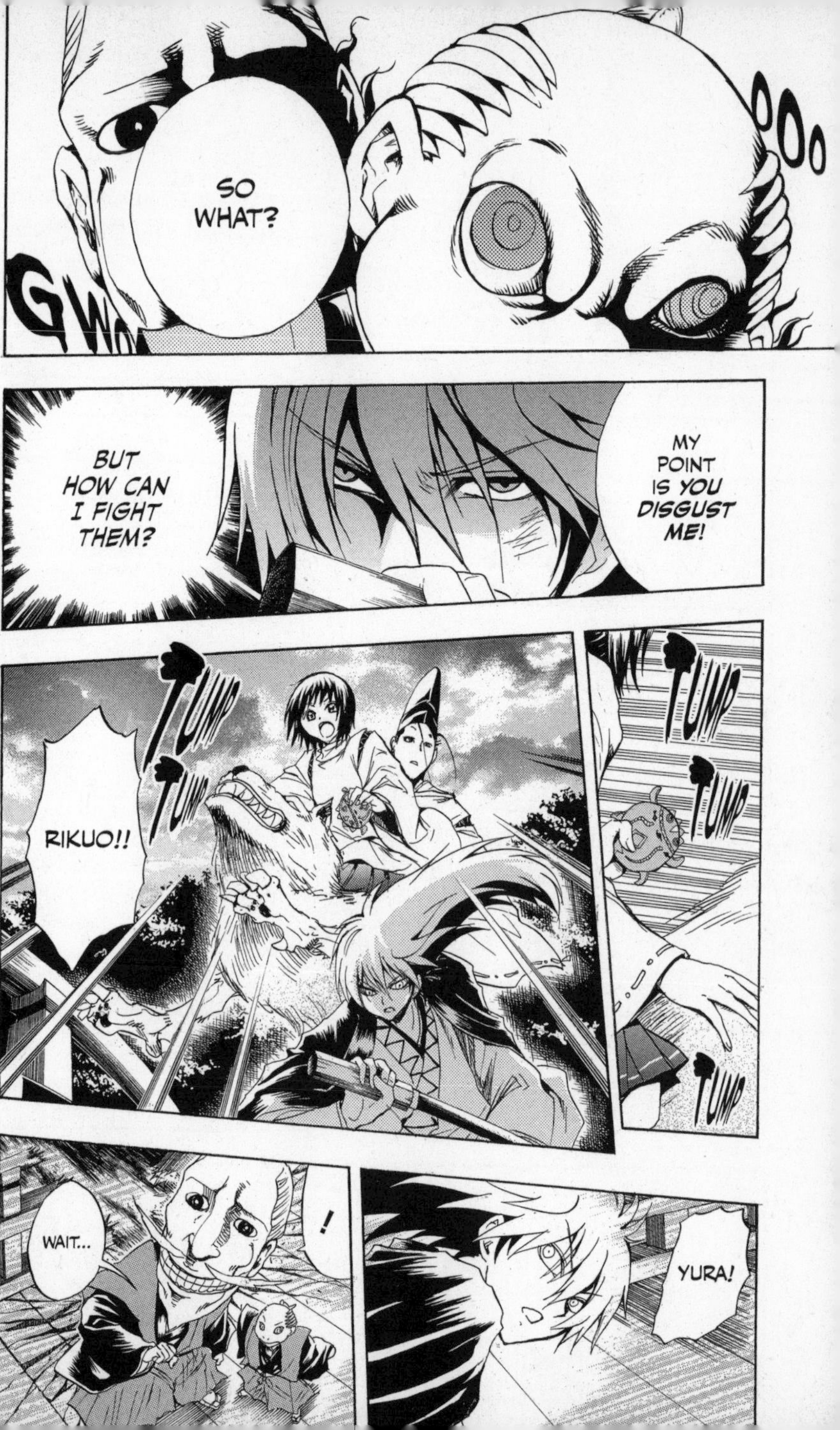
OOO
SO WHAT?
GWO
MY POINT IS YOU DISGUST ME!
BUT HOW CAN I FIGHT THEM?
TUMP
TUMP
TUMP
TUMP
TUMP
RIKUO!!
YURA!
!
WAIT...

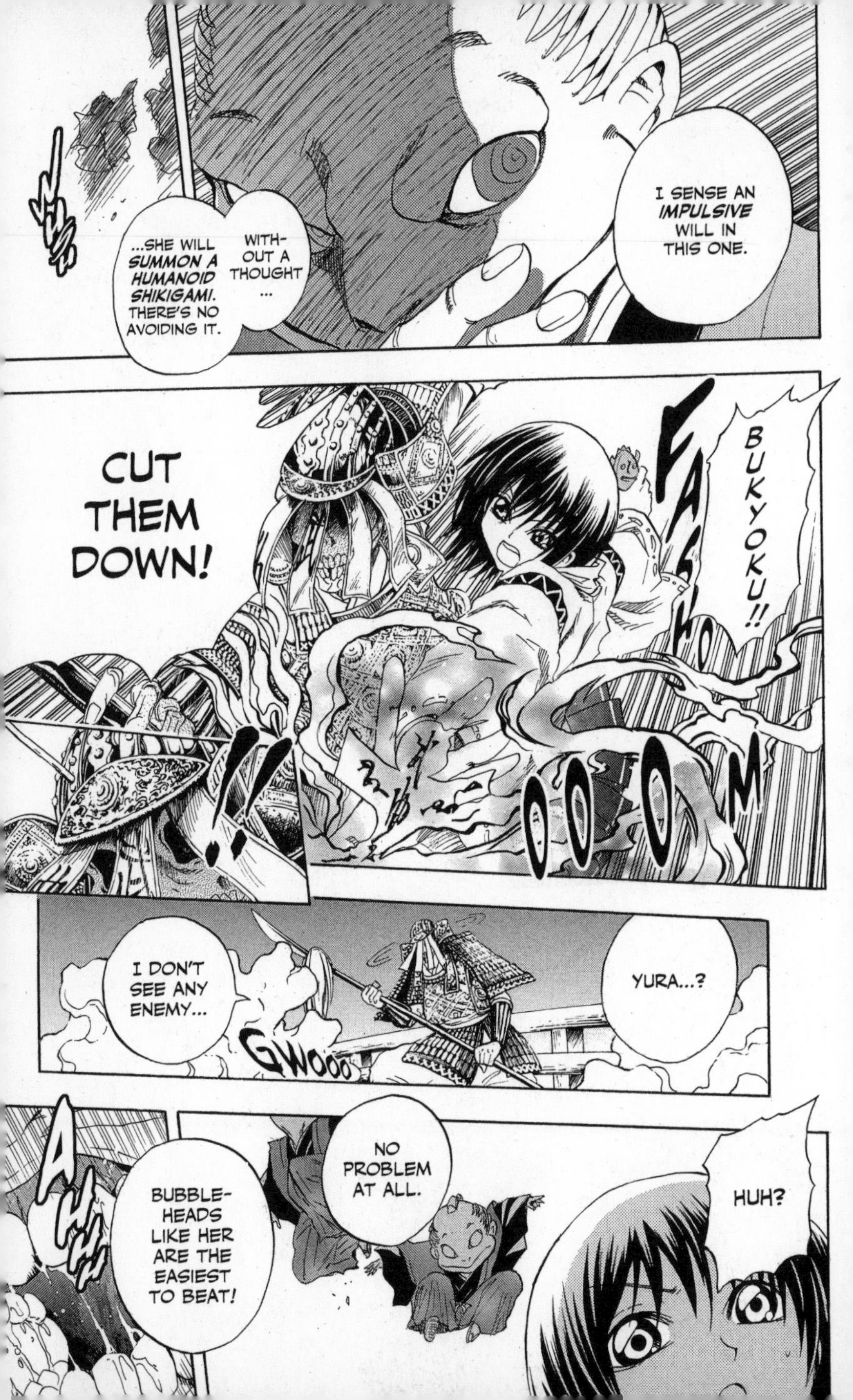
I SENSE AN *IMPULSIVE* WILL IN THIS ONE.
WITHOUT A THOUGHT...
...SHE WILL *SUMMON A HUMANOID SHIKIGAMI.* THERE'S NO AVOIDING IT.
BUKYOKU!!
FASHOOOOOM
CUT THEM DOWN!
YURA...?
I DON'T SEE ANY ENEMY...
GWOOO
HUH?
NO PROBLEM AT ALL.
BUBBLEHEADS LIKE HER ARE THE EASIEST TO BEAT!

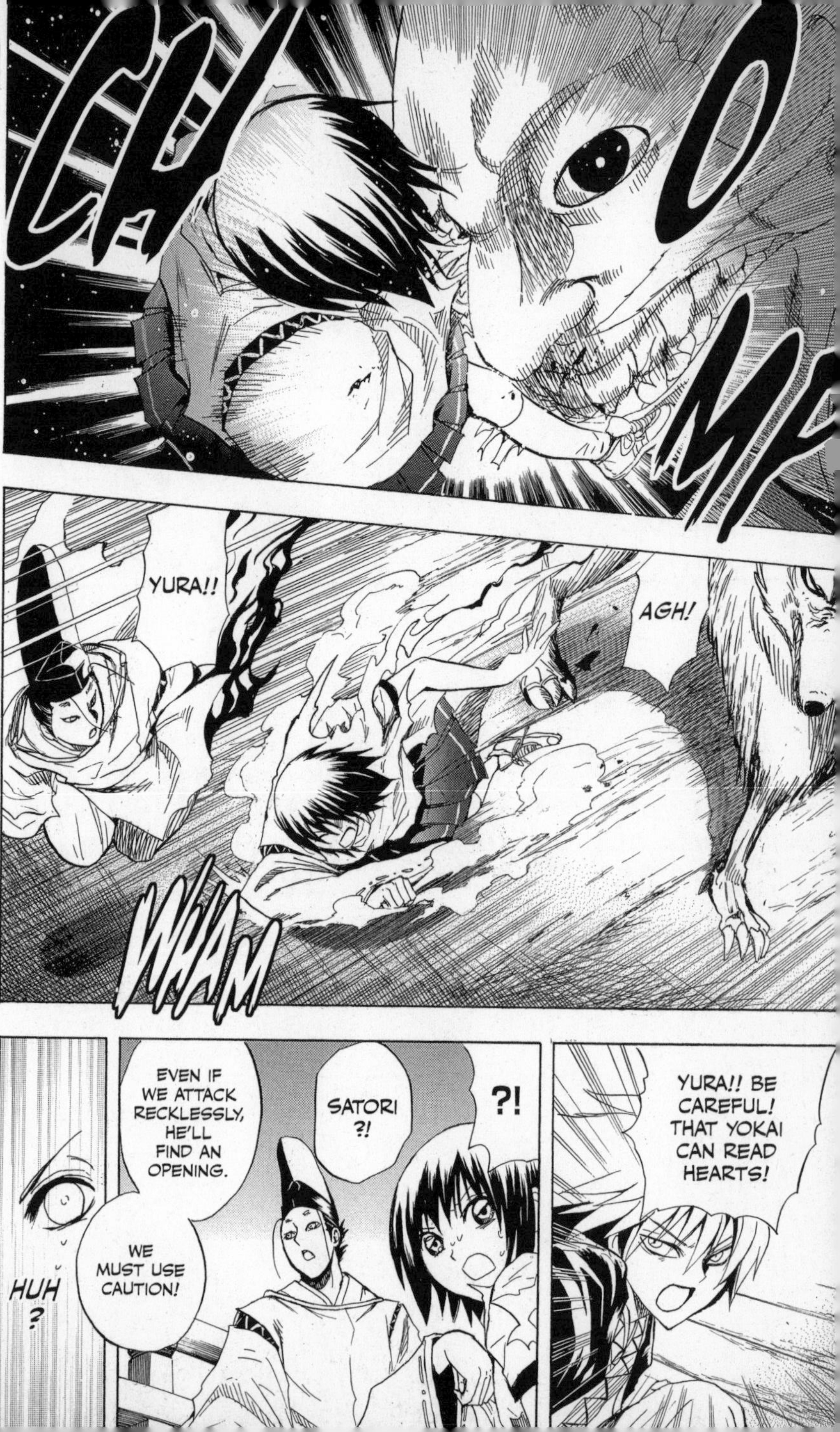
CHOMP
AGH!
YURA!!
WHAM
YURA!! BE CAREFUL! THAT YOKAI CAN READ HEARTS!
?!
SATORI ?!
EVEN IF WE ATTACK RECKLESSLY, HE'LL FIND AN OPENING.
WE MUST USE CAUTION!
HUH ?

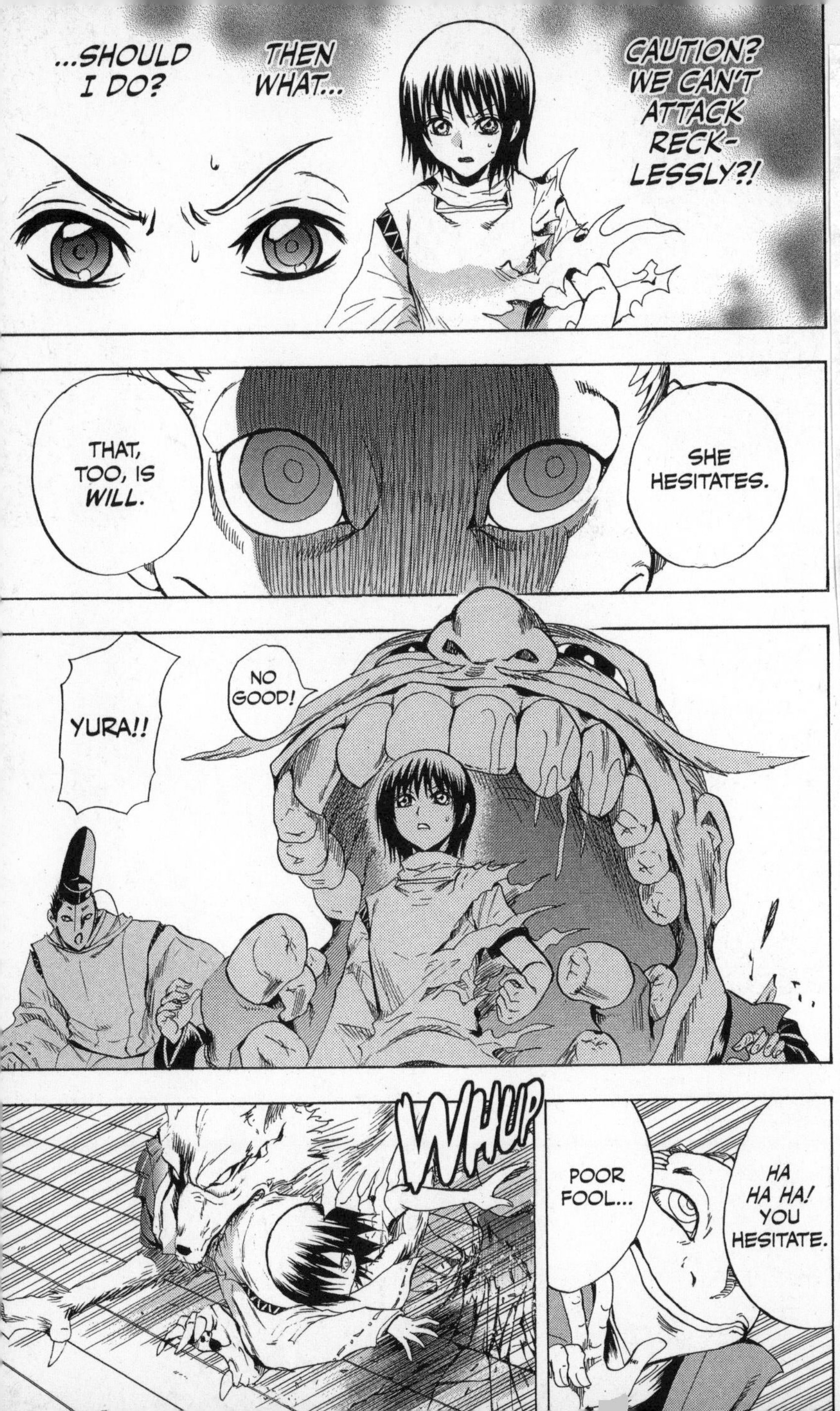
CAUTION? WE CAN'T ATTACK RECK-LESSLY?!
THEN WHAT...
...SHOULD I DO?
SHE HESITATES.
THAT, TOO, IS WILL.
NO GOOD!
YURA!!
HA HA HA! YOU HESITATE.
POOR FOOL...
WHUP

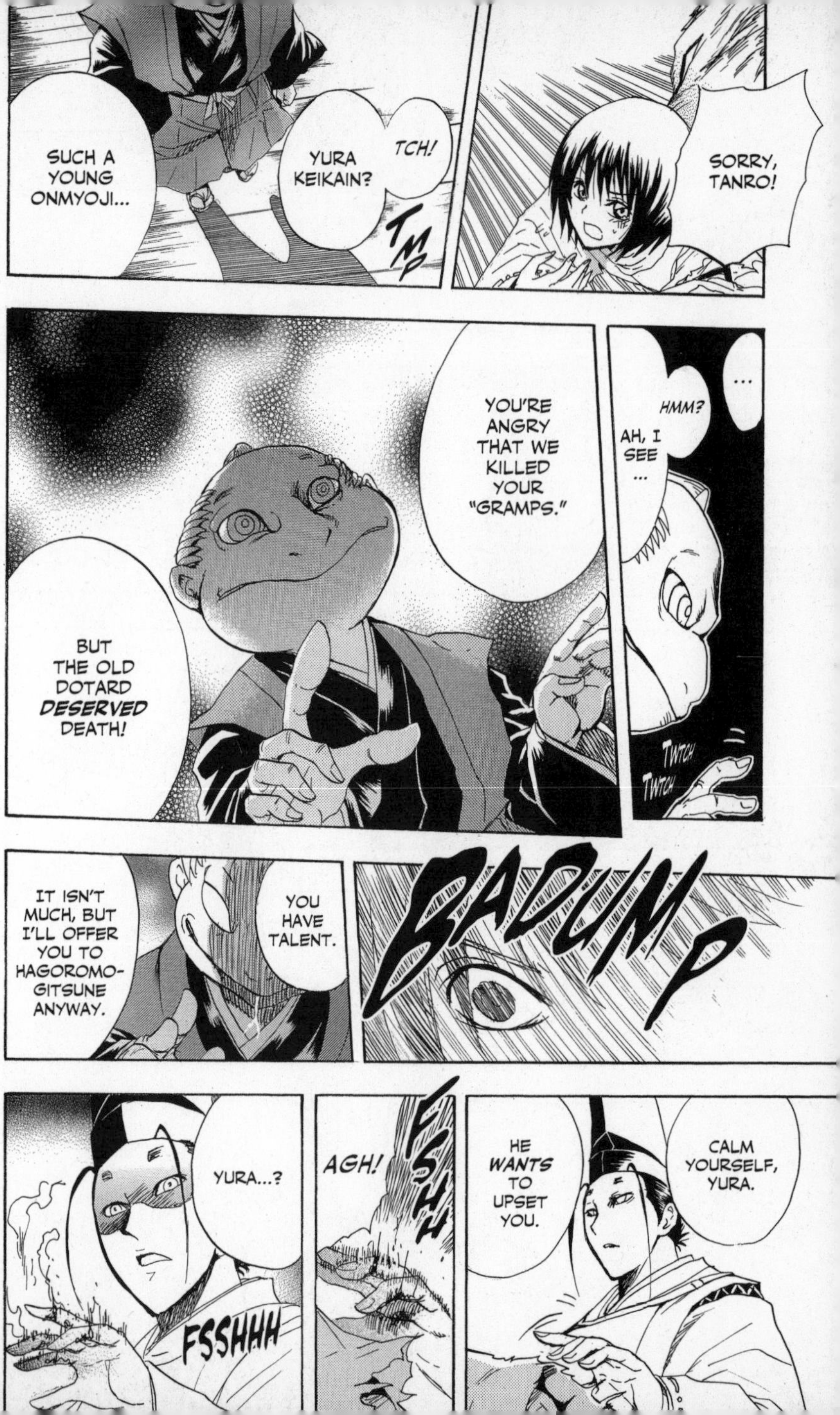
SORRY, TANRO!
TCH!
YURA KEIKAIN?
SUCH A YOUNG ONMYOJI...
TMP
...
HMM?
AH, I SEE ...
TWITCH TWITCH
YOU'RE ANGRY THAT WE KILLED YOUR "GRAMPS."
BUT THE OLD DOTARD *DESERVED* DEATH!
BADUMP
YOU HAVE TALENT.
IT ISN'T MUCH, BUT I'LL OFFER YOU TO HAGOROMO-GITSUNE ANYWAY.
CALM YOURSELF, YURA.
HE *WANTS* TO UPSET YOU.
FSHH
AGH!
YURA...?
FSSHHH

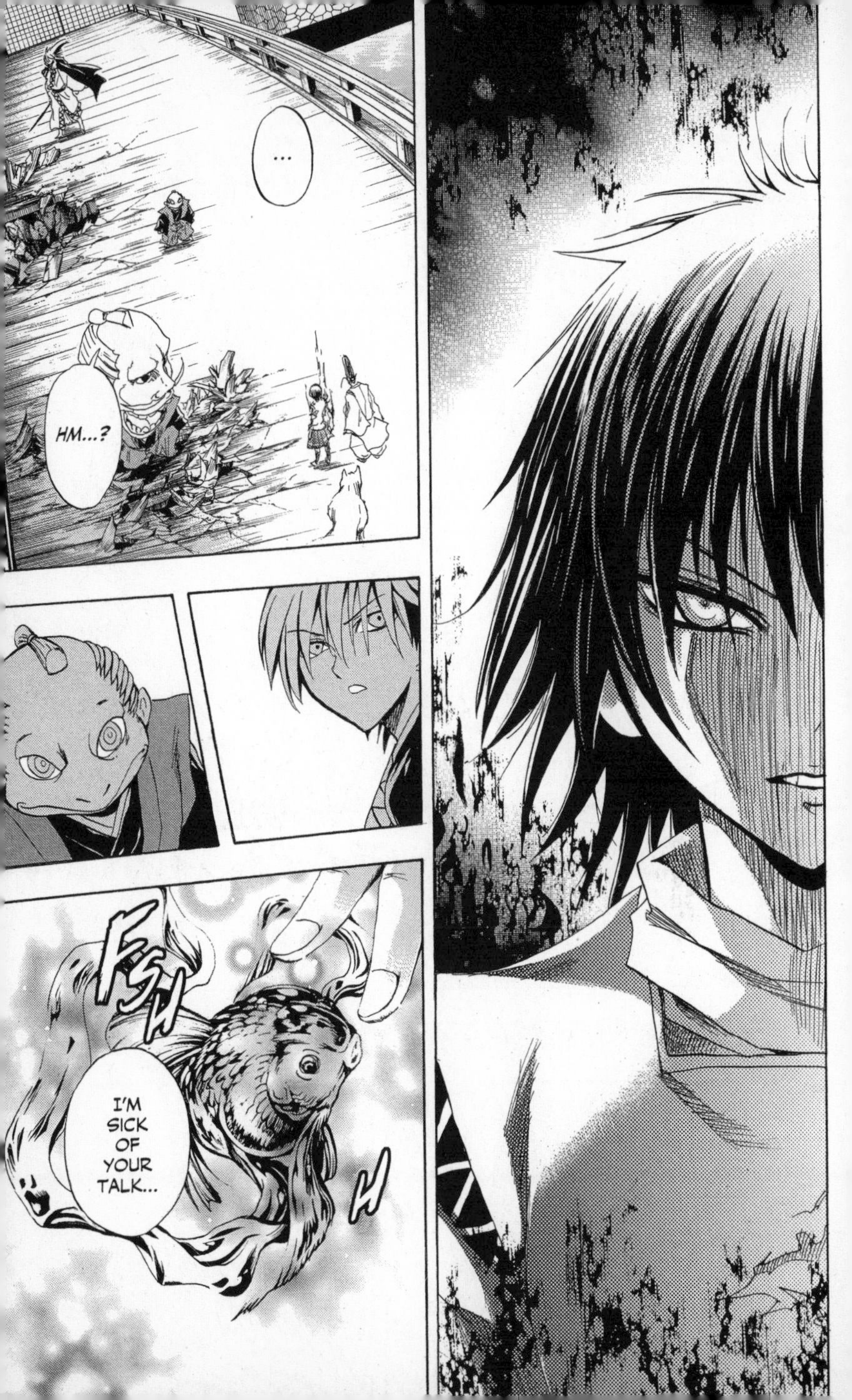
...
HM...?
FSH
I'M SICK OF YOUR TALK...
H

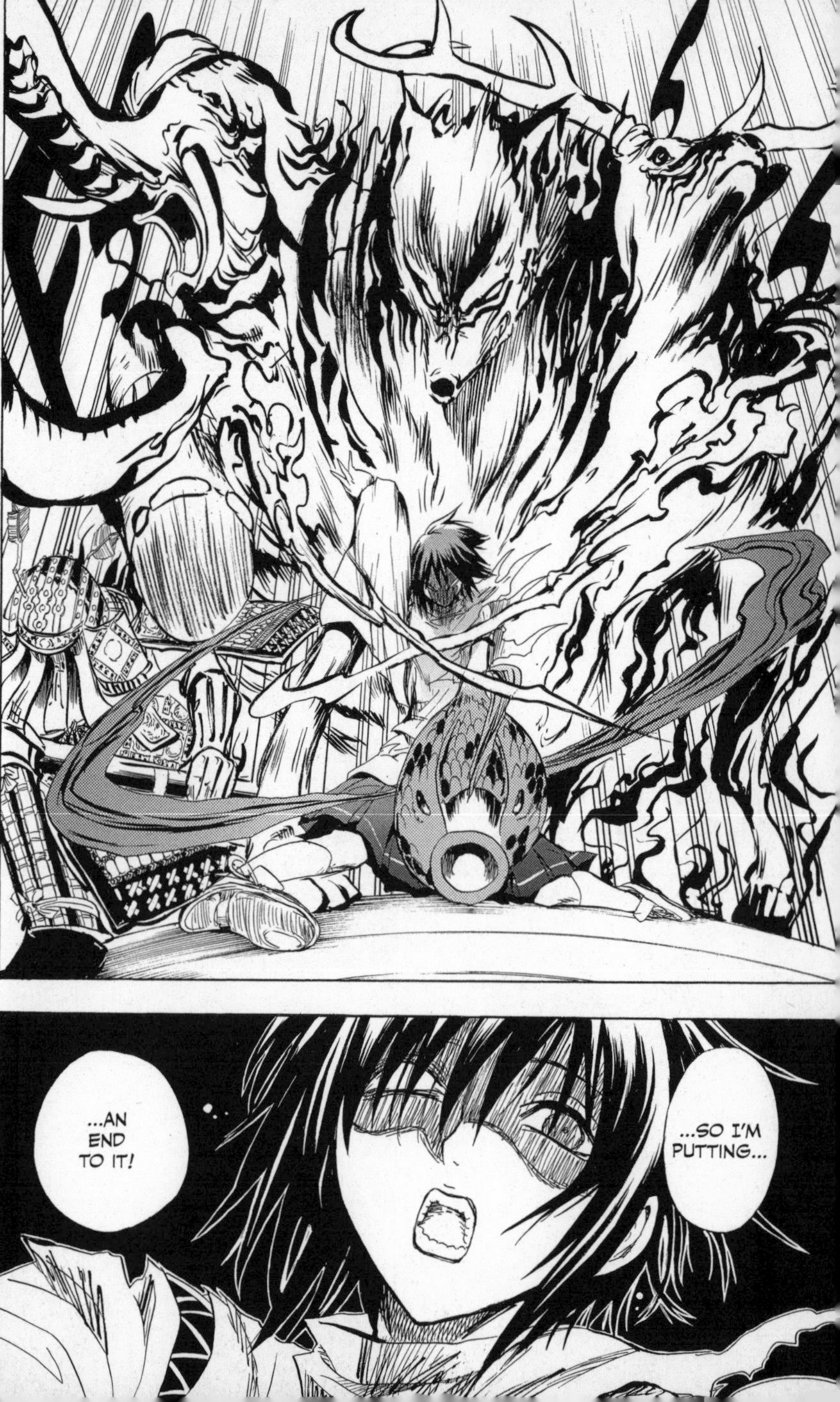
...SO I'M PUTTING...
...AN END TO IT!

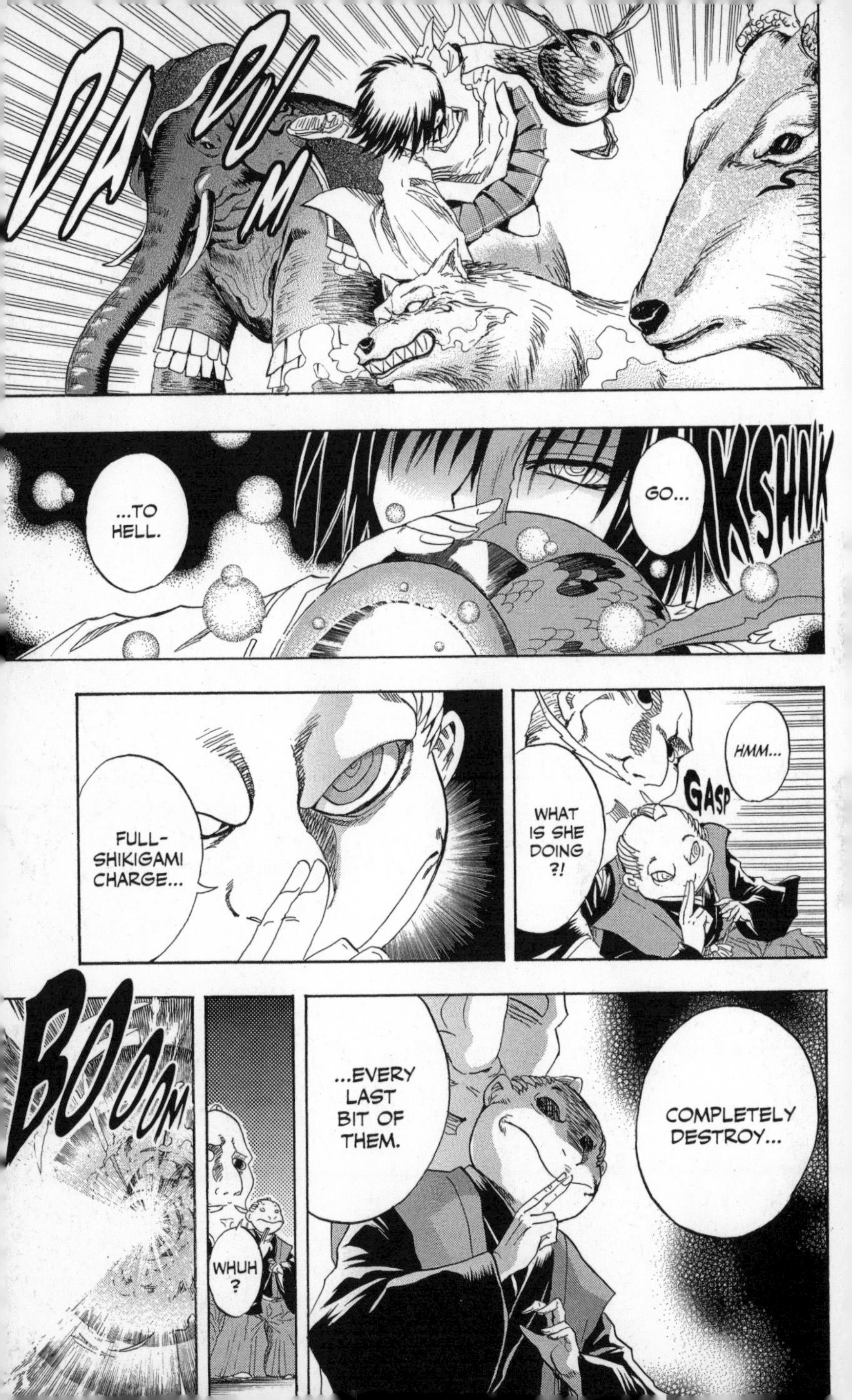
DA-DUM
KSHNK
GO...
...TO HELL.
HMM...
GASP
WHAT IS SHE DOING?!
FULL-SHIKIGAMI CHARGE...
COMPLETELY DESTROY...
...EVERY LAST BIT OF THEM.
WHUH?
BOOOM

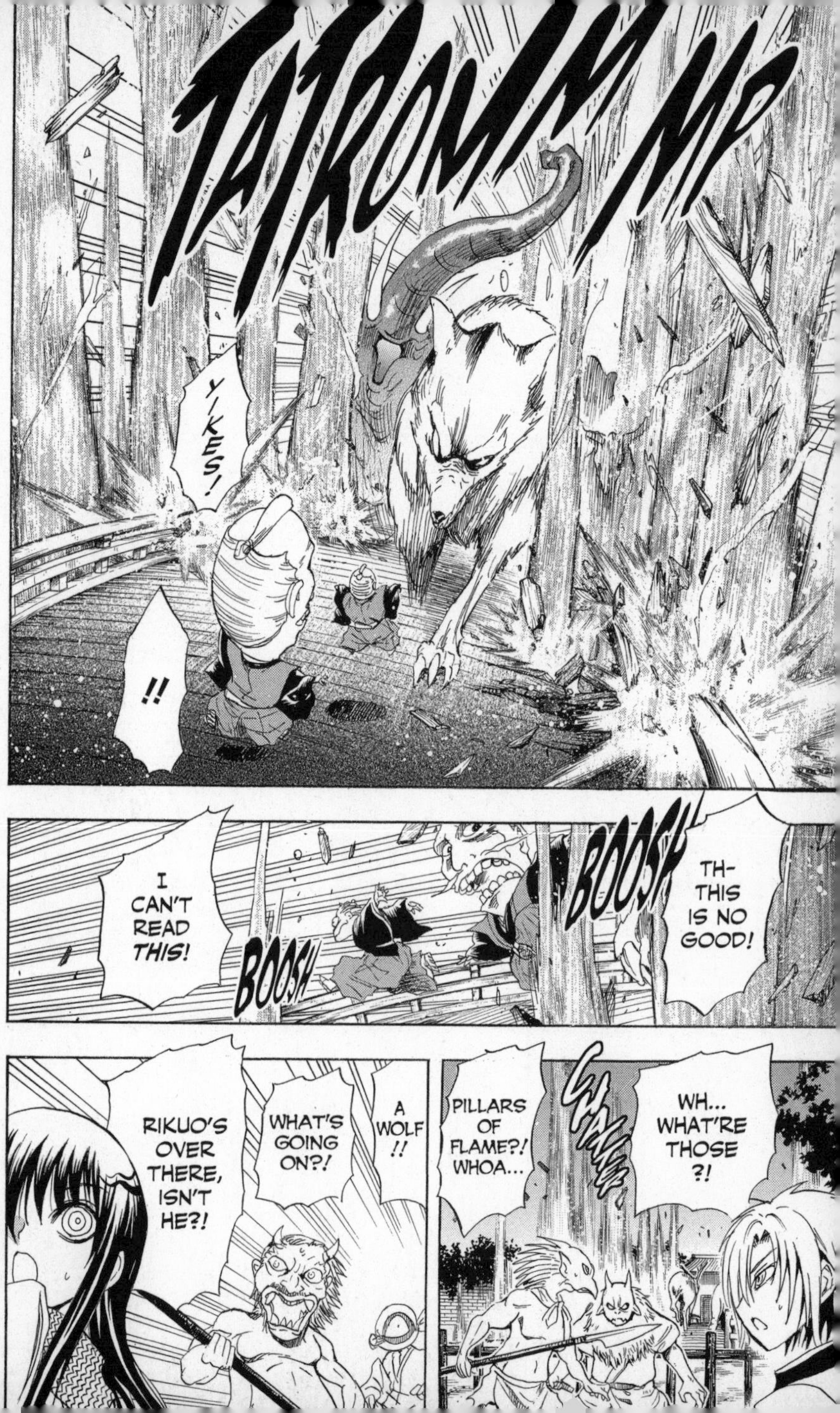
YIKES!
!!
TH-THIS IS NO GOOD!
BOOSH
BOOSH
I CAN'T READ THIS!
WH... WHAT'RE THOSE?!
PILLARS OF FLAME?! WHOA...
A WOLF!!
WHAT'S GOING ON?!
RIKUO'S OVER THERE, ISN'T HE?!

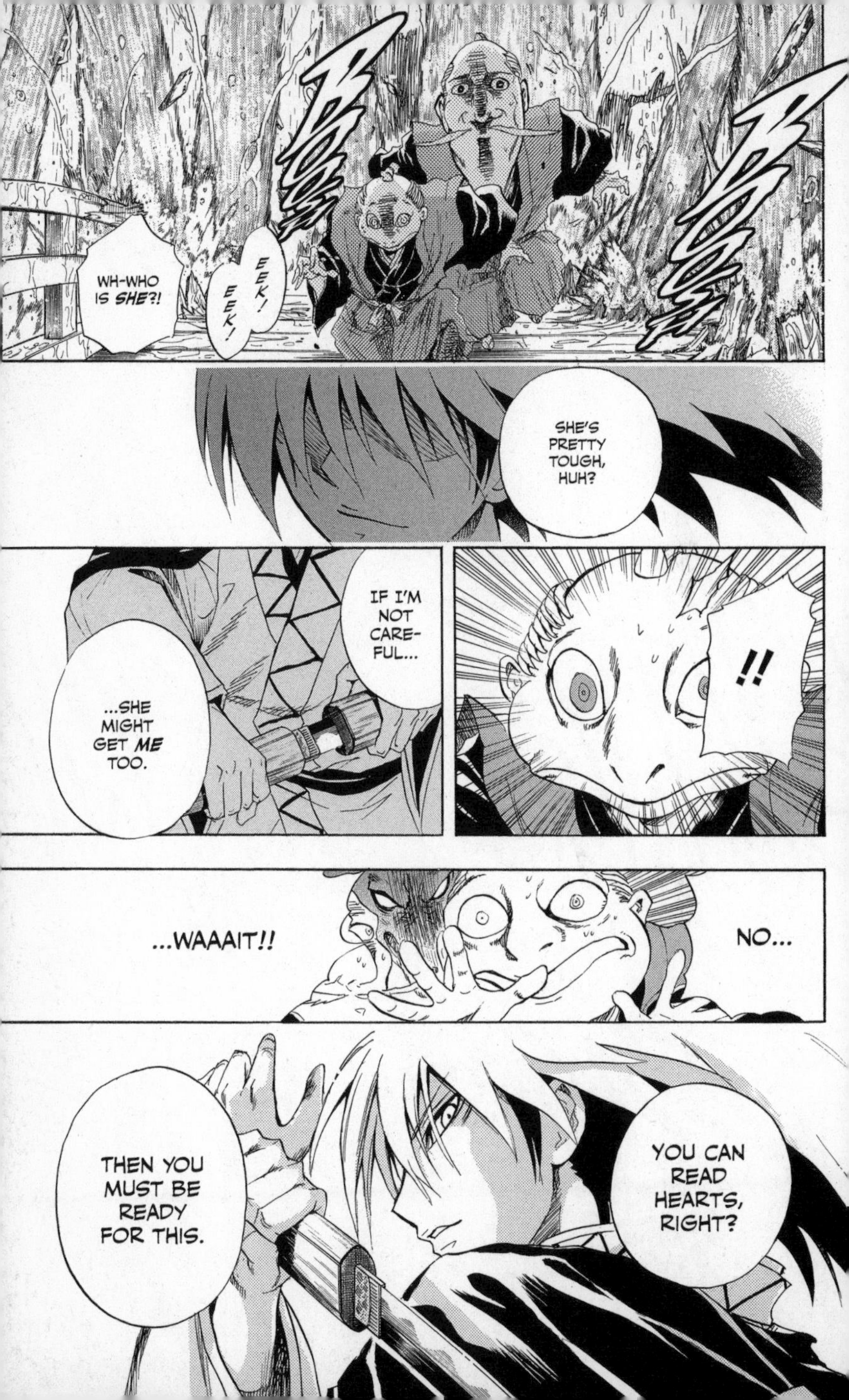
EEK! EEK!
WH-WHO IS SHE?!
SHE'S PRETTY TOUGH, HUH?
!!
IF I'M NOT CAREFUL...
...SHE MIGHT GET ME TOO.
NO...
...WAAAIT!!
YOU CAN READ HEARTS, RIGHT?
THEN YOU MUST BE READY FOR THIS.

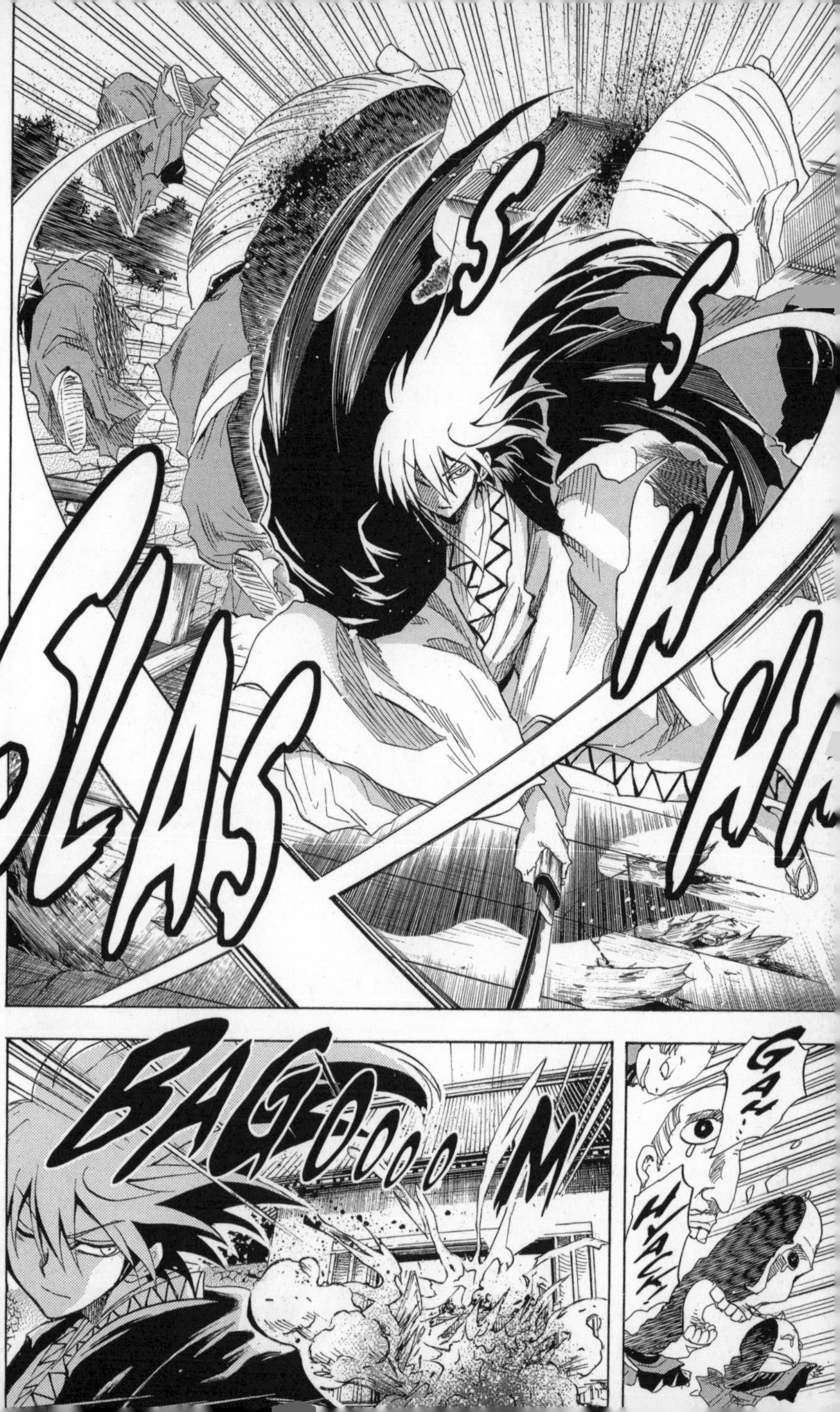
BAGOOOOM
GAH...
HAAK!

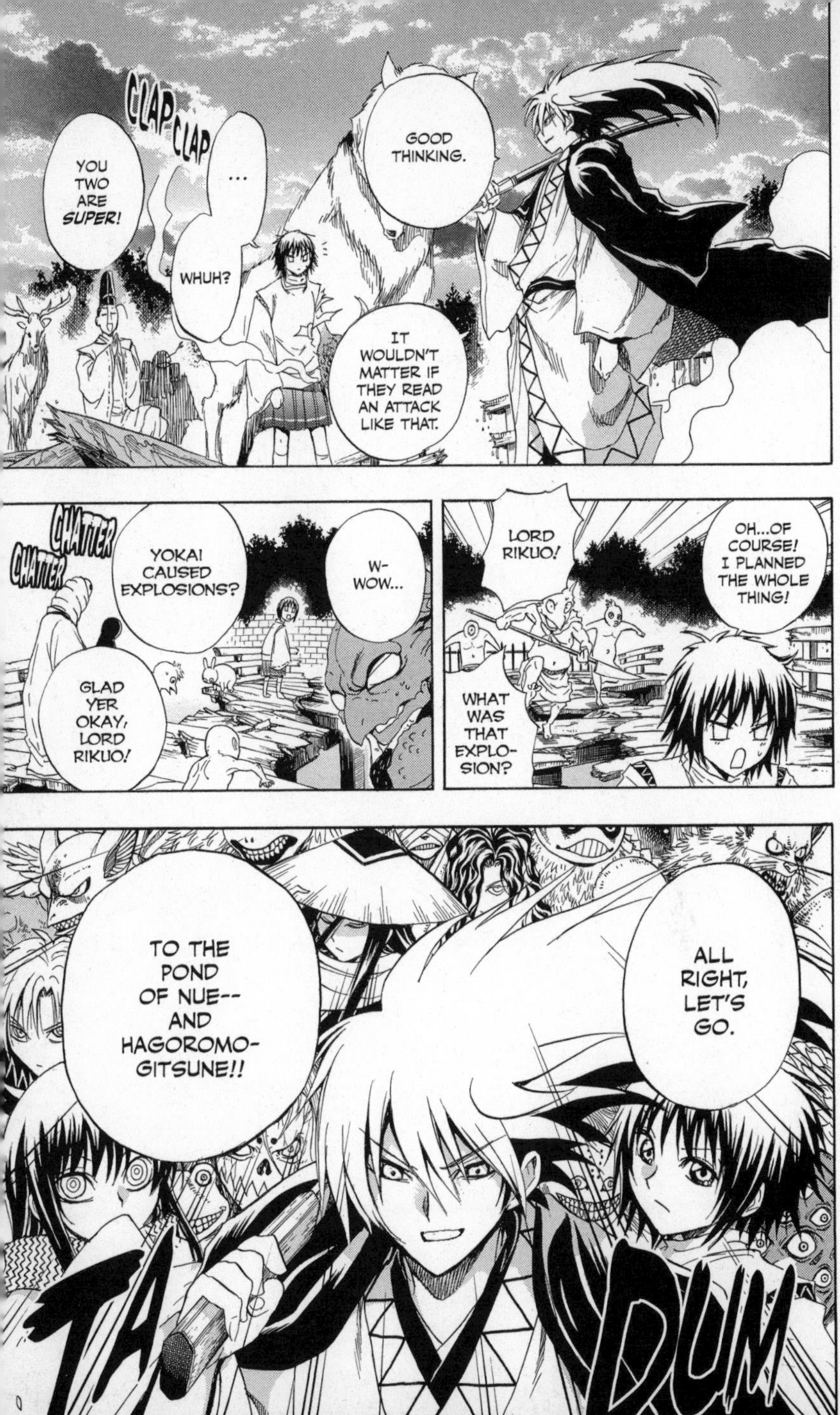
GOOD THINKING.
IT WOULDN'T MATTER IF THEY READ AN ATTACK LIKE THAT.
...
CLAP CLAP
YOU TWO ARE SUPER!
WHUH?
OH...OF COURSE! I PLANNED THE WHOLE THING!
LORD RIKUO!
WHAT WAS THAT EXPLOSION?
W-WOW...
YOKAI CAUSED EXPLOSIONS?
CHATTER CHATTER
GLAD YER OKAY, LORD RIKUO!
ALL RIGHT, LET'S GO.
TO THE POND OF NUE-- AND HAGOROMO-GITSUNE!!
TA-DUM

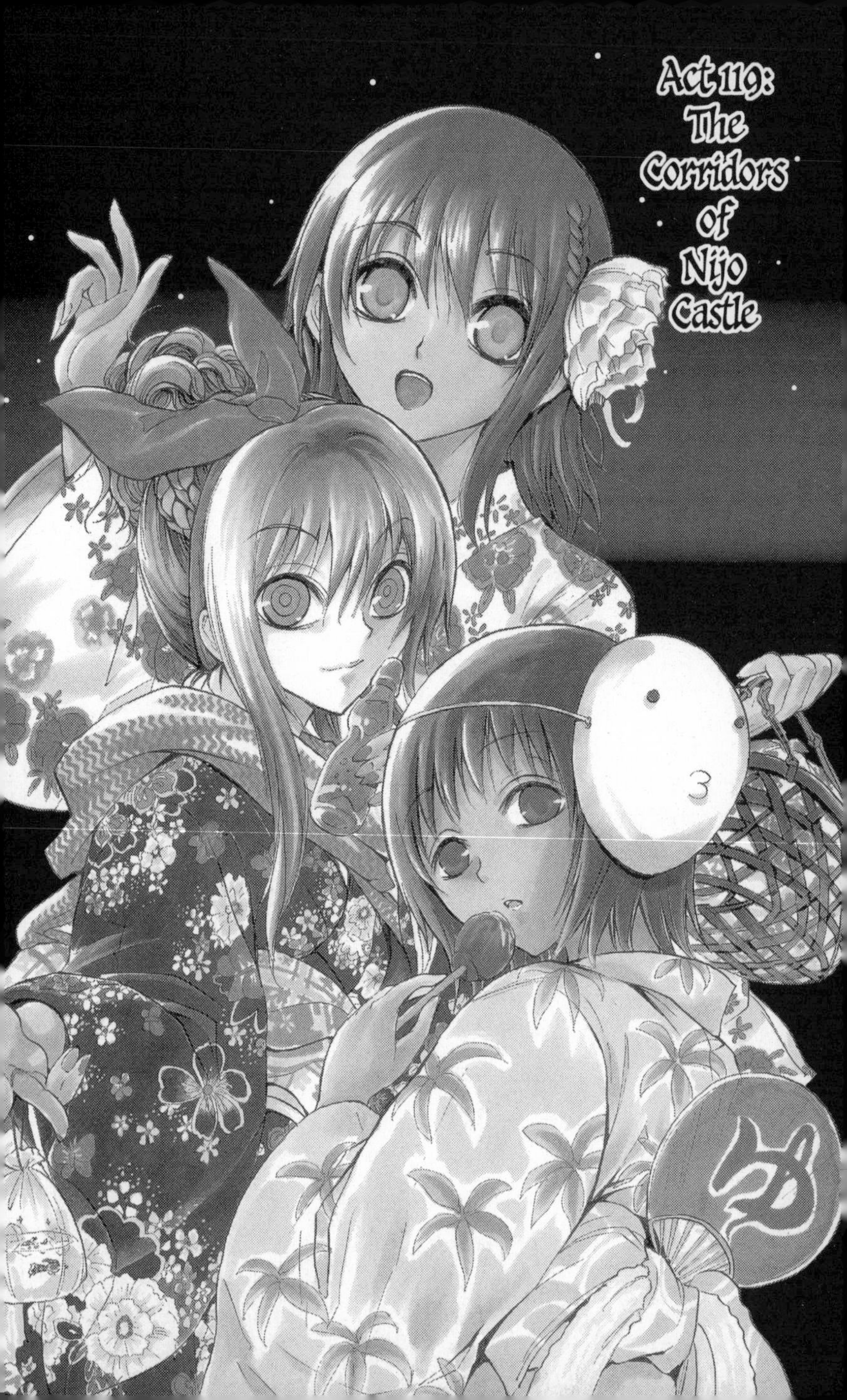
Act 119:
The Corridors of Nijo Castle

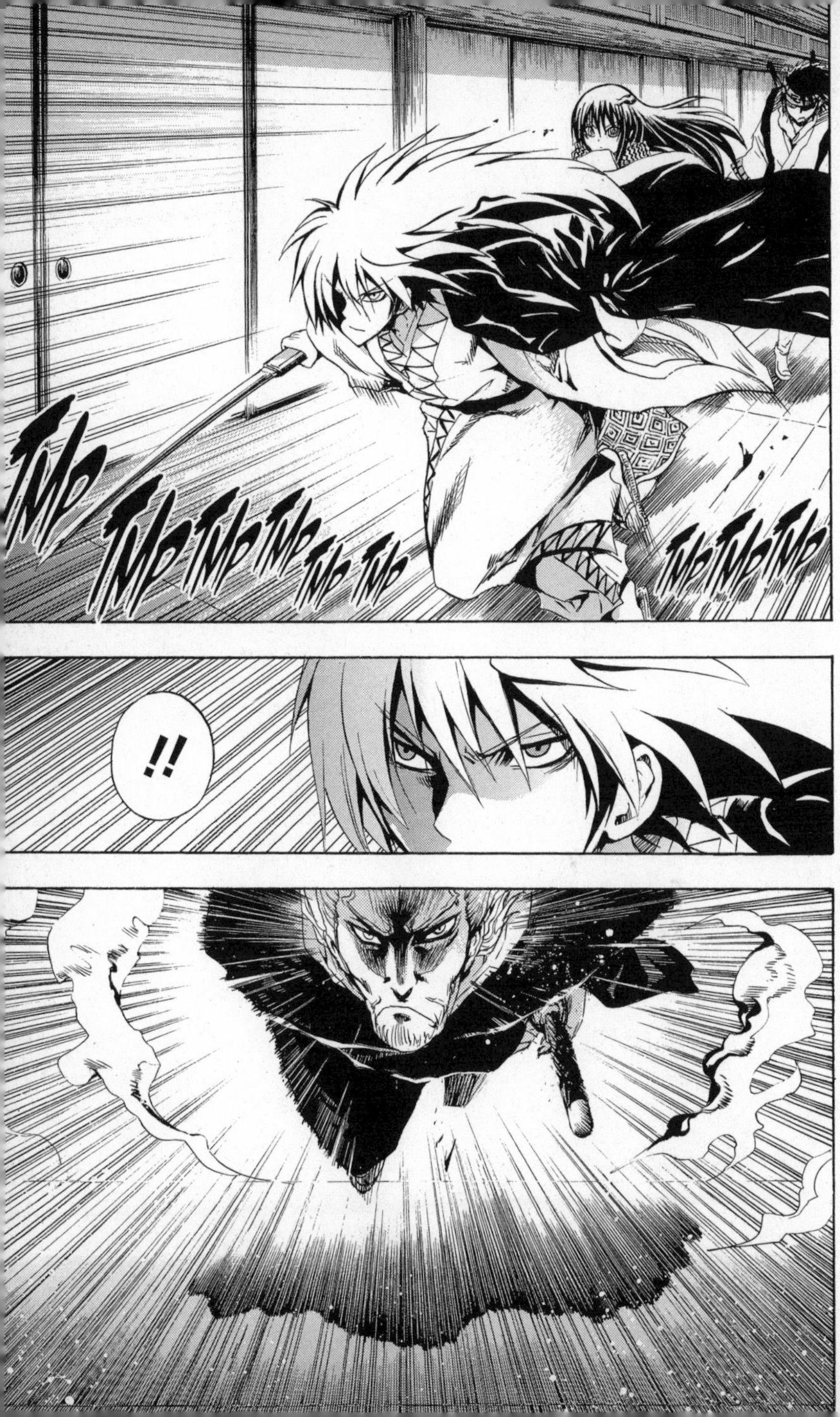
TMP TMP TMP
TMP TMP TMP TMP TMP TMP
TMP
!!

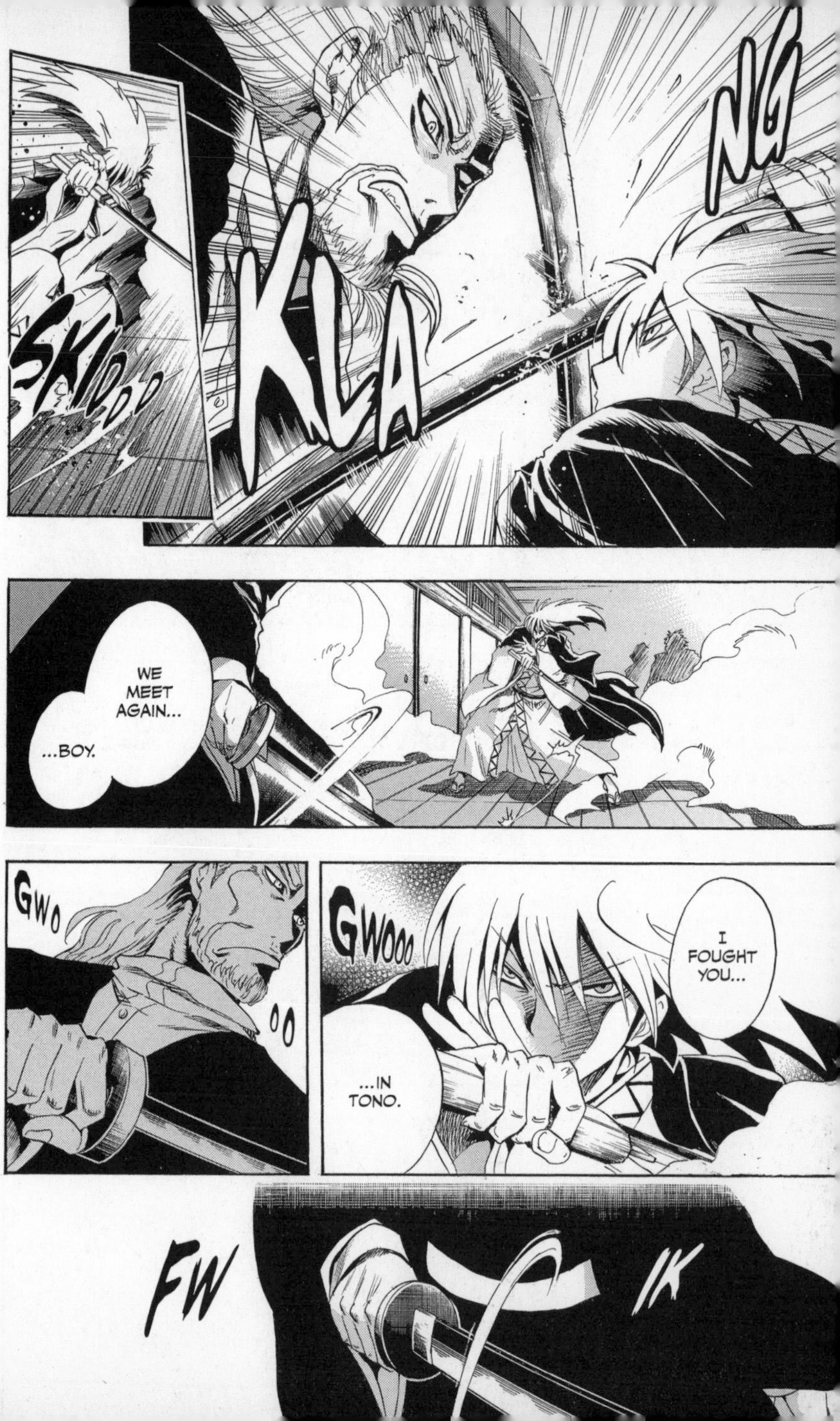
NG
KLA
SKIDDD
WE MEET AGAIN...
...BOY.
I FOUGHT YOU...
GWOOO
...IN TONO.
GWO
OO
FW
IK

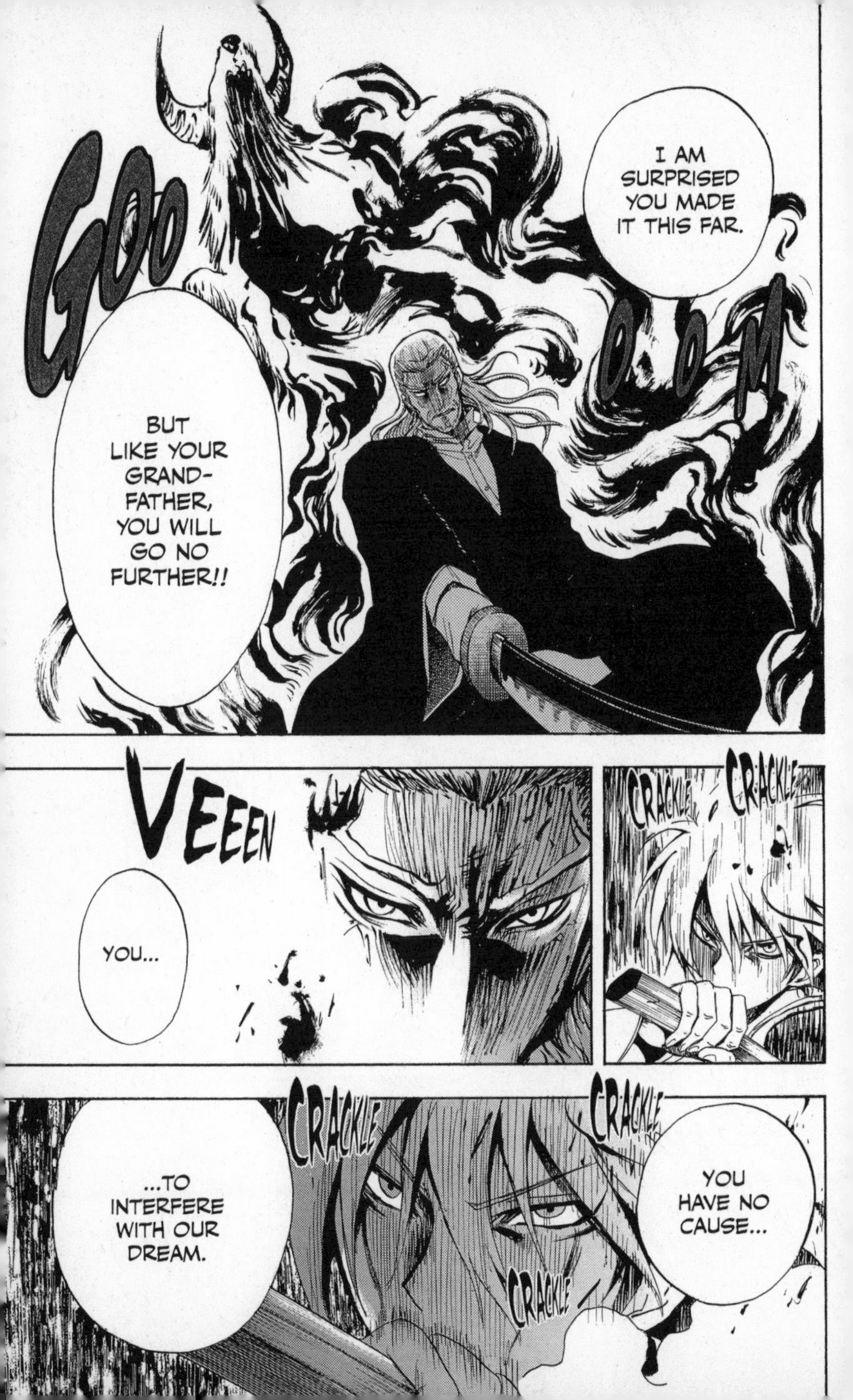
I AM SURPRISED YOU MADE IT THIS FAR.
GOOOOM
BUT LIKE YOUR GRAND-FATHER, YOU WILL GO NO FURTHER!!
CRACKLE
CRACKLE
VEEEN
YOU...
CRACKLE
YOU HAVE NO CAUSE...
CRACKLE
CRACKLE
...TO INTERFERE WITH OUR DREAM.

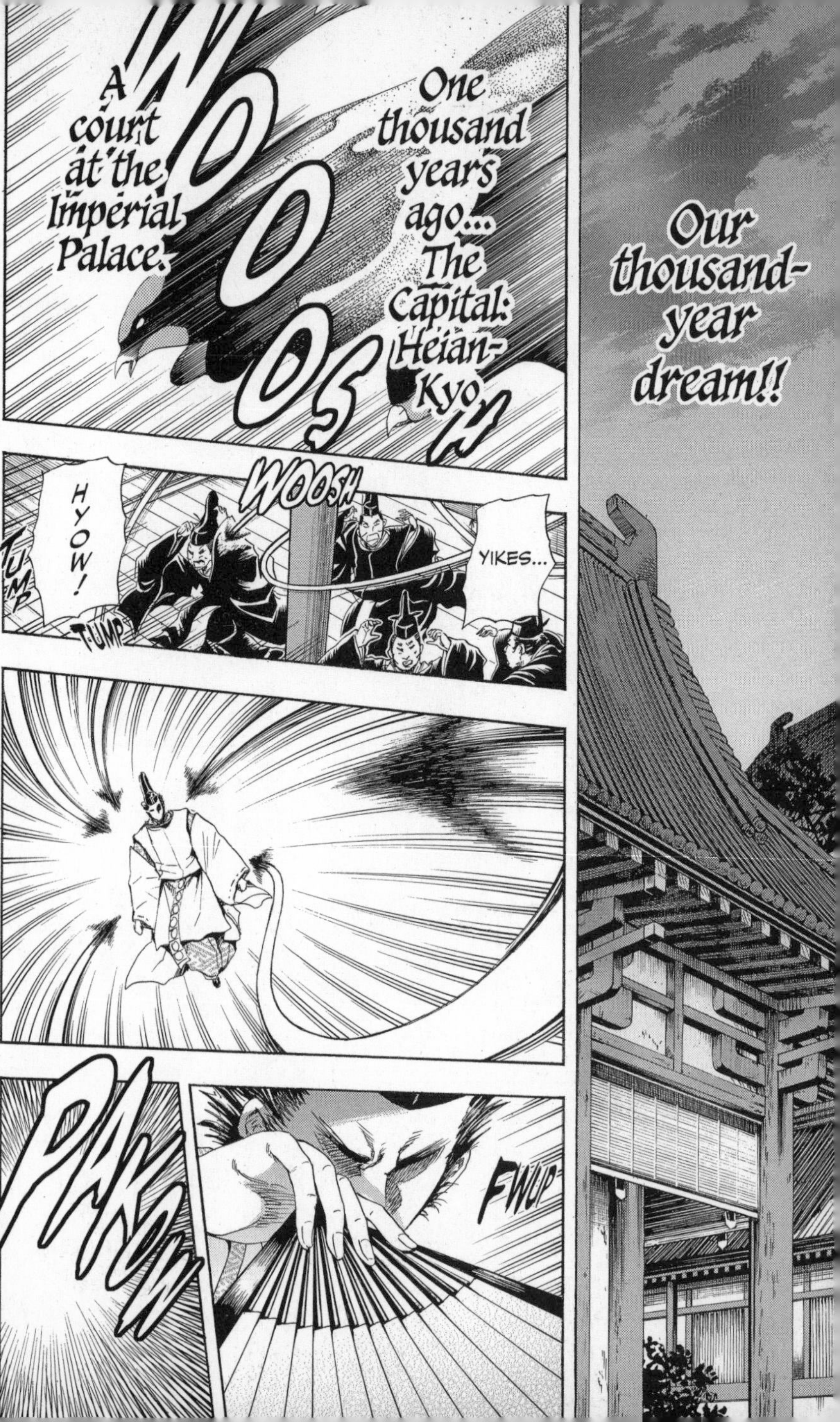

Our thousand-year dream!!
One thousand years ago... The Capital: Heian-Kyo
A court at the Imperial Palace.
WOOOSH
YIKES...
WOOSH
HYOW!
TUMP
TUMP
FWUP

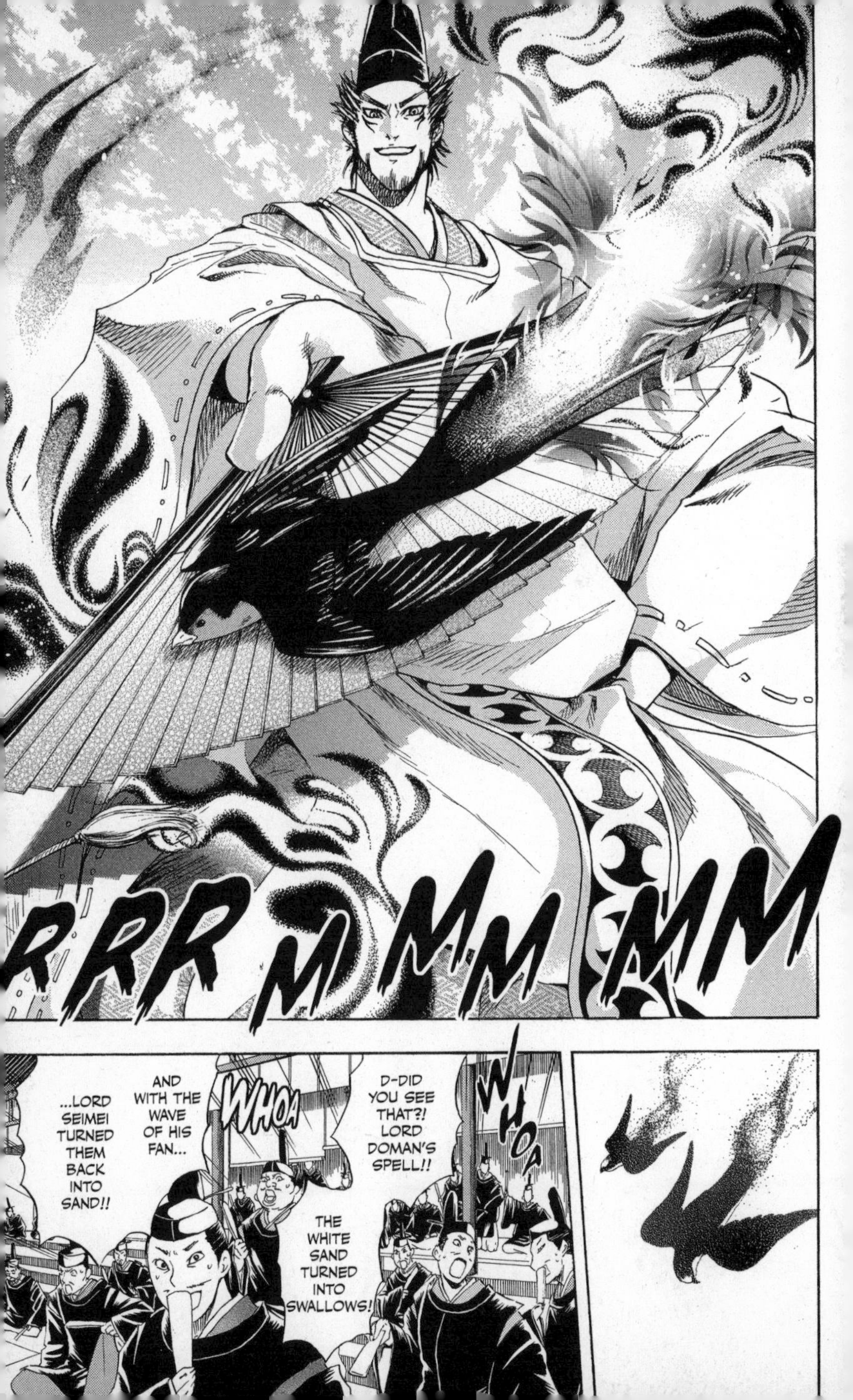
RRRMMMMMM
WHOA
D-DID YOU SEE THAT?! LORD DOMAN'S SPELL!!
THE WHITE SAND TURNED INTO SWALLOWS!
WHOA
AND WITH THE WAVE OF HIS FAN...
...LORD SEIMEI TURNED THEM BACK INTO SAND!!

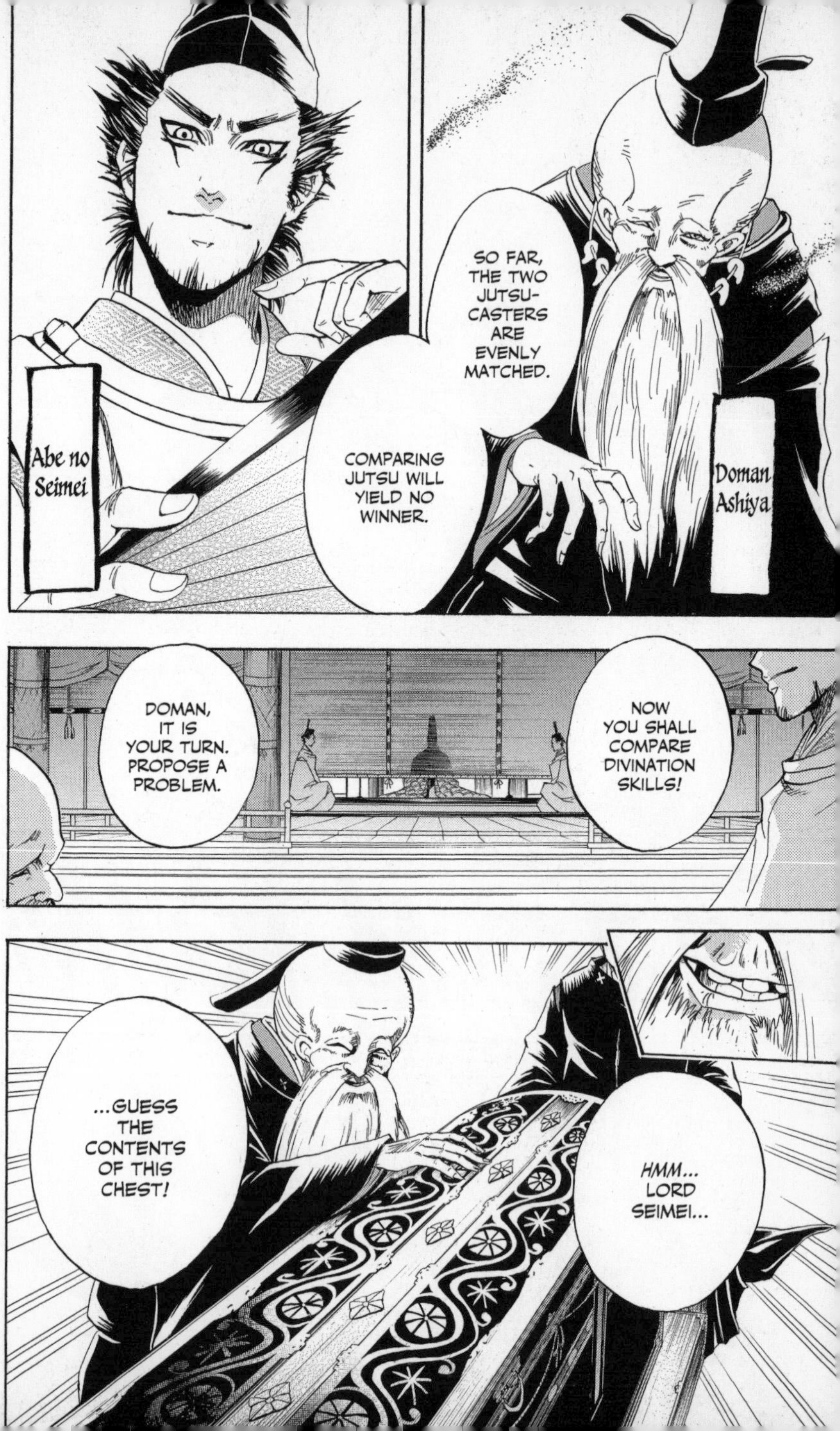
SO FAR, THE TWO JUTSU-CASTERS ARE EVENLY MATCHED.
Doman Ashiya
COMPARING JUTSU WILL YIELD NO WINNER.
Abe no Seimei
NOW YOU SHALL COMPARE DIVINATION SKILLS!
DOMAN, IT IS YOUR TURN. PROPOSE A PROBLEM.
HMM... LORD SEIMEI...
...GUESS THE CONTENTS OF THIS CHEST!

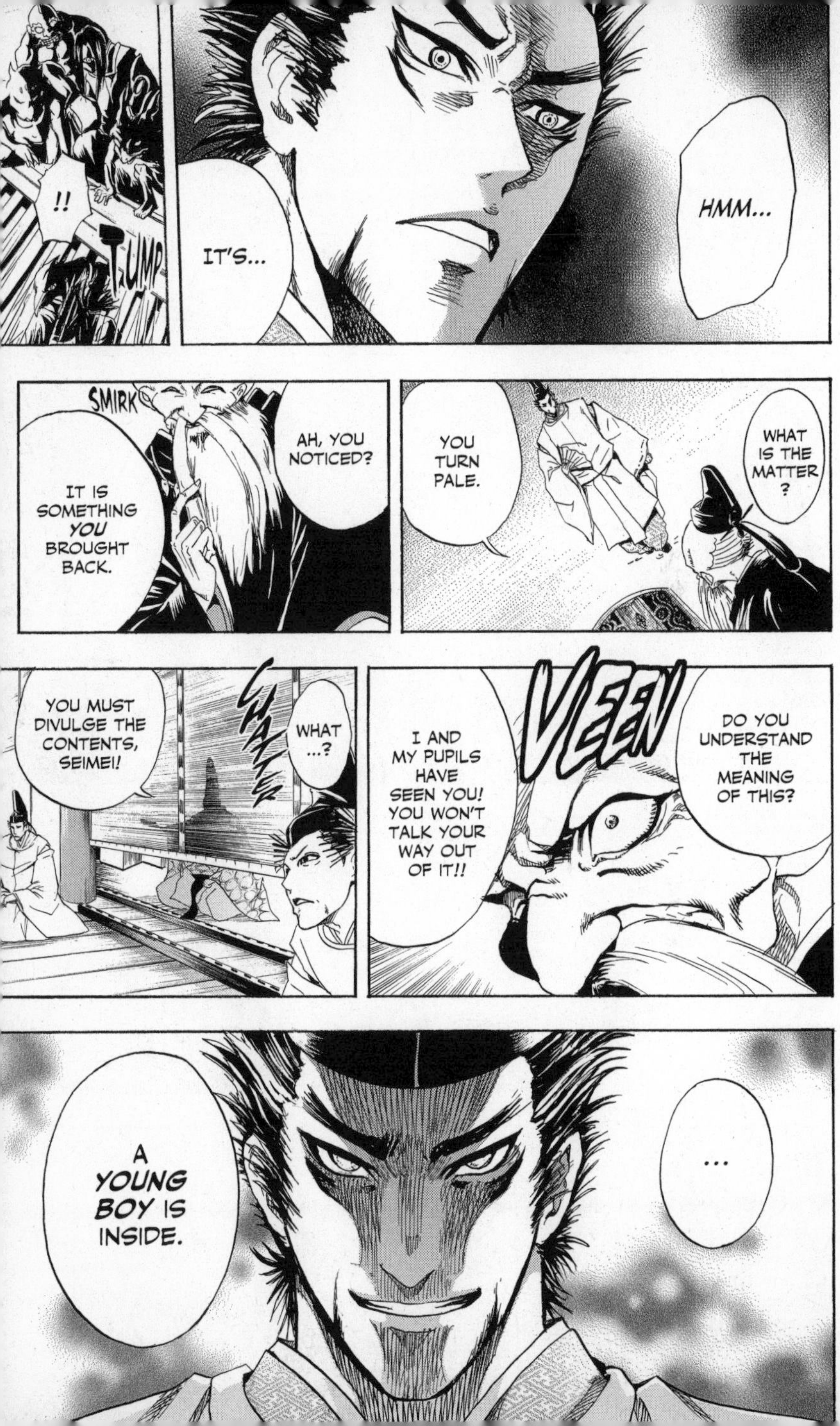
HMM...
IT'S...
!!
TUMP
WHAT IS THE MATTER?
YOU TURN PALE.
AH, YOU NOTICED?
SMIRK
IT IS SOMETHING *YOU* BROUGHT BACK.
DO YOU UNDERSTAND THE MEANING OF THIS?
VEEN
I AND MY PUPILS HAVE SEEN YOU! YOU WON'T TALK YOUR WAY OUT OF IT!!
WHAT ...?
YOU MUST DIVULGE THE CONTENTS, SEIMEI!
...
A *YOUNG BOY* IS INSIDE.

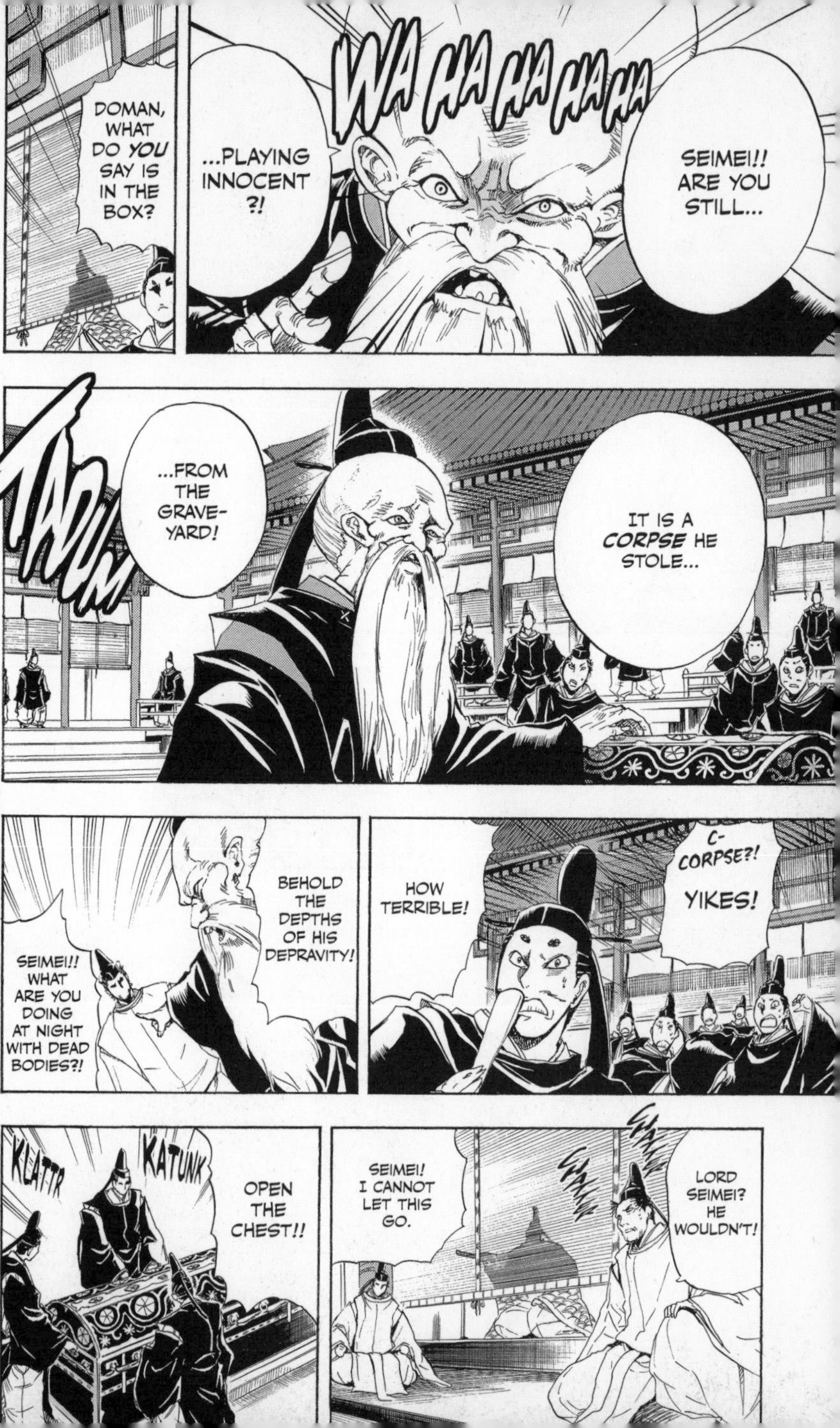
SEIMEI!! ARE YOU STILL...
WA HA HA HA HA
...PLAYING INNOCENT ?!
DOMAN, WHAT DO YOU SAY IS IN THE BOX?
IT IS A CORPSE HE STOLE...
...FROM THE GRAVEYARD!
C- CORPSE?!
YIKES!
HOW TERRIBLE!
BEHOLD THE DEPTHS OF HIS DEPRAVITY!
SEIMEI!! WHAT ARE YOU DOING AT NIGHT WITH DEAD BODIES?!
LORD SEIMEI? HE WOULDN'T!
SEIMEI! I CANNOT LET THIS GO.
KATUNK
OPEN THE CHEST!!
KLATTR

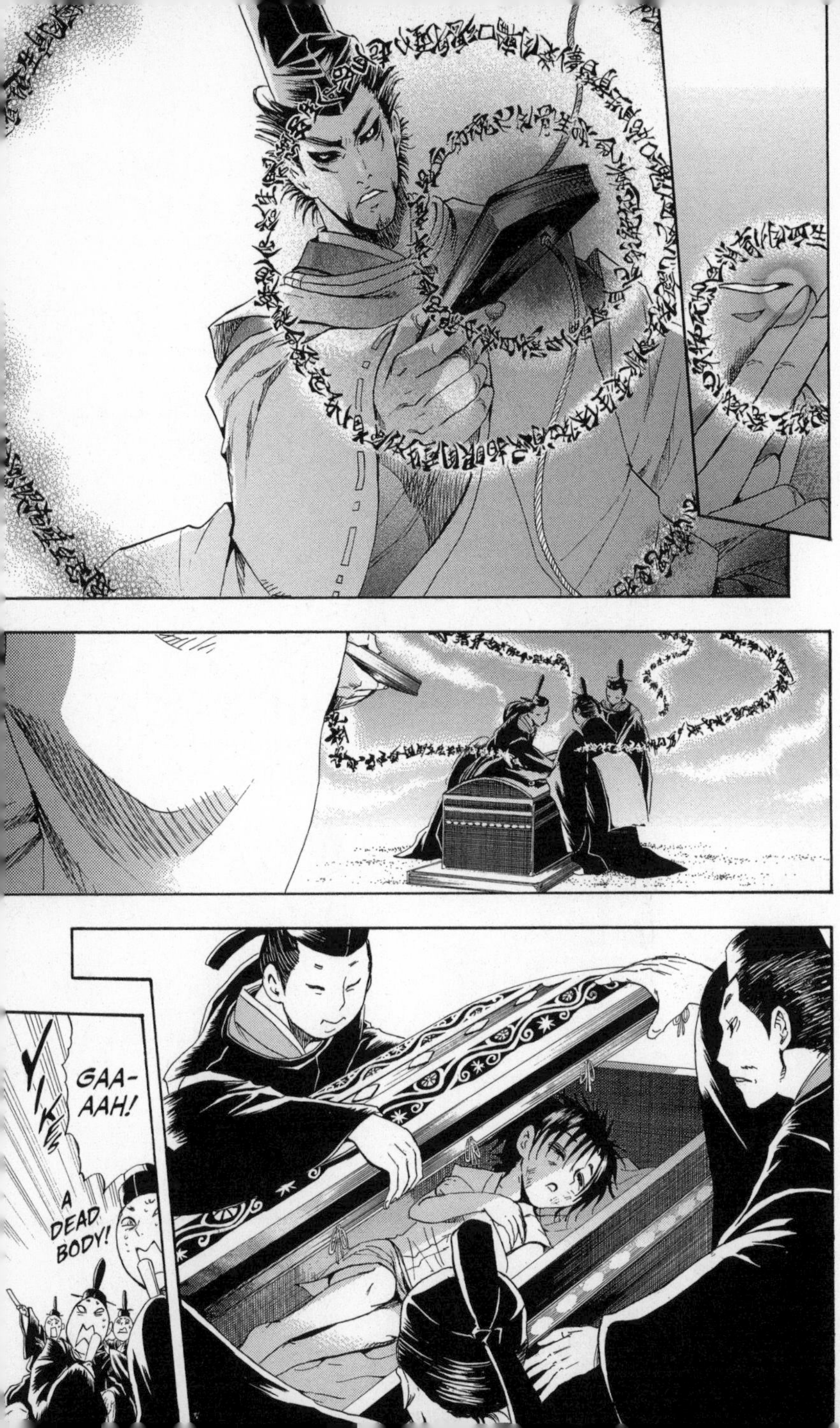
YIKES
GAA-
AAH!
A DEAD BODY!

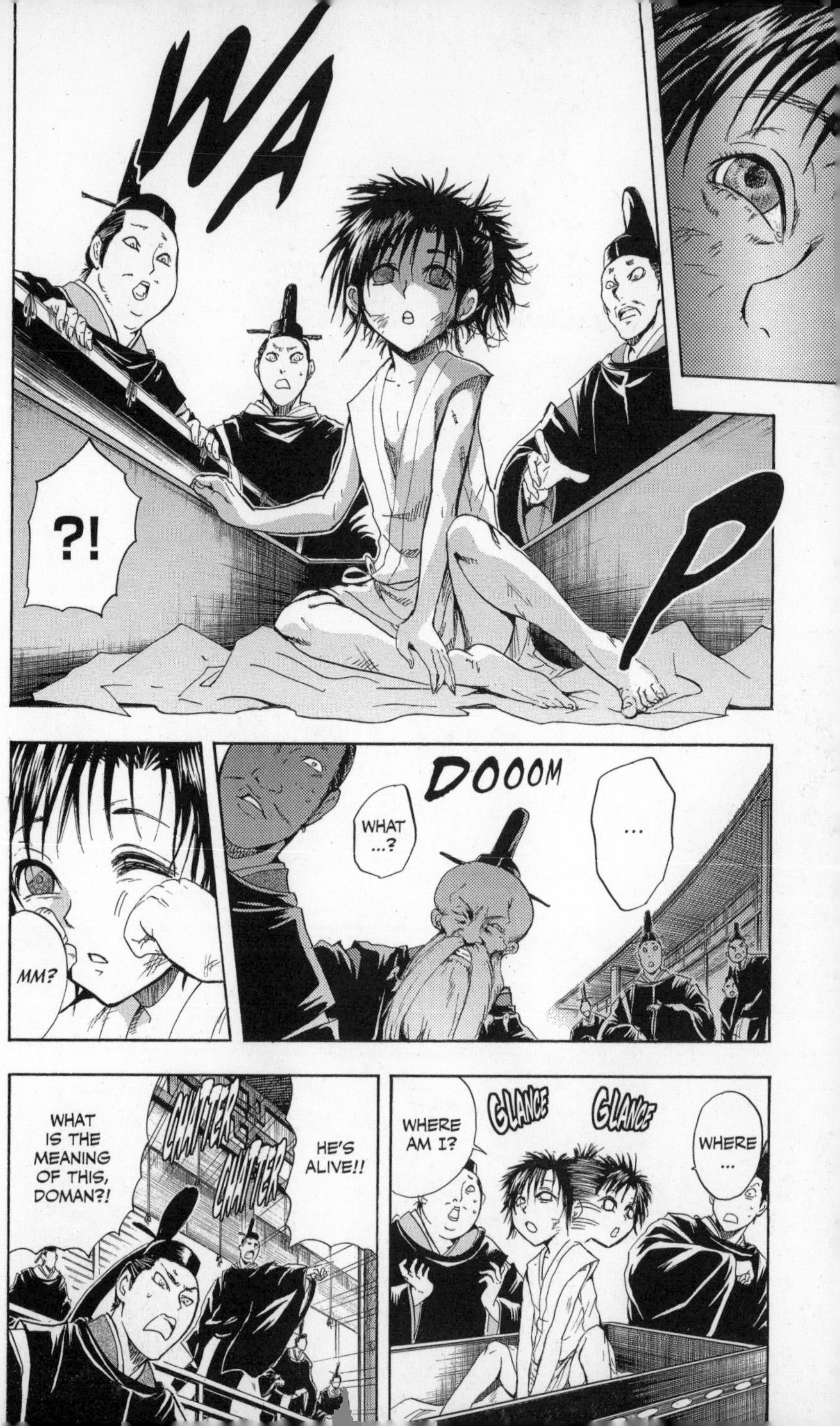
WA
P
?!
...
DOOOM
WHAT ...?
MM?
WHERE ...
GLANCE
GLANCE
WHERE AM I?
HE'S ALIVE!!
CHATTER
CHATTER
WHAT IS THE MEANING OF THIS, DOMAN?!

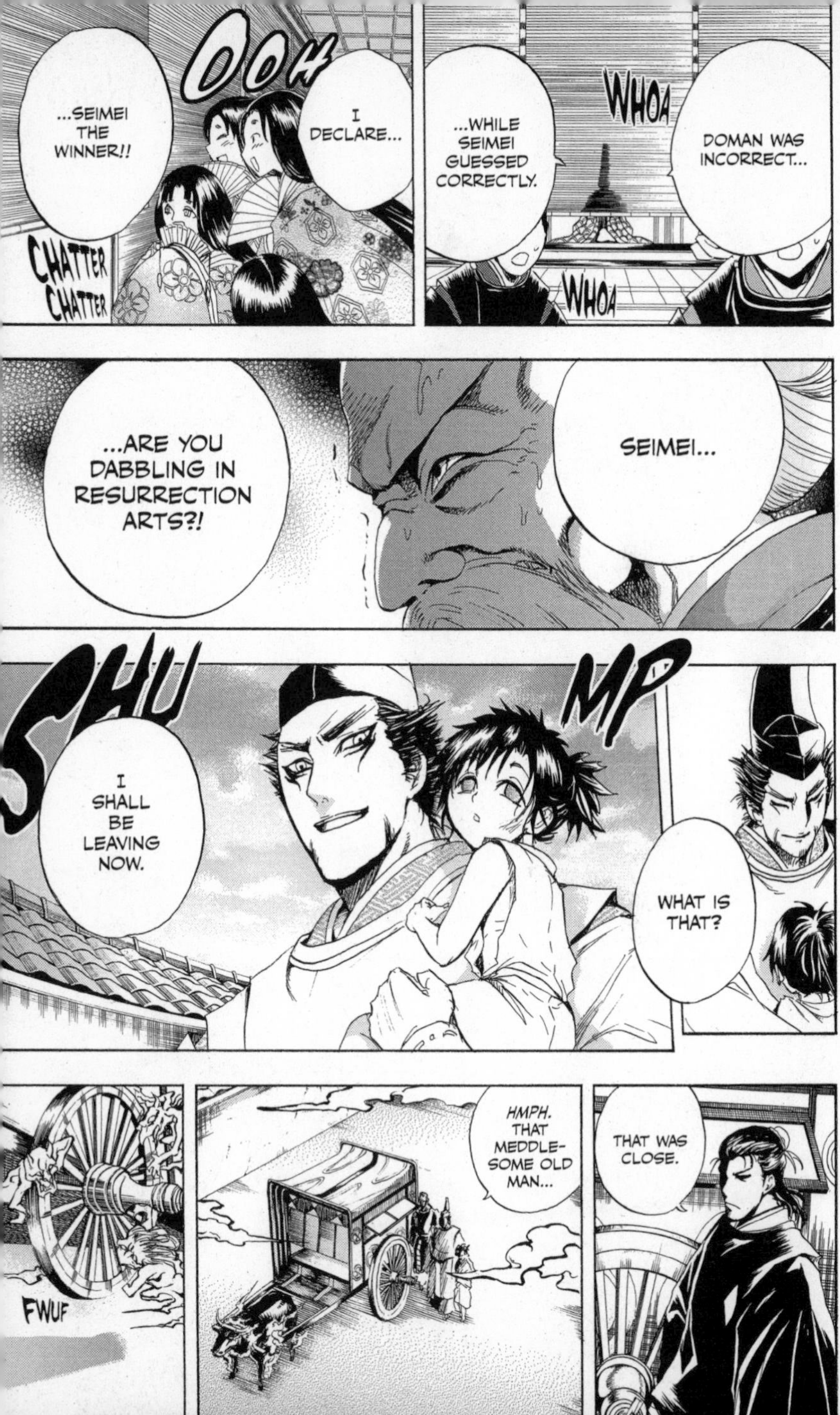
DOMAN WAS INCORRECT...
WHOA
...WHILE SEIMEI GUESSED CORRECTLY.
WHOA
I DECLARE...
OOH
...SEIMEI THE WINNER!!
CHATTER CHATTER
SEIMEI...
...ARE YOU DABBLING IN RESURRECTION ARTS?!
WHAT IS THAT?
SHUMP
I SHALL BE LEAVING NOW.
THAT WAS CLOSE.
HMPH. THAT MEDDLE-SOME OLD MAN...
FWUF

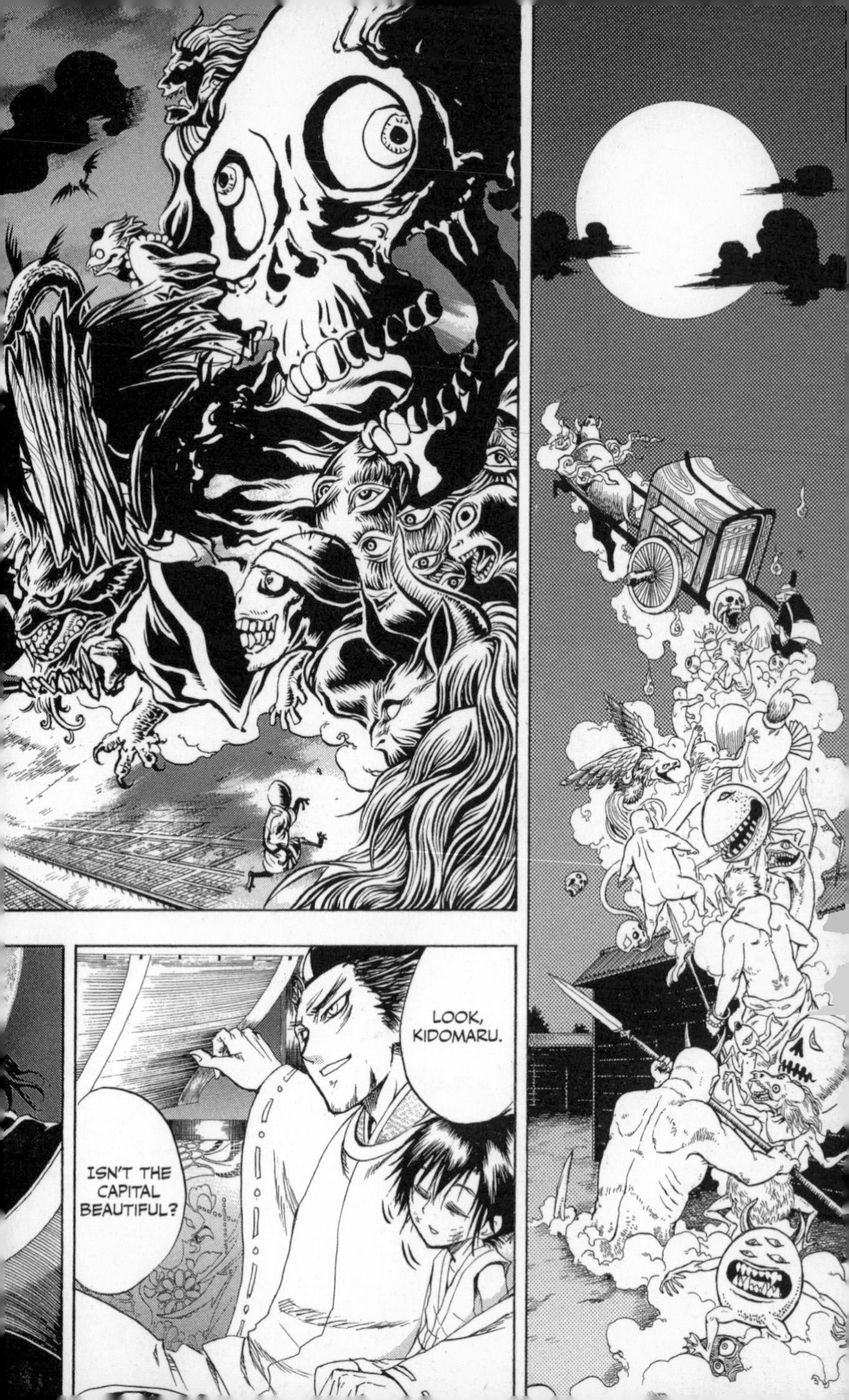
LOOK, KIDOMARU.
ISN'T THE CAPITAL BEAUTIFUL?

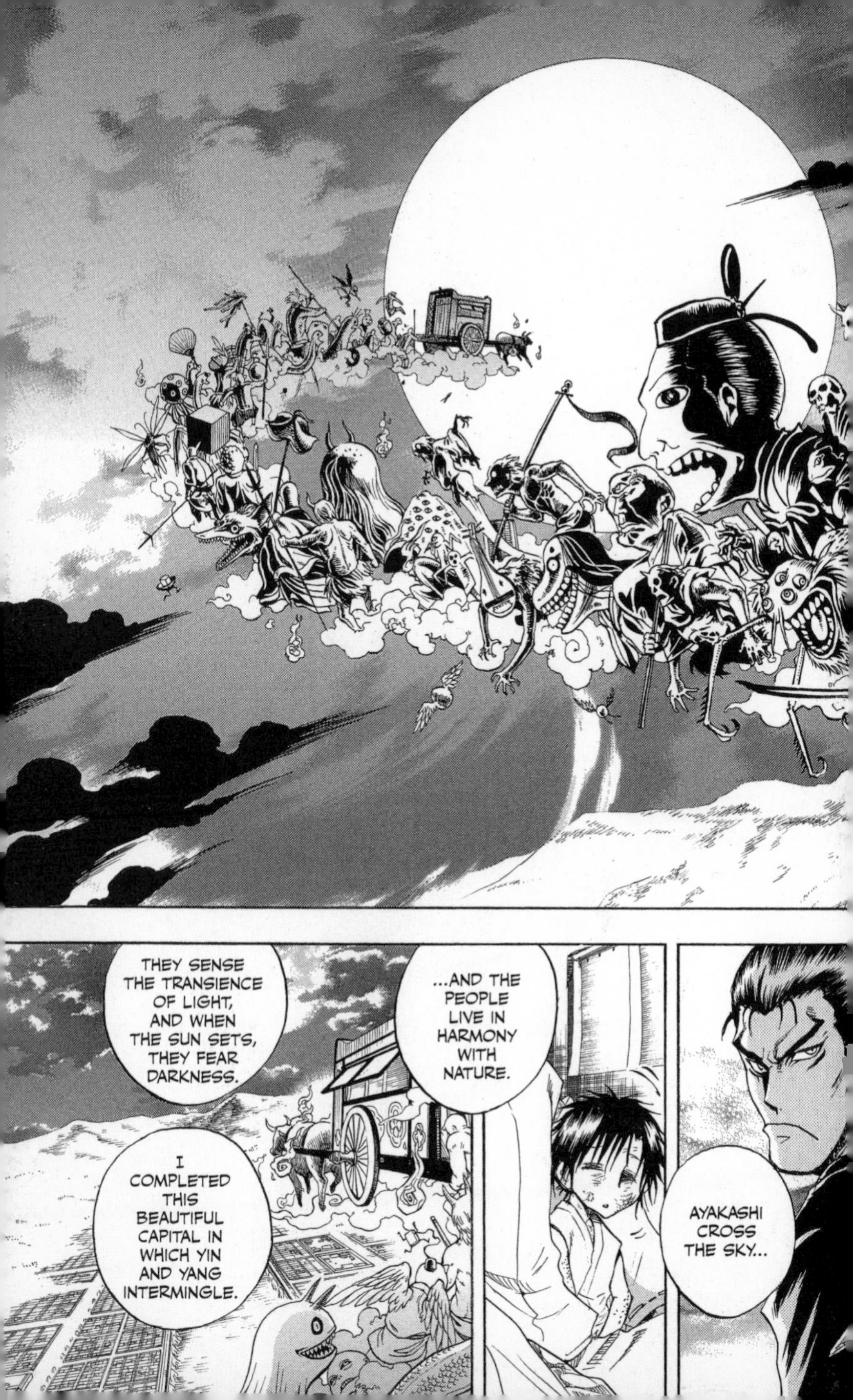
AYAKASHI CROSS THE SKY...
...AND THE PEOPLE LIVE IN HARMONY WITH NATURE.
THEY SENSE THE TRANSIENCE OF LIGHT, AND WHEN THE SUN SETS, THEY FEAR DARKNESS.
I COMPLETED THIS BEAUTIFUL CAPITAL IN WHICH YIN AND YANG INTERMINGLE.

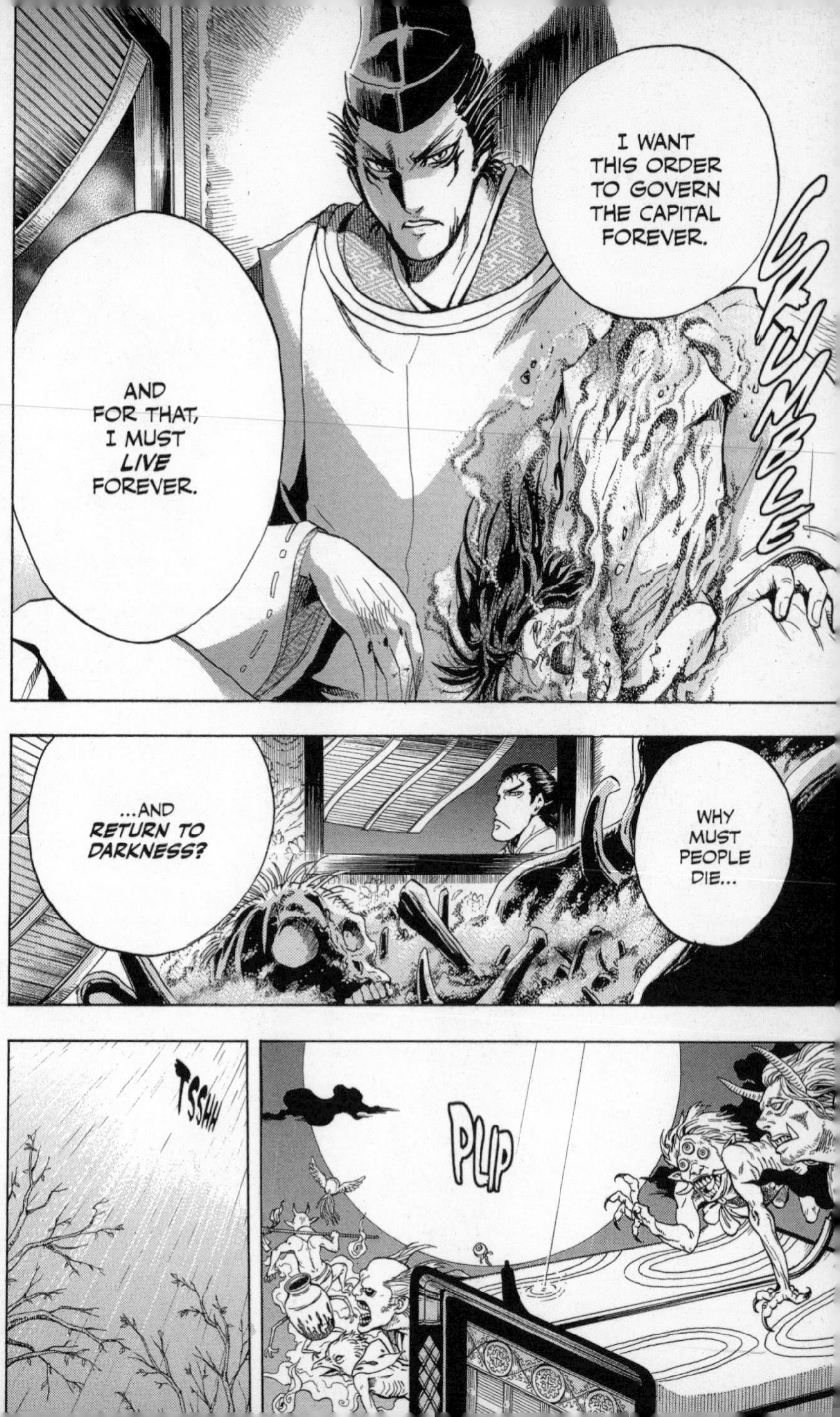
I WANT THIS ORDER TO GOVERN THE CAPITAL FOREVER.
AND FOR THAT, I MUST *LIVE* FOREVER.
WHY MUST PEOPLE DIE...
...AND *RETURN TO DARKNESS?*
PLIP
TSSHH

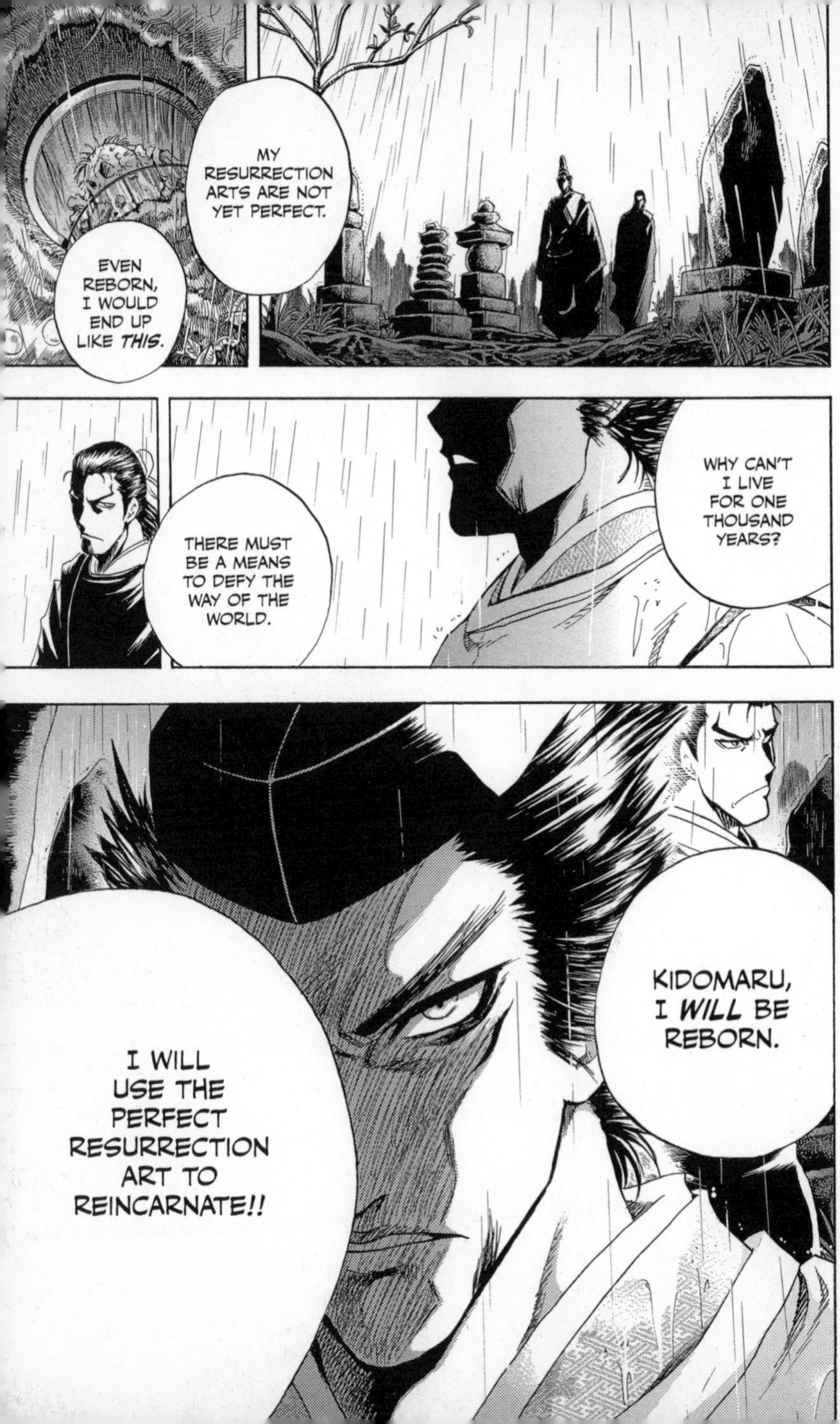
MY RESURRECTION ARTS ARE NOT YET PERFECT.
EVEN REBORN, I WOULD END UP LIKE *THIS*.
WHY CAN'T I LIVE FOR ONE THOUSAND YEARS?
THERE MUST BE A MEANS TO DEFY THE WAY OF THE WORLD.
KIDOMARU, I *WILL* BE REBORN.
I WILL USE THE PERFECT RESURRECTION ART TO REINCARNATE!!

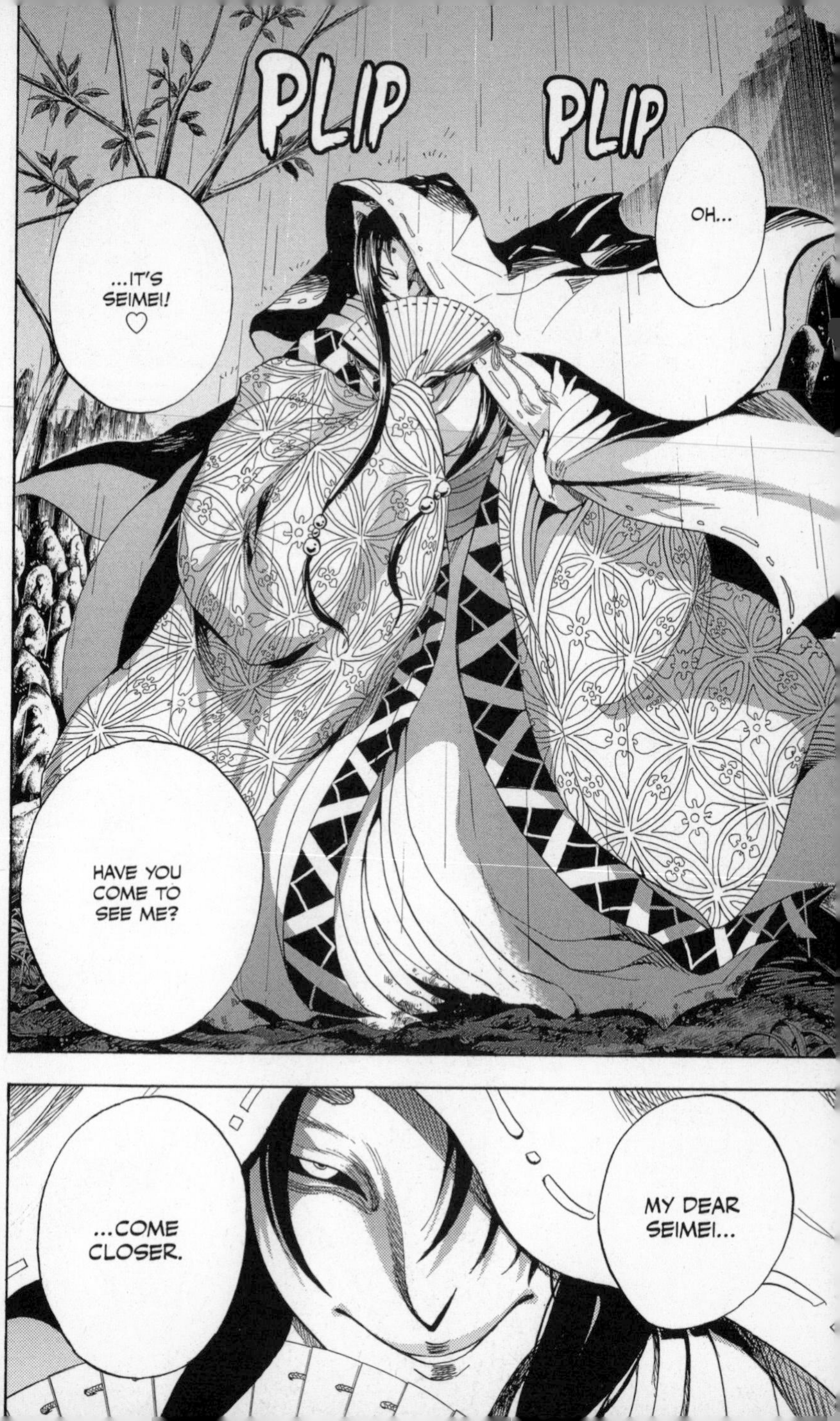
PLIP
PLIP
OH...
...IT'S SEIMEI! ♡
HAVE YOU COME TO SEE ME?
MY DEAR SEIMEI...
...COME CLOSER.

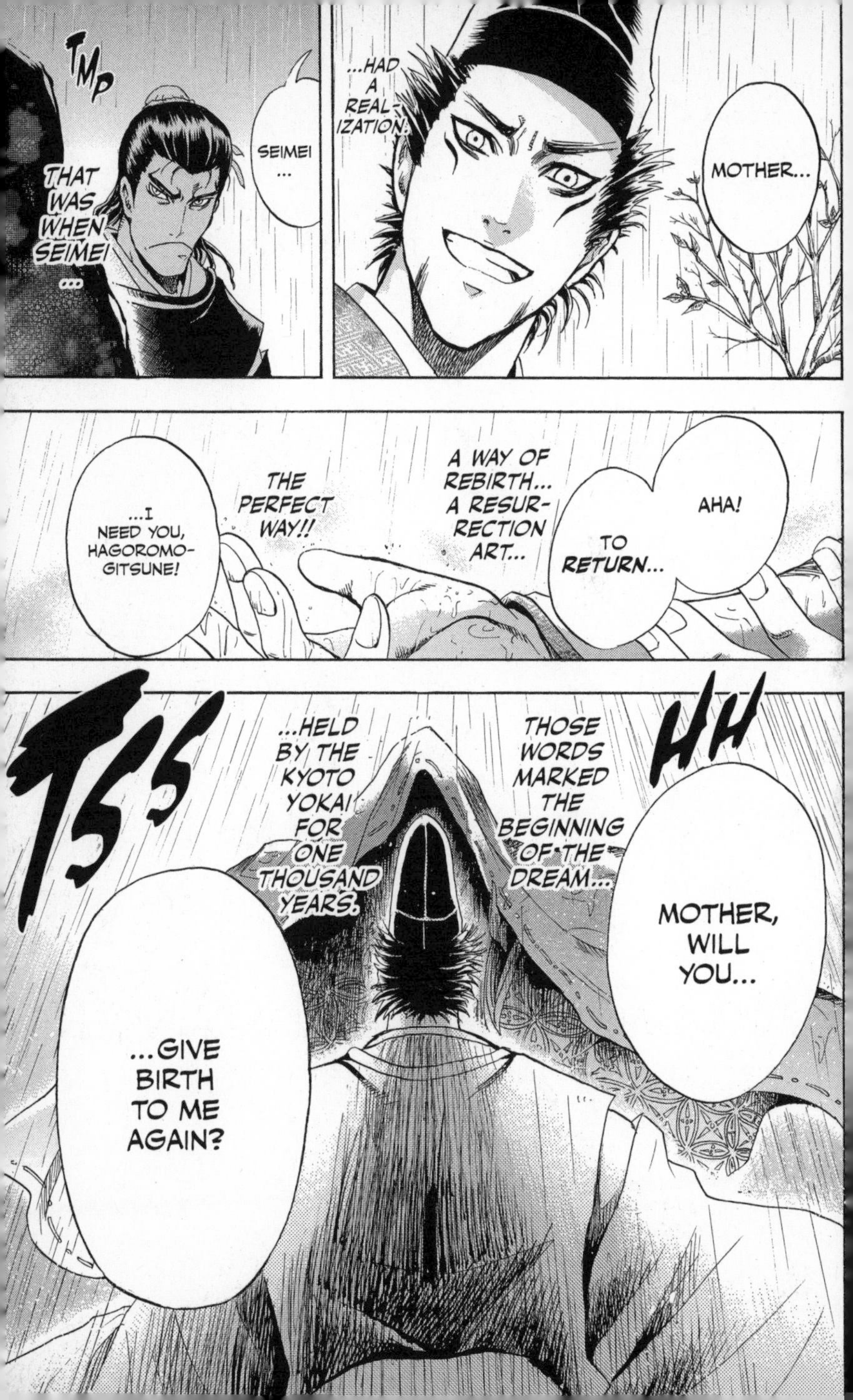

MOTHER...
...HAD A REALIZATION.
SEIMEI...
TMP
THAT WAS WHEN SEIMEI...
AHA!
TO RETURN...
A WAY OF REBIRTH... A RESURRECTION ART...
THE PERFECT WAY!!
...I NEED YOU, HAGOROMO-GITSUNE!
HH
MOTHER, WILL YOU...
THOSE WORDS MARKED THE BEGINNING OF THE DREAM...
...HELD BY THE KYOTO YOKAI FOR ONE THOUSAND YEARS.
TSS
...GIVE BIRTH TO ME AGAIN?

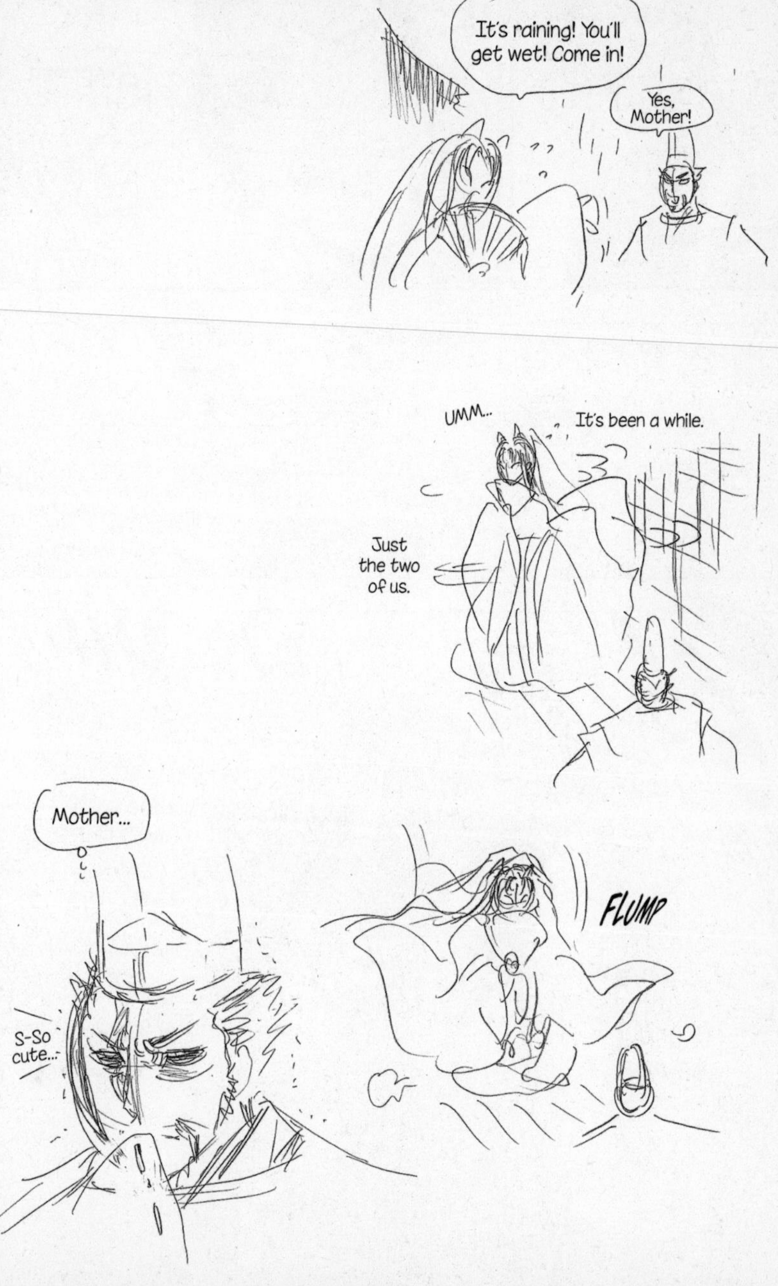
It's raining! You'll get wet! Come in!
Yes, Mother!
It's been a while.
UMM...
Just the two of us.
FLUMP
Mother...
S-So cute...

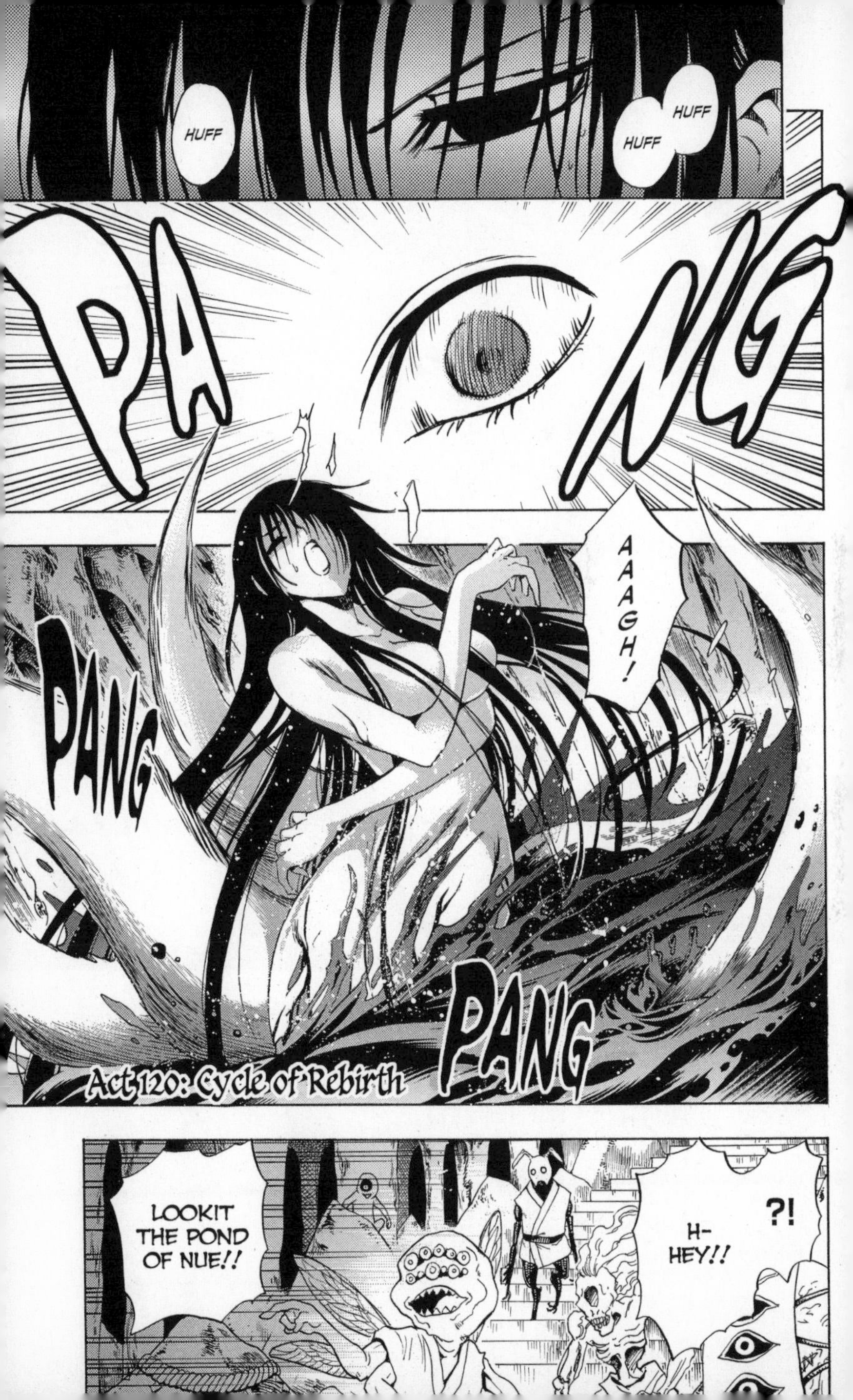
HUFF
HUFF
HUFF
PANG
AAAAGH!
PANG
PANG
Act 120: Cycle of Rebirth
?!
H-HEY!!
LOOKIT THE POND OF NUE!!

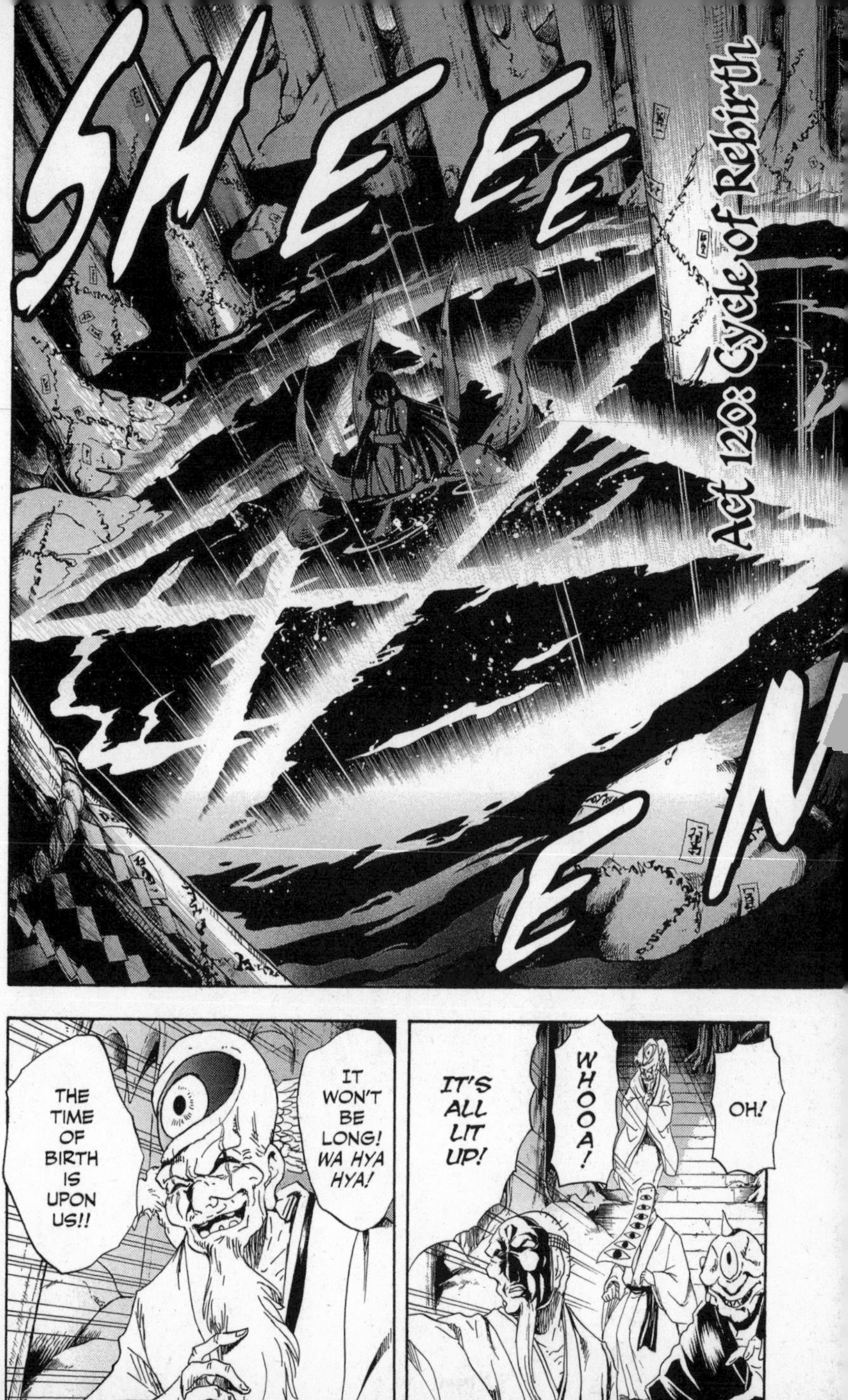
Act 120: Cycle of Rebirth
SHEEEEN
OH!
WHOOA!
IT'S ALL LIT UP!
IT WON'T BE LONG! WA HYA HYA!
THE TIME OF BIRTH IS UPON US!!

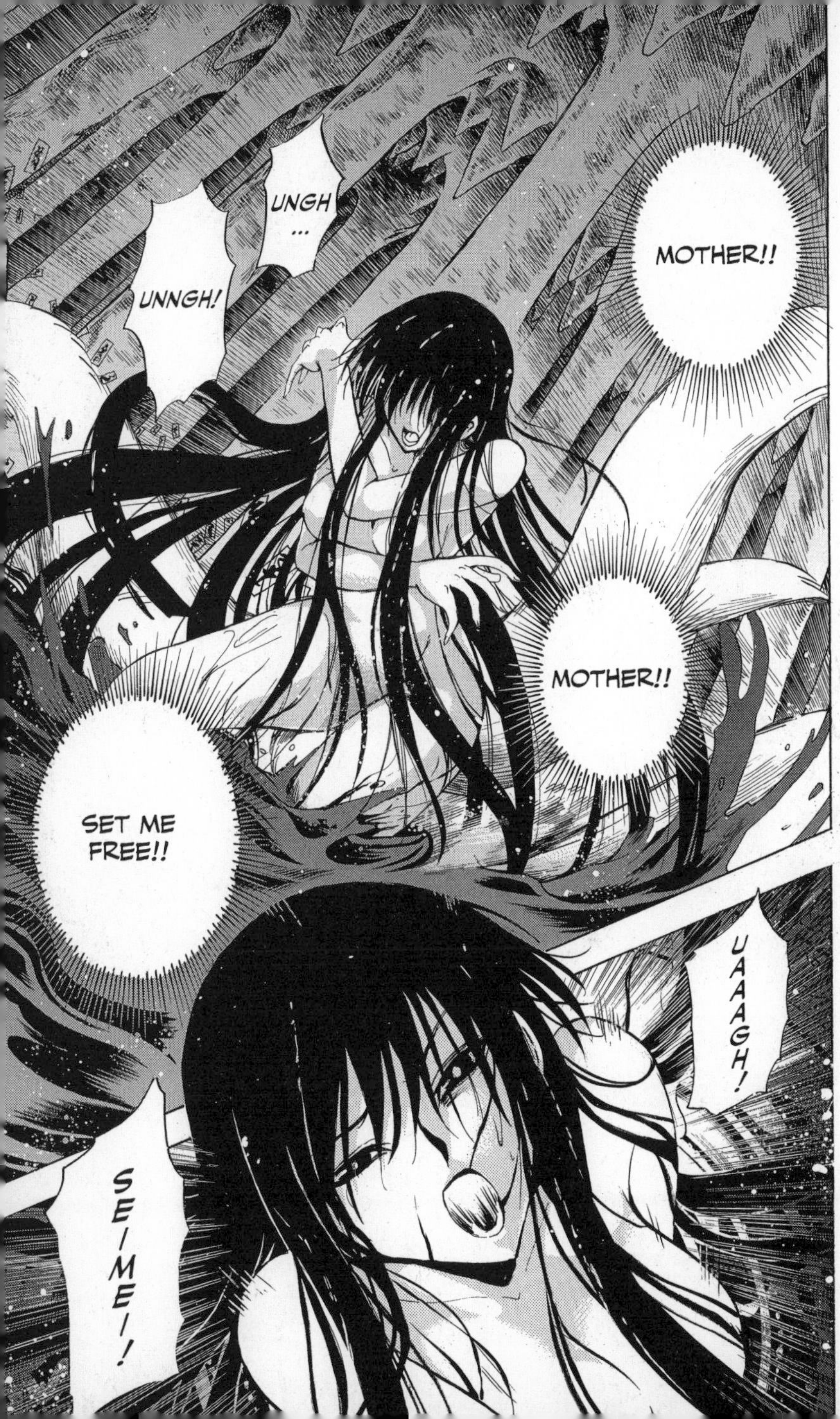
MOTHER!!
UNGH ...
UNNGH!
MOTHER!!
SET ME FREE!!
UAAAGH!
SEIMEI!!

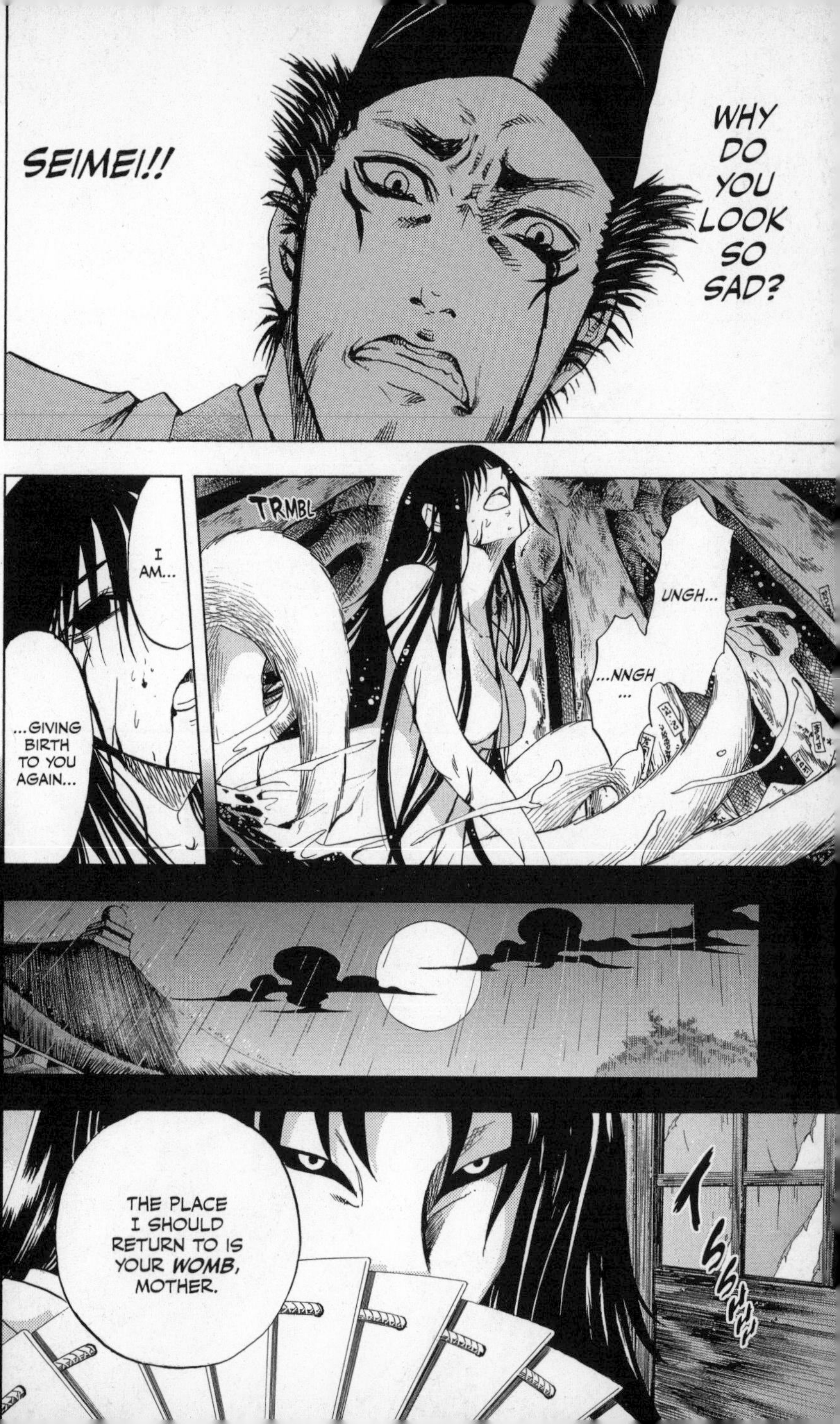
WHY DO YOU LOOK SO SAD?
SEIMEI!!
TRMBL
UNGH...
...NNGH...
I AM...
...GIVING BIRTH TO YOU AGAIN...
THE PLACE I SHOULD RETURN TO IS YOUR **WOMB**, MOTHER.

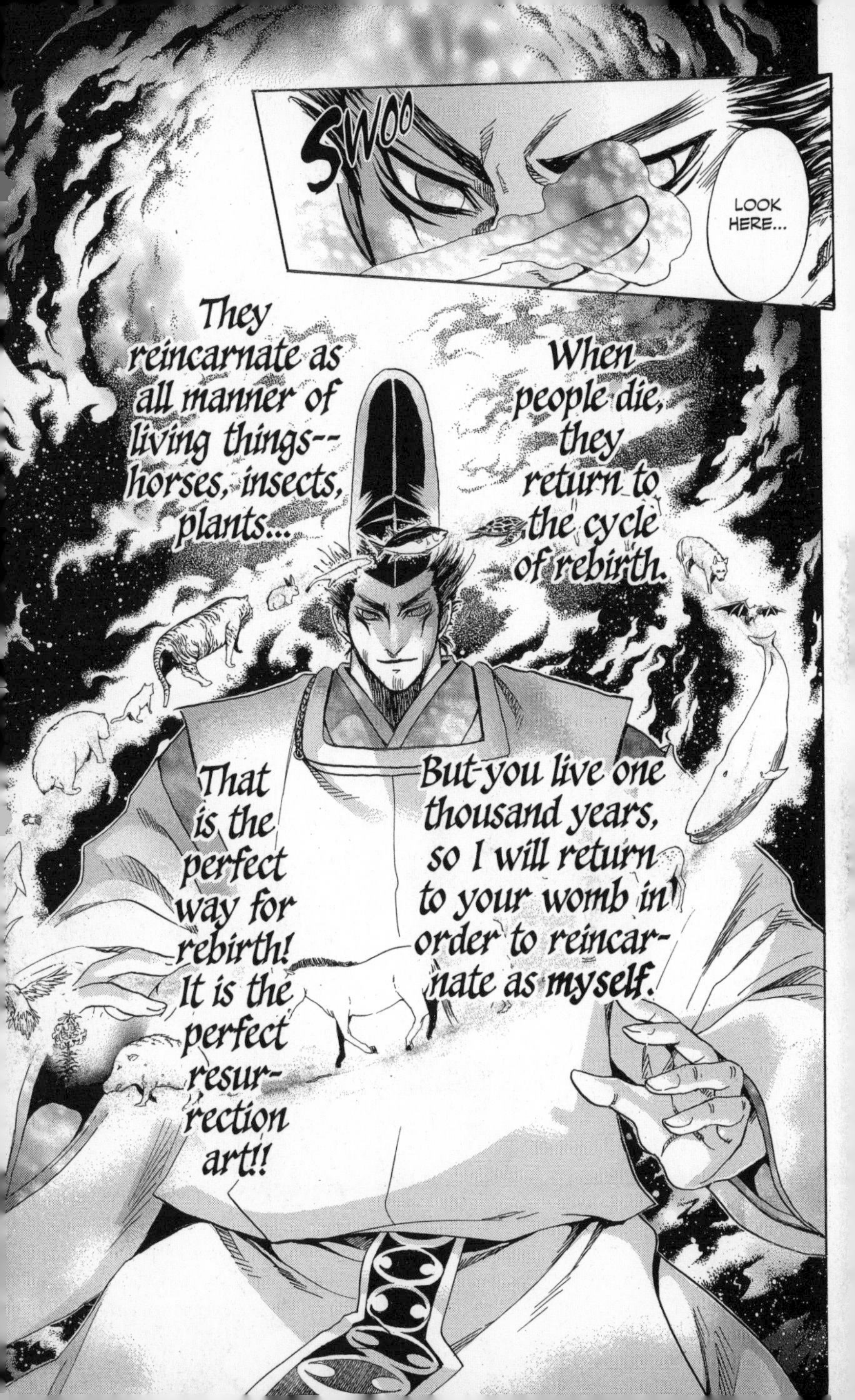
LOOK HERE...
SWOO
When people die, they return to the cycle of rebirth.
They reincarnate as all manner of living things--horses, insects, plants...
But you live one thousand years, so I will return to your womb in order to reincar-nate as myself.
That is the perfect way for rebirth! It is the perfect resur-rection art!!

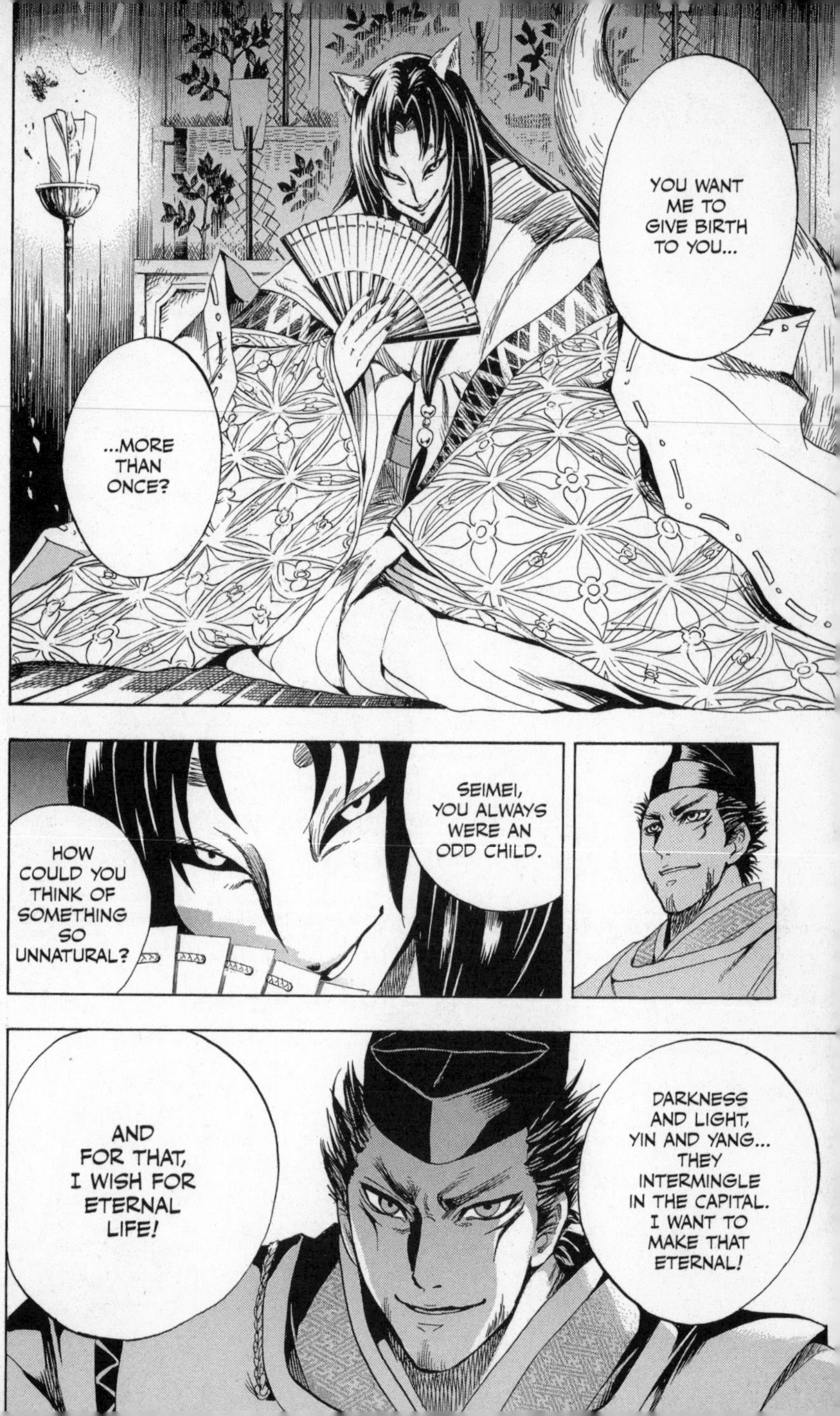
YOU WANT ME TO GIVE BIRTH TO YOU...
...MORE THAN ONCE?
SEIMEI, YOU ALWAYS WERE AN ODD CHILD.
HOW COULD YOU THINK OF SOMETHING SO UNNATURAL?
DARKNESS AND LIGHT, YIN AND YANG... THEY INTERMINGLE IN THE CAPITAL. I WANT TO MAKE THAT ETERNAL!
AND FOR THAT, I WISH FOR ETERNAL LIFE!

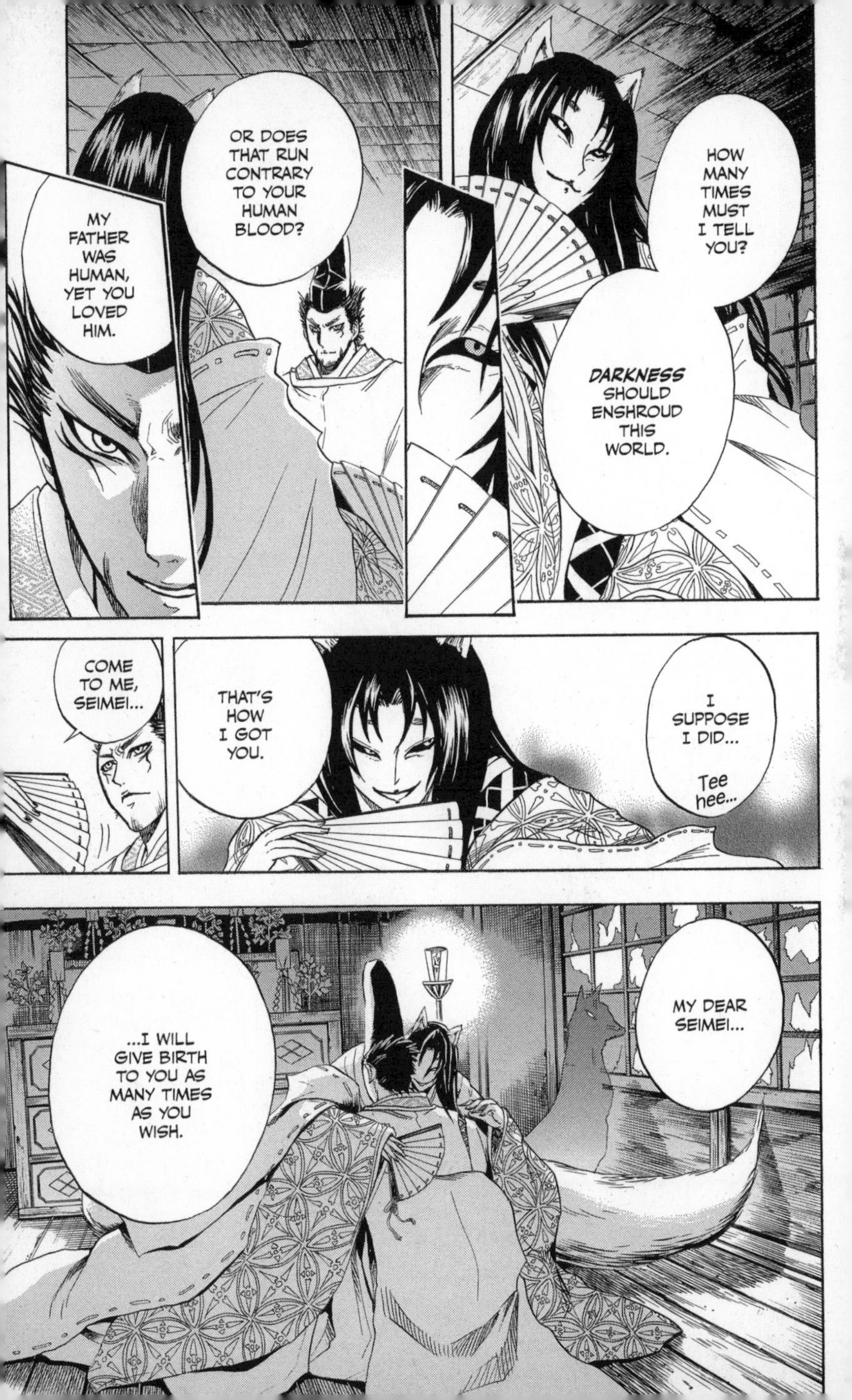
HOW MANY TIMES MUST I TELL YOU?
DARKNESS SHOULD ENSHROUD THIS WORLD.
OR DOES THAT RUN CONTRARY TO YOUR HUMAN BLOOD?
MY FATHER WAS HUMAN, YET YOU LOVED HIM.
I SUPPOSE I DID...
Tee hee...
THAT'S HOW I GOT YOU.
COME TO ME, SEIMEI...
MY DEAR SEIMEI...
...I WILL GIVE BIRTH TO YOU AS MANY TIMES AS YOU WISH.

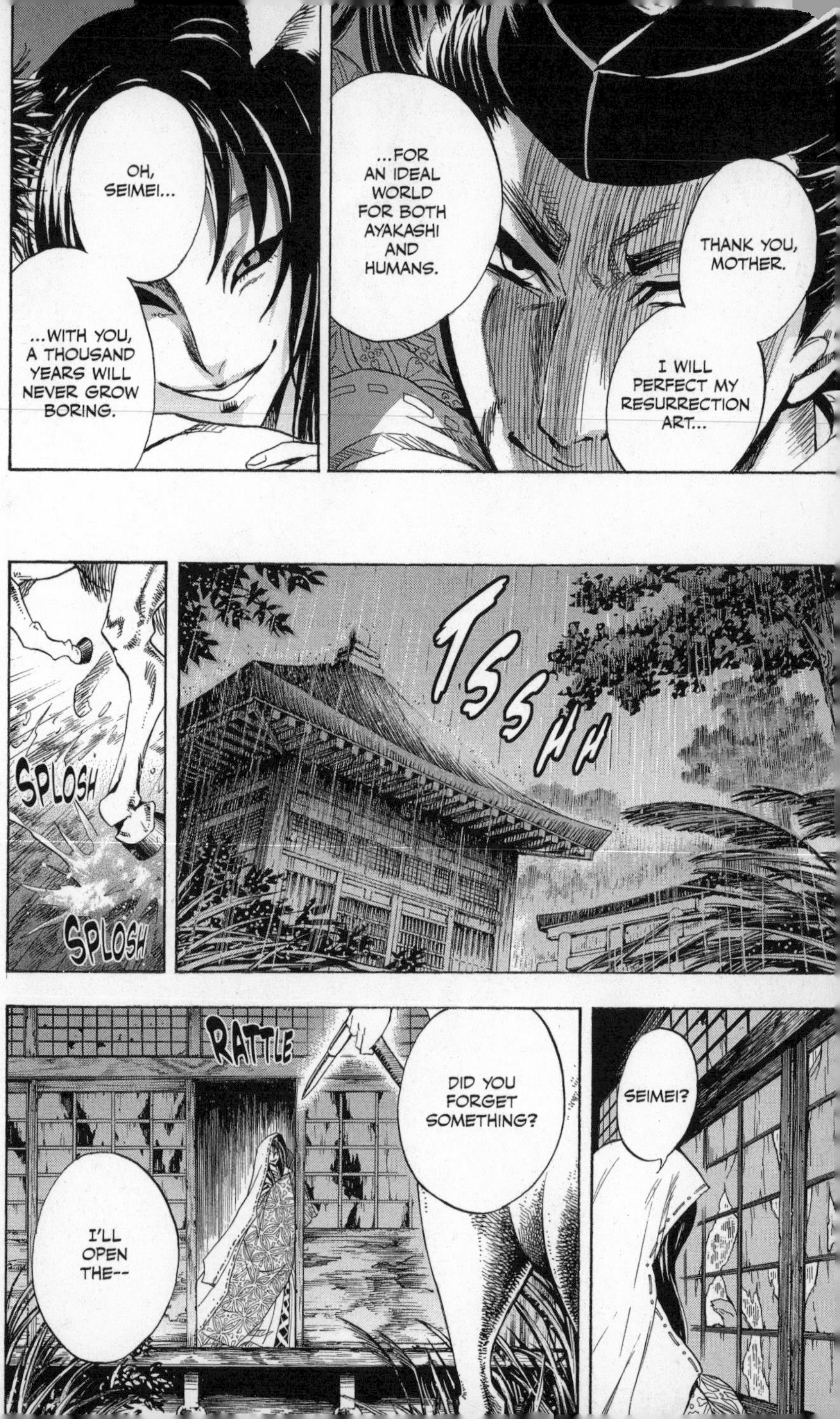
THANK YOU, MOTHER.
I WILL PERFECT MY RESURRECTION ART...
...FOR AN IDEAL WORLD FOR BOTH AYAKASHI AND HUMANS.
OH, SEIMEI...
...WITH YOU, A THOUSAND YEARS WILL NEVER GROW BORING.
TSSHH
SPLOSH
SPLOSH
SEIMEI?
RATTLE
DID YOU FORGET SOMETHING?
I'LL OPEN THE--

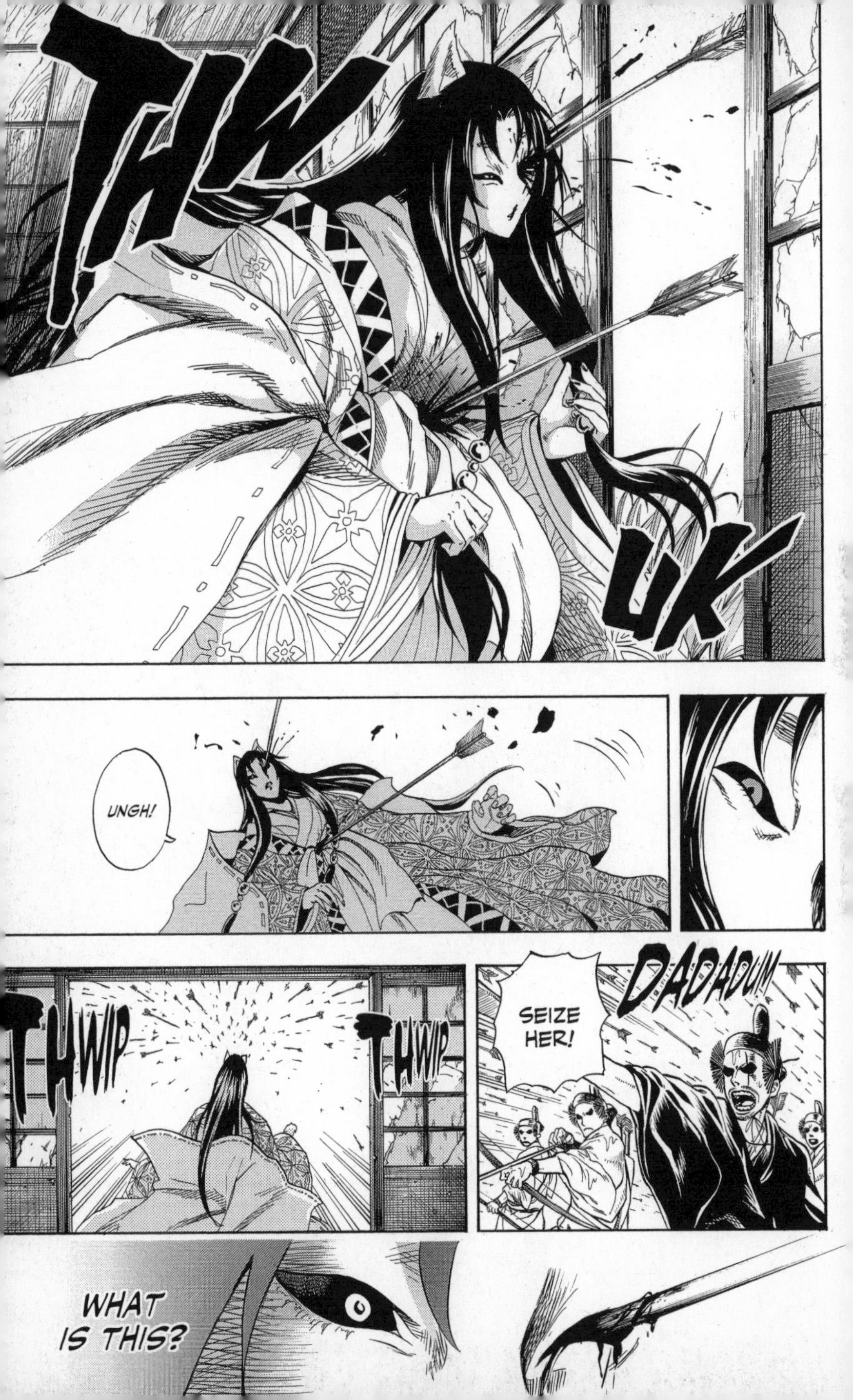
THWK
UK
UNGH!
DADADUM
SEIZE HER!
THWIP
THWIP
WHAT IS THIS?

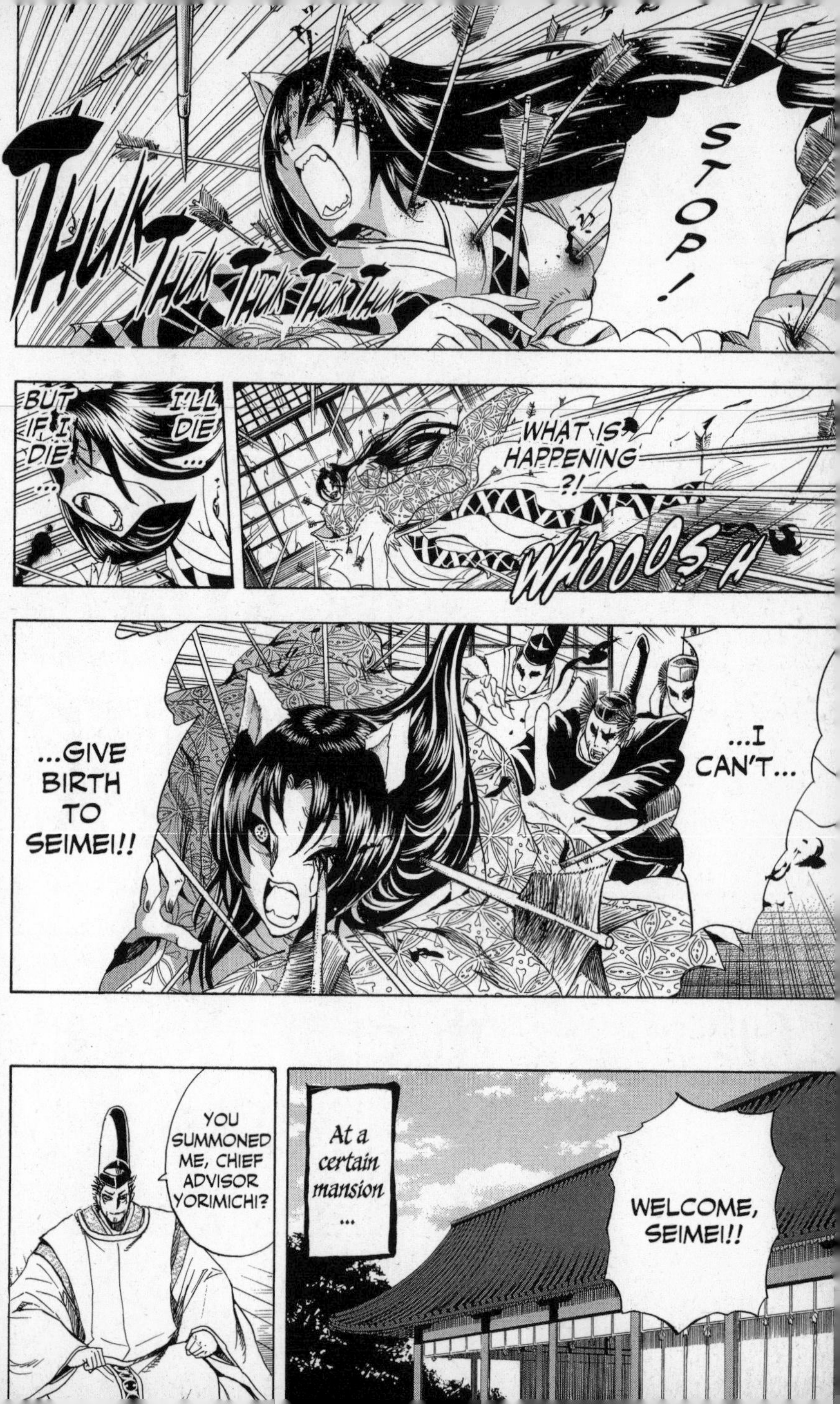
STOP!
THUK THUK THUK THUK THUK
WHAT IS HAPPENING?!
WHOOOSH
I'LL DIE...
BUT IF I DIE...
...I CAN'T...
...GIVE BIRTH TO SEIMEI!!
At a certain mansion...
WELCOME, SEIMEI!!
YOU SUMMONED ME, CHIEF ADVISOR YORIMICHI?

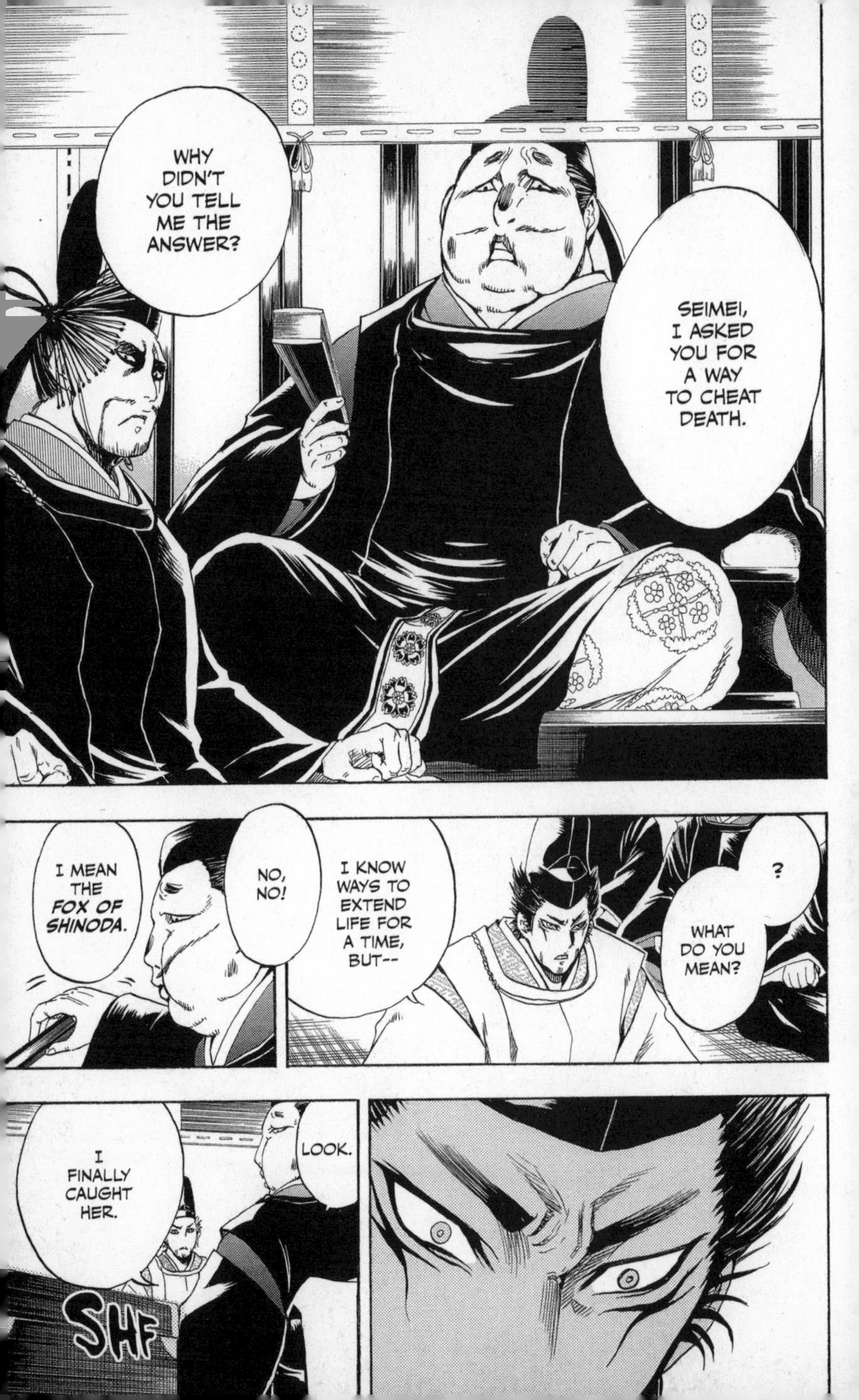
SEIMEI, I ASKED YOU FOR A WAY TO CHEAT DEATH.
WHY DIDN'T YOU TELL ME THE ANSWER?
?
WHAT DO YOU MEAN?
I KNOW WAYS TO EXTEND LIFE FOR A TIME, BUT--
NO, NO!
I MEAN THE *FOX OF SHINODA*.
LOOK.
I FINALLY CAUGHT HER.
SHF

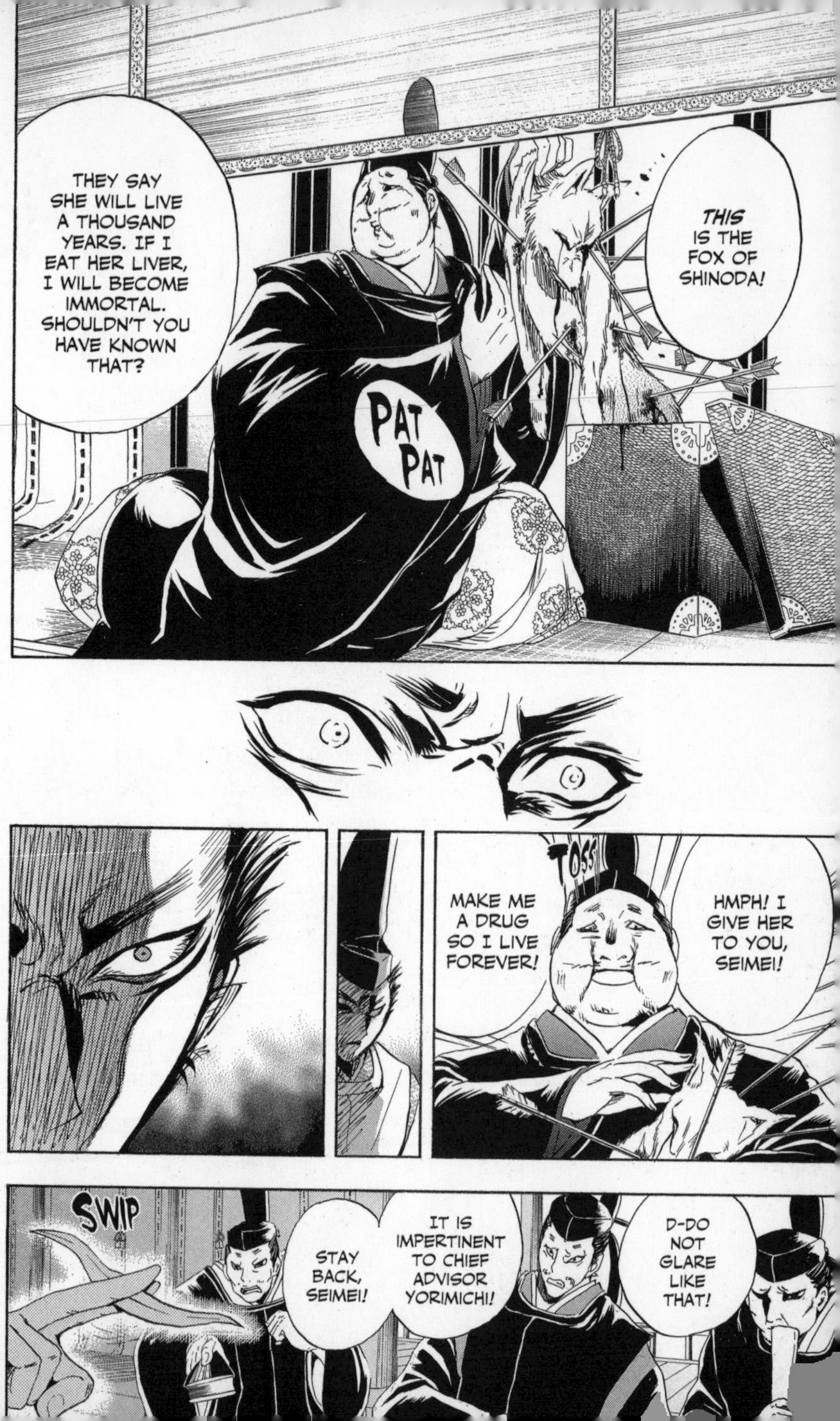
THIS IS THE FOX OF SHINODA!
THEY SAY SHE WILL LIVE A THOUSAND YEARS. IF I EAT HER LIVER, I WILL BECOME IMMORTAL. SHOULDN'T YOU HAVE KNOWN THAT?
PAT PAT
TOSS
HMPH! I GIVE HER TO YOU, SEIMEI!
MAKE ME A DRUG SO I LIVE FOREVER!
D-DO NOT GLARE LIKE THAT!
IT IS IMPERTINENT TO CHIEF ADVISOR YORIMICHI!
STAY BACK, SEIMEI!
SWIP

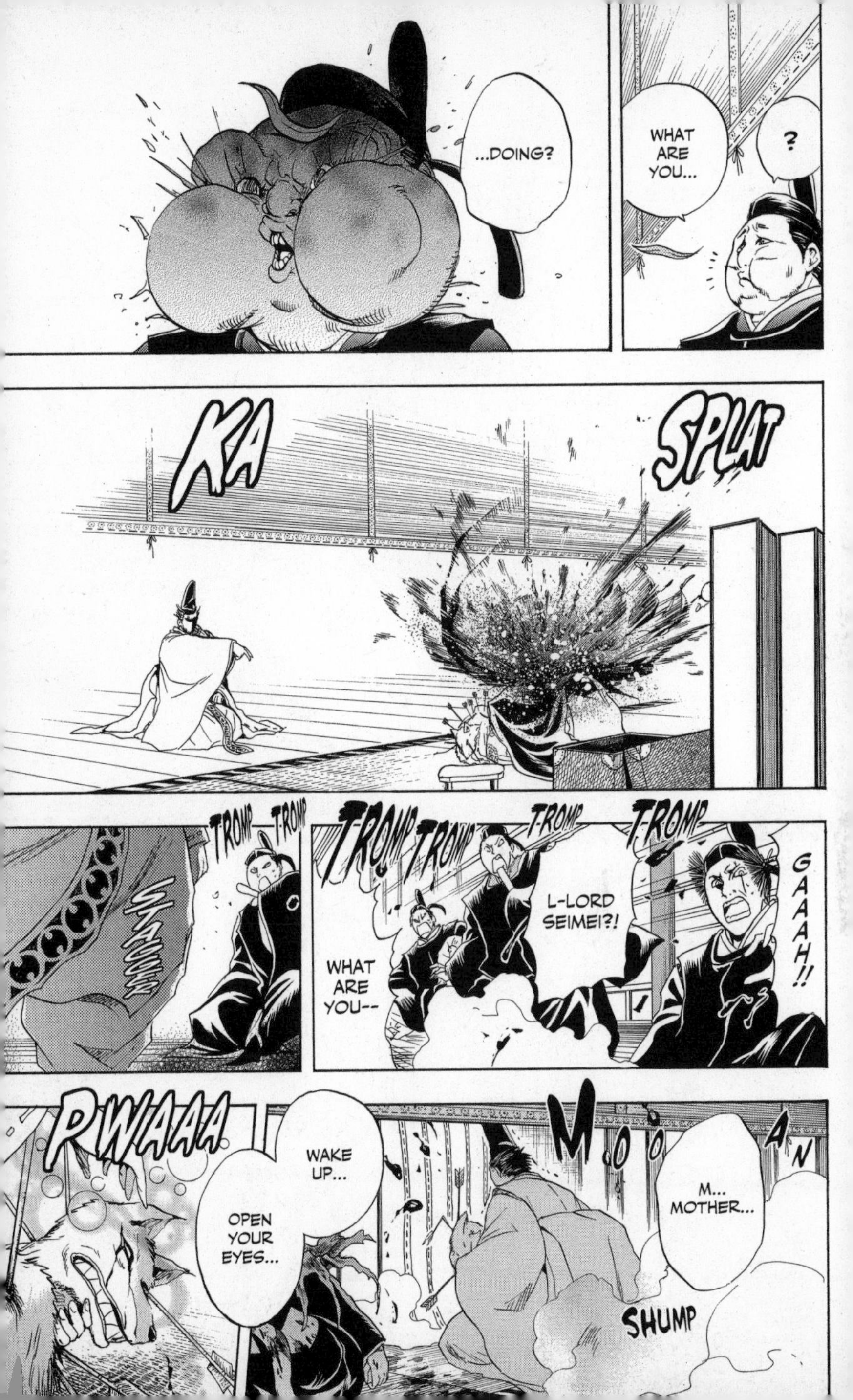
?
WHAT ARE YOU...
...DOING?
SPLAT
KA
GAAAH!!
T-TROMP
T-ROMP
L-LORD SEIMEI?!
TROMP TROMP
WHAT ARE YOU--
T-ROMP T-ROMP
AN
M... MOTHER...
MOOAN
SHUMP
WAKE UP...
OPEN YOUR EYES...
RWAAAA

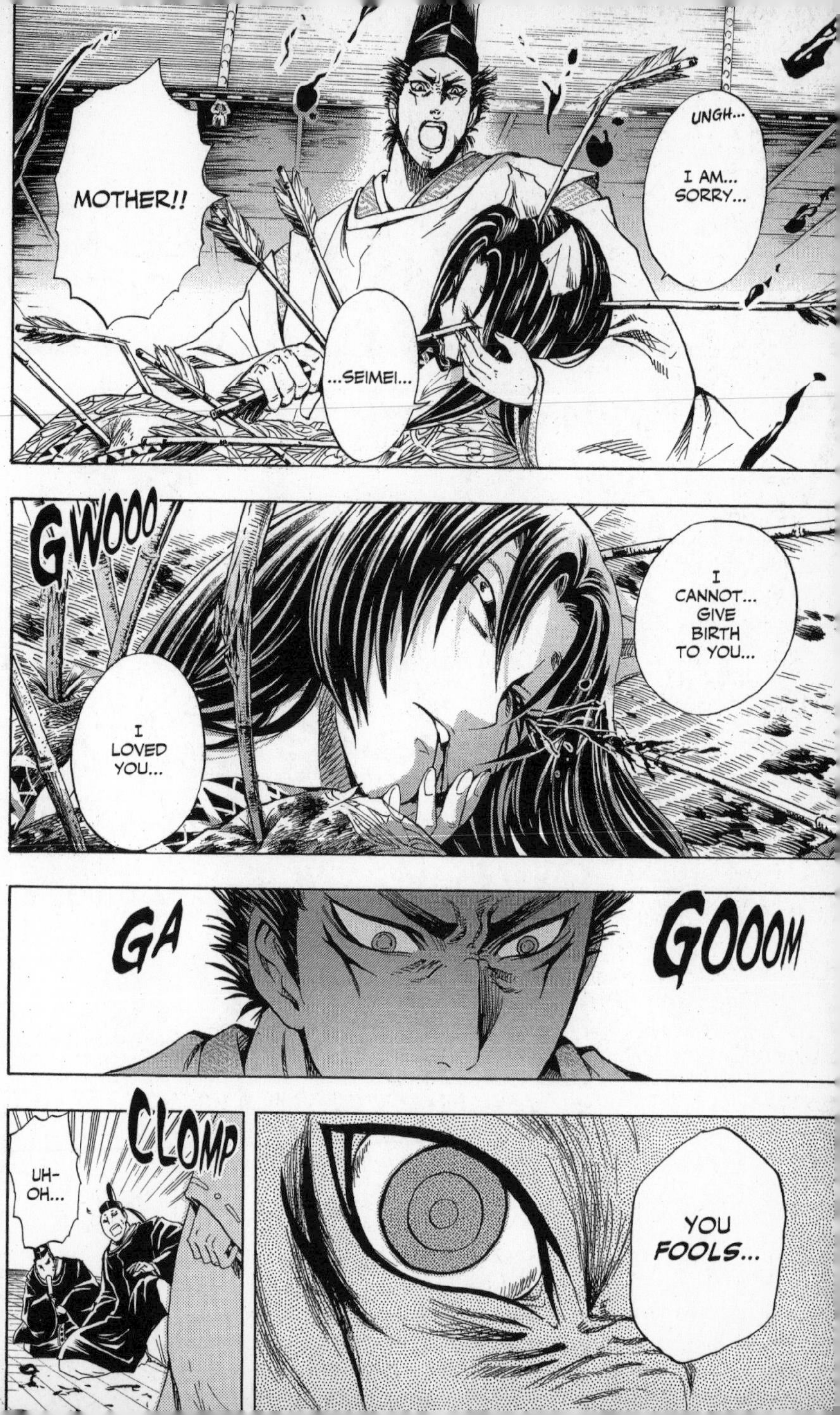
UNGH...
I AM... SORRY...
...SEIMEI...
MOTHER!!
I CANNOT... GIVE BIRTH TO YOU...
I LOVED YOU...
GWOOO
GA GOOOM
YOU FOOLS...
CLOMP
UH-OH...

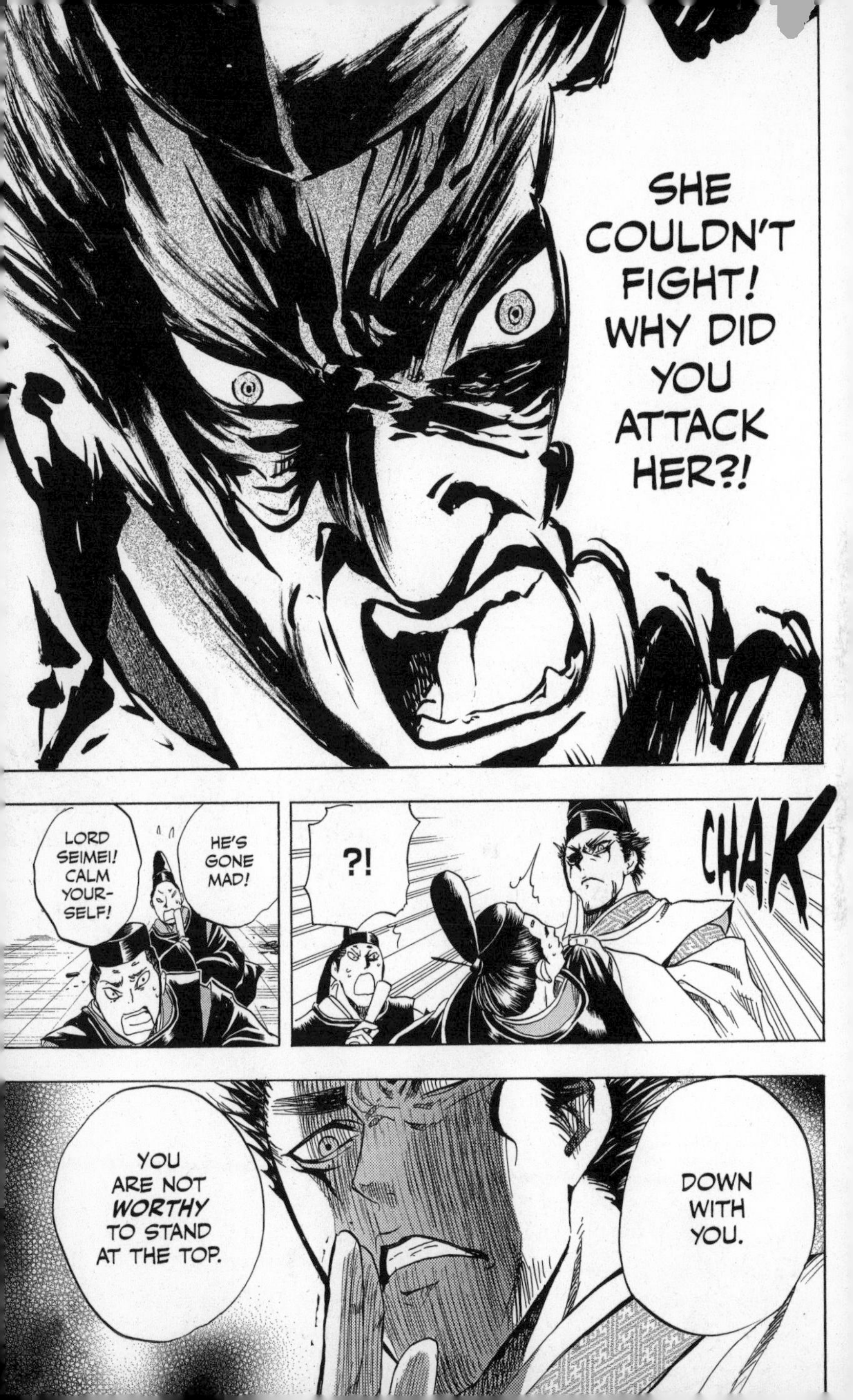
SHE COULDN'T FIGHT! WHY DID YOU ATTACK HER?!
CHAK
?!
HE'S GONE MAD!
LORD SEIMEI! CALM YOURSELF!
DOWN WITH YOU.
YOU ARE NOT *WORTHY* TO STAND AT THE TOP.

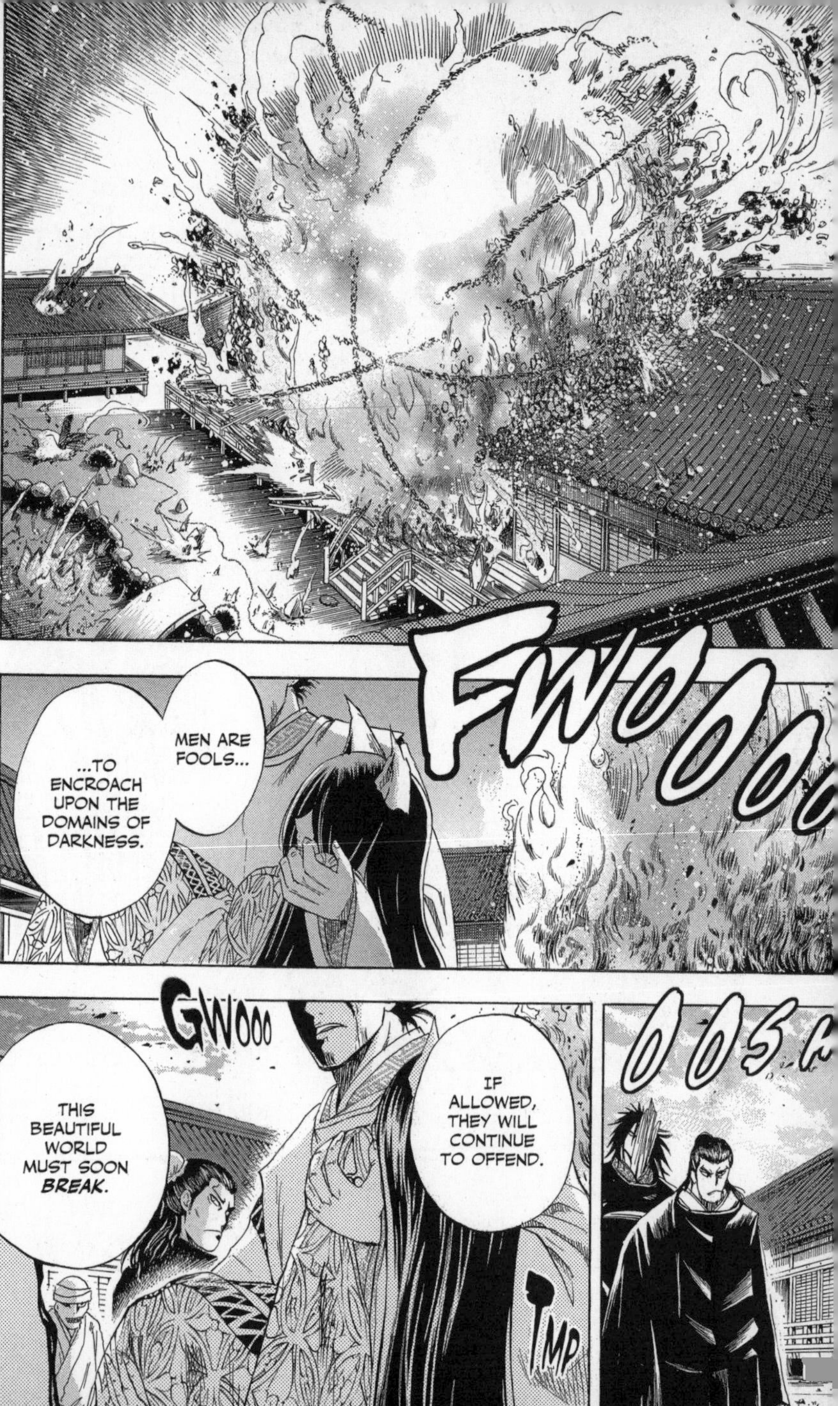
FWOOOO
MEN ARE FOOLS...
...TO ENCROACH UPON THE DOMAINS OF DARKNESS.
OOSH
GWOOO
IF ALLOWED, THEY WILL CONTINUE TO OFFEND.
THIS BEAUTIFUL WORLD MUST SOON *BREAK*.
TMP

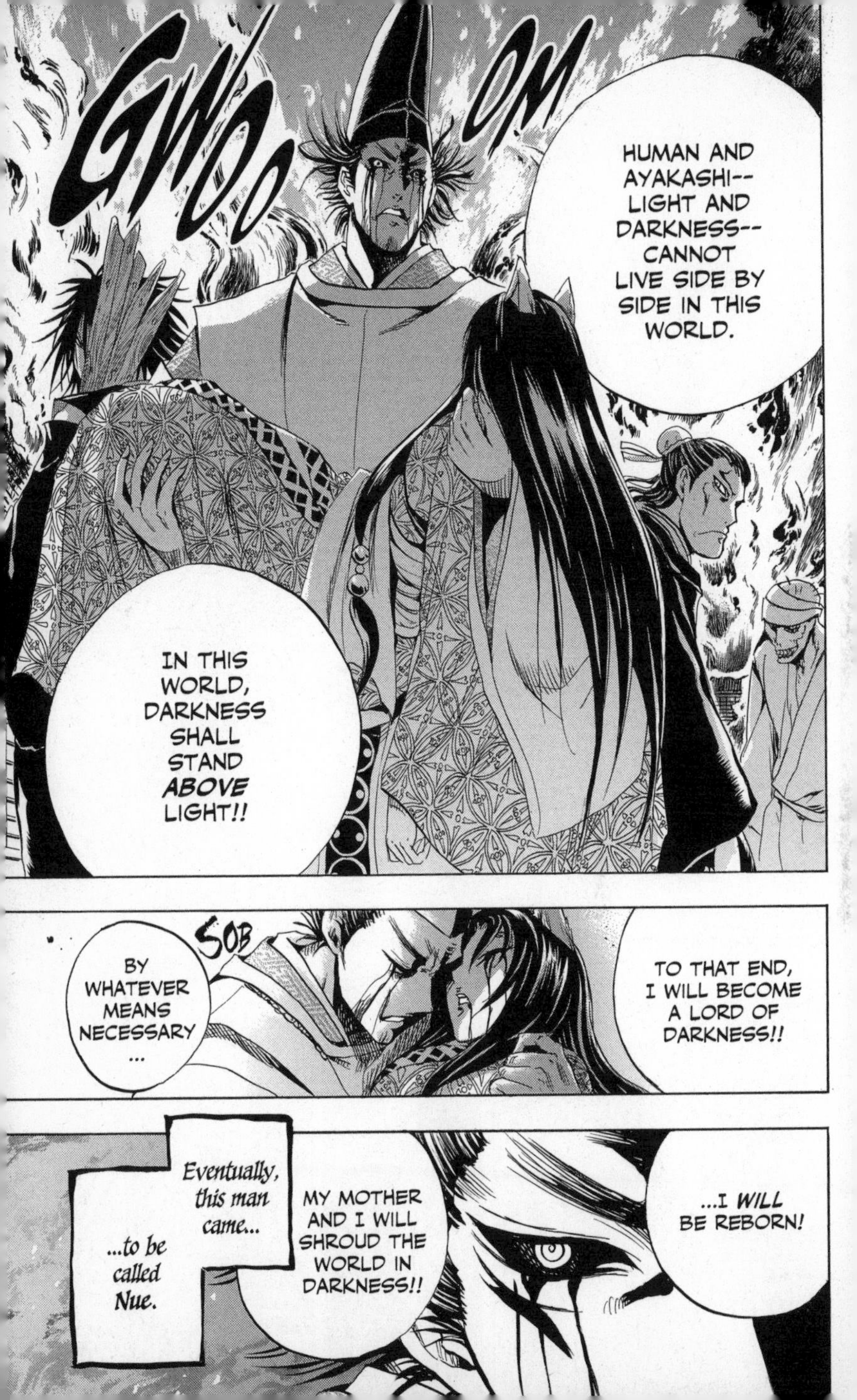
GWOOOM
HUMAN AND AYAKASHI-- LIGHT AND DARKNESS-- CANNOT LIVE SIDE BY SIDE IN THIS WORLD.
IN THIS WORLD, DARKNESS SHALL STAND *ABOVE* LIGHT!!
TO THAT END, I WILL BECOME A LORD OF DARKNESS!!
SOB
BY WHATEVER MEANS NECESSARY ...
...I *WILL* BE REBORN!
MY MOTHER AND I WILL SHROUD THE WORLD IN DARKNESS!!
Eventually, this man came...
*...to be called **Nue.***

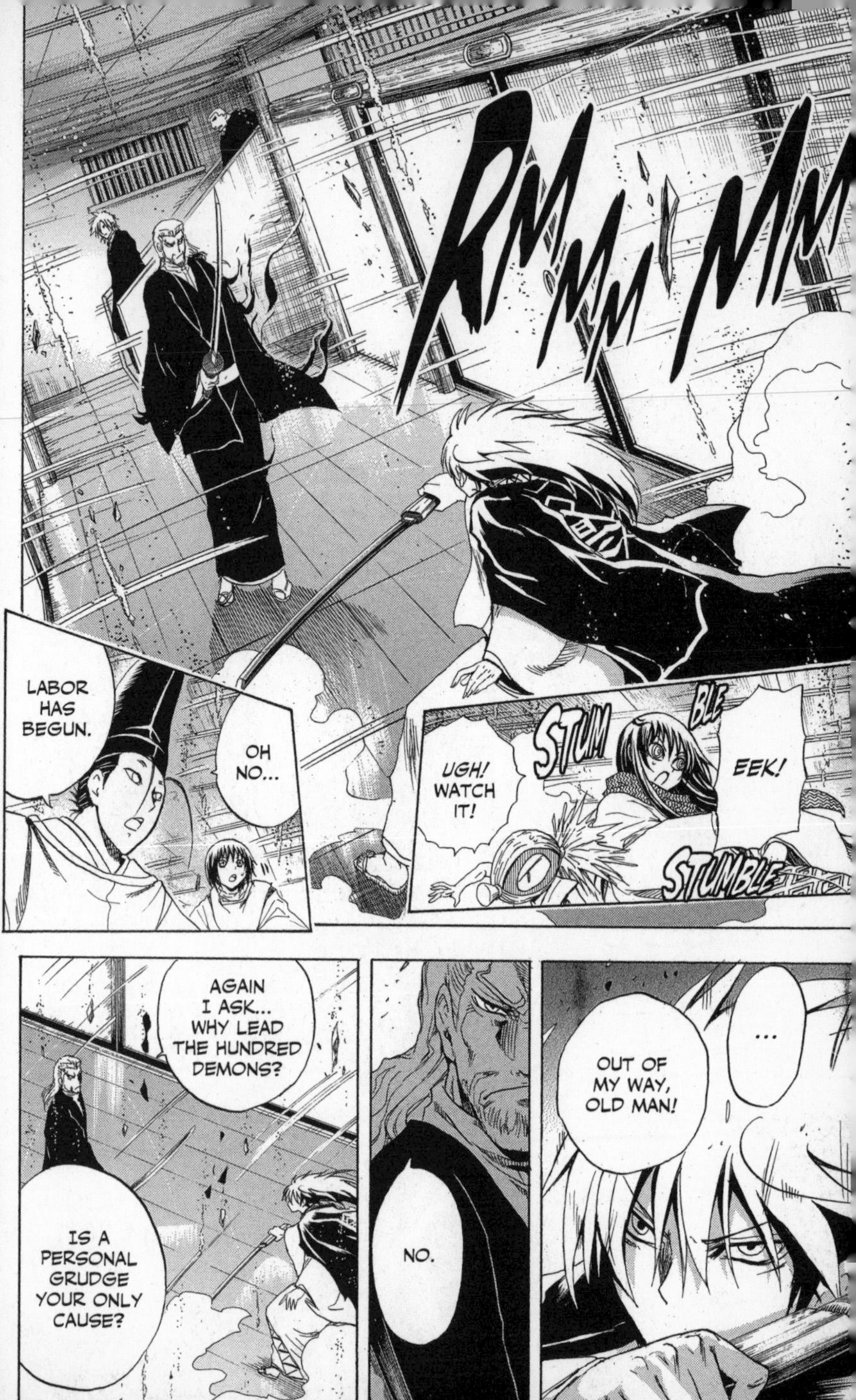
RMMMMM
STUMBLE
EEK!
UGH! WATCH IT!
STUMBLE
OH NO...
LABOR HAS BEGUN.
...
OUT OF MY WAY, OLD MAN!
NO.
AGAIN I ASK... WHY LEAD THE HUNDRED DEMONS?
IS A PERSONAL GRUDGE YOUR ONLY CAUSE?

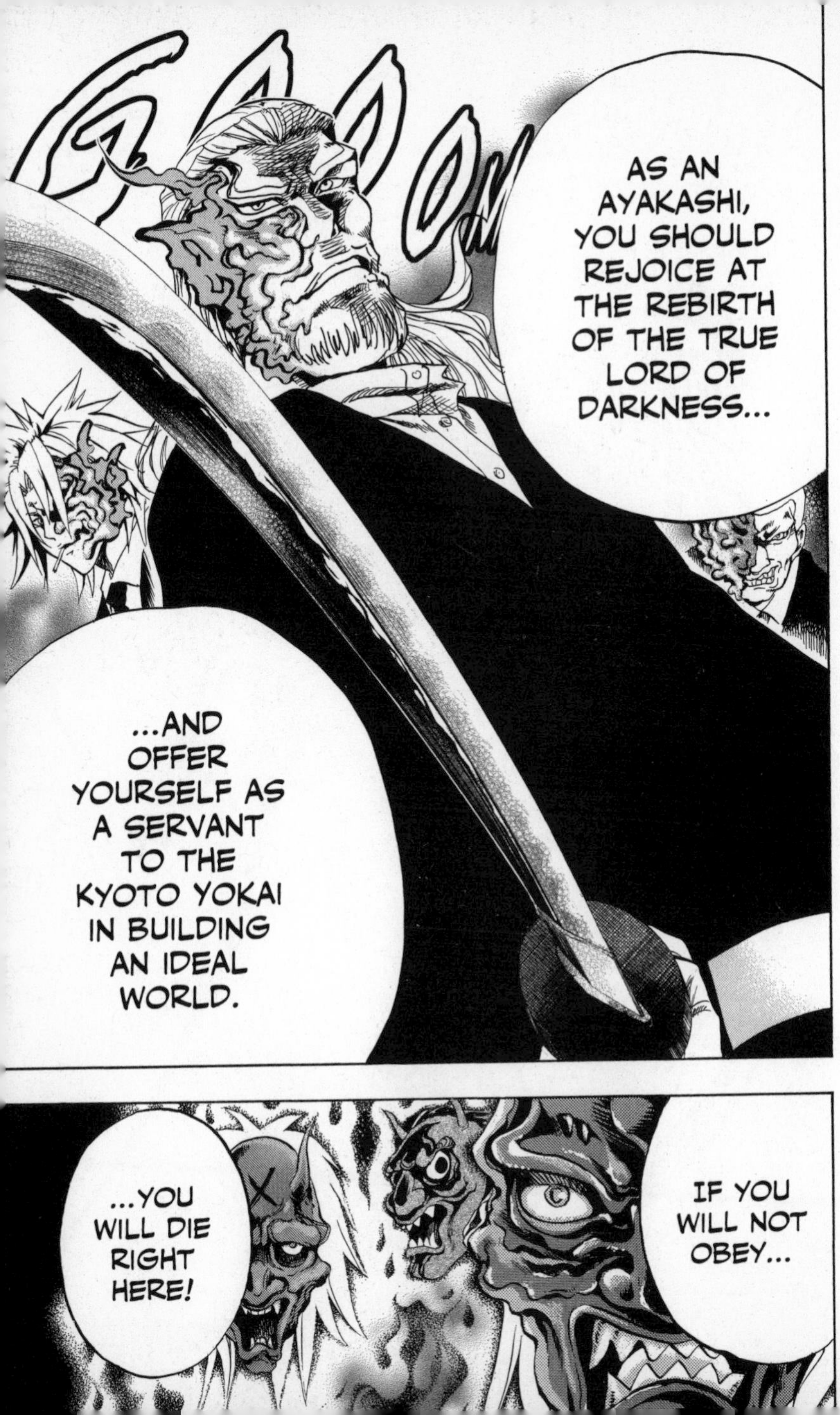
AS AN AYAKASHI, YOU SHOULD REJOICE AT THE REBIRTH OF THE TRUE LORD OF DARKNESS...
...AND OFFER YOURSELF AS A SERVANT TO THE KYOTO YOKAI IN BUILDING AN IDEAL WORLD.
IF YOU WILL NOT OBEY...
...YOU WILL DIE RIGHT HERE!

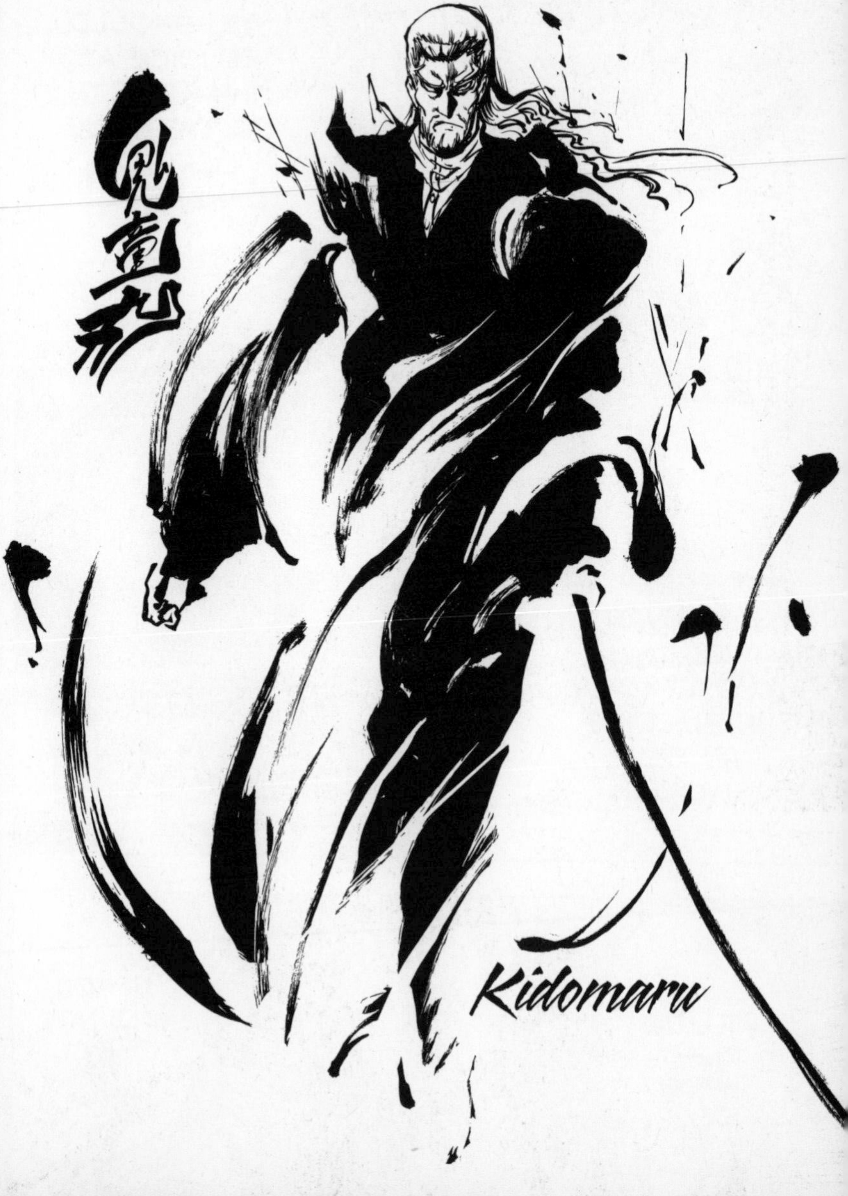
鬼童丸
Kidomaru

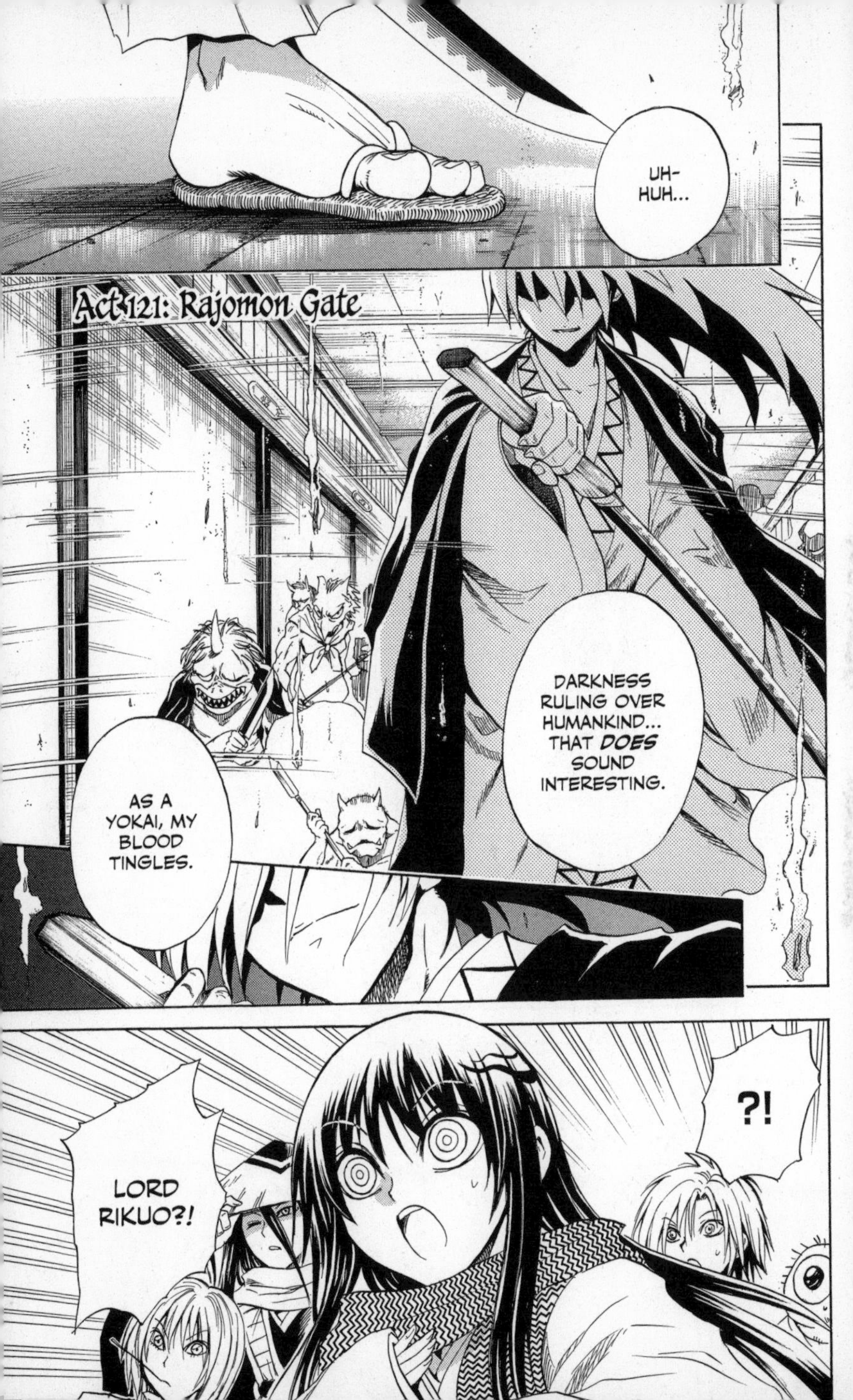
UH-HUH...
Act 121: Rajomon Gate
DARKNESS RULING OVER HUMANKIND... THAT DOES SOUND INTERESTING.
AS A YOKAI, MY BLOOD TINGLES.
?!
LORD RIKUO?!

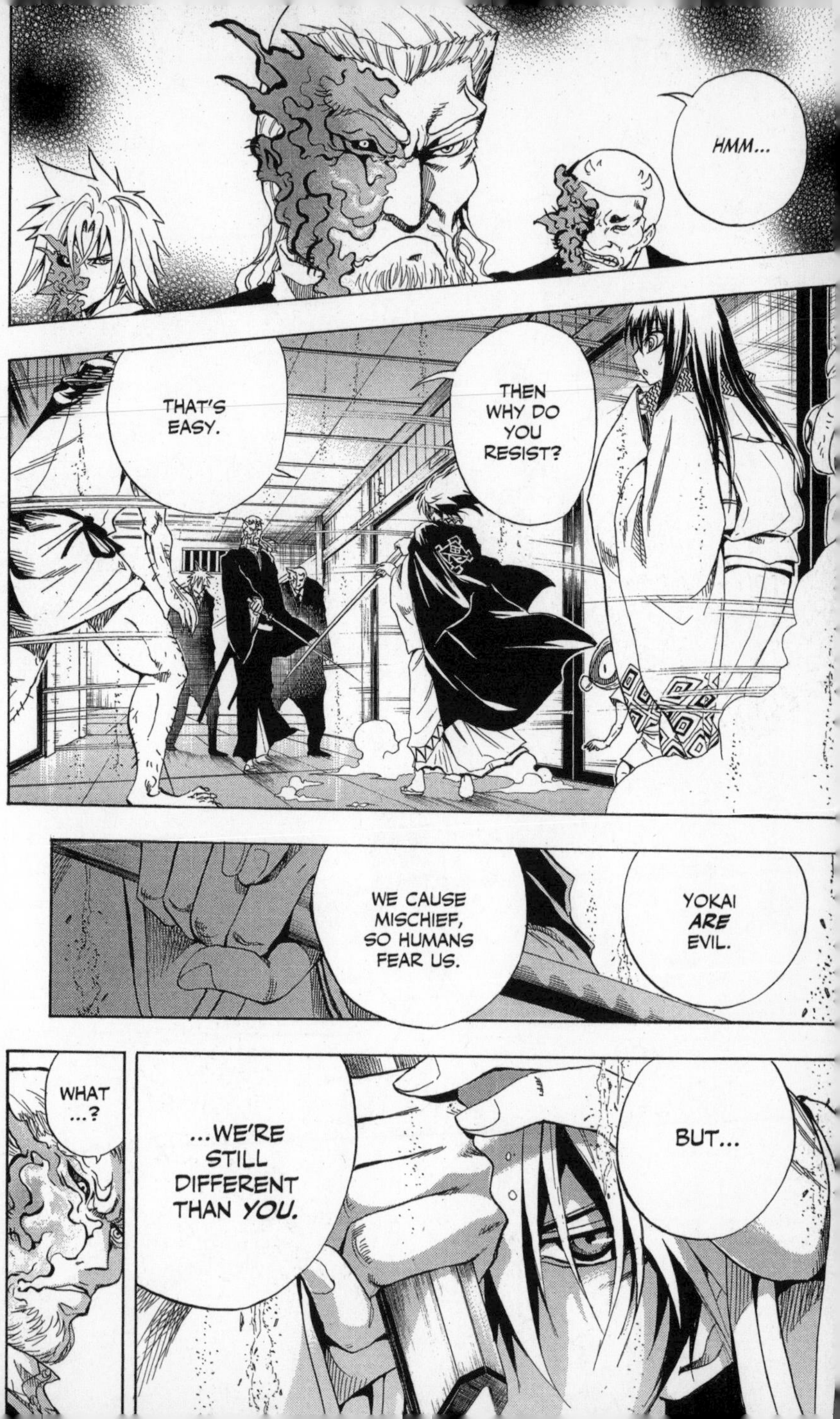
HMM...
THEN WHY DO YOU RESIST?
THAT'S EASY.
YOKAI *ARE* EVIL.
WE CAUSE MISCHIEF, SO HUMANS FEAR US.
BUT...
...WE'RE STILL DIFFERENT THAN *YOU.*
WHAT ...?

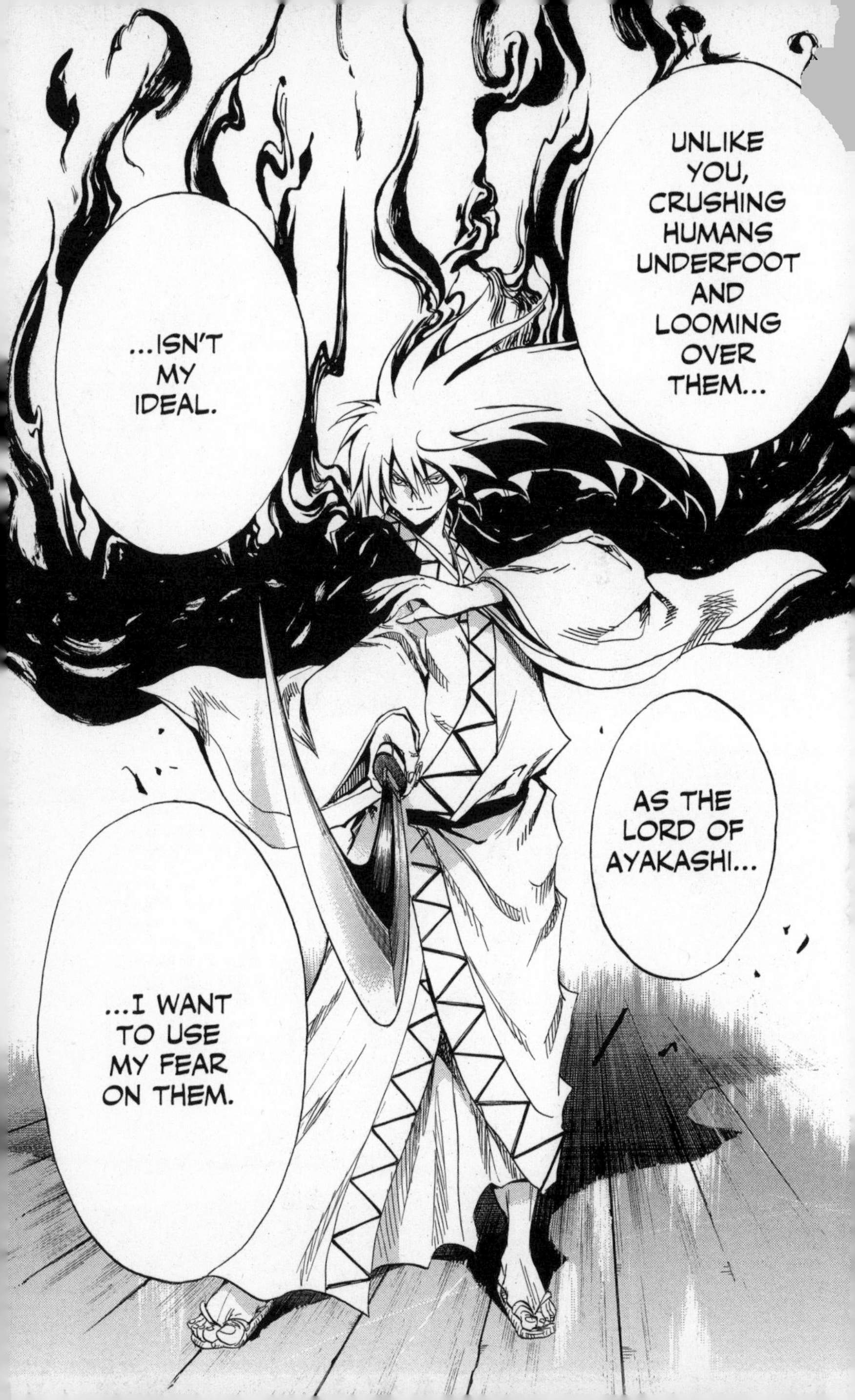
UNLIKE YOU, CRUSHING HUMANS UNDERFOOT AND LOOMING OVER THEM...
...ISN'T MY IDEAL.
AS THE LORD OF AYAKASHI...
...I WANT TO USE MY FEAR ON THEM.

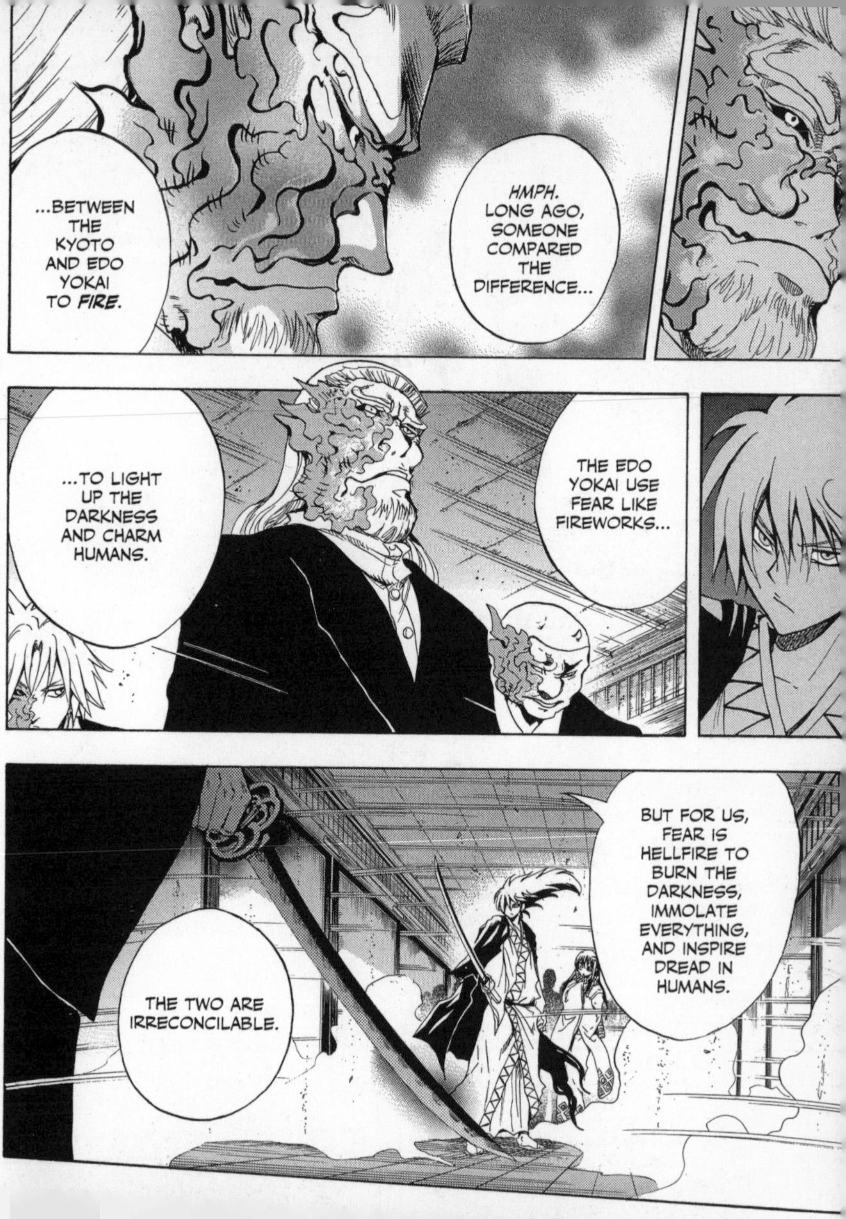
HMPH. LONG AGO, SOMEONE COMPARED THE DIFFERENCE...
...BETWEEN THE KYOTO AND EDO YOKAI TO *FIRE*.
THE EDO YOKAI USE FEAR LIKE FIREWORKS...
...TO LIGHT UP THE DARKNESS AND CHARM HUMANS.
BUT FOR US, FEAR IS HELLFIRE TO BURN THE DARKNESS, IMMOLATE EVERYTHING, AND INSPIRE DREAD IN HUMANS.
THE TWO ARE IRRECONCILABLE.

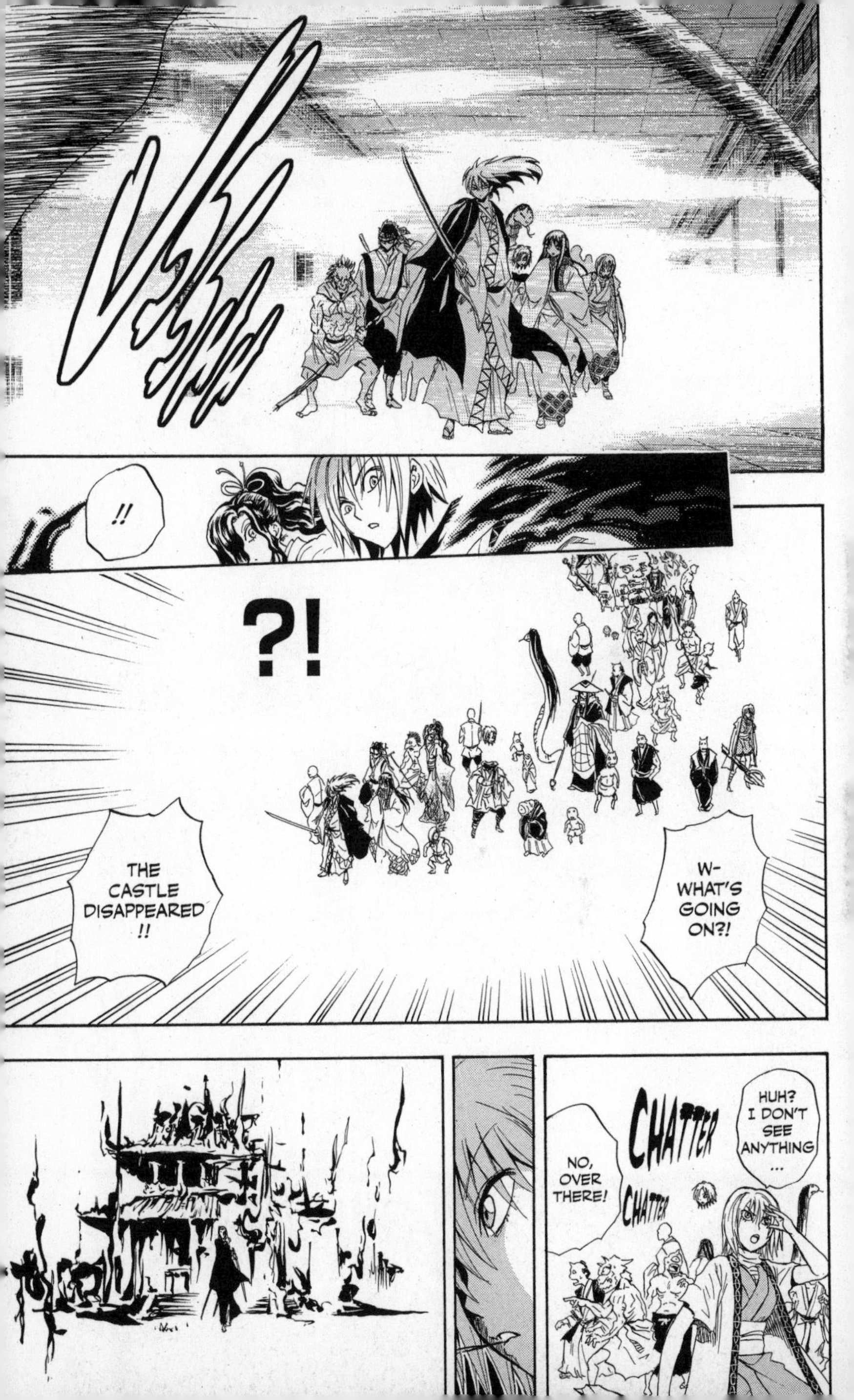
!!
W-WHAT'S GOING ON?!
?!
THE CASTLE DISAPPEARED!!
HUH? I DON'T SEE ANYTHING...
CHATTER
CHATTER
NO, OVER THERE!

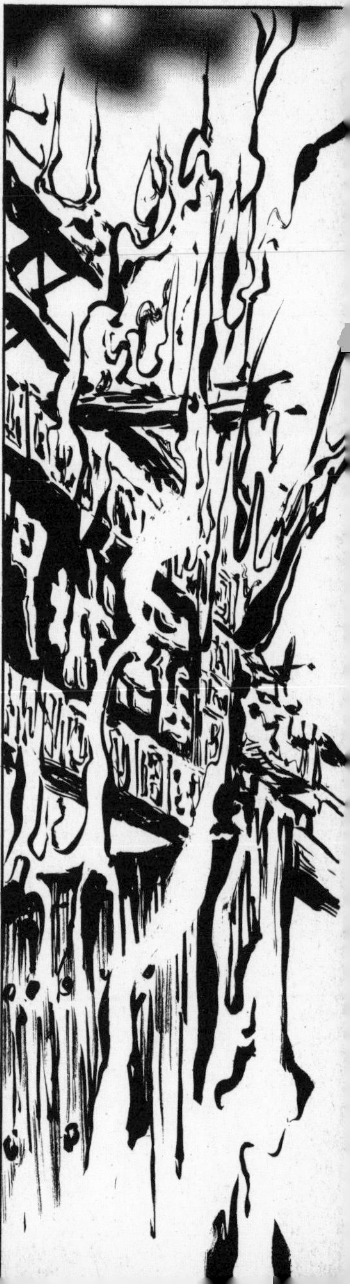

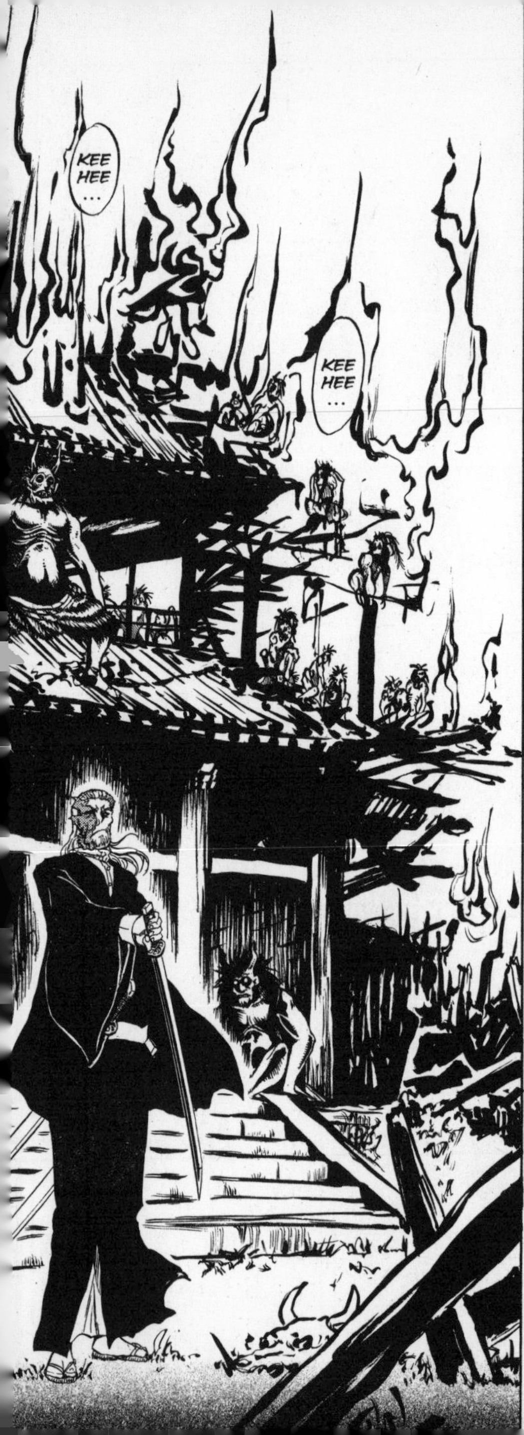
KEE HEE ...
KEE HEE ...

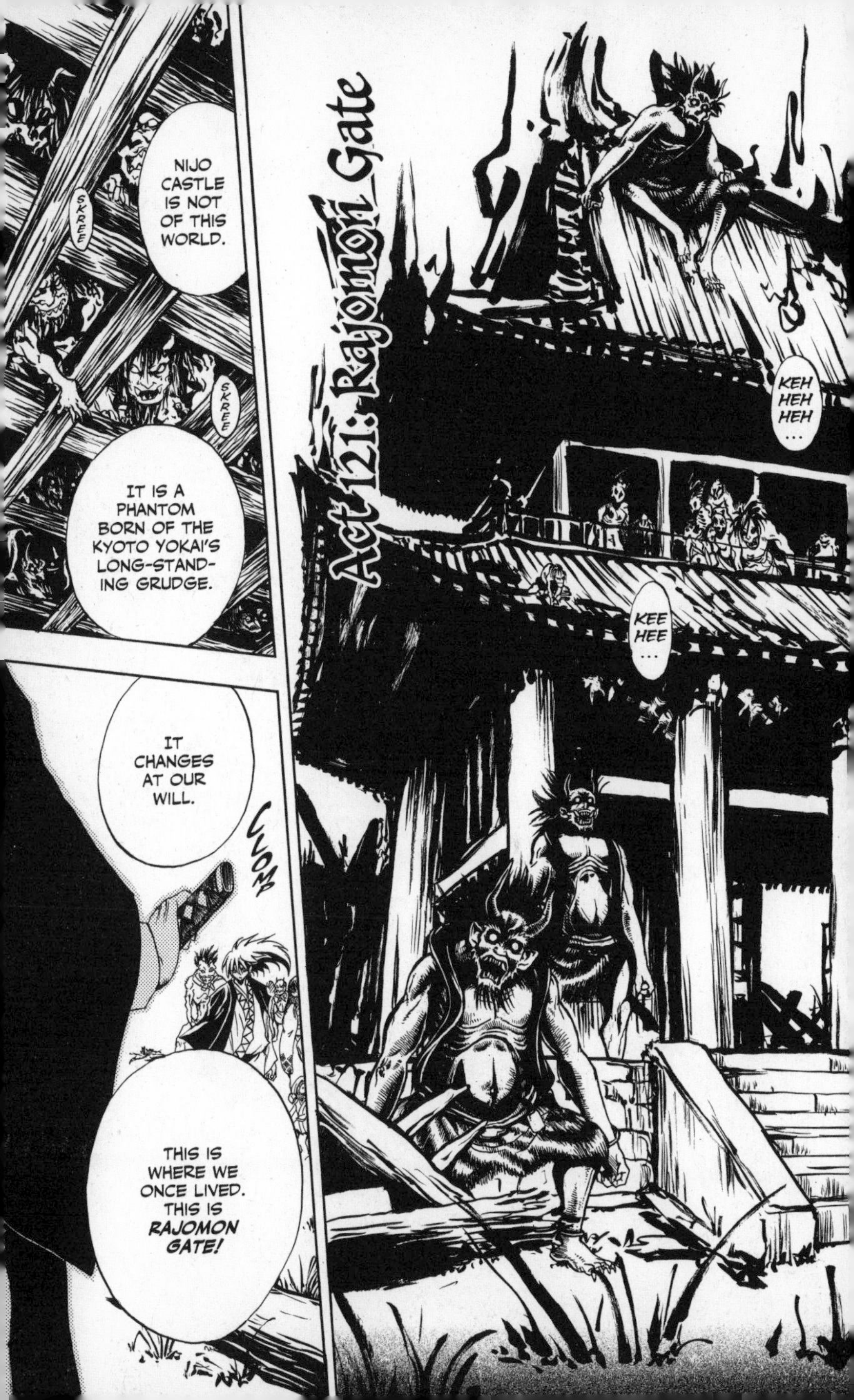
Act 121: Rajomon Gate
KEH HEH HEH ...
KEE HEE ...
NIJO CASTLE IS NOT OF THIS WORLD.
SKREE
SKREE
IT IS A PHANTOM BORN OF THE KYOTO YOKAI'S LONG-STANDING GRUDGE.
IT CHANGES AT OUR WILL.
VWOM
THIS IS WHERE WE ONCE LIVED. THIS IS *RAJOMON GATE!*

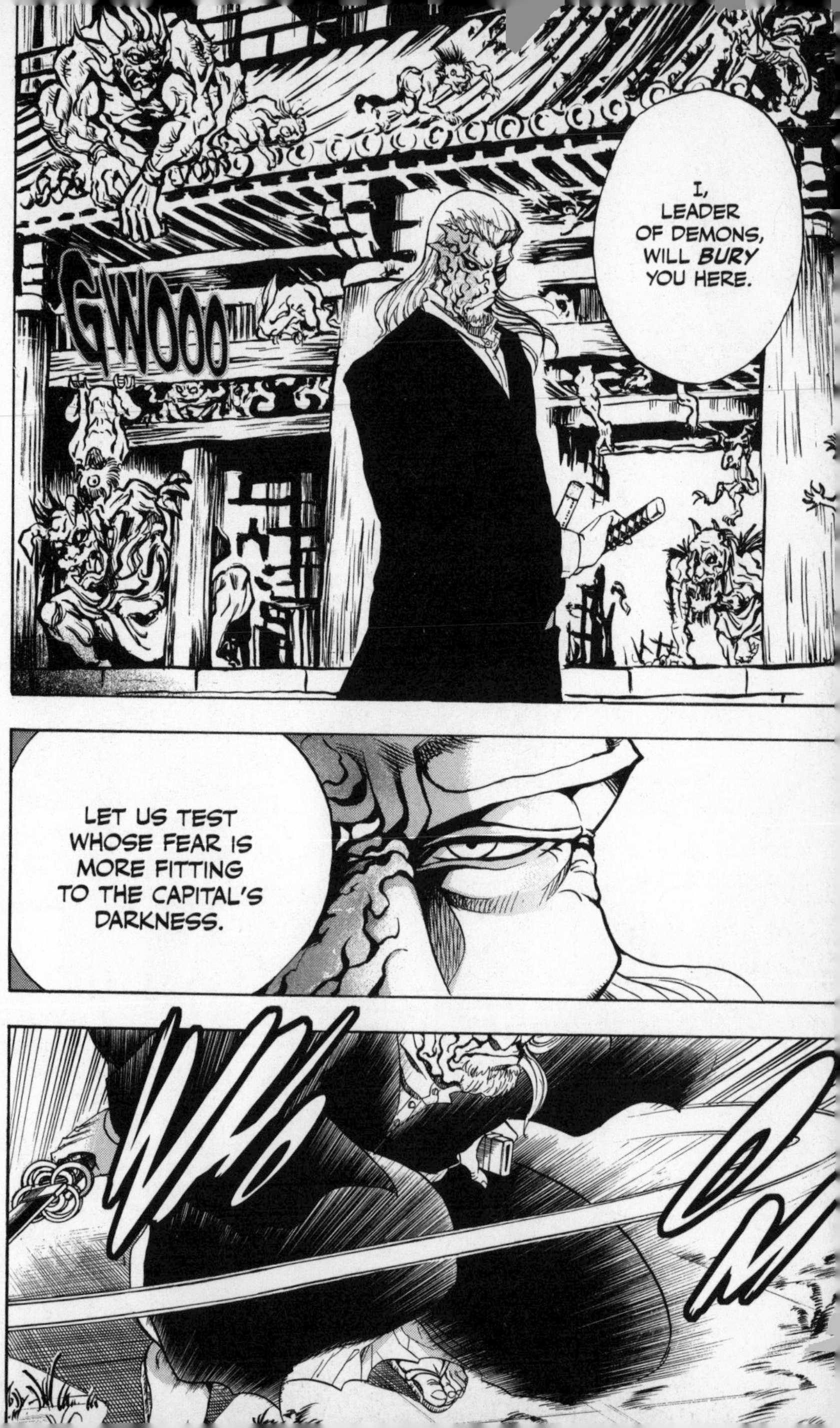
I, LEADER OF DEMONS, WILL *BURY* YOU HERE.
GWOOO
LET US TEST WHOSE FEAR IS MORE FITTING TO THE CAPITAL'S DARKNESS.

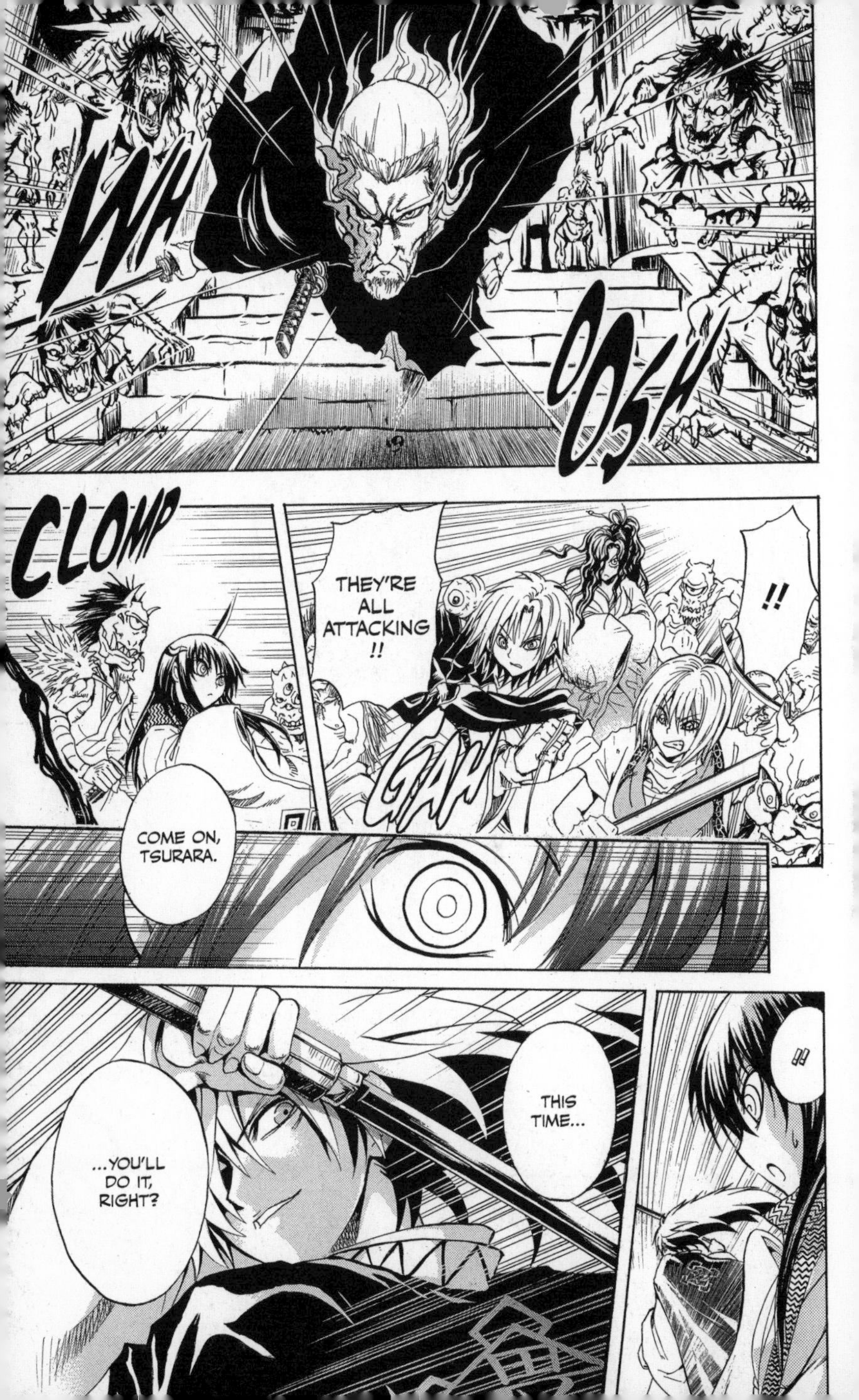
WH
OOSH
!!
THEY'RE ALL ATTACKING !!
GAAH
CLOMP
COME ON, TSURARA.
!!
THIS TIME...
...YOU'LL DO IT, RIGHT?

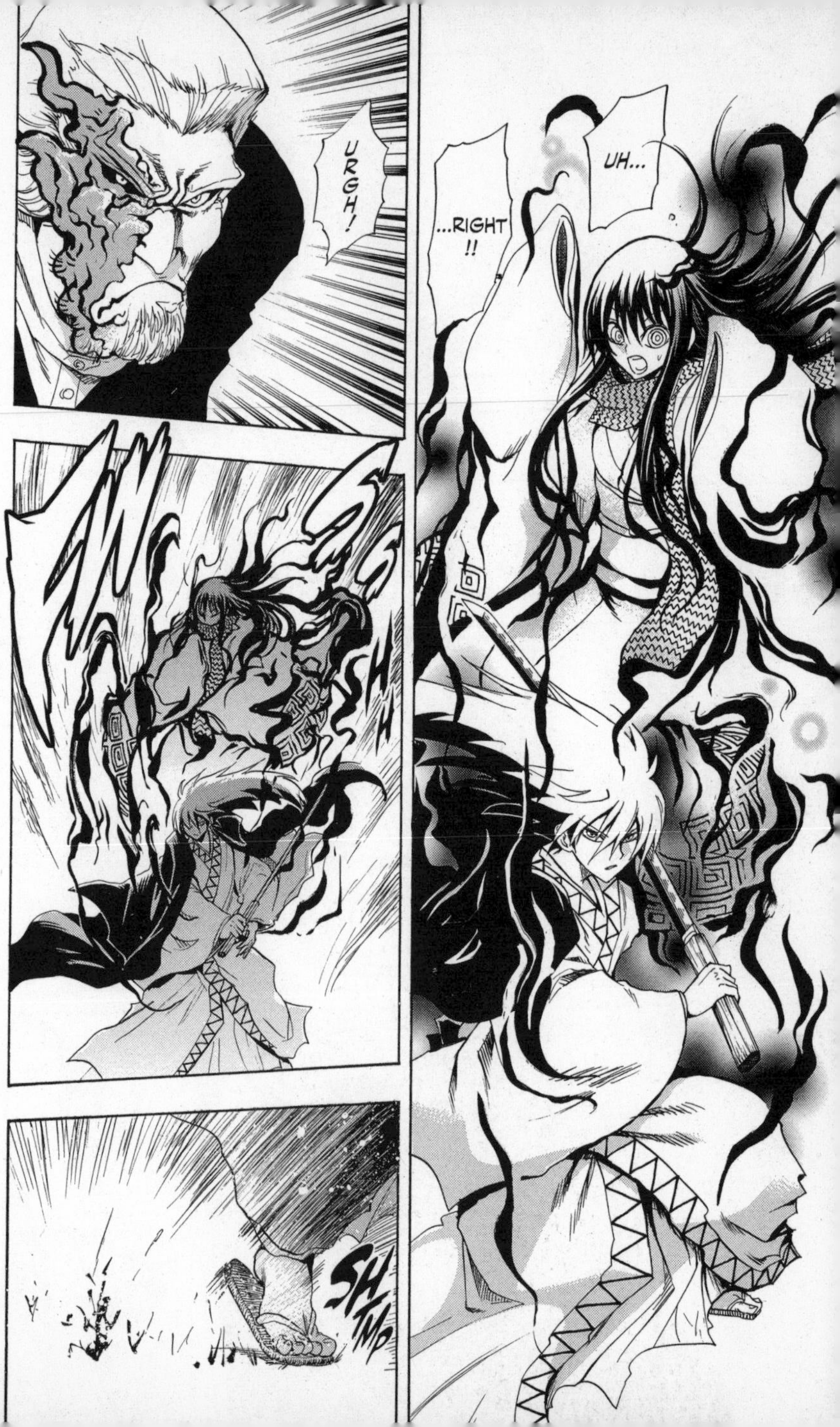
UH...
...RIGHT !!
URGH!
SHTMP

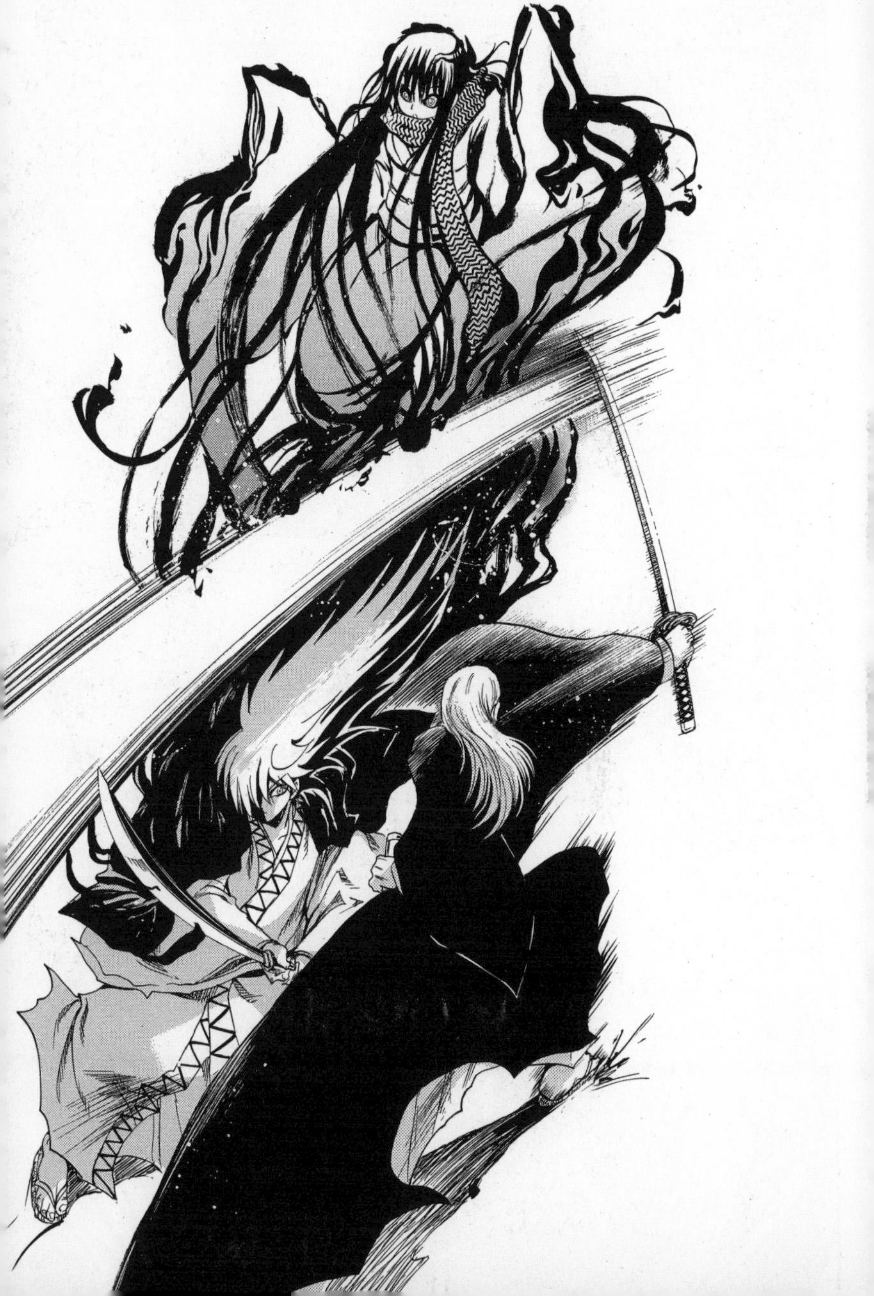

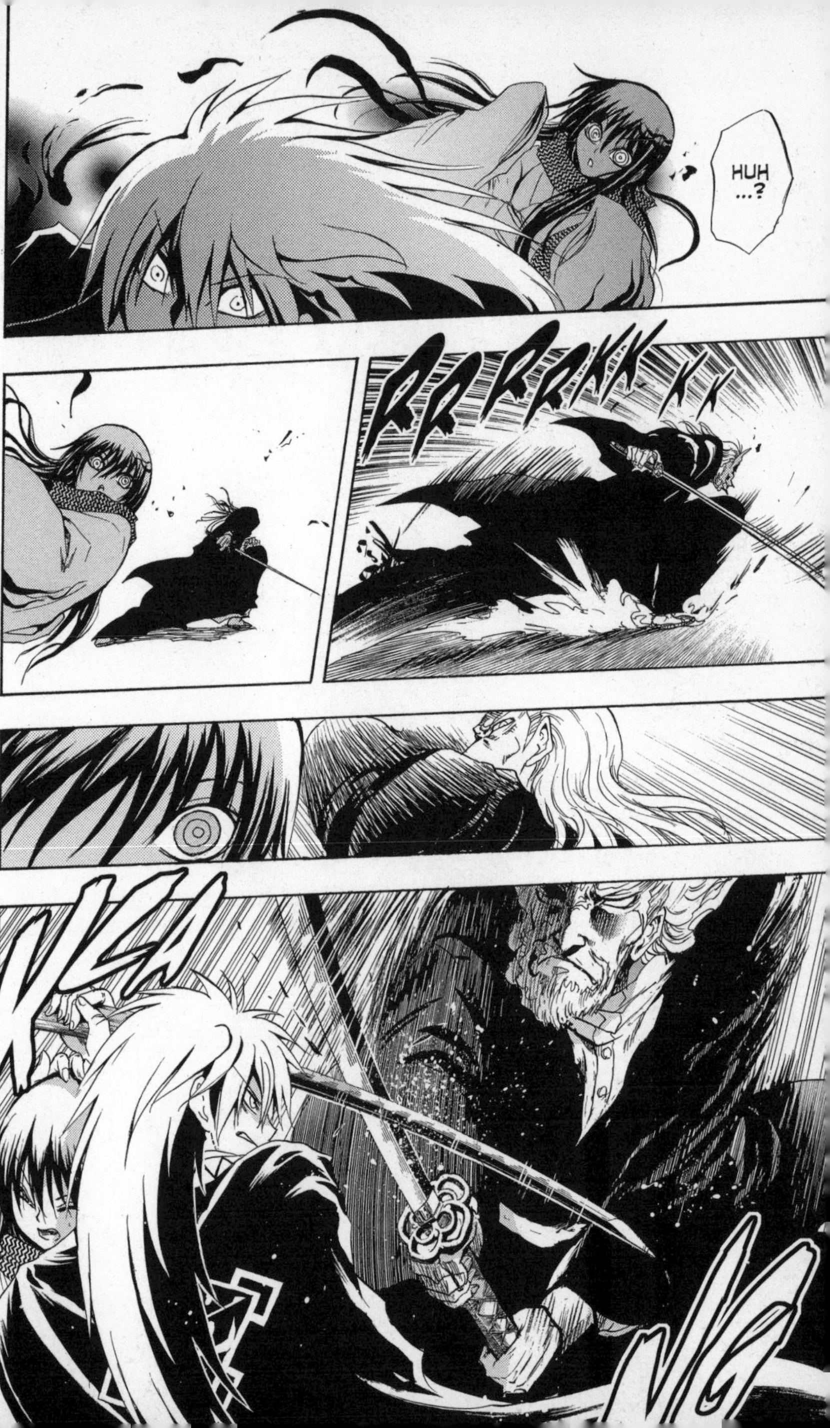
HUH ...?

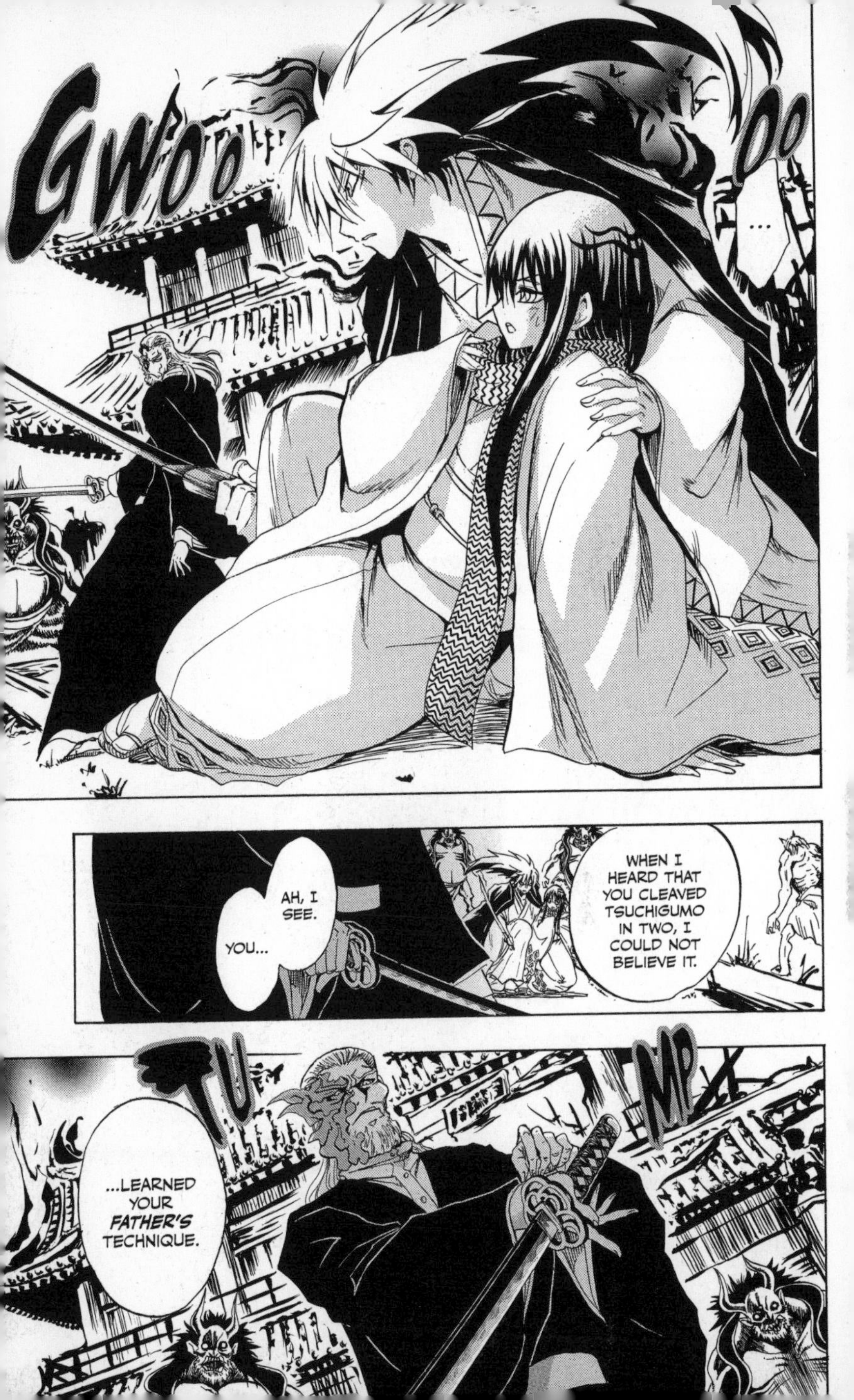
GWOOOO
...
WHEN I HEARD THAT YOU CLEAVED TSUCHIGUMO IN TWO, I COULD NOT BELIEVE IT.
AH, I SEE.
YOU...
TUMP
...LEARNED YOUR *FATHER'S* TECHNIQUE.

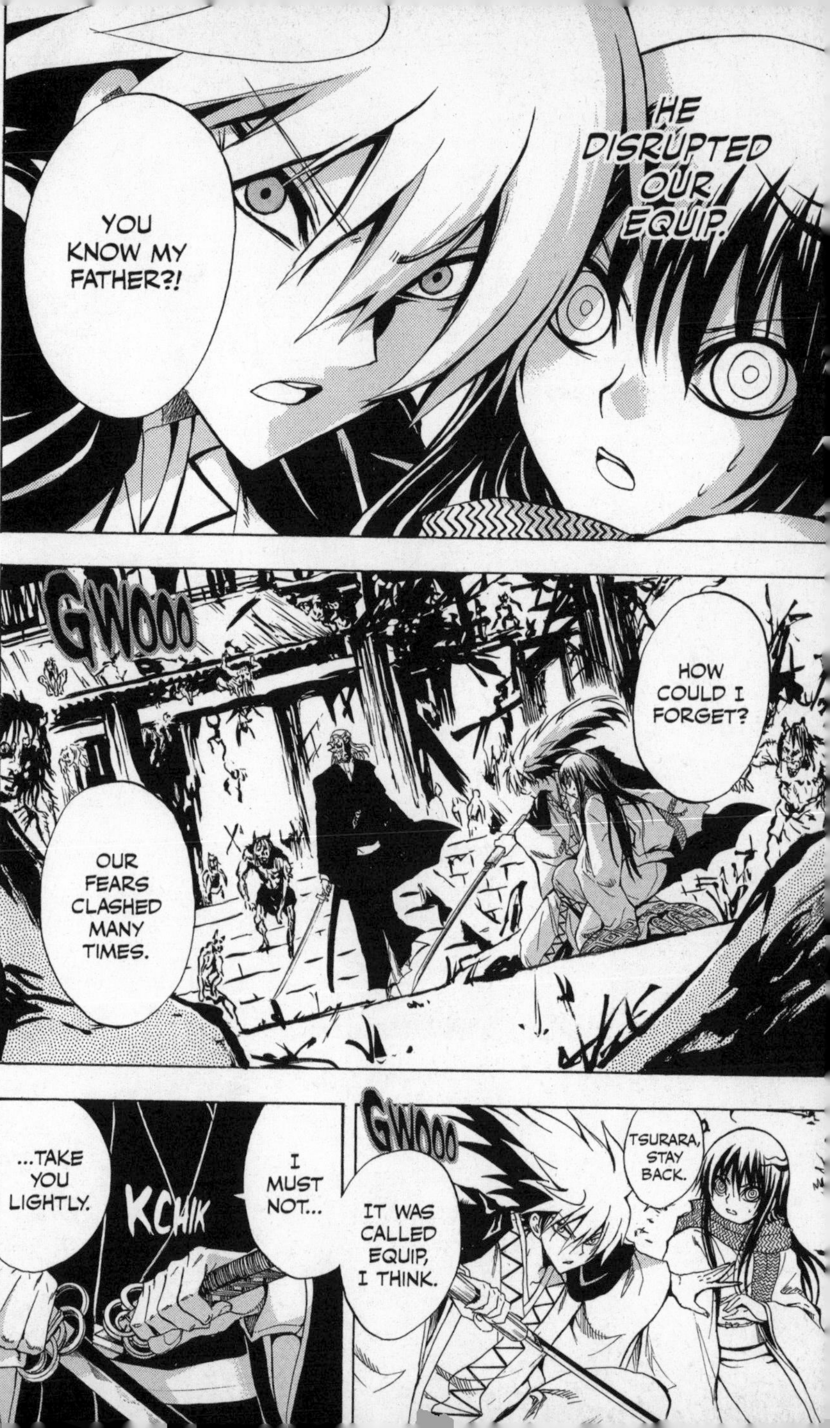
HE DISRUPTED OUR EQUIP.
YOU KNOW MY FATHER?!
HOW COULD I FORGET?
GWOOO
OUR FEARS CLASHED MANY TIMES.
GWOOO
TSURARA, STAY BACK.
IT WAS CALLED EQUIP, I THINK.
I MUST NOT...
KCHIK
...TAKE YOU LIGHTLY.

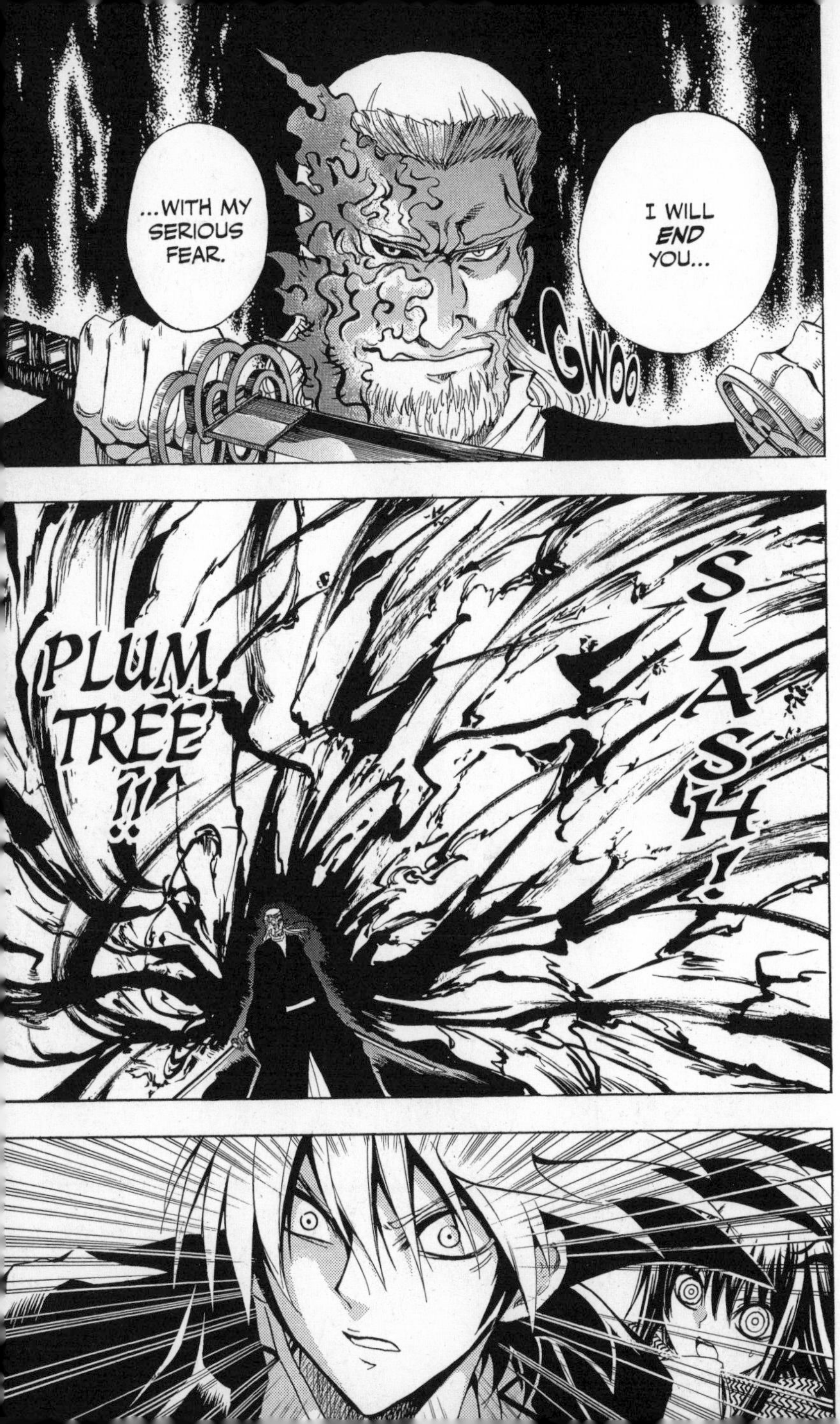
I WILL END YOU...
GWOO
...WITH MY SERIOUS FEAR.
SLASH!
PLUM TREE !!

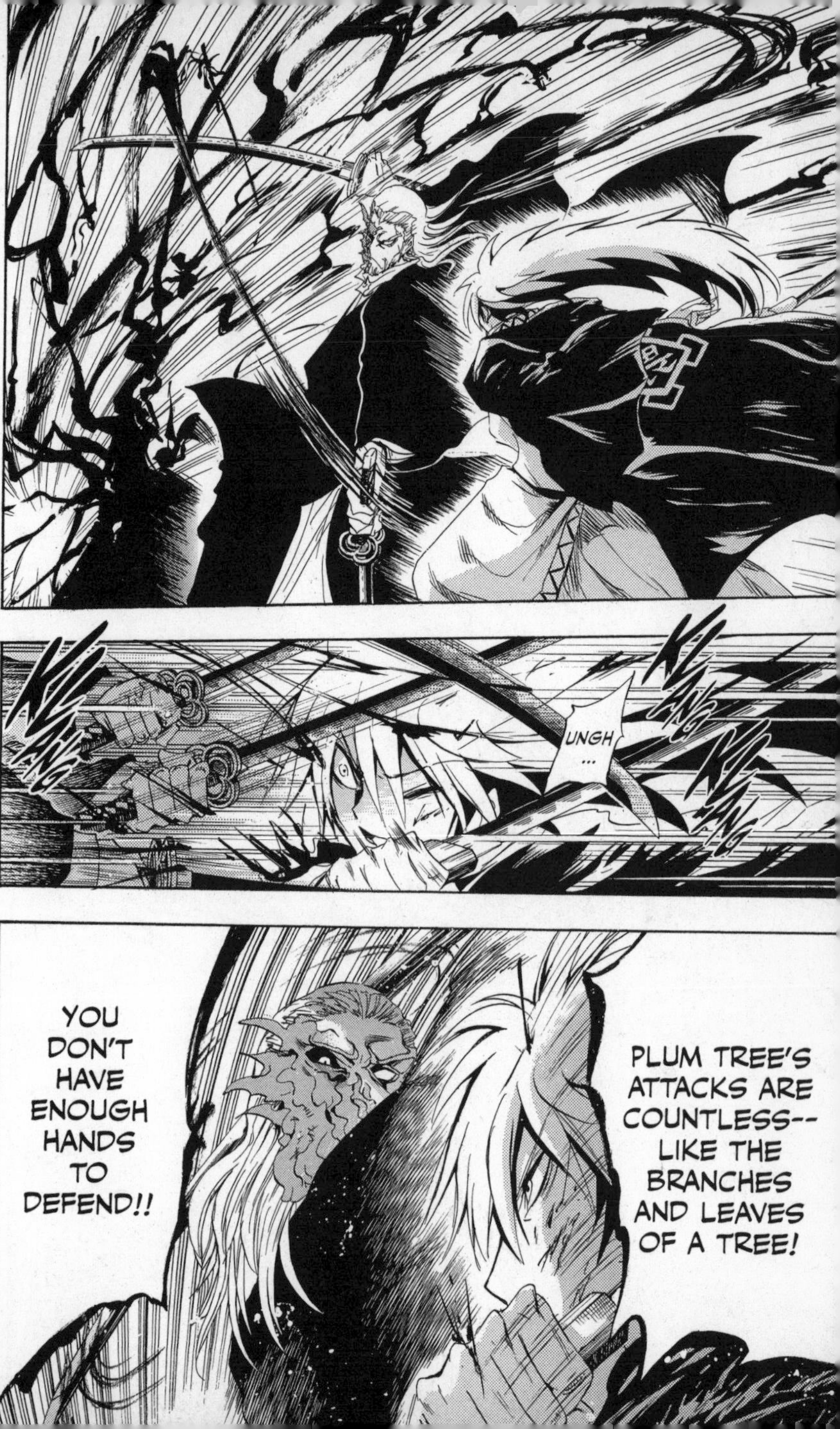
KWANG KWANG
UNGH ...
KWANG
PLUM TREE'S ATTACKS ARE COUNTLESS-- LIKE THE BRANCHES AND LEAVES OF A TREE!
YOU DON'T HAVE ENOUGH HANDS TO DEFEND!!

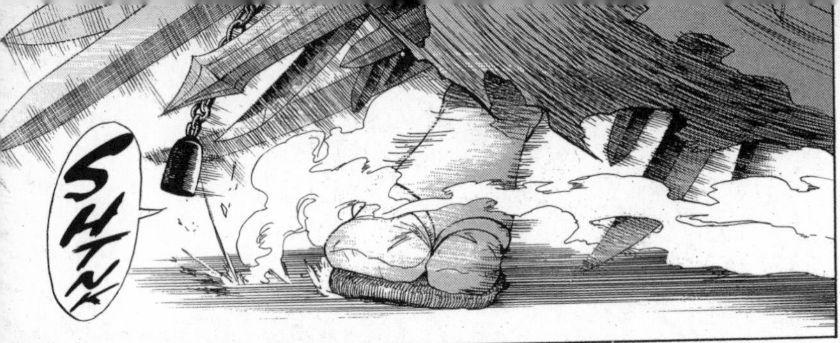
SHINK
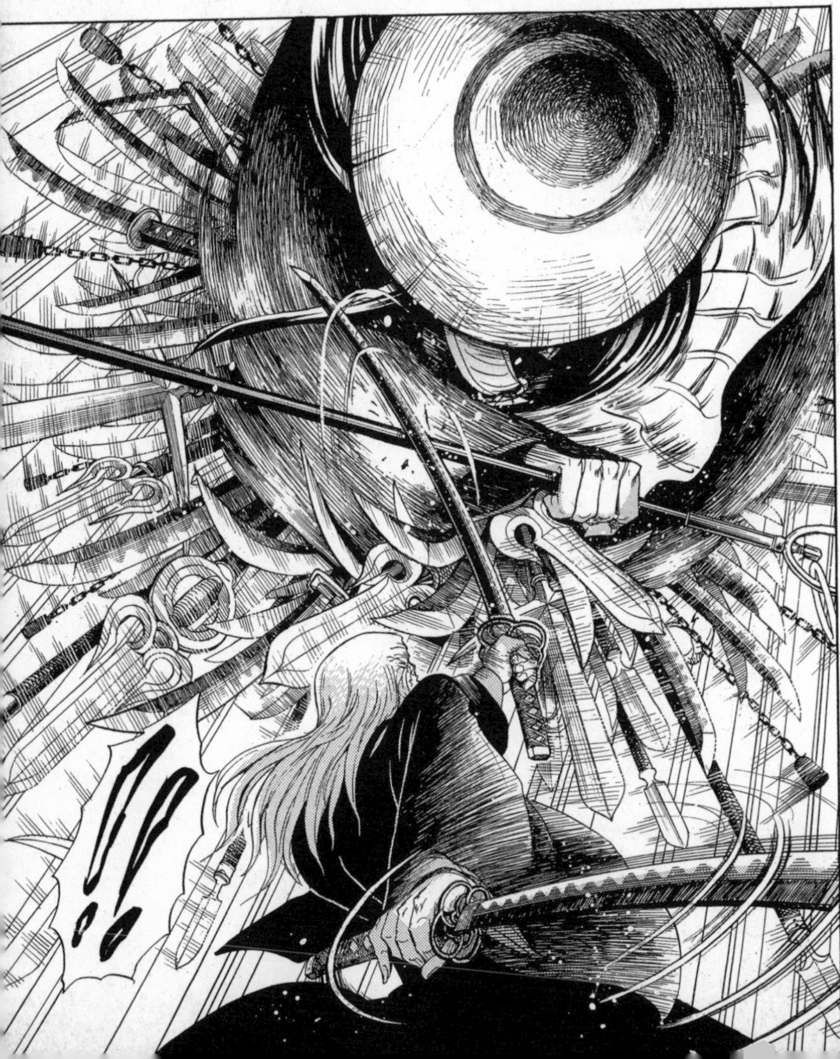
!!

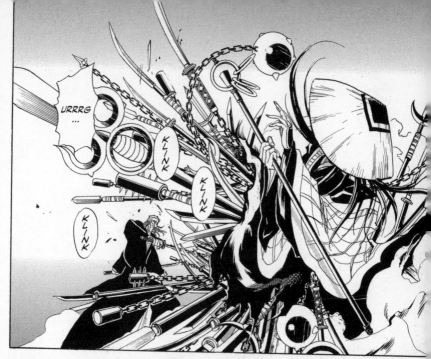

URRRG
...

KLINK

KLINK

KLINK

TRMBL

TRMBL

TRMBL

LORD RIKUO, IT APPEARS YOU HAVE LEARNED EQUIP.

I'M SURPRISED. SUCH GROWTH FOR ONE ONLY 12.

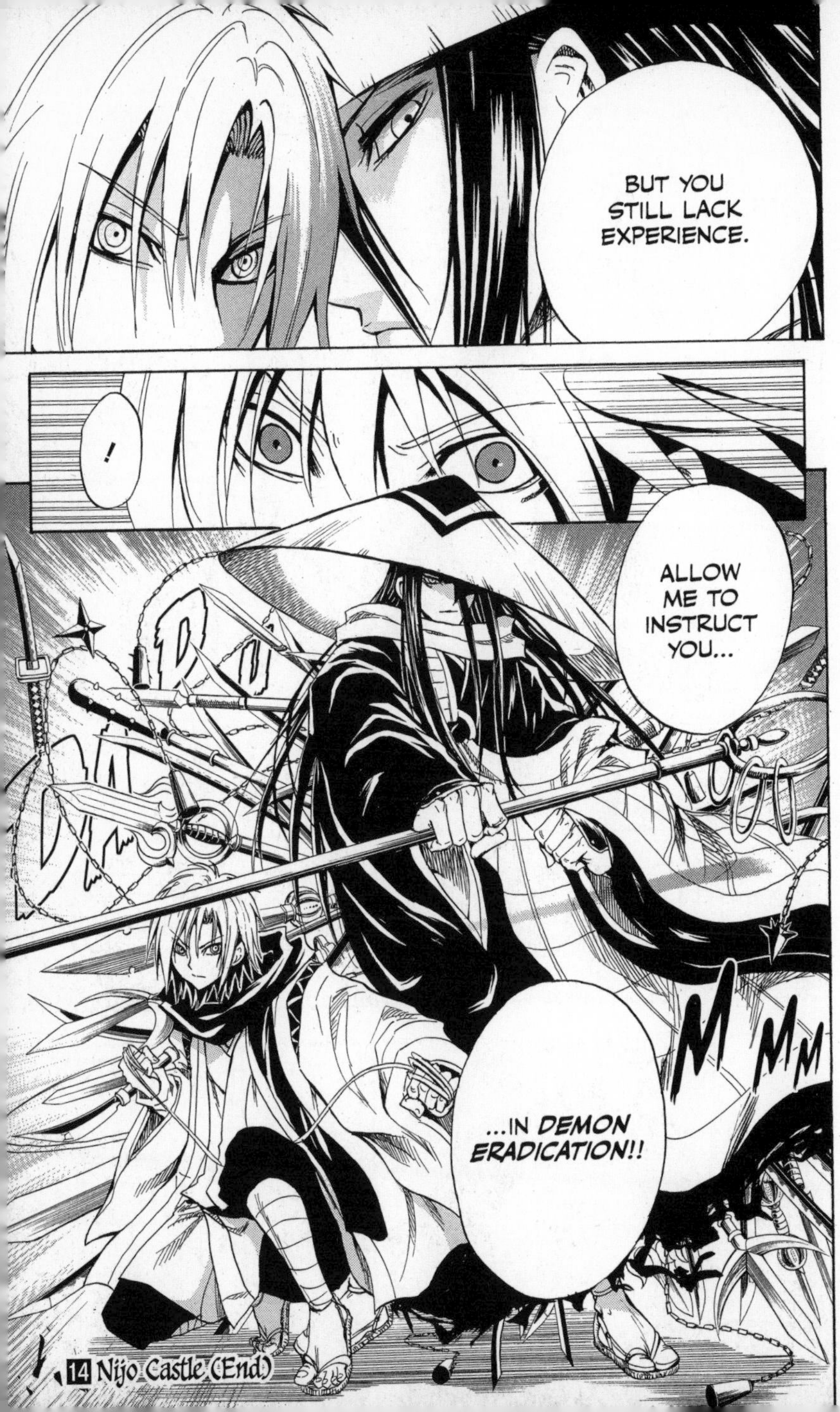
BUT YOU STILL LACK EXPERIENCE.
!
ALLOW ME TO INSTRUCT YOU...
...IN *DEMON ERADICATION*!!
14 Nijo Castle (End)

From chapter 1 of the novel Nura: Rise of the Yokai Clan: Kyoto Mugenya

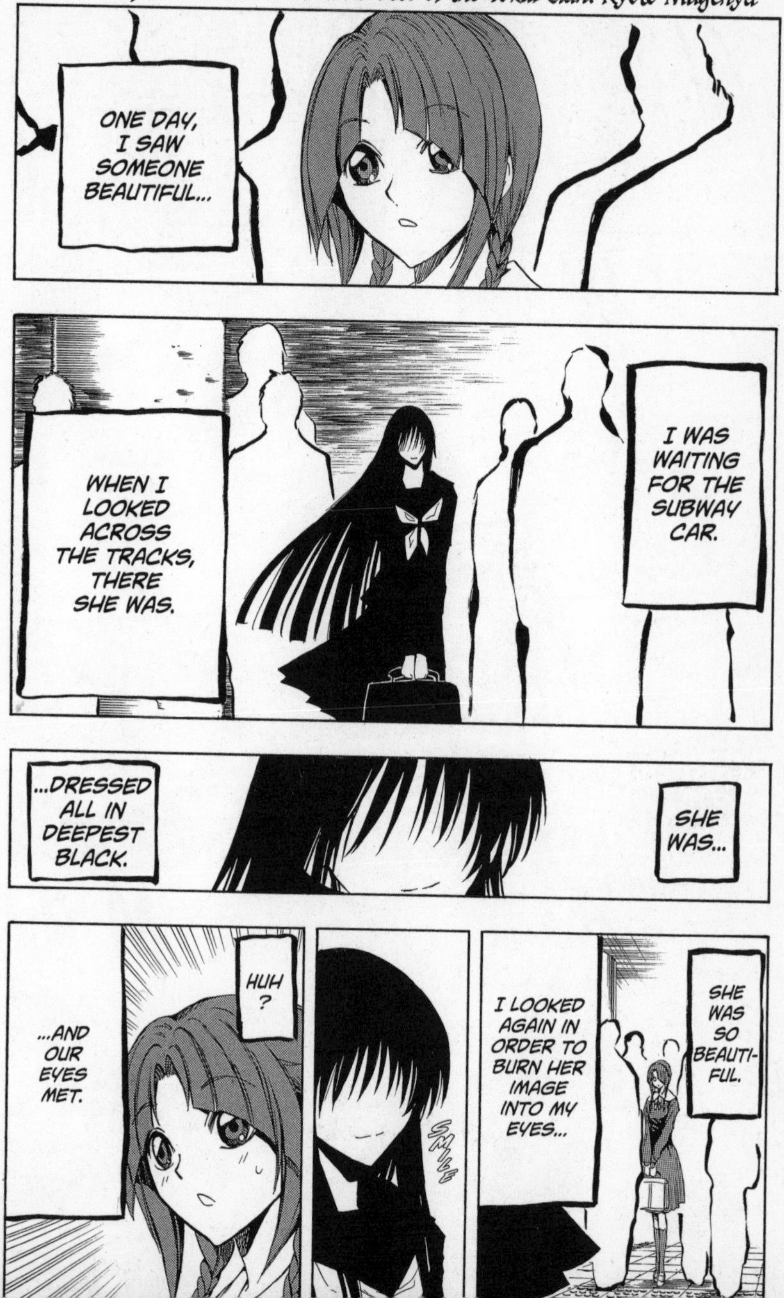
ONE DAY, I SAW SOMEONE BEAUTIFUL...
I WAS WAITING FOR THE SUBWAY CAR.
WHEN I LOOKED ACROSS THE TRACKS, THERE SHE WAS.
SHE WAS...
...DRESSED ALL IN DEEPEST BLACK.
SHE WAS SO BEAUTI-FUL.
I LOOKED AGAIN IN ORDER TO BURN HER IMAGE INTO MY EYES...
SMILE
HUH?
...AND OUR EYES MET.

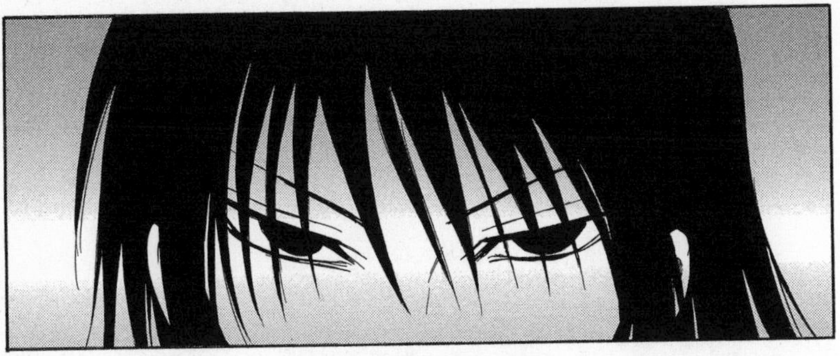

From Chapter 2

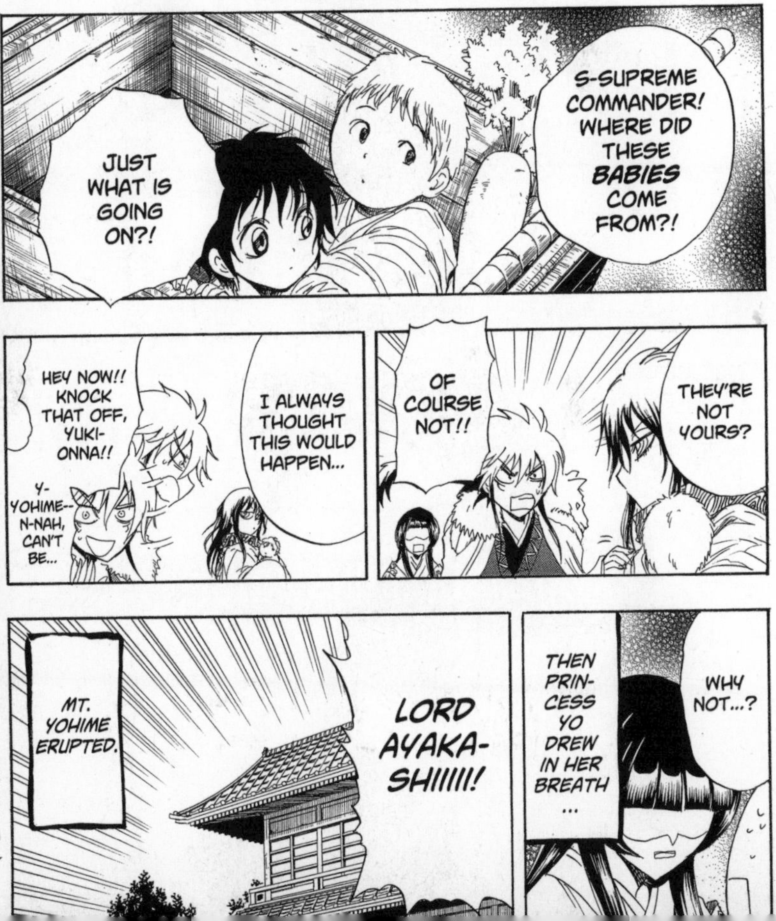

S-SUPREME COMMANDER! WHERE DID THESE BABIES COME FROM?!
JUST WHAT IS GOING ON?!
THEY'RE NOT YOURS?
OF COURSE NOT!!
I ALWAYS THOUGHT THIS WOULD HAPPEN...
HEY NOW!! KNOCK THAT OFF, YUKI-ONNA!!
Y-YOHIME--N-NAH, CAN'T BE...
WHY NOT...?
THEN PRINCESS YO DREW IN HER BREATH ...
LORD AYAKASHIIIIII!
MT. YOHIME ERUPTED.

☆ I TURNED A COUPLE SCENES FROM THE NOVEL INTO MANGA. CHECK IT OUT!

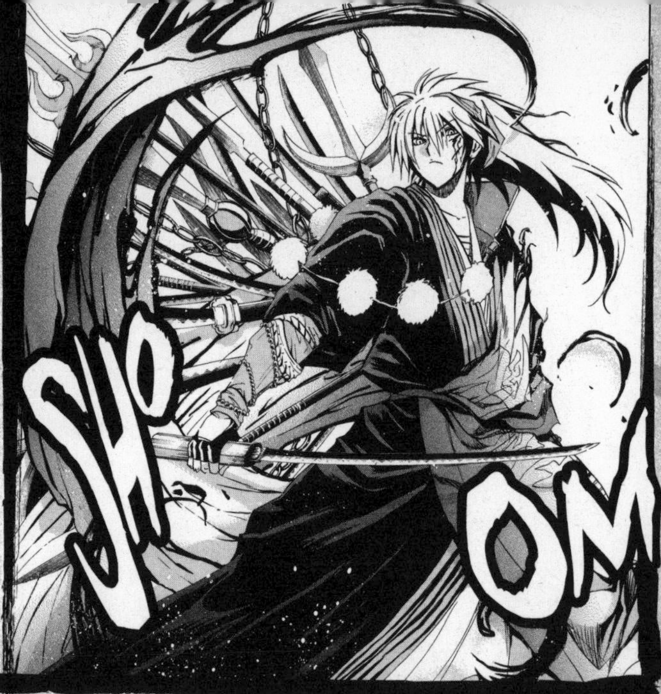
SHO
OM

IN THE NEXT VOLUME...

FRAGMENTS OF THE PAST

As the ancient yokai Hagoromo-Gitsune prepares to give birth to the new reincarnation of Nue, ancestor to the world-killing Gokadoin clan, Rikuo rushes to learn new skills and battle moves that will ready him for his biggest battle yet.

AVAILABLE JUNE 2013!